HANDBOOK OF PERCEPTION

Volume I

Historical and Philosophical Roots of Perception

This is Volume 1 of

HANDBOOK OF PERCEPTION

EDITORS: *Edward C. Carterette and Morton P. Friedman*

HANDBOOK
OF PERCEPTION

VOLUME I

HISTORICAL AND PHILOSOPHICAL ROOTS OF PERCEPTION

EDITED BY

Edward C. Carterette and Morton P. Friedman

Department of Psychology
University of California
Los Angeles, California

ACADEMIC PRESS   New York   San Francisco   London   1974
A Subsidiary of Harcourt Brace Jovanovich, Publishers

ACADEMIC PRESS, INC.
111 Fifth Avenue, New York, New York 10003

United Kingdom Edition published by
ACADEMIC PRESS, INC. (LONDON) LTD.
24/28 Oval Road, London NW1

Library of Congress Cataloging in Publication Data

Carterette, Edward C
    Historical & philosophical roots of perception.

    (His Handbook of perception, 1)
    Includes bibliographies.
    1.   Perception.   I.   Friedman, Morton P., joint
author.   II.   Title.
BF311.C29   153.7   73-21837
ISBN 0-12-161901-X

PRINTED IN THE UNITED STATES OF AMERICA

CONTENTS

PART I. PHILOSOPHICAL ROOTS

Chapter 1. Sense Experience

Roderick Firth

Chapter 2. Some Philosophical Problems of Perception

R. M. Yost

Chapter 3. Epistemology

Gilbert Harman

Chapter 4. Some Questions in the Philosophy of Mind

Max Deutscher

PART II. HISTORICAL BACKGROUND OF CONTEMPORARY PERCEPTION

Chapter 5. The Problem of Perceptual Structure

Michael Wertheimer

Chapter 6. Association (and the Nativist-Empiricist Axis)

Bruce Earhard

Chapter 7.   Consciousness, Perception, and Action

Wolfgang Metzger

Chapter 8.   Attention

D. E. Berlyne

Chapter 9.   Cognition and Knowledge: Psychological Epistemology

Joseph R. Royce

PART III.   CONTEMPORARY VIEWS OF PERCEPTION

A.   Modern Classical Tradition

Chapter 10.   Organization and the Gestalt Tradition

Julian Hochberg

Chapter 14. The Visual System: Environmental Information

R. M. Boynton

Chapter 15. A Note on Ecological Optics

James J. Gibson

Chapter 16. Information Processing

Ralph Norman Haber

Chapter 17. Automata

Patrick Suppes and William Rottmayer

LIST OF CONTRIBUTORS

Numbers in parentheses indicate the pages on which the authors' contributions begin.

D. E. BERLYNE (123), Department of Psychology, University of Toronto, Toronto, Ontario, Canada

R. M. BOYNTON* (285), University of Rochester, Rochester, New York

KENT DALLET (387), Department of Psychology, University of California, Los Angeles, California

MAX DEUTSCHER (57), Department of Philosophy, Macquarie University, North Ryde, New South Wales, Australia

W. J. DOWLING (243), Department of Psychology, University of California, Los Angeles, California

BRUCE EARHARD (93), Department of Psychology, Dalhouise University, Halifax, Nova Scotia, Canada

RODERICK FIRTH (3), Department of Philosophy, Harvard University, Cambridge, Massachusetts

DAGFINN FØLLESDAL (377), Department of Philosophy, University of Oslo, Oslo, Norway, *and* Department of Philosophy, Stanford University, Stanford, California

JAMES J. GIBSON (309), Department of Psychology, Cornell University, Ithaca, New York

RICHARD L. GREGORY (255), Brain and Perception Laboratory, Department of Anatomy, The Medical School, University of Bristol, Bristol, England

RALPH NORMAN HABER (313), Department of Psychology, University of Rochester, Rochester, New York

GILBERT HARMAN (41), Department of Philosophy, Princeton University, Princeton, New Jersey

* Present address: Department of Psychology, University of California, San Diego, California.

JULIAN HOCHBERG (179), Department of Psychology, Columbia University, New York, New York

WOLFGANG METZGER (109), Psychologisches Institüt, University of Münster, Münster, West Germany

KELYN ROBERTS (243), Department of Psychology, University of California, Los Angeles, California

WILLIAM ROTTMAYER (335), Department of Philosophy, Eastern Washington State College, Cheney, Washington

JOSEPH R. ROYCE (149), Center for Advanced Study in Theoretical Psychology, University of Alberta, Edmonton, Alberta, Canada

WM. W. ROZEBOOM (211), Center for Advanced Study in Theoretical Psychology, University of Alberta, Edmonton, Alberta, Canada

PATRICK SUPPES, (335), Institute for Mathematical Studies in the Social Sciences, Stanford University, Stanford, California

ELIANE VURPILLOT* (363), Laboratoire de Psychologie Experimentale et Comparée, Université René Descartes, Paris, France

MICHAEL WERTHEIMER (75), Department of Psychology, University of Colorado, Boulder, Colorado

R. M. YOST (19), Department of Philosophy, University of California, Los Angeles, California

* Present address: 28 rue Serpente, Paris 6e, France.

FOREWORD

The problem of perception is one of understanding the way in which the organism transforms, organizes, and structures information arising from the world in sense data or memory. With this definition of perception in mind, the aims of this treatise are to bring together essential aspects of the very large, diverse, and widely scattered literature on human perception and to give a précis of the state of knowledge in every area of perception. It is aimed at the psychologist in particular and at the natural scientist in general. A given topic is covered in a comprehensive survey in which fundamental facts and concepts are presented and important leads to journals and monographs of the specialized literature are provided. Perception is considered in its broadest sense. Therefore, the work will treat a wide range of experimental and theoretical work.

The first part of the treatise deals with the fundamentals of perceptual systems. It is comprised of six volumes covering (1) historical and philosophical roots of perception, (2) psychophysical judgment and measurement, (3) the biology of perceptual systems, (4) hearing, (5) seeing, and (6) feeling, tasting, smelling, and hurting.

Another six volumes will cover the perceiving organism, which takes up the wider view and generally ignores specialty boundaries. The major areas will include speech and language, perception of space and objects, perception of form and pattern, cognitive performance, information processing, perceptual memory, perceptual aspects of thinking and problem solving, esthetics, and the ecology of the perceiver. Coverage will be given to theoretical issues and models of perceptual processes and also to central topics in perceptual judgment and decision.

The "Handbook of Perception" should serve as a basic source and reference work for all in the arts or sciences, indeed for all who are interested in human perception.

EDWARD C. CARTERETTE
MORTON P. FRIEDMAN

PREFACE

... Any quality of a thing which affects our sense-organs does also more than that: it arouses processes in the hemispheres which are due to the organization of that organ by past experiences, and the result of which in consciousness are commonly described as ideas which the sensation suggests. The first of these ideas is that of the *thing* to which the sensible quality belongs. *The consciousness of particular material things present to sense* is nowadays called *perception.*

WILLIAM JAMES
*(in The Principles of Psychology,
Volume 2, 1890)*

Perception is a rich, diverse, and difficult field. The concerns of perception range from problems of knowing on through sensory processes to the perception of events in time and space.

In this volume we consider some of the main persisting conceptual issues. We begin with some philosophical problems of perception, of sense experience, of epistemology, and include some questions on the philosophy of mind. From a definitely psychological point of view we consider some origins of contemporary work in perception, in particular of perceptual structure, association, attention, cognition and knowledge, consciousness and action. We conclude with a series of chapters emphasizing several contemporary views of perception.

EDWARD C. CARTERETTE
MORTON P. FRIEDMAN

CONTENTS OF OTHER VOLUMES

Volume III: Biology of Perceptual Systems

HANDBOOK OF PERCEPTION

Volume I

Historical and Philosophical Roots of Perception

Part I

Philosophical Roots

Chapter 1

SENSE EXPERIENCE

RODERICK FIRTH

A psychologist who picks up a contemporary book or article on the philosophy of perception is likely to be baffled by what he finds. Some of it may seem trivial. Why should philosophers wonder so subtly and at such length whether the statement "The mountain looks purple" has the same meaning as "The mountain has a purple look," and whether either of these has the same meaning as "The mountain appears purple" or "The mountain seems purple"? Why should it matter so much whether "The mountain looks purple" is synonymous with "The mountain looks the way purple things look under normal conditions"? Even if these problems turn out to be puzzling and intriguing ones, why have philosophers chosen *them* to worry about? They seem quite remote from anything that a psychologist is likely to call "the problem of perception." Are they, indeed, related in any important way to the problems that have dominated the philosophy of perception throughout the history of Western thought?

These are all fair questions and I should like to do what I can to answer them. In the pages at my disposal I cannot write a comprehensive essay entitled "The Concept of Sense Experience in Contemporary Philosophy." If I had space for such an essay it would surely be criticized by other philosophers as narrow, provincial, and not sufficiently appreciative of the recent work of Professors X, Y, and Z. But it is possible, I believe, to make a few observations that will help, at the very least, to explain the motivation behind *some* of the recent developments in the philosophy of perception, in particular some of the recent work on the concept of sense experience.

I. THE EPISTEMOLOGICAL PROBLEM OF PERCEPTION

There is no traditional branch of philosophy broad enough to embrace every problem that might be called a "philosophical problem of perception." Philosophers in our Western tradition, however, have been interested in perception primarily because they have wanted to answer the question "What is knowledge?"—the central question of epistemology. This is an ancient philosophical question. Plato raises it explicitly in the *Theaetetus,* and then turns the dialogue immediately into a discussion of sensation and perception. The question "What is *empirical* knowledge?," which has dominated the history of modern philosophy, leads even more certainly to problems of perception. For if "empirical knowledge" means knowledge based on some form of observation, then all empirical knowledge of the "external world" is presumably based on perception. If psychologists will keep this in mind they will find it easier to understand the special point of view from which philosophers look at perception. From the point of view of an empirical science the problem of perception is, roughly speaking, a *causal* problem. The editors of this *Handbook* have defined it as "the problem of understanding the way in which the organism transforms, organizes, and structures information arising from the world in sense data or memory." But the philosophical question "What is knowledge?" calls for an examination of the *concept* of knowledge. Thus philosophers tend to be interested in causal questions about perception only to the extent that these seem to be relevant to conceptual questions.

We can be much more specific than this, however, about the interests of the philosopher. In order to answer the question "What is knowledge?" it is first necessary to answer the question "What makes a belief warranted (or justified)?" This is not because knowledge is constituted, as some philosophers have thought, only of true, warranted beliefs. There seem to be special circumstances in which someone can be said to know that so-and-so is the case even though he is not justified in believing that so-and-so is the case. But in normal circumstances the fact that a particular person *A* is not warranted in believing a particular proposition *p*, is a sufficient reason for concluding that *A* does not know *p*. I may believe right now, for example, that it is snowing in northern New Hampshire. I may believe this with deep conviction, and my belief may in fact be true. But if my belief is wishful thinking or a lucky guess, if it is not a warranted belief, then I do not *know* that it is snowing in northern New Hampshire. Thus the question "What is knowledge?" cannot be answered unless we first discover what makes a belief warranted. And if all empirical knowledge is somehow based on perception, it becomes a matter of special importance for epistemology to know what makes a *perceptual* belief (or judgment) warranted. It is fair to say, I think, that this is what most philosophers have in mind when they speak of "the problem of perception." Most of them are not inclined to be skeptical. They have no serious doubt that the vast majority of our perceptual beliefs *are* warranted, and that these beliefs constitute an important part of our empirical knowledge. But the problem of perception is to explain, so to speak, how it is *possible* for them to be warranted. If they are warranted because there is evidence for them, just what can this evidence be? And by what valid principles of inference can this evidence confer warrant on perceptual beliefs?

It should be noted at this point that terms like "perceptual belief" and "perceptual judgment" are ambiguous. If I assert "I see a lighthouse" or "I hear a bell" it is natural to say that I am expressing a perceptual belief—a belief to the effect that I am perceiving something of such and such a kind. Such judgments might well be called "psychophysical perceptual judgments." They entail the existence of objects like lighthouses and bells that constitute part of the subject-matter of the physical sciences. They also entail the existence of perceptual experiences (seeing, hearing, etc.) that constitute part of the subject-matter of psychology. The term "perceptual judgment," however, has traditionally been applied to judgments of quite another kind—to judgments that can be expressed in "observation statements" such as "That is a lighthouse" or "This is a bell." Statements like these may identify and characterize the things that I perceive. Unlike "psychophysical perceptual judgments," however, they do not assert or entail that I perceive the things (e.g., the lighthouse and the bell) that are identified and characterized. Many philosophers seem to have thought that the epistemological problem of perception can be defined by reference to perceptual judgments in this traditional sense of the term. The problem of perception, as they have construed it, is to explain how such judgments acquire the high degree of warrant that they so often have. But there is, in fact, no way to identify a class of such judgments that is distinctively perceptual. The fact that they can be expressed in demonstrative statements of the form "This (or that) is a ———," is not sufficient. It is quite possible to point at an object that one cannot see at the moment (e.g., an object behind one's back) and assert with conviction "That is my favorite book." In such a case it would be more appropriate to say that the judgment is based on memory than perception (although perception may play some role). To meet this difficulty we might be tempted to add what looks like a minor qualification. The problem of perception, we might say, is to explain how such judgments acquire warrant when we actually perceive the things referred to by the words "this" and "that." But this qualification introduces a consideration that is epistemologically irrelevant. Even if the statement "That is a lighthouse" is warranted by perception, its warrant does not

depend on what we actually perceive but on what we are justified in thinking that we perceive. We may sometimes be justified in thinking that we see
a lighthouse when in fact we are seeing a distant sail. The fact that we
actually see a sail and not a lighthouse is irrelevant to the question "Why is
the statement 'That is a lighthouse' warranted?"

The epistemological problem of perception, therefore, must be formulated by reference to what I have called "psychophysical perceptual judgments." Such judgments often seem to be highly warranted. I seem right
now, for example, to be thoroughly justified in believing that I see a sheet
of white paper. The problem of perception is to explain exactly why this
belief is warranted. If we can do this we shall also have explained, at least
in part, why I am justified in asserting the observation statement "This is a
sheet of white paper." For if I am justified in believing that I really *see* a
sheet of white paper in a certain place, then I am justified in believing that
there *is* a sheet of white paper in that place. This brings us to sense experience.

II. CARTESIANISM AND ITS CRITICS

Most of the major philosophers in modern times have agreed that sense
experience must play a central role in any plausible solution to the epistemological problem of perception. They have disagreed among themselves
on many important issues, but they have accepted the following three theses
about sense experience.

(i) We have a sense experience whenever (or at least almost whenever) we make a psychophysical perceptual judgment of the form "I now
perceive such and such a physical thing."

(ii) Such a psychophysical judgment derives its warrant from its inferential relations to warranted propositions about the intrinsic character
of the accompanying sense experience.

(The term "inferential relations" is used here to avoid suggesting that
the warrant of a psychophysical perceptual judgment is supposed to depend
on its causation, in particular on its being made as a result of an actual
process of inference. To say that such a judgment is warranted by inferential relations implies that it *can* be reached by valid inference, but not that
it actually has been. Nor does (ii) imply that propositions about sense experience are sufficient to account for the inferential warrant of psychophysical perceptual judgments. Presumably memory also plays an important
role.)

(iii) These propositions about sense experience do not derive their warrant primarily from their inferential relations to still *other* propositions. They are, in short, epistemically basic—or, as we might say, self-warranted.

Because of the historical influence of Descartes' methodology, I shall call the position defined by these three theses "Cartesianism," and I shall say that anyone who accepts these three theses is a Cartesian in his theory of perception. Serious objections have been raised to each of these theses in recent years, and the best way to understand some of the recent developments in the philosophy of perception is to examine some of these objections. I shall discuss the three theses in the order in which they are listed.

A. The Identification of Sense Experience

Thesis (i) of the Cartesian doctrine has been attacked on a number of grounds in recent years, perhaps most effectively by John Austin in his lectures entitled *Sense and Sensibilia* (1962), published after his death. It is important to observe that Austin's arguments are not directed merely against some particular *analysis* of sense experience or against some particular *description* (phenomenology) of sense experience. He calls into question the very *existence* of any kind of experience that could satisfy thesis (i). This may not be obvious at first. On the surface Austin's objections to the Cartesian tradition are directed only against doctrines formulated in what philosophers today often call a "sense datum terminology." This terminology, as traditionally understood, entails an "act-object analysis" of sense experience—an analysis that construes sense experience as the perceiving or sensing or just the "experiencing" of a particular kind of object called an impression, an idea, a percept, a sensum, a sense datum, and so forth. It has been criticized on a variety of grounds. It is said to have misled philosophers into confusing the sense of "perceive" in which we perceive an afterimage with the sense of "perceive" in which we perceive a chair. It is said to have distorted the epistemological problem of perception by interposing an impenetrable "curtain of sense data" between the knower and the external world, thus leading philosophers into skepticism or subjectivism. It is said to have raised pseudoproblems by permitting us to ask questions about sense data (e.g., "Can they exist unsensed?") that can be raised meaningfully only of other kinds of things. It is said to violate Occam's maxim by multiplying entities beyond necessity. These are not objections to Cartesianism in general but only to a particular form of it that might be called "Sense Datum Cartesianism." If a Cartesian finds enough merit in these objections, therefore, he can easily abandon the act-object analysis in favor of what is sometimes called an "adverbial analysis." Instead of saying that we have or experience a red sense datum, he can say, for example, that we experience redly or in a red manner. Austin has a more basic line of argument, however, that cannot be avoided in this way.

If Cartesians are convinced that there is a sensory constituent in perceptual experience they should be able, Austin thinks, to identify it in some effective way. But this, he says, they have not been able to do. They have employed an ancient argument, "The Argument from Illusion," that is intended to show the existence of sense experience by comparing cases of normal perception with cases of hallucination and other abnormal perception. But they have invariably failed in their purpose, primarily because they have misused key words like "illusion," "delusion," "material," "looks," "appears," "seems," and "real." I shall not attempt to summarize or evaluate Austin's arguments here; but whether or not they are correct they raise an interesting and instructive methodological problem that deserves independent consideration.

The term "Argument from Illusion" is sometimes applied to an argument against Naive Realism, an epistemological position that no philosopher has ever defended without qualification. Early in the *Dialogues between Hylas and Philonous,* for example, Berkeley argues that the characteristics that belong to our sense experience—to our "sensible ideas," in Berkeley's terminology—cannot always be characteristics of the external object we are perceiving. For if they were, he says, there would be no perceptual illusions. Green mountains would not look purple as they sometimes do. Warm water would not feel cold as it sometimes does. And so on. Whatever its merits this is certainly a genuine argument, and an argument from illusion. From the fact that illusions occur, Berkeley concludes that Naive Realism is false. But this argument is not an attempt to prove the *existence* of sense experience. In fact it explicitly assumes the existence of sense experience in order to prove something about the relationship between sense experience and the external objects of perception.

Philosophers and psychologists have also appealed to illusion and hallucination, however, in an effort to *identify* sense experience. To distinguish sense experiences from perceptual judgments they have asked us to note that similar experiences may "mean" different things in different circumstances, may be "interpreted" differently, may "give rise to" different perceptual judgments, and so on. The most dramatic examples are cases of hallucination. Thus at the beginning of his soliloquy Macbeth was inclined to judge that he really saw a dagger before him. At the end he decided that he was having a hallucination. Yet throughout this radical change in belief there was, so it is "argued," something that remained relatively constant—something that we may call, without any causal implications, "sense experience." This appeal to the independent variation of sense experience and "interpretation," although very different from Berkeley's argument against

Naive Realism, has also been called an "Argument from Illusion." It is said to be an argument to *prove the existence* of sense experience, more particularly, an argument to prove that perceptual experience contains a "sensory" as well as a "judgmental" element. But this is a very misleading way to describe the role played by such an appeal to illusion or hallucination in the development of a Cartesian theory of knowledge.

For the Cartesian, as stipulated in Thesis (iii), sense experiences are among the ultimate data on the basis of which each of us is justified in believing propositions about people and things in the external world. The proposition that *someone else* has sense experiences may be construed as a theory or hypothesis that is warranted for me to the extent that it explains his behavior and thus, when I perceive his behavior, explains my own sense experiences. But that *I* have sense experiences, which is what the Cartesian is trying to show me when he appeals to cases of illusion or hallucination, is not for me, according to the Cartesian, a theory. It is not something that can be "proved" to me by appealing to further empirical data which are evidence for it. (Some Cartesians hold that propositions about my past sense experiences are necessarily theoretical, but this is a complication that I shall pass over.) Strictly speaking, therefore, the so-called Argument from Illusion is not an argument at all. When used by the Cartesian to identify sense experience it is merely an elaborate form of *ostensive definition.* Since he cannot point at sense experience with his finger or other physical pointer, the Cartesian must use a technique that might be called "ostensive definition by description." This is a familiar technique in lexicography. One of my dictionaries, for example, defines "red" as "the color of arterial blood" and "white" as "the color of new-fallen snow." These definitions are clearly not intended as conceptual analyses. It is surely possible to understand the meaning of "red" and "white" without knowing that blood is red and snow is white. The definitions tell us, so to speak, where to look in order to find samples of the two colors. They *describe an environment* in which each of the colors is manifested. It is in this sense that the Cartesian's appeal to illusion and hallucination can be construed as an ostensive definition by description. He describes a type of situation in which (he hopes) we shall have no difficulty identifying the kind of experience that is to be labeled "sense experience." In the end, of course, the attempt at ostensive definition may fail. We cannot be compelled by force of logic to find a sensory constituent within our perceptual experience. There are, according to the Cartesian himself, no more ultimate empirical data on which to base an argument for the existence of sense experience.

The chief lesson to be learned from Austin, I believe, is that the traditional techniques for the ostensive definition of "sense experience" are laden with loopholes and confusions. This does not mean that they have been generally unsuccessful. Those of us who think that we understand the term "sense experience" as Cartesians use it, will naturally grant that the techniques have worked for us. But how shall we improve those techniques to overcome various kinds of resistance? What shall we say, for example, to someone like Austin who denies that he can find a common "sensory element" in hallucinatory experiences and "veridical perception"? Suppose he holds that the only thing that Macbeth's hallucinatory experience has in common with the normal perceptual experience of a real dagger is a feeling of *inclination to believe* that one is seeing a dagger. Suppose he denies that there is anything in the experiences that causes this inclination or even seems to cause it. Any causal explanation, he maintains, will have to be a physiological one. Such a challenge need not render us completely speechless (Firth, 1964). It is a matter of some importance, however, to recognize the limits within which it is possible to debate an issue of this kind.

The problem is by no means an isolated one. It can be raised in a more specialized form if we ask what our response should be to someone who proposes in all seriousness that we can dispense with the traditional concept of "negative afterimage." For when we say that we have a green afterimage, he argues, the only thing to which we can be referring is a feeling of inclination to believe that part of some local physical object (a wall, a screen, or whatever we are looking at) is really green. We learn to resist this inclination when we discover that we can produce it more or less at will by staring for a while at a red object. But the inclination remains. To suppose that there is something else present, a so-called image that causes (or seems to cause) this inclination, is to postulate an unnecessary middleman in accord with some ancient psychological theory. If the term "afterimage" is to denote anything at all, an afterimage is just a certain feeling of inclination, produced in a certain special way, to believe that something in the external world has a certain color property. What could we say in reply to such an argument?

Or consider the term "itch," which is defined by one of my dictionaries as "a sensation in the skin that causes a desire to scratch." Here again, it might be argued, we see evidence of the unfortunate tendency of psychologists, both professional and amateur, to multiply entities beyond necessity —and beyond reality. If the term "itch" is to have any denotion at all, an itch is not something that causes (or seems to cause) a desire to scratch. It *is* a desire (at least a feeling of desire) to scratch. It is not, of course, just any feeling of desire to scratch. We may desire to scratch for some ulterior purpose, perhaps as a signal in accord with some prearranged code. But an itch, it might be said, is a feeling of desire to scratch for the sake of scratching, and not for some further end. To suppose that this feeling is caused by a so-called itch, or that scratching relieves a so-called itch, is again to postulate an unnecessary middleman. It should be noted that the kind of "reductionism" proposed here, as in the other cases we have considered, is quite independent of issues concerning the reduction of the phenomenal to the physical. To reduce an itch to a feeling of desire is to reduce one kind of phenomenal experience to another.

When the traditional analysis of perceptual experience is challenged by this kind of reductionism, the Cartesian is likely to turn for help to the idioms of everyday speech. He may fail by more direct means to persuade his critic that hallucinations and "veridical perceptual experiences" have something in common that can be called "sense experience"—something other than a feeling of inclination to believe that one is perceiving something. But sense experience is not something, he may insist, known only to philosophers and psychologists, much less something invented by them in the hope of solving problems in epistemology or learning theory. The fact that the common man can identify a sensory constituent in perceptual experience is reflected in the distinctions we all draw between things as they "really are" and things as they appear, seem, look, feel, smell, taste, sound, etc. In fact some writers have introduced technical terms for talking about sense experience by defining them merely as convenient substitutes for expressions containing the words "appear," "seem," "look," etc. Bertrand Russell, a good Cartesian according to my definition, introduced the term sense data in that way in his early book *The Problems of Philosophy* (1912). (Russell seems to have been responsible for the subsequent popularity of this term.) From the Cartesian point of view definitions that appeal to such "looks-expressions," as I shall call them, must still be construed as ostensive. We are told, in effect, how to find an instance of sense experience. We are told to pick out the experience that leads us to say "That mountain looks purple to me" even on occasions when we know that the mountain is not "really purple." The word "looks" is used here, so to speak, as a pointer to draw our attention to a visual sense experience.

Unfortunately for this handy method of ostensive definition, all such looks-expressions have more than one use in everyday speech. The Cartesian will have to admit, at the very least, that they have two very different uses. Suppose, for example, that we are looking at the well-known Müller-Lyer figure drawn in large scale on the blackboard. I might say, quite correctly, "The long horizontal lines look (or appear) unequal to me," thus indicating that I am subject to the usual optical illusion. But suppose, now, that someone offers to bet me that I cannot tell from where I am sitting whether or not the horizontal lines on the board are *really* equal—equal, let us say, within a 1-inch margin of error. After studying the diagram for some time I may finally say, perhaps with some hesitation, "They look (appear) equal to me. I may be mistaken but I'm willing to bet that they

are equal." When I say "They look equal to me" I do not intend to assert
that my sense experience has changed so that I am no longer subject to the
illusion. (Of course my sense experience may have changed, but this is not
implied by my statement.) The statement "They look equal to me" is a
tentative way of saying "I think they are (really) equal" or perhaps something like "I am inclined to think they are equal." If the Cartesian holds
that "looks" is used in the first case to describe sense experience, he must
nevertheless agree that it is used in the second case to make a tentative
commitment—a tentative statement about the character of the object perceived. And once he has admitted this he is in trouble again. For Austin
and others will deny that there is any use of looks-expressions in everyday
speech that allows the Cartesian to say what he wants to say about sense
experience. All the idioms that he tries to use are in fact idioms that express
a tentative commitment or some related attitude of doubt or uncertainty.
None of them is ordinarily used to describe what the Cartesian calls "sense
experience."

The problem for the Cartesian at this point arises from the fact that
Thesis (ii) of the Cartesian doctrine requires that we be able to formulate
propositions about the "intrinsic character" of sense experience, propositions from which psychophysical perceptual judgments derive their warrant. A statement like "The apple looks red to me" does not fulfil the
requirement for it already entails or presupposes that I am seeing an apple.
It thus presupposes a proposition that sense experience is supposed to
justify. What is needed, therefore, is some idiom like "I seem to see a red
apple" or "There appears to me to be a red apple before me"—some idiom
that does not beg the epistemological question by presupposing from the
outset that I actually see some real physical thing. But these two idioms, it
can plausibly be argued, are ordinarily used to express tentative beliefs
about what I am actually seeing—not beliefs about something called "sense
experience" but beliefs about physical objects in the external world. If I
say "I seem to see a red apple" I usually mean to express, albeit cautiously
or doubtfully, the belief that I do see a red apple. Or on some occasions
I may even use this statement when I think that I do not see a red apple.
I may use it to indicate that I am somewhat inclined, perhaps tempted, to
think that I see a red apple, when in fact I am sure that I do not. Thus I
might say: "When I stand here and look at that glass ball on the Christmas
tree, I seem to see a red apple." Other looks-expressions in everyday
speech, it can be argued, function in the same way.

Now the Cartesian will of course object that there is a reason why we are
inclined to think that we see a red apple, or tempted to think that we see a
red apple when we know we see something else. We are inclined or tempted
because of the character of our sense experience. Or at least, to play it safe,

our sense experience is what we naturally *think to be* the cause of our inclination or temptation. But to reply in this way may merely return the issue to its original state. The critic of Cartesianism will simply deny that there is anything in perceptual experience that plays, or seems to play, such a causal role, and we may be no closer at all to finding an effective ostensive definition of "sense experience." This is why philosophers have given so much attention in recent years to the everyday use of words like "appears," "looks," and "seems." Some of us are convinced that looks-expressions are ordinarily used *in some contexts* to describe sense experience. In my judgment the expression "It looks as if I am seeing a red apple" is sometimes used for that purpose. (In conversation Austin once suggested to me that my case might be strengthened by inserting the word "exactly" after the word "looks.") But in the end, as I have already said, there is no way to compel anyone to find a sensory constituent in his perceptual experience. Nor is there, on the other hand, any way to compel the Cartesian to conclude that he has been mistaken in his analysis of perceptual experience. Surely no arguments about the use of words in everyday speech can compel such a conclusion.

B. Inference from Sense Experience

I turn next, much more briefly, to Thesis (ii) of the Cartesian doctrine of perception. This thesis raises immense epistemological problems that have dominated the history of modern philosophy. Most of the major philosophers since the time of Descartes have been convinced that our psychophysical perceptual judgments (e.g., the judgment that I now see a sheet of white paper) derive warrant from the sense experiences that accompany them. The fact that it looks as if I am seeing a sheet of white paper is, under present conditions, a good reason for thinking that I do see a sheet of white paper. But they have found it difficult to explain how this is possible. For in order to argue inductively from sense experience to external object, it is necessary to know some general laws correlating sense experience with objects in the external world. But how do we acquire knowledge of these psychophysical laws? In order to learn these laws must we not be able to generalize from individual cases? Must we not discover by perception that in this case and that case and that case a certain kind of sense experience was associated with a certain kind of physical object, *A*? But how can we identify an object of kind *A* by perception? If Thesis (ii) is true, how can we ever be justified in thinking that we perceive a physical object of kind *A* unless we *already* know the very psychophysical laws that we hope to justify by perception? This is the "vicious circle" that generates what has traditionally been called by philosophers "the problem of perception."

Whether the circle is as vicious as it seems is an extremely complicated question that I shall not attempt to discuss here. But Cartesians have generally considered it vicious and have responded in one of three ways. A few, like Hume, have settled for skepticism, concluding that our so-called knowledge of the external world is, in Santayana's words, a matter of "animal faith." The second alternative is to hold that perceptual knowledge requires us to recognize the validity of at least one irreducible principle of nondeductive inference that is not needed within the physical sciences, i.e., a principle not needed to account for the warrant that statements about physical objects or events confer on other statements about physical objects or events. Descartes chooses this alternative when he appeals to the goodness of God to justify inference from sense experience (adventitious ideas) to physical reality. Locke chooses this alternative when he assumes, in effect, without offering proof, that there are certain "resemblances" between sense experiences and their physical causes. And Russell in his *Human Knowledge* (1948) seems to treat his "Structural Postulate" as an irreducible principle of inference only because it enables us to avoid solipsism and subjectivism. The third alternative, adopted by Berkeley, Kant, Mill, C. I. Lewis, and many others, is to construe physical reality in a way that allows inference from sense experience to physical objects, without further premises, by ordinary inductive principles. This has meant to them that in one way or another propositions about physical reality must be construed as propositions about sense experience—a "reduction" that realists like Descartes, Locke, and Russell would consider to be no better than skepticism.

The obvious alternative to all these alternatives is to abandon Cartesianism by rejecting Thesis (ii) and with it the unique evidential status traditionally accorded to sense experience. The "pure coherence theory," as I shall call it, broadens the evidential base to a maximum degree by attributing some "initial" warrant or "self-warrant" to every empirical proposition that we happen to believe. All the empirical propositions that I happen to believe have some degree of warrant for me merely because I believe them; and their inferential interdependence (coherence) allows them to confer further warrant on one another in varying degrees. This avoids the problems posed by Cartesian Thesis (ii), for it permits us to include psychophysical laws among the ultimate premises that justify perceptual beliefs. If I happen to believe (as I do) that a visual sense experience of the kind I am now having is usually caused by a sheet of white paper, then I have *ipso facto* some justification for believing that my present sense experience is caused by a sheet of white paper. The psychophysical law does not have to be established from scratch by inductive generalization and the Cartesian's "vicious circle" is therefore broken.

Most philosophers seem to believe, however, that the circle is broken at the expense of denying to perception the special role that it actually plays in the justification of empirical knowledge. Perceptual beliefs have a special authority in confirming and disconfirming other beliefs about the external world, and this authority seems to be incompatible with the egalitarianism of the pure coherence theory. This has led to the development of positions that are, from the point of view of the Cartesian, *compromises* between his own position and the coherence theory. One that deserves special mention in a handbook of perception has been defended in recent years by H. H. Price (1933) and R. M. Chisholm (1957). These philosophers have maintained, in effect, that we can avoid skepticism by attributing a degree of self-warrant to our psychophysical perceptual beliefs. Thus the mere fact that I now believe that I see a sheet of white paper is enough to give that belief some degree of warrant. This warrant is literally *self*-warrant, warrant that is not derived by inductive inference from propositions about sense experience or from propositions about anything else. It enables us, so it is argued, to account for our knowledge of the external world without adopting the pure coherence theory and yet without falling into the vicious circle entailed by Cartesian Thesis (ii). It should be noted, however, that this way of breaking the circle seems to have no advantage over the assumption of a special principle like Locke's or Russell's that allows direct inference from sense experience to physical cause. If the one solution strikes us as an *ad hoc* way of avoiding skepticism, so will the other.

C. Self-warrant and Conceptual Parasitism

Thesis (iii) of the Cartesian doctrine of perception has also provoked some interesting debate in recent years. On the one hand there is a strong *prima facie* case for the doctrine that warranted propositions about the intrinsic character of sense experience are to a considerable degree self-warranted. They may be warranted in part by inference, but they usually seem to us to have a higher degree of warrant than we can account for by appealing to anything we know about our physical environment or the condition of our nervous system. In fact inductions about such casual conditions are often incompatible with highly warranted beliefs about our own sense experience. I may have good inductive reasons to believe that a certain object should look white to me under present conditions, yet I may have no doubt at all that the object now looks red to me and that I am justified in believing that it looks red. In such a case there are inferential grounds for thinking that my belief about my sense experience is false, yet I do not for that reason think that I should abandon it. If I am rational I look for a causal explanation. I try to explain the occurrence of the unexpected sense experience, not to explain it away. Later, of course, I may have reason to doubt my memory. (This is a point that often confuses the issue.) But if I now believe that I am having a certain kind of sense experience, my belief, while I have it, surely seems to be self-warranted.

The critic of Cartesianism can argue, however, that an analysis of the meaning of "looks-expressions" will show that there is something wrong with the Cartesian doctrine of self-warrant. Looks-expressions, he may say, are "parasitic" on expressions used to designate objective properties in perceived objects. They are parasitic even if we concede Cartesian Thesis (i) by granting that there is a distinguishable sensory element in perceptual experience. For suppose I describe my present sense experience by asserting:

(a) I now have a white sense experience.

Does not this mean something like the following:

(b) I now have a sense experience of the kind that white objects would characteristically produce under standard conditions of observation?

There may be questions about the term "standard conditions," and other details of formulation. But it can be argued that the close relation in meaning between (a) and (b) becomes obvious if we try to assert (a) while denying (b). It seems flatly self-contradictory to say "I now have a white sense experience but not a sense experience of the kind that white objects would characteristically produce under standard conditions of observation. If (a) and (b) mean essentially the same thing, however, then (a) cannot be self-warranted. For surely (b) is a statement that can be warranted only by inductive inference. To know how white objects look under various conditions of observation it is necessary to observe them under various conditions and then draw inductive conclusions from those observations.

It would take many pages to treat this issue in an adequate way or even to formulate it with precision. I shall conclude, therefore, only by noting that there seem to be two alternative ways in which the Cartesian may respond to this argument. On the one hand he may grant that (a) and (b) have the same meaning. In that case he will have to deny that (b) is a statement that can be warranted only by inductive inference. He can argue that (b) follows *deductively* from (a) in virtue of the meaning of the word "white" when applied to physical objects. As Locke maintained, he can say, a white object is by definition an object that would produce a white sense experience under standard conditions of observation. Thus, substituting definiens for definiendum, (b) means the same as

(c) I now have a sense experience of the kind that objects that would produce a white sense experience under standard conditions of observation would produce under standard conditions of observation.

If (a) is self-warranted then so is (c), for to assert (c) is just to assert (a) in a roundabout way. (c), and therefore (b), can be warranted without inductive support. This reply to his critic, however, has the disadvantage of committing the Cartesian to Locke's "dispositional" analysis of color concepts. This is a very controversial analysis, for nobody has yet shown that it is possible, without circularity, to define "standard conditions" so that a white object will always look white under standard conditions.

The Cartesian who does not accept Locke's analysis of "secondary qualities" has the alternative of denying that (a) and (b) have the same meaning. This allows him to maintain that (a) is self-warranted and that (b) is warranted by induction. But he must then explain why it seems self-contradictory to assert (a) and deny (b). A plausible answer can be given, I believe, if we draw a distinction between semantic rules and what I shall call "baptismal rules." The statement "This piece of paper is square but not rectangular" is paradoxical because it breaks a semantic rule. In English the word "square" designates the same shape as "equilateral rectangle," so that according to this rule we contradict ourselves in asserting "This piece of paper is square but not rectangular." On the other hand a man does not contradict himself if he utters the paradoxical statement: "This is my youngest daughter, John Smith, Jr." He is a man, let us suppose, who very much wanted a son and finally decided to name his twelfth daughter after himself. He has broken an accepted baptismal rule in selecting a name for his daughter; but once she has been appropriately baptized he breaks no further linguistic rule when he calls her "John Smith, Jr."

The Cartesian can maintain, employing this distinction, that there is indeed a baptismal rule that requires us to name our sense experiences after the objects that produce them under standard conditions. A sense experience of the kind produced by white physical objects under standard conditions, for example, is baptized "white." But alternative baptismal rules are of course quite conceivable. We might have learned to differentiate types of sense experience by using the letters of the Greek alphabet in some random way. And in that case, the Cartesian could maintain, there would be no air of paradox in asserting (a) while denying (b). There would be no air of paradox, that is to say, if we are convinced that Locke's analysis of seconddary qualities is false. For if the term "alpha sense experience" is defined ostensively, and if we are really convinced that Locke's analysis of secondary qualities is false, then it should not seem self-contradictory to assert "I now have an alpha sense experience but not a sense experience of the kind that white objects would characteristically produce under standard conditions of observation." This statement would be false if we meant by "alpha sense experience" what we now mean by "white sense experience." But with no baptismal rule connecting "alpha sense experience" with "white object," there would be no inclination to think that the statement is false because it is self-contradictory. There is, to be sure, much more to be said about this argument in defense of Cartesian Thesis (iii). But then there is also much more to be said about all the issues I have discussed.

References

Austin, J. L. *Sense and sensibilia*. London & New York: Oxford Univ. Press (Clarendon) 1962.

Chisholm, R. M. *Perceiving*. Ithaca, New York: Cornell Univ. Press, 1957.

Firth, R. Austin and the argument from illusion. *Philosophical Review*, 1964, 73, 372-382.

Price, H. H. *Perception*. New York: McBride, 1933.

Russell, B. *The problems of philosophy*. New York: Holt, 1912.

Russell, B. *Human knowledge: Its scope and its limits*. New York: Simon & Schuster, 1948.

Chapter 2

SOME PHILOSOPHICAL PROBLEMS OF PERCEPTION

R. M. YOST

I. INTRODUCTION

The purpose of this chapter is to suggest that there are problems about perception that are not dealt with by either the sciences, the fine arts, or common sense. Traditionally, these problems have been dealt with by people called philosophers. Attempts to solve them have disappointed nearly everyone who has shown any interest in them. The disappointment has arisen mainly because the solutions have appeared either to involve irresponsible metaphysical speculations or to trivialize the problems away by superficial linguistic maneuvers. A proper understanding of the nature of the problems will show, I think, that both these appearances are misleading. I shall try to suggest what some of them are, why everyone who is concerned about perception has them whether he realizes it or not, and what their "solutions," if there were any, would be like. In what follows there is room for only a sketch. Distinctions will have to be drawn too coarsely, and positions will have to be formulated too briefly to be true, or perhaps even very plausible.*

II. GENERAL SCHEMA OF A COMMON KIND OF PHILOSOPHICAL PROBLEM OF PERCEPTION

A common kind of philosophical problem about perception may be schematized in the following general way.

> That part of our knowledge which is applicable to perceptual situations is distributed among three "departments," namely, common sense, science (especially theoretical science), and analytic inspection of sensory fields. Many pieces of this knowledge, each considered within its own "department," seem indefeasible. Each piece of it is expressible by means of a sentence, yet many sets of such sentences, drawn from different "departments," are internally inconsistent. Although the inconsistency in one set can be removed by reformulating one or more of its sentences, the reformulation, if extended elsewhere, usually generates inconsistency in some other set. There seems to be no systematic, familiar way of formulating our total knowledge about perceptions, drawn from all three "departments," so that all the inconsistencies of its formulation are removed at once. Any set of sentences with these features constitutes a philosophical problem of perception.

The foregoing general schema will be illustrated in the course of the chapter by particular examples, which, though various, will be limited for convenience mainly to sight.

III. PRELIMINARY CLARIFICATION OF THE ORDINARY CONCEPT OF PERCEPTION

No attempt will be made to define "perception," but attention could be drawn to what I mean by "perception" by saying that it applies especially

---

* The philosophical problems of perception that I shall present are those that mainly engaged the attention of British philosophers during the first half of this century. I have drawn especially heavily from the writings of G. E. Moore, Bertrand Russell, C. D. Broad, and H. H. Price. To my knowledge the best anthology of writings in this tradition, including some that are critical of it, is Robert J. Swartz' *Perceiving, Sensing, and Knowing* (1956).

well to situations in which a person sees a table under optimum conditions, i.e., the table is nearby, his body is functioning normally, the light is strong and white, the medium is uniform and transparent, etc. Or by characterizing it in a general way as the sort of event in which we can acquire direct knowledge of the physical world.

A. Direct Knowledge as an Essential Ingredient of Perception

1. THE DISTINCTION BETWEEN DIRECT KNOWLEDGE AND INDIRECT KNOWLEDGE

In our paradigm of the perception of a table a person would normally be prepared to claim that he knows that there is a table nearby. If his claim were challenged, he would respond by saying that he sees, or observes, or notices, that a table is nearby. Very few claims to knowledge can be defended this briefly. One might defend the claim to know that there is a fire in the hills by saying that one sees that smoke is billowing up from behind the ridge; the claim to know that a man walked along a beach by saying that one sees that there are footprints on it; the claim to know that an aircraft is approaching the field by saying that one sees that a blip is moving on a radar scope in the right sort of way; the claim to know that nuclear units passed through a cloud chamber by saying that one sees that there are certain marks on a photographic plate. The distinction I have been drawing between what one observes and what one knows only on the basis of what one observes is universally recognized, though there is much debate over its proper formulation. At the risk of raising many hackles, I propose to say that when one observes some fact, one has direct knowledge of it, and that when one defends a belief in, or a claim to know, an unobserved fact by appealing to an observed fact, the knowledge about the unobserved fact is indirect.

2. THE EVIDENTIAL SUPERIORITY OF DIRECT KNOWLEDGE OVER INDIRECT KNOWLEDGE

It is also widely accepted that claims to direct knowledge are more cogent than claims to indirect knowledge. Rival claims to indirect knowledge cannot be settled merely by appeals to degrees of internal elegance; they must be settled mainly by appeals to direct knowledge, that is, to observed, or noticed, facts. In short, knowledge of unobserved facts about the world must have an empirical foundation. The contrary view that some unobserved facts about the world can be known without any empirical foundation may be called a Delphic theory of knowledge, after the ancient priestesses at

Delphi, who were widely supposed to acquire their knowledge of unobserved facts by imbibing fumes from a holy grotto and going into trances. Doubtless, no sensible well-informed person today holds a specifically Delphic theory of knowledge, but there may be many people whose fundamental beliefs about perception imply that knowledge of the physical world can be acquired only in a nonempirical, if not specifically Delphic, manner.

Ordinary perceiving is not quite the same as direct knowing, nor does it have the same object as direct knowing. Yet a perceptual situation is supposed to be an event of the kind that anchors our knowledge of the physical world. And if so, it must contain an ingredient that is directly known.

B. The Importance and Difficulty of Formulating Direct Knowledge Carefully

It is very easy to be careless in formulating direct knowledge. Indeed, it is often very difficult, even for an experienced investigator, to report only what he observes and to exclude what he merely takes for granted, believes, or indirectly knows. Yet it is only what he observes, or directly knows, that can settle rival claims to indirect knowledge, and hence serve as empirical grounds for knowledge. The soundest empirical knowledge must be based upon the reports of observers who have taken the greatest care to distinguish their direct from their indirect knowledge. But the tendency of the average observer to confuse what he observes with what he knows only indirectly is so strong that it will be worthwhile to consider briefly two species of it.

1. THE TENDENCY TO CLAIM DIRECT KNOWLEDGE OF DISPOSITIONAL PROPERTIES

First to be dealt with are dispositional properties, that is, powers, capacities, susceptibilities, and the like. Although a person can know indirectly that a thing has a certain dispositional property, it is logically impossible for him to observe that a thing has a dispositional property; yet many people claim to observe the dispositional properties of things. I shall not fully define "dispositional property," but I shall try to indicate what it means by reference to a familiar example, namely, solubility. To say that a thing is soluble at a certain time is to say that if it were then in water, it would be dissolving. Nobody can observe that a cube of sugar is soluble, not even the greatest living physicist, not even an archangel physicist, though they all may have overwhelmingly sound indirect knowledge that it is. On the other hand, dissolving, as compared with being soluble, is readily observable by anyone. In this example "solubility" is the name of a dispositional property, and it is definable in terms of "dissolving," which is the name of a nondispositional property. Most adjectival expressions are used in most contexts as names of dispositional properties. Consider, for example, metric adjectives such as "3 feet long" or "circular." They are used to say what the outcome would be if certain measuring devices were applied to a thing in a prescribed way. Thus, to say that a thing is 3 feet long might be to say that a foot rule would have to be laid off on it three times in order to make their extremities coincide. A great many non-metrical adjectives are used to assert that a thing would match a certain standard object in a certain respect. Thus, the sentence "This is reddish orange" is often used to say that a thing would match a certain Munsell color chip under standard conditions. And again, although we may have well-founded indirect knowledge of these facts, we cannot observe, or notice, them. Yet many people report their observations in such a way that their hearers, and even themselves, end up talking as if they believed that dispositional properties had been observed.

2. The Tendency to Claim Direct Knowledge of Hidden Parts

Under normal circumstances, if one were handed a 1-dollar bill, one would scarcely hesitate to say that one observed a 1-dollar bill even though the profferer's thumb covered part of it. Suppose, however, that a person familiar with currency were handed a 500-dollar bill in payment of a debt. He would not be likely to say that he observed a 500-dollar bill until the profferer had removed his thumb so that all parts of the bill could be inspected. His reluctance would be due partly to his specific knowledge of what to expect beneath the thumb, but mainly to the high stakes involved. Another example: suppose that a person is in a public garage looking at the engine of an old automobile. Its fan is rotating, its tappets bobbing rhythmically, its bedplate trembling. He would scarcely hesitate to say that he was observing the operation of an internal combustion engine. But he would not be observing that there is such an operation, for the internal combustion would be hidden from him. In an engineering museum he might hesitate to say this, even though he observed the same sort of facts, because he might suspect that the engine was a facsimile driven by a concealed electric motor. In general, the facts that anyone strictly observes, or notices, on a single occasion are very few and thin, and only under special circumstances does one bother to confine one's reports strictly to them.

IV. INCONSISTENT SETS OF SENTENCES THAT CONSTITUTE PHILOSOPHICAL PROBLEMS OF PERCEPTION

Without further preliminaries, let us now proceed directly to the consideration of particular sets of sentences that constitute philosophical problems about perception. I shall first present four examples, with a minimum of commentary, and then make some general remarks about the sources of their internal inconsistency.

A. List of Examples

1. APPROACHING AND LOOKING AT A FIXED PENNY

Suppose that under normal conditions an observer looks obliquely, and from several feet away, at an old British penny that lies on a table in a well-lighted room. Keeping his eyes—the example would be better if he were using only one eye—on the penny, he approaches the table until he is looking straight down at it. He would now probably claim to know that the following sentences are true:

(i) The penny was round and brown throughout the interval of his approach to the table.

(ii) What was presented to him in the center of his visual field throughout his approach was at first thinly elliptical and a bright whitish yellow, then increasingly fatter and darker, until at the end it was circular and brown.

(iii) What was presented to him in the center of his visual field throughout the approach was identical with the penny, or at least the top surface of the penny.

For any commonsensical person under these circumstances would claim to know that what he was directing his eyes toward was a round brown coin. If he were also a very careful observer, striving to exclude indirect knowledge from his report, he would probably accept the second sentence as a description of what he inspected in his visual field. For when many people look at a penny very obliquely and inspect the centers of their visual fields carefully, they notice something thinly elliptical in them, something whose vertical stretch traverses much less of their visual fields than its horizontal stretch. The sense of "stretch" and "traverse" may be roughly illustrated by a person who looks with one eye at a clear blue sky through a pane of glass on which a thin ellipse has been painted with transparent yellow ink. His visual field is entirely blue except for a thinly elliptical green expanse in its center, whose vertical stretch is much less than its horizontal stretch; so that if the expanse were enlarged at the same rate in all directions in the visual field, its horizontal extremities would blot out the blue long before its vertical extremities would do so. Finally, if the observer were commonsensical, he would probably claim to know that the third sentence is true on the grounds that if we are to have well-founded knowledge about the system of physical objects in our world, we must sometimes see some of them face to face directly, and notice what properties they have, and that in our example he is in the best possible position to do this.

A commonsensical person who on appropriate occasions tries to describe his visual fields as carefully as possible would be unwilling to give up any of the three sentences. But he must give up one or more of them, for taken together they imply that one and the same particular, namely, what the observer was aware of, both did and did not change shape, and both did and did not change color, during the interval of his approach to the table.

2. SIMULTANEOUSLY LOOKING AT AND FEELING A TILTING PENNY

Let us take another example. A single observer curls this thumb and forefinger around the rim of the penny so that he can simultaneously feel and see its rim. He begins by holding the penny inclined away from him so that he looks at it obliquely, and then gradually rights it until finally its near surface is at right angles to his line of sight. If the observer is commonsensical and careful, he will probably claim to know that the following four sentences are true:

(i) The shape of the penny did not change while it was being tilted.

(ii) What was presented in the center of his visual field was thinly elliptical at the beginning of the tilting, then became steadily fatter, and ended up round.

(iii) What was presented to him in his tactual field remained fixed and round throughout the tilting.

(iv) The boundary of what was presented to him in the center of his visual field and what was presented to him in his tactual field were both identical with the near rim of the penny.

The first and fourth sentences are readily acceptable by common sense, and the second, like its analog in the previous example, is readily acceptable to many people who try to describe the contents of their visual fields as carefully as possible. Most of us may balk at the third one, however, for most sighted people have poorly developed tactual discrimination, and can hardly believe that a blind and deaf person like Laura Brigman was able to recognize another person by shaking hands with him a whole year after the only other time when she had shaken hands with him. She would not have found it difficult to recognize circular rims or to distinguish ellipses with many degrees of eccentricity. But even a person with poor tactual discrimination should be able to notice that what was in his tactual fields did not change its shape during an interval. He should therefore be troubled by the fact that jointly the sentences imply that something both did and did not change its shape during a certain interval; and consequently, one or more of them are false, or at least must be reformulated.

3. LOOKING AT AN OAR HALF IMMERSED IN WATER

A third example is generated by the ancient puzzle about looking at an oar half immersed in water. It consists of the following sentences:

(i) The oar is straight.

(ii) What is presented in the observer's visual field is a long, thin, cylindrical, bent surface.

(iii) The surface in his visual field is identical with the near surface of the oar.

Taken together, they imply that some particular both is and is not bent.

4. Looking at a Penny, Which Consists Entirely of Elementary Theoretical Units

The preceding examples drew only on the "departments" of common sense and analytic inspection. The next example draws upon that of theoretical science as well. Merely looking at one side of the penny under optimum normal conditions can help generate belief in the following sentences:

(i) The near side of the penny consists of a vast number of elementary theoretical units at relatively enormous distances from one another; neither any one of them nor any aggregate of them is brown; and the whole array of them is radically discontinuous.

(ii) What is presented in the center of the observer's visual field is continuously and uniformly brown.

(iii) What is presented in the center of his visual field is identical with the near side of the penny.

Taken together, they imply that something both is and is not brown, and both is and is not continuous.

B. Three General Presuppositions that Underlie These Inconsistent Sets

Three general presuppositions underlie the problems we have just listed, although they have not been explicitly formulated and included in the sets. Two of them seem to be metaphysical, for they seem to be a priori judgments about the world; and the other seems to be linguistic, for it seems to be a semantic rule for the use of basic sentences about perception. It should be noted in passing that even the wariest investigators often find it difficult to keep these categories distinct. The three presuppositions will be stated below and their bearing on the problems brought out.

1. A Perceiver Must Notice a Fact about a Particular External to Himself

This presupposition underlies the distinction normally drawn between perception and introspection. Thus, if a person notices that he feels melancholy, he is not perceiving but introspecting. On the other hand, he is perceiving when he sees his own hand, or feels the warmth induced in it by a physiotherapist's lamp. There are many borderline cases, like stomach-aches, but we shall not examine the reasons for drawing the line in one place rather than another.

2. BOTH PHYSICAL OBJECTS AND THE EXTERNAL PARTICULARS THAT PERCEIVERS NOTICE FACTS ABOUT ARE ALL IN THE SAME SPACE

This presupposition is a fertile source of inconsistency, because if the properties we ascribe in perceptual reports are incompatible with one another, it greatly increases the likelihood that we shall ascribe incompatible properties to the same region. The likelihood is increased still further if the second presupposition is taken in conjunction with the third.

3. THE BASIC SENTENCES THAT EXPRESS A PERCEIVER'S DIRECT KNOWLEDGE OF PARTICULARS OTHER THAN HIMSELF MUST EITHER ASCRIBE QUALITIES TO THEM OR ASSERT RELATIONS HOLDING AMONG THEM

An example of the first would be the subject-predicate sentence "This is blue," and an example of the second would be the relational sentence "This is larger than that."

Recall the perceptual situation of approaching and looking at a fixed penny. Many of us—maybe all of us when we are unwary—would be tempted to say that a perceiver would notice the real shape and color of the penny only when he looked at it under normal conditions from directly overhead. We would also be tempted to say that it would continue to be round and brown after he had left this optimum position and begun to look at it obliquely. And if the top surface of the penny and the particular presented to him in the center of his visual field were in the same region of space, then his assertion about the real shape and color of the penny and his descriptive reports about the particulars presented to him in the centers of his visual fields would be incompatible with one another. Usually, the incompatibility is ignored, but whenever it is not, it may be immediately overcome by the stipulation that the predicates "is round" and "is brown" are applied to physical objects only in a dispositional sense, whereas they are applied to particulars in a perceiver's visual fields only in a nondispositional sense. Thus, if the sentence "This is round and brown" were about a physical object, it would be an abbreviation of some longer sentence like "If this were looked at by a perceiver under normal conditions from directly overhead, it would produce a round brown particular in his visual field," in which "round" and "brown" would be used in a nondispositional sense. But if the sentence "This is round and brown" were an abbreviation for some such longer sentence, it would no longer be a basic sentence. Accordingly, it would no longer satisfy our third presupposition, and hence could not participate in the inconsistent set constituted by our first example.

Analogous remarks apply to sentences about the atomic constitution of a penny. If a scientist in a commonsensical frame of mind were looking down at a penny under optimum conditions, he would be tempted to say that the region of space he was looking at was occupied by something uniformly and continuously brown. And if, while continuing to look at it, his frame of mind were to turn scientific, he would probably say that the region of space he was looking at was occupied by nothing but a widely scattered multitude of tiny theoretical units, say, atoms. But if he were to make these statements by means of nondispositional predicates, he would be contradicting himself. Some scientists who have felt disturbed about contradicting themselves in this way have gone so far as to say that theoretical units do not really exist, that sentences which seem to ascribe nondispositional properties to them are really abbreviations for much longer sentences which assert how pieces of apparatus would be observed to behave under certain conditions.

Every moderately educated person sometimes explicitly accepts, at least in rough form, the picture of the world offered by theoretical science; sometimes he also is, or could readily become, an analytic inspector of his sensory fields; and most of the time he is commonsensical. Moreover, the chances are that he implicitly makes the three presuppositions formulated above. If such a person were to consider any of the sentences in our inconsistent sets, each sentence separately from the rest, he would probably accept it. Thus, if a scientist were describing some experiment to him and said, "This coin is wholly constituted of atoms . . . ," he would doubtless accept the description explicitly. If a numismatist told him that a coin was round, smooth, brownish green, etc., he would doubtless accept this description. And if an expert in perspective drawing told him that when he looks obliquely at a coin, its field-of-vision contour is elliptical, he would doubtless, after some reflection and trial of his own, accept that. The inconsistent sets constitute problems only because each sentence in them would be accepted separately in this way. They do not constitute problems in the sense that prima facie solutions are hard to come by.

V.   FOUR PRIMA FACIE SOLUTIONS TO PROBLEMS CONSTITUTED BY THE INCONSISTENT SETS; EACH SOLUTION REJECTS ONE OR MORE OF THE THREE GENERAL PRESUPPOSITIONS

Solutions to our problems are not like solutions of other kinds of problems. Although I shall try to explicate their nature mainly by sketching some examples, a few general characterizations may be of help here. A solution must alter one or more of the sentences that constitute a problem. Thus, one cannot solve the example of the oar by explaining why there is a bent surface in the observer's visual field; that would leave the inconsistency untouched, even strengthen it. A solution must be generalizable to all problems. It must be as systematic and logically economical as possible. And it must disturb careful formulations of our knowledge, in whatever "departments," as little as possible. It cannot be found by acquiring more empirical knowledge. Indeed, an archangel who possessed all empirical knowledge would not thereby possess solutions to philosophical problems of perception. He would instead possess more such problems than we now have.

A. First Solution: The Theory of Appearing

1. Exposition of the "Theory"; Mechanics of the Solution

The so-called Theory of Appearing begins by rejecting the third presupposition, and so at the outset it looks like a merely linguistic solution. In its simplest form, it asserts that in perception a person's direct knowledge of something other than himself should be formulated by a sentence like "O appears Φ to S," where "O" is the name of a physical object, "S" is the name of a person, and "Φ" is the name of a property.

A word or two must be said about the sense of "appear" in this formulation. According to one familiar sense of "appear," to say that a pear appears ripe to someone is to say that as a result of a cursory inspection of it, he is inclined to believe that it would taste sweet. According to another familiar sense, everything appears rosy to a person wearing red spectacles, even though he has no inclination to believe that everything is rosy, indeed is convinced to the contrary. It is in this second sense that many people claim to know that a tilted round coin appears elliptical. And this is the sense of "appear" that is intended in the new formulation of direct perceptual knowledge.

Armed with this formulation, one can transform our inconsistent sets into consistent ones by turning the second sentences of the sets into, respectively, the following:

(ii) What was presented to him in the center of his visual field throughout his approach at first appeared thinly elliptical and whitish yellow to him, then increasingly fatter and darker, until at the end it appeared circular and brown.

(ii) What was presented to him in the center of his visual field appeared thinly elliptical to him at the beginning of the tilting, then appeared to become steadily fatter, and ended up appearing round.

(ii) What is presented in the observer's visual field appears long, thin, cylindrical, and bent to him.

(ii) What is presented in the center of his visual field appears continuously and uniformly brown to him.

As a result of these changes, the corresponding sets become consistent.

2. DIFFICULTIES

a. DREAMS AND HALLUCINATIONS. But though the adoption of the "appearing" formulation for direct perceptual knowledge solves the particular problems we have been concerned with, it will not solve others, and indeed it generates others. A standard objection against it is that it does not allow us to describe dreams or hallucinations. It is widely held that when a person dreams of, say, a cow, there is no physical object that is appearing bovine to him, and that when there is a vivid, opaque hallucinatory object, say, a dagger in a person's visual field, there is no physical object that is appearing daggerish to him. Yet suppose that during a 12-hour period a person briefly looks at a cow, looks at a dagger, dreams of a cow, and hallucinates a dagger, and is asked how many bovinish objects and how many daggerish objects occurred in his visual fields during this period. He would be strongly inclined to say that two of each had occurred. For there may have been no qualitative internal difference between what he noticed of a real cow and what he noticed of a dream cow, or between what he noticed of a real dagger and what he noticed of a hallucinatory dagger. We can even assume here that while dreaming and hallucinating he had no inclination to believe that physical objects were appearing bovine or daggerish to him. Yet on the Theory of Appearing our observer would have to report that during that period something appeared bovine to him on only one occasion and something appeared daggerish to him on only one occasion.

b. POSITIONAL PROPERTIES. A second objection arises from the fact that if the "appearing" formulation is to have sufficient scope, "Φ" must take positional properties as values, not just shapes, colors, etc. But if it does, then once again there are cases in which an observer would not be able to formulate his direct perceptual knowledge. In order to bring out this implication, let us take the case of seeing something in a mirror.

Suppose that an observer holds a finger a few inches in front of a mirror, so that he can see both the finger and its reflection. Now if a physical object can appear to be where it is not, then it can appear to be in several places at the same time. Although our observer has indirect knowledge that a single finger is appearing him in two places, he has no direct knowledge of it. That is, he cannot notice whether a single finger is appearing to him in two places, or two fingers are appearing to him each in a different place from the other's. And so he would be unable to describe the grounds on which he bases his indirect knowledge that a single finger is appearing to him in two places.

That such knowledge is indirect may be illustrated by the famous Mirror Scene from the Marx Brothers' film *Duck Soup*. Groucho has become the dictator of a mythical state in Central Europe, and Harpo has broken into his mansion at night to steal some documents. Aroused by the noise, Groucho gets out of bed and prowls the mansion in his nightclothes looking for intruders. Harpo, trying to escape, runs into a huge full-length mirror and shatters it. He quickly puts on a nightcap, a long nightshirt, and a pair of steel-rimmed glasses; and he paints heavy black eyebrows and a mustache on his face. Thus rigged, he looks exactly like Groucho. As Groucho approaches the place where the mirror was, Harpo resolves to make him think that the mirror is still there, and so behaves so as to look just as Groucho's reflection in the mirror would have looked. Groucho suspects that something is fishy, but he can't be sure. Instead of removing his doubts the easy way, i.e., by trying to touch the mirror, he resolves to remove them by performing capers that would normally be beyond the powers of an intruder to imitate. But Harpo imitates them all, and the hilarity becomes excruciating as the capers become wilder. The philosophical point here is that Groucho is unable to notice whether he is appearing to himself to be in two places, or he and some other person are appearing to him, each in his own, and different, place. But in fact he notices a great deal. And so there is much direct knowledge here that the Theory of Appearing cannot formulate.

The Theory of Appearing can be patched up to avoid this difficulty by incorporating in it an ad hoc postulate that a physical object can appear only in the place where it really is. But such a patch would generate new problems, i.e., have implications that are incompatible with other claims to knowledge, either in the form of general presuppositions or in the form of special bits drawn from the three "departments." Imagine that on his return from the moon, Neil Armstrong shaved by using a mirror fastened to the inner wall of his spaceship. How could he describe the direct knowledge he acquired by looking in the mirror? According to the ad hoc postulate, he could not say that his own face was appearing to him in a place a foot behind the mirror. For according to it, if any physical object appeared to him in that place, it would have had to be there. But since the spaceship was moving through a vacuum, there was no physical object in that place. His claim to acquiring direct knowledge by looking in the mirror could be sustained only if the Theory of Appearing were patched up still further, say, by supposing that some volume of space outside the spaceship were appearing facelike to him. But this is, in effect, to incorporate in the Theory of Appearing the old Absolute, or Newtonian, Theory of Space. According to the Absolute Theory, space consists of a set of points which may or may not be occupied by physical objects, and it would continue to exist, in a nondispositional way, even if there were no physical objects in it. At the present time this theory is in disfavor, having been replaced by a Relational, or Leibnizian, Theory, according to which space is nothing over and above whatever physical objects there are and their interrelationships of distance and direction. And so this attempt to patch a once-patched Theory of Appearing will make it capable of formulating our direct perceptual knowledge only by violating what is now a general presupposition about the nature of physical space.

The fortunes of the Theory of Appearing illustrate the fact that although philosophical theories of perception become elaborate, they need not become so wantonly or irrationally. Each step in its elaboration is made to accommodate some claim to knowledge that almost anyone, considering it in isolation, would be strongly inclined to accept.

c. DIRECT KNOWLEDGE OF FACTS ABOUT PHYSICAL OBJECTS. There is a third and more typically philosophical objection to the unpatched Theory of Appearing. According to it, the direct knowledge a person acquires in perception is that there is a certain physical object which is appearing to him in a certain way. But there are strong reasons for saying that nobody can have direct knowledge of the existence of physical objects. The conjuror's old trick of hiding coins under a cup depends on the fact that his audience cannot have direct knowledge of what is hidden from them by the opaque inverted cup. He then arranges matters so that, despite their claims, they do not even have indirect knowledge about what is thus hidden from them. Tricks with coins alone often make use of a thin shell which fits snugly over a standard coin and whose outer surface exactly resembles that of the coin. The audience do not directly know either that what they are looking at is a standard coin, with a full complement of hidden parts, or that it is only a resembling shell. But every opaque physical object, even the shell, must have some hidden parts. And if an observer can have only indirect knowledge of a physical object's hidden parts, he can have only indirect knowledge that a physical object exists. In the perception of opaque physical objects, an observer can have direct knowledge only that a surface exists. If he assumed a priori the postulate that every surface is the surface of a physical object, he could often acquire invincible indirect knowledge that a physical object, including its hidden parts, exists. But I see no reason to make such an assumption.

There are many other objections to the Theory of Appearing. For example, allowing temporal qualities to be values of "Φ" has many awkward implications. But the ones I have mentioned, or something like them, have made several careful writers decline to accept it. If it is not accepted, another prima facie plausible way of making the sets of sentences consistent must be found.

B. Second Solution: Minds, Physical Objects, and Sensa

1. EXPOSITION

Let us begin by reasserting the third general presupposition, according to which we must formulate the direct knowledge in perception by saying that a certain particular *does have* a certain property instead of only *appearing to have* it. And then let us deny the last sentence in each set, namely, the sentence in each set that identifies what is presented in a perceiver's sensory field with the physical object that he is perceiving, or with some aspect of it. This step would prevent the remaining sentences in each set from implying a contradiction. But initially it would also require one to find another location in physical space for what is presented in one's sensory field, and thereby give rise to new and powerful difficulties. In the first place, locating what is presented in one's sensory field—we may call this particular a "sensum"—at a specific place in physical space does not seem to be a merely linguistic proposal; nor does it seem to be the outcome of scientific procedures; it seems, rather, to be a piece of metaphysical postulation. Since one cannot locate a visual sensum in empty physical space without presupposing the Absolute Theory of Space, one must locate it in, or on, some physical object. If it is to be located in or on any physical object external to the sensory end organs, it would have to be located in or on the physical object that is being perceived. But since this has already been found untenable, it would have to be located in some physical object internal to the sensory end organs. Some writers who took this line have identified it with the retina or with some region in the visual cortex. Other writers have balked at this proposal for various reasons. One reason is its implication that whenever an observer is looking at a blue object under normal conditions, part of his retina, or part of his visual cortex would *be* blue, in the same sense in which the sensum in his visual field would be recognizably blue; whereas it seems certifiable by physiology that no aspect of those physical objects is blue in that sense. Another reason is its implication that in normal perception a person would be directly aware of his retina or visual cortex and would notice facts about them; whereas it seems certifiable by physiology that an observer could become directly aware of his retina or visual cortex only under extraordinary circumstances, perhaps with some sort of autoophthalmoscope or autocerebroscope. Having found no resting place in physical space for sensa, some writers have taken the radical step of rejecting the second general presupposition that underlay our inconsistent sets of sentences, namely, the presupposition that all particulars, other than ourselves, that we are aware of in perception are in the same space that physical objects are in. And this sounds very metaphysical indeed. Let us briefly explore the consequences of taking this radical step.

It opens the way to what seems to have been the prevailing, though tacit, philosophy of perception in the sciences since Newton's time, which may be roughly reconstructed as follows. Physical space contains nothing but elementary physical units, and they are deemed to have only those properties, dispositional or nondispositional, that current theoretical science ascribes to them. No sensa are in physical space. For example, the array of colored particulars that constitutes a person's visual field at a particular time is generated in complete detail by a state of his brain, but it is not in his brain or anywhere else in physical space. The perceiver himself is characterized only by such mental properties as cognizing, conating, and emoting. He may inspect the particulars in his visual field, for example, and notice what colors they have, but he is not himself characterized by colors. Sensory fields belonging to different persons have no particular in common.

Theoretical science by itself does not imply this view. It has been held because it seemed to go farthest toward accommodating consistently the corpus of theoretical science, the corpus of analytic inspection of sensory fields, part of the corpus of common sense, and two, i.e., the first and third, of the general presuppositions underlying our inconsistent sets of sentences.

2. DIFFICULTIES

a. INFERENCE FROM DIRECT KNOWLEDGE TO INDIRECT KNOWLEDGE OF PHYSICAL OBJECTS. Traditionally, two serious objections have been raised against it. One is that if it is true, nobody could know that it is. For many writers have felt that it is impossible to formulate an acceptable principle of inference that would allow one to infer either strictly or probably from direct knowledge of one's private sensory world to indirect knowledge of a physical world that does not overlap it anywhere.

b. EXCESSIVE DUPLICATION OF PARTICULAR ENTITIES. Another objection is that the view is too complex, and its main parts improperly connected. For according to it, the physical world is partially duplicated for each person; the array of particulars in a person's visual field, for example, corresponds in complete detail to one of his brain states, but its properties are not reducible to those of the brain. These objections have been motivated partly by a concern for formal systematic elegance and partly by the commonsensical conviction that in addition to minds and physical objects there is not a third category of particulars, namely, sensa.

C. Third Solution: Only Minds and Physical Objects

1. EXPOSITION

The commonsensical conviction seems to have led some writers to reject the first two general presuppositions underlying our inconsistent sets of sentences, and perhaps the third as well. That is, because of it they seem to have held that in addition to physical objects, as described by theoretical science, the only other particulars are minds, and that in perception each mind has direct knowledge only of some fact about itself.* Thus, in perception direct knowledge is acquired by an act of introspection, not by an act of inspection directed upon particulars other than the perceiver. A person may express such direct knowledge either by saying what properties he has or by saying what properties he appears to himself to have. On the first alternative it would be expressed by a sentence of the form "S is Φ"; on the second, by a sentence of the form "S appears Φ to S." There are plenty of familiar introspective sentences of the first form, such as "I am melancholy"; and in sophisticated circles there are even familiar introspective sentences of the second form, such as "I appear to myself to be melancholy" or "I seem melancholy to myself." The program of the third solution would rewrite all the sentences in our sets except one, namely, the sentence stating that the penny consisted entirely of elementary theoretical units; and it would thereby remove the initial inconsistency of the sets. Since each new sentence would either ascribe a wholly mental property to a mind, or ascribe a wholly theoretical property to a physical object, or assert a correlation between them, the danger of introducing new inconsistencies seems prima facie to be small.

2. DIFFICULTIES

a. SIMPLE ASSIMILATION OF PERCEPTION TO INTROSPECTION. Nevertheless, the attempt to assimilate basic perceptual sentences to these intro-

---

* Something like this view seems to have been explicitly, though reluctantly, held by William James. See his unabridged *The Principles of Psychology* (1950, Ch. VI, 181). In that place he said, after reviewing several views on the mind-body relation, "I confess . . . that to posit a soul influenced in some mysterious way by the brain-states and responding to them by conscious affections of its own, seems to me in the line of least logical resistance, so far as we yet have attained."

spective ones in a simple way fails at once because it yields falsehoods. If a person is looking up at a clear blue sky, he cannot express his direct perceptual knowledge by means of the sentences "I am blue" or "I appear blue to myself," for these are clearly false. Similarly, if he is looking at his hand, he cannot use the sentences "I am handlike" or "I appear hand-like to myself." If the assimilation can be carried out at all, it must be done by devious devices, to all of which there are strong prima facie objections. We shall now consider a few of them.

b. MODEST LINGUISTIC DEVICES. Suppose one were to express one's direct perceptual knowledge by means of "I am having a blue sensation" or "I am having a handlike sensation." Whatever other shortcomings these sentences may have, they not only fail to have the prescribed form; they also seem to introduce into the world of minds and physical objects a new category of particulars, namely, sensations. But it was the intention of the present scheme to limit the categories of particulars to minds and physical objects. The trouble about the form could be gotten around orthographically by a liberal use of hyphens, so as to yield the new sentences "I am having-a-blue-sensation" or "I am having-a-handlike-sensation." But hyphenation alone cannot get rid of act–object relationships in perception, any more than it could fool the telegraph operator in the joke about the impecunious traveling salesman who wanted to telegraph his wife just his name and claimed that he was an Indian chief named Will-Not-Be-Home-Until-Tuesday. Nor will simply recasting a sentence into subject-predicate form get rid of relations. Thus, one cannot get rid of a relation between a perceiver and his hand by simply recasting "I see my hand" into the form "I am characterized by the property of seeing my hand." Another proposal, "It appears to me that this is a hand," fails not only because of its form, but also because in it "this" occurs as the name of a particular other than the perceiver.

c. RADICAL LINGUISTIC DEVICES; THE ANNULMENT OF FAMILIAR AD-JECTIVES. As a basic perceptual sentence some writers have favored something like "It is to me as if I were seeing a hand," which can be turned into a sentence of the proper form as "I am as-if-I-were-seeing-a-hand." Similarly, "It is to me as if I were seeing something blue" can be turned into "I am as-if-I-were-seeing-something-blue." But by now these hyphenated predicates can no longer be regarded as names, or even as definitions, of qualities that characterize perceiving minds. The predicate "as-if-I-were-seeing-something-blue," for example, does not name a complex quality one of whose constituents is blueness, in some such way as the predicate "Union-Jacklike" does so. In uttering the sentence "I am as-if-I-were-seeing-something-blue" a perceiver is, rather, drawing attention to some quality Ψ by indicating that he is normally characterized by it whenever the conditions expressed by the predicate hold. Unfortunately, any knowledge to this effect would be indirect; a corresponding piece of direct knowledge would be of the form "I am Ψ." It would follow that so far as perception is concerned nearly all the familiar adjectives of common sense and analytic inspection would be relegated to the language we use for expressing indirect knowledge about the physical world. But if particulars in the physical world have only those properties ascribed to them by theoretical science, then these familiar adjectives—"blue," "warm," "rough," etc.—could not even be used for that purpose, and thus for no purpose whatever. Any person—and not only a theoretical scientist—would more correctly draw attention to the fact that he is characterized by Ψ if he were to utter the sentence "I am as-if-my-brain-were-in-condition-C." On the present view the only properties we notice instances of in perception are like Ψ, and none of them have names. But many people find this consequence too great a price to pay for reducing the population of the world to minds and physical objects, especially since this rejection aggravates the difficulty of finding an acceptable principle for inferring from our direct knowledge to our indirect knowledge of the physical world.

D. Fourth Solution: Only Elementary Theoretical Units

1. EXPOSITION

Those who are partial to systematic elegance would not be contented with the preceding solution, for they would prefer one which requires the world to consist of only one category of particulars. And if the category were exhaustively comprised by the elementary units of theoretical science, the solution would be doubly attractive. For it seems to many that science has indeed discovered that there are no things over and above theoretical units, and no properties over and above theoretical properties. If this view were true, then all the sentences of the inconsistent sets would have to be rewritten wholly in the language of theoretical science, and if they could be thus rewritten, without gain or loss of meaning, the resulting sets would doubtless be consistent. However attractive this outcome may be to theoretical scientists, while their minds are on theoretical science, it is difficult to defend philosophically. There is no room here even to sketch some of its recent ingenious formulations, but they all, so it seems to me, suffer from the same traditional liabilities, namely, that they cannot rewrite the sentences of our sets without radically changing their meanings, and that they presuppose a Delphic-like theory of knowledge.

2. DIFFICULTIES

a. DISSOLUTION OF BLUENESS. In the world of the fourth solution there is no room for most of the qualities that participate in the direct knowledge claimed by the "departments" of common sense and analytic inspection. Nothing in this world is blue, for example, in the sense in which analytic inspection would attribute blueness to something. If all properties are theoretical ones, "blue" means nothing over and above wave trains of a certain sort, or retinal stimulus patterns of a certain sort, or energy distributions in the visual cortex of a certain sort, or certain overt responses of an observer to certain stimuli. But these meanings are flatly incompatible with the meaning that common sense or analytic inspection assigns to "blue."

The tendency to suppose that the latter is identical with one or another of the former may have arisen from the feeling that science has discovered what being blue *is*. There is a sense, of course, in which science has done this, but there is an equally good sense in which it has done nothing of the sort. Imagine an ace theoretical scientist who knows everything there is to know about being blue. His knowledge has been acquired over a long period of time extending back to the day when he first went to school. When, as a preschool child, he looked up at a clear sky, he noticed that something was characterized by blueness. As he got older, acquiring more and more indirect theoretical knowledge about the world, he continued to look up at clear skies from time to time. It is not true that in the course of these sky-viewings the blueness of his preschool years gradually changed into some webby pattern of elementary theoretical units. The blueness noticed by the ace theoretical scientist is the same as the blueness noticed by the preschool child.

b. INEXPLICABILITY OF SCIENTIFIC LABOR AND UNJUSTIFIABILITY OF THEORETICAL SCIENTIFIC DOCTRINE. If a person could notice the webby patterns of theoretical units in the same sense as he can notice the blueness of the sky, then the long, arduous history of scientific discovery would be inexplicable. For it would be folly to construct long chains of support for indirect knowledge of some fact when we can notice it directly. If, on the other hand, our knowledge in theoretical science is ineluctably indirect, as it certainly is, then if blueness were fully reducible to theoretical units, our theoretical knowledge could have no empirical grounds; we should have to acquire it by Delphic means. The tendency to suppose that the acquisition of theoretical knowledge dissolves the nontheoretical, and noticeable, facts that suport it should be resisted. The view that there is nothing but the elementary units of theoretical science achieves systematic elegance at the expense of credibility.

References

James, W. *The Principles of Psychology*. Vol. I. New York: Dover, 1950. (Originally published New York: Holt, 1890.)

Swartz, R. J. *Perceiving, Sensing, and Knowing*. Garden City, New York: Anchor Books, 1956.

Chapter 3

EPISTEMOLOGY

GILBERT HARMAN

I. RADICAL SKEPTICISM

Much of epistemology (the theory of knowledge) in philosophy is best seen as a response to the thesis that one never has the slightest reason to believe anything. This radical skepticism must be distinguished from the more commonsensical idea that nothing can be known *for certain* and that one can never be *absolutely sure* of anything. Common sense assumes that practical certainty is possible even if absolute certainty is not. Radical skepticism departs from common sense and denies that even practical certainty is ever attainable. Indeed, it denies that anything is ever even the slightest bit more likely to be true than anything else.

The problem is not that there are radical skeptics who need to be convinced that they are wrong. There aren't and, if there were, one could not argue with them, since they would have to be insane. The problem is that an extremely natural line of argument seems to lead inevitably to radical skepticism. Common sense keeps one from accepting such a conclusion. That leaves the philosophical problem of finding what goes wrong with the reasoning that seems to lead there. To repeat, the problem is not to find an argument against skepticism, it is to find out what is wrong with an argument for skepticism.

One such argument begins by asking how you know that the color red looks to someone else as it looks to you. Perhaps things that look red to you look green to him, things that look blue to you look orange to him, and similarly for other colors. His spectrum may be inverted, where compared with yours; and there may be no way to discover this, since he may call what is for you the experience of red the experience of green. He may describe colors exactly as you do, despite the systematic difference between his and your experience of color. This suggests you have no more reason to suppose that others see the world as you do rather than as the man with an inverted spectrum.

Further reflection suggests that you may not have the slightest reason to suppose that visual perception gives other people experiences that are anything like your visual experiences. Perhaps someone else has what would be for you auditory experiences. When he looks at the blue sky it is like what hearing middle C on the piano is for you. There seems to be no way to tell, since he would have been brought up to call that sort of experience the experience of blue. Indeed it is not clear that you have the slightest reason to suppose that others have anything you could recognize as experience. When others see things, their visual experience may be something you could not even imagine.

But then is there any reason to suppose that others have experience at all? The suggestion is that, even if you could know that the people around you were made of flesh and blood, born of women, and nourished by food, they might for all you know be automatons, in the sense that behind their elaborate reactions to the environment there might be no experience. But the suggestion is not merely that you do not *know* whether other people have any experience but also that you haven't the slightest reason to suppose they do.

Similarly, it might be suggested that you haven't the slightest reason to believe you are in the surroundings you suppose you are in, holding a book, reading an article on epistemology. It may look to you and feel as it would look and feel if you were in those surroundings, holding a book, and reading an article. But various hypotheses could explain how things look and feel. You might be sound asleep and dreaming, or a playful brain surgeon might be giving you these experiences by stimulating your cortex in a special way. You might really be stretched out on a table in his laboratory with wires running into your head from a large computer. Perhaps you have always been on that table. Perhaps you are quite a different person from what you seem: you are a volunteer for a psychology experiment that involves having the experiences of someone of the opposite sex reading an article about epistemology in English, a language which in real life you do not understand. Or perhaps you do not even have a body. Maybe you were in an accident and all that could be saved was your brain which is kept alive in the laboratory. For your amusement you are being fed a tape from the twentieth century. Of course, that is to assume you have to have a brain in order to have experience; and that might be just part of the myth you are being given.

You might suppose that there is actually little difference between these hypotheses. After all, you have the same experiences on all of them. So you may feel that, no matter what is actually the case, everything will work out fairly well if you continue to act on the assumption that things are roughly what they seem. But that is to go beyond your evidence. It may be that up until now everything has worked out well on the assumption that things are roughly what they seem to be. But what reason is there to suppose that things will continue to work out well on that assumption? An inductive inference is needed here: "Things have worked out well in the past; so they can be expected to work out well in the future." But how could you justify this use of induction? You might argue that, since inductions have generally worked out well in the past, you are entitled to expect them to work out well in the future. But that would be circular. You would be giving an inductive argument in order to defend induction.

Furthermore, do you really have any reason to suppose that things have worked out well in the past? You may seem to remember that they have. But how can you justify relying on your memory? Surely not on the grounds that your memory has been reliable in the past, for what reason do you have to think that it has been? The fact that you seem to remember that memory has been reliable in the past is irrelevant. You cannot legitimately appeal to memory to justify memory. You seem to have no reason to suppose that things have worked out well if and when in the past you have acted as if things are much as they seem.

Such reflections lead to the philosophical problems of other minds, the external world, induction, and memory. It is important that these problems are not simply whether we could ever know for sure or be absolutely certain of various matters. They are more radical: Do we have the *slightest reason* to continue to believe as we do? Is there any more reason to believe what we do about the world than to believe anything else, no matter how incredible it may seem?

II. THE APPEAL TO MEANING

Some philosophical theories of knowledge appeal to meaning in the attempt to answer skepticism. For example, *philosophical behaviorism* is the view that statements about experience have the same meaning as certain statements about behavior. On this view, the problem of the inverted spectrum is meaningless. It is suggested that what it *means* for someone to see the world in the way that you see the world is that you and he are disposed to behave in the same way in the same perceptual situations. The supposition that you and he have roughly the same responses to color but that his spectrum is inverted with respect to yours would have no meaning.

According to philosophical behaviorism one can inductively discover someone's behavioral dispositions (how he is disposed to behave) on the basis of purely behavioral evidence. One is supposed to be able to know about that person's experience because one is supposed to know that having certain experience is equivalent to having certain behavioral dispositions. This equivalence is supposed to hold almost by virtue of the very definitions of words like "pain," "anger," "hunger," and so on. One is supposed to know the equivalence holds because one knows what these words mean.

Similarly, a *phenomenalist* claims that statements about physical objects are equivalent in meaning to complex statements about possible sensory experience. According to a phenomenalist, to say that there is a typewriter on my desk is to say that under certain conditions it would look as if there is a typewriter on my desk, that certain experiences of seeming to type can be followed by experiences of seeming to read something freshly typed, and so forth. Phenomenalists argue that one knows about these equivalences simply by virtue of knowing the meaning of statements about the external world. One uses induction to justify statements asserting the possibility of sensory experience. Then one uses the meaning equivalences to justify one's views about the world.

It is true that philosophical behaviorism and phenomenalism appeal to induction as well as to meaning; but some philosophers have argued that inductive conclusions are themselves justified simply by virtue of the meaning of "justified." To reach a conclusion by induction is supposed to be almost by definition one of the ways one can justify a conclusion. Similarly, to say that something is probable is supposed to be to say that there are good reasons for it; and in this context, "good reasons" is supposed to mean "good inductive reasons." It is said to be "analytic" (i.e., true solely by virtue of meaning) that inductive reasons are good reasons, analytic that inductive conclusions are probably true, and analytic that inductive conclusions can be used to justify belief.

Some philosophers, not wishing to accept strict philosophical behaviorism, make a similar but weaker claim. These philosophers say that to understand the meaning of statements about someone else's experience one must realize that certain kinds of behavior will provide good, but not absolutely conclusive, evidence of that experience. According to these philosophers, it is part of the meaning of the word "pain" that certain behavior, such as moaning, is evidence that one is in pain. Such evidence is said to be a "criterion" of pain. One is supposed to be able to know that others are in various psychological states because one can observe their behavior and knows criteria for these states. One is supposed to know the criteria, not by virtue of any empirical investigation, but simply because one knows the meaning of one's words. So, for these philosophers, certain statements relating behavioral evidence and psychological states are analytic, true by virtue of meaning and known to be true by virtue of one's knowledge of meaning.

Similarly, a philosopher who does not wish to accept phenomenalism can still argue that there are purely sensory criteria for statements about physical objects. Certain experience is evidence for certain claims about the external world, where the evidential relationship can be said to hold by virtue of meaning. Perhaps it is supposed to be analytic that, if one seems to be seeing a blue book, that is adequate reason to believe that one is seeing a blue book, other things equal. One is said to know an analytic truth like that because one knows the meaning of the claim that one is seeing a blue book. One is said to be able to use experience as evidence about the external world because one knows the meanings of one's words.

The reliability of memory can also be defended by an appeal to meaning. The more radical view, corresponding to philosophical behaviorism and phenomenalism, is that statements about the past are equivalent in meaning to statements about present evidence that certain things have happened in the past. The weaker version has it that it is analytic of the notion of an apparent memory that apparent memories are good but not absolutely conclusive evidence for what is apparently remembered.

III. THE REVOLT AGAINST MEANING

According to philosophical behaviorism, statements about another person's experiences can be translated without loss of meaning into statements about his behavioral dispositions. Similarly, according to phenomenalism, statements about objects in the external world can be translated without loss of meaning into statements about the possibility of one's own experience. In either case, knowledge of truths about the experiences of others or about objects in the world is supposed to be made possible by knowledge of these translations; and that knowledge is supposed to be available simply by virtue of the fact that one knows the meanings of one's words. It was always embarrassing to philosophical behaviorism and to phenomenalism that no one was ever able to give a single example of such a translation. If knowledge of other minds and of the external world were based on knowledge of translation relations, the latter knowledge would have had to be unconscious.

Lately it has become clear that the required sort of translation is impossible. No single simple psychological statement is equivalent in meaning to any nonpsychological statement that is purely about behavioral dispositions. And no statement about objects in the external world can be translated without loss of meaning into a statement that is purely about one's own possible experience.

A belief is not a simple behavioral disposition. At best, it is a disposition to behave in certain ways *given certain desires.* On the other hand, a desire is at best a disposition to act in certain ways *given certain beliefs.* This means there can be no noncircular way to give a purely behavioristic analysis of belief or desire. There is no way to translate a simple statement about belief or desire without loss of meaning into a statement that speaks only of purely behavioral dispositions. The same point holds for simple statements about other psychological states and about experiences.

Similarly, to say there is a typewriter on my desk is not to say, among other things, that under certain *purely experiential* conditions it would look to me as if there is a typewriter on my desk. For these conditions must include such things as that my eyes are open, that nothing opaque intervenes between me and the typewriter, that I have not just taken a hallucinogenic drug, and so on. A statement of relevant conditions must speak not only of possible experience but also of things in the external world. There is no way to translate simple statements about objects in the external world without loss of meaning into statements that are solely about possible experience.

Psychological statements are to statements about behavioral dispositions, and statements about the external world are to statements about possible experience, as statements of theory are to statements of possible evidence. The failure of philosophical behaviorism and phenomenalism illustrates the fact that individual theoretical statements cannot be translated without loss of meaning into purely evidential statements. The point goes back to Duhem (1906), who noted that an individual theoretical statement does not have evidential consequences all by itself but only in conjunction with other theoretical assumptions.

What is prima facie a different objection can be raised against other philosophical appeals to meaning mentioned above. These theories depend on the supposed analyticity of certain statements about good reasons. It is supposed to be true solely by virtue of meaning that an inductive argument gives one reason to believe its conclusion, that certain behavior is a good reason for believing that someone is having certain experiences, that certain sensory experience provides a good reason to think one is perceiving objects of a certain sort, and that the experience of seeming to remember something gives one a good reason to believe that it actually happened. One objection to the idea that such connections hold by virtue of meaning is that this would enable one to derive normative conclusions from purely factual premises. The claim that there are *good* reasons to believe something is normative; it has implications for what one *ought to* believe. The claim that a conclusion is the outcome of a given procedure, that certain behavior has occurred, that one has had a kind of experience, or that one seems to remember something is a purely factual claim.

Many philosophers have argued that it is impossible to derive a normative conclusion from purely factual premises. Any suggestion that there is an analytic connection between statements of fact and normative conclusions is said to commit "the naturalistic fallacy." However, philosophers have not always been agreed that every such suggestion represents a fallacy.

On one interpretation, the naturalistic fallacy consists in supposing that the meaning of a normative expression is a matter of the factual criteria used in applying that expression rather than a matter of typical reactions to the acceptance of conclusions containing that expression. It is argued that, on the contrary, the meaning of "good" and "ought" is closely connected with the fact that one tries to get things that one thinks are "good" and also tends to do something if one thinks one "ought" to do it. The point is sometimes made by appeal to how to translate the words of a foreign people if one of their expressions has the same factual criteria of application as our expression "morally ought" but does not have the same implications for action, whereas another of their expressions tends to be associated with action in the way that "morally ought" is for us but is used with quite a different set of factual criteria. Should one say that, unlike us, they have no tendency to do what they conclude they morally ought to do? Or should one say that they have a different morality? It has been argued that only the latter possibility would be plausible and therefore that our expression "morally ought" cannot be analytically tied to the factual criteria one uses in deciding what one morally ought to do.

Similarly, suppose that a foreign people did not guide their conduct by inductive procedures but by appeal to their witchdoctor. They acknowledge that the witchdoctor has often been wrong in the past. Their reason for thinking he will be right in the future is that he assures them he will be. They have an expression in their language which they use if and only if there are what we take to be good inductive reasons for a hypothesis that is under consideration. However, having thus used the expression, they have no tendency to go on to accept the relevant hypothesis. On the other hand, they have another expression which is associated with going on to accept hypotheses in the way that "good reasons" is for us. However, the latter expression is not associated with inductive methods but with appeal to the witchdoctor. Here again it would seem that we ought to translate the second and not the first of these expressions as "good reasons" and that, therefore, it cannot be true by virtue of meaning alone that inductive methods yield good reasons for accepting conclusions.

The translation argument does not work well when deployed against the remaining philosophical appeals to meaning. It is not easy to imagine a foreign people with a conception of the external world who do not treat sensory data as evidence much in the way that we do. Nor is it easy to imagine that they could have a conception of the psychological states and experiences of others unless they use behavioral evidence for these states that is like the sort of evidence that we use. Finally, it is difficult to suppose that one of their expressions should be translated as "seem to remember" if that implies they have no tendency to believe that what they "seem to remember" actually occurred.

But a more basic objection can be raised against philosophical theories that attempt to answer skepticism by appealing to meaning. Quine (1963, Ch. II; 1966, Chs. 9, 10) argues that there is no such thing as analytic truth, that nothing is true solely by virtue of meaning and that nothing is ever known to be true simply by virtue of one's knowledge of the meaning of one's words.

Skepticism maintains that one never has the slightest reason to believe one thing rather than another. In attempting to meet skeptical arguments, one eventually reaches a point at which (a) one wishes to claim that certain evidence provides a good reason to believe a particular conclusion, but (b) one cannot offer further grounds for this claim in response to any further skeptical challenge. In another age, one might have said that one can intuit the connection between evidence and conclusion; but it is no longer felt that an appeal to intuition can explain one's knowledge of such a connection any better than an appeal to magic would. In this context analyticity seems to provide just what one is looking for. If the connection between evidence and conclusion holds by virtue of meaning, it would seem that one can know that the connection holds simply by virtue of knowing what one means.

Two questions immediately arise: (1) How does one know what one means? (2) How does knowledge of that meaning give one knowledge of the connection between evidence and conclusion? Unless these questions can be satisfactorily answered, the appeal to analyticity will turn out to be as empty as an appeal to magic or to intuition.

On the most plausible account of analyticity, the meaning of a person's words is determined by the way in which he intends to use those words. That a person can know what he means by his words would on this view be an instance of the more general point that a person can know what his intentions are. This account claims that sometimes the relevant intention can be expressed as an explicit definition, if one intends to use an expression solely as an abbreviation of another. It is admitted that usually, one's intentions cannot be represented simply as such an explicit definition. But in that case it is suggested that one's intentions can be expressed by "meaning postulates," basic principles which one supposedly accepts as "implicitly defining" the meaning of some of the expressions occurring in those postulates. One is supposed to intend to use those words in such a way that those meaning postulates will be true.

There is obviously something to this account. The meaning of the expressions used to set forth any theory depend heavily on the basic principles of the theory. In explaining one's theory by citing the principles that give meaning to one's theoretical terms, one gives one's audience to understand that one is intending to use those words in such a way that those principles will be true.

The problem is that intending that certain principles be true does not make them true, even when those principles give meaning to the terms used in stating them. What a person's words mean depends on *everything* he believes, on *all* of the assumptions he is making. This is a consequence of the fact that one takes another to mean the same by his words as one does only if this does not lead to the conclusion that certain of his beliefs are radically different from one's own. In the latter case, if there is a relatively simple way to construe the other person's words such that he would then have similar beliefs to one's own, one will thus construe his words. This allows no room for a distinction between analytically true assumptions and others. For any assumption one makes, it can happen that the best way to understand another person's view has him denying that assumption.

Applied to oneself, the point becomes the Duhemian thesis that undermined philosophical behaviorism and phenomenalism. There is no way to divide one's assumptions into those possibly disconfirmable by the evidence and others not susceptible to disconfirmation because they are analytically true. One's total view faces the evidence together as a unit. In the face of contrary evidence, some part of that view must be changed; and no part is immune to revision. The history of science teaches that lesson. Euclidean geometry, which was once taken as a paradigm of something which could be intuited to be true, was abandoned with the coming of relativity theory. Scientists do not hesitate to abandon a definition if that seems to be the best way to improve a going theory. And it has even

been suggested that basic principles of logic are shown false by considerations of quantum physics.

The appeal to analyticity was supposed to be an improvement over an
appeal to magic or intuition. It now turns out to involve the supposition
that assuming that something is true can make it true. One is not told how
this is possible. One might as well have stuck with intuition and magic.

IV. PSYCHOLOGISM

Any skeptical argument can be turned on its head. That the argument
leads to skepticism can be taken to show either that the argument is invalid
or that one of its premises is false. If the argument is clearly valid, it can
be used to demonstrate the falsity of one of the premises.

For example, how does one know that other people have the same sort
of experience one has? Let us suppose that one infers that they do on the
basis of their behavior. What justifies that inference? How can one rule
out the inverted spectrum, the experienceless automata? If such questions
are approached directly, one must say, e.g., that inductive inference infers
the simplest and most plausible explanation. Then one must show that the
usual hypothesis is simpler and more plausible than the others. But what
criteria of simplicity and plausibility could one appeal to in order to
complete the argument?

The present suggestion is to turn the matter around. One is to use the
fact that we accept a hypothesis as a sign that that hypothesis is simpler
and more plausible than alternatives. The fact that we accept our usual
hypothesis about other minds, as opposed to the inverted spectrum hypothesis, shows that the usual hypothesis is simpler, less ad hoc, and more
plausible. The suggestion is that, if one studies this and other hypotheses
we accept, one might begin to learn something about what makes a
hypothesis better for us, i.e., better.

Similarly with knowledge of the external world. That we accept the
hypothesis of the external world shows that it is reasonable to accept it.
More specifically, as the result at least in part of your perceptual experience, you believe that you are now reading an article on epistemology.
Applying the suggested strategy, it follows that there is a warranted inference here. The hypothesis that you are now reading an article on epistemology provides the best explanation of your experience, given other things
you believe. It provides a better explanation than the supposition that you
are now dreaming or that you are being deceived by an evil computer.
If one wishes to learn more about this sort of inference to the best explanation, one must examine this and other cases of perceptual knowledge.

The old problem of induction was to justify the inductive inferences on which one's knowledge rests. What Goodman (1965) calls "the new riddle of induction" is to discover what the criteria of good inductive inference are. We are inclined to think that, if all observed A's are B's, that is a good reason to think that all A's are B's, especially if A's have been observed in various circumstances under various conditions. We have examined a great number of emeralds from various places and all of them have been found to be green. So we infer that all emeralds are green. But suppose one defines a predicate "grue" as follows: "x is grue at t" $= df$ "Either x is examined before the year 2000 A.D. and x is green at t or x is not examined before the year 2000 A.D. and x is blue at t." Notice that every emerald that has been examined has been found to be grue; and a great many emeralds have been examined from various places. What prevents the inference that all emeralds are grue? Something must be wrong with that conclusion since it conflicts with the earlier conclusion that all emeralds are green, at least for emeralds unobserved before the year 2000 A.D. For according to the first conclusion such emeralds are green, while according to the second they are blue. But how can the one hypothesis be any more supported by the evidence than the other? It can seem that the evidence should support the one exactly as well as it supports the other.

Despite the large literature on this question, there seems to be little that one can say here except that one does treat the inferences differently. The mind finds the one inference better than the other, even though in some sense there is equal evidence for the two hypotheses. It is a fact about the mind that one hypothesis is, to use Goodman's term, more "projectible" than the other.

Goodman claims that projectibility is a function of past projection. Since "green" has figured in more actual inferences than "grue," his theory entails that the hypothesis with "green" in it is more projectible than the one with "grue." In fact, Goodman's theory may not go much beyond the nontheory of the previous paragraph. In order to find the principles of inductive inference, one must look to actual practice. The correct principles are those that account for the inferences that have actually been made. It follows that projectible predicates are those that get projected. If the mind treats one predicate differently from another, that will have had an effect on past projection. In the past one will have projected one but not the other. There is a correlation between projectibility and past projection, not because past projection determines projectibility but because projectibility has led to the past projection.

What is being suggested here is a kind of *psychologism:* the valid principles of inference are those principles in accordance with which the mind works. Of course, a simple statement like that is an idealization. Things can go wrong: one may fail to consider all the evidence; one can be biased; one commits fallacies. Still, the test of good inference does not seem to be whether it corresponds with rules that have been discovered a priori. The test can only be whether the inference seems right to someone who does his best to exclude things that can lead him astray.

Some philosophers criticize psychologism in logic on the grounds that it detracts from the certainty of logical truths and even makes them false, since some people reason invalidly. Some of this charge is answered by pointing out that the relevant rules concern the working of the mind when nothing goes wrong: how it works ideally. As for the rest of the complaint, that psychologism detracts from the certainty of logical truths, that holds only if one is talking about principles of deductive "inference." The present topic is induction. Principles of deduction can be clearly stated; and they are probably more certain than any generalizations one might discover about the working of the mind. It would be wrong to take those principles to be principles about the working of the mind. But the principles of induction are not even known; so, of course, they cannot be clearly stated; and no statement of an inductive rule could have the sort of certainty that attaches to the principles of deduction. There cannot be the same objection to identifying inductive principles with principles about the idealized working of the mind.

V. SENSE DATA AND UNCONSCIOUS INFERENCES

Many philosophers reject the idea that knowledge is ultimately based on inference from data derived from immediate sensory experience. One objection is that the concept of sensory data only makes sense on a *homunculus theory of perception,* which holds that one perceives things in the world by perceiving an image of those things in one's head. Such an account always provides an unilluminating theory of perception because it leaves unexplained one's perception of the image. It is to suppose that one can see something because an image is flashed into one's head where it is seen by a little man or homunculus. How does the little man see the image? If we have to explain the visual perception of a tree by supposing an awareness of a sensory image of a tree, how do we explain the awareness of the image without assuming that an awareness of an image of the image: a homunculus inside a homunculus. If we do not need to assume the image of the image, why assume the original image in the first place?

Some defenders of sense data reply that a different sort of perception is involved. One has a complete awareness of the image of the tree, only an incomplete awareness of the tree. The image is postulated in order to explain the ways in which one can go wrong about the tree. For example, in hallucination there may be an image of a tree which is not the result of the perception of a tree. However, there is a problem here. Suppose one fails to notice how many branches or how many leaves the tree has within one's line of sight. Does one's image of the tree have a definite number of branch images, a definite number of leaf images? If one does not notice exactly what shade of color the tree trunk is, or some leaves are, does the trunk have a definite color in one's image? Do the leaves? If so, one can be wrong about one's image; and presumably the same argument that leads to the postulation of the image leads to the postulation of the image of the image, and so on. If not, the image is a strange thing, having color but no definite color, having a number of branches and leaves but no definite number of branches and leaves.

This does not mean that it is wrong to speak of sensory data. Many philosophers simply deny that sensory data necessarily involve images. They say instead that data are about how things look, sound, smell, taste, feel, and so on. Some philosophers object that this is to misconstrue the use of statements containing words like "look," "sound," etc., which are often used to make guarded statements about how things are. ("Given the evidence he looks guilty.")

Moreover some philosophers who agree that such statements *can* be used to describe immediate sensory experience deny that such statements represent data on which one's knowledge is in any ordinary case based. Ordinarily one is completely unaware of how things look, sound, smell, taste, feel, etc. It takes a great deal of training before a painter gets so that he can see things as they look. (How often does one notice that shadows have color?) But if one is rarely aware of what the sensory data are, how can one's knowledge of the world be based on inference from such data?

Many philosophers go on to say that in ordinary cases of (visual) perception one does not *infer* that something is there, one simply *sees* that it is there. They would argue that you do not need to infer that there is printing on this page, you can see that there is. "If you were blind or the lights were out, you might infer that there is printing on this page. You do not need to make an inference when you can see every word." They say that the word "inference" is misapplied here. It is clear that there is no conscious reasoning in ordinary perception. How could there be if one is not conscious of the premises of this reasoning? And philosophers have suggested that it is pure obscurantism to suggest that there is unconscious reasoning from unconscious premises, especially since such reasoning would have to be "instantaneous" (as soon as you saw this page you knew there was printing on it).

A difficulty with such arguments is that they require the assumption that one has an independent way to tell when inference has occurred and when it has not. It is not clear why that assumption is any more acceptable than the skeptical assumption that one knows ahead of time what the valid principles of inference are. In fact the only way one can discover what those principles are is to discover what principles account for the inferences we actually make. Similarly, the only way to discover when a person makes inferences is to discover what assumptions about inference are needed to account for his knowledge. One can turn the arguments just considered on their heads. Knowledge of the world is based on inference. If there is knowledge of the world in perception, then there is inference in perception. If one is not conscious of the inference, then there is unconscious inference. If it would have had to have been instantaneous, then inference takes no time. If one was not aware of the premises, then one can make inferences without being aware of the premises of those inferences.

VI. KNOWLEDGE AND INFERENCE

Gettier (1963) demonstrates that the ordinary concept of knowledge cannot be defined as justified true belief. Gettier describes a pair of situations in which a person believes something. In both situations, what he believes is true; and he is equally justified in believing as he does in the two situations. However, a speaker of English is inclined to say that the person would know something in the one situation but not in the other. Any such pair of situations is often called a *Gettier example.*

Here is a typical Gettier example. Sometimes one comes to know something by being told it by someone else. Consider any such situation. Then consider a situation like the first except that the speaker does not believe what he says. Suppose that, despite the speaker's intentions, what he says is true; and suppose that the hearer is as justified in believing the speaker in this case as in the first. Even so, any one who knows English will be more inclined to say that the hearer comes to know something in the first situation than in the second.

It has been suggested that the hearer can infer the truth of what the speaker says only if he also infers that the speaker believes what he is saying. The hearer gains knowledge only if everything he must infer is true. Since the speaker believes what he is saying in the first situation but not in the second, the hearer can come to know in the first but not the second situation. If such a suggestion is correct, Gettier examples can be used to discover something about inference. The principles of inference must account for the fact that the hearer can only infer that what the speaker says is true if he also infers that the speaker believes what he is saying.

One idea (Harman, 1973) is that a person is to infer the most coherent explanatory account that makes the least change in his antecedent beliefs. For example, the hearer infers that the speaker says what he does because he believes it, and believes it because he saw it happen. Such a theory of inference provides an answer to radical skepticism. One is justified in continuing to believe something unless one has a special reason to change one's mind. The alternative hypotheses the skeptic mentions are not equally reasonable, since one of them is already believed.

It is interesting to notice that there are Gettier examples involving simple perceptual knowledge. A person may see that there is a candle a few feet in front of him. Another person may be equally justified in believing that there is a candle in front of him and he may be right too, although a mirror intervenes between the second person and his candle so that what he sees is the reflection of a different candle off to one side. A speaker of English is inclined to say that the first perceiver knows that there is a candle in front of him but the second does not, even though both have justified true belief.

One cannot easily account for perceptual Gettier examples unless one assumes that even simple perceptual knowledge is based on inference. In that case, the perceiver can be assumed to infer that the explanation of there seeming to be a candle ahead is that he is seeing a candle there. He comes to know that there is a candle there only if he is right about why it seems to him that there is a candle there.

That perception involves inference comes as no surprise to a perceptual psychologist who studies the cues used in depth perception. What is interesting is the connection between that idea and an investigation into the ordinary use of the word "know." Harman (1973) argues that this shows psychology must take the ordinary concept of knowledge seriously.

References

Duhem, P. *La théorie physique: Son object et sa structure*. Paris, Rivière: 1906.
Gettier, E. Is justified true belief knowledge? *Analysis*, 1963, **23**, 121–123.
Goodman, N. *Fact, fiction, and forecast*. New York: Bobbs Merrill, 1965.
Harman, G. *Thought*. Princeton University Press, 1973.
Quine, W. V. *From a logical point of view*. (2nd rev. ed.) New York: Harper, 1963.
Quine, W. V. *The ways of paradox*. New York: Random House, 1966.

Chapter 4

SOME QUESTIONS IN THE PHILOSOPHY OF MIND

MAX DEUTSCHER

I. INTRODUCTION

A. Psychological Theories

Some, particularly the psychologists for whom this book is intended, may think that the only way to understand more of the nature of "mind" is to consider and test one of the current general theories explaining human behavior or to postulate another theory if what we have is not good enough. It would be presumptuous of me to add to the disputes among S–R theorists, Gestaltists, those who would think that only direct neurophysiological investigations can work, and so on. Any advance must be made by those who are equipped to make it.

B. Ordinary and Technical Psychological Terms

Though professional psychologists generally have been taught at least to wrinkle their noses at the psychological terms of ordinary language, the reasons for the wrinkles are rarely made clear. Nothing is more vague than the usual charge that ordinary terms are "vague." Of course, our notions of motives, reasons, intentions, beliefs, prejudices, knowledge, memory and so on *may* be vague; but it is none too easy to establish this. It is sometimes thought, too, that various superstitions or otherwise "unscientific" preconceptions about mind are wrapped up in these notions. Mostly this is claimed without proof or any kind of evidence.

In the hands of observant, articulate, and honest people, our everyday concepts are employed to give subtle, accurate, and precise descriptions and explanations of individual and group conduct. People can make fairly good predictions and retrodictions of the behavior of others and even of themselves. This is done without the aid of a commonsense counterpart to psychological *theory*. There are those who do use such a counterpart, viz., the cluster of "wise sayings," and proverbs, and verbal jugglery expressed as conventional generalizations. But anyone can abuse the best of concepts, even those which have pride of place in fully articulated theoretical systems. It may well be that the suspicion of everyday psychological concepts exists mainly because, being used by all, they are more often inaccurately used than are specialists' concepts.

C. A Main Division of Aims in the Philosophy of Mind

The philosophy of mind divides into (*1*) general questions about "mind," or mental events and processes—whether they are correlated with, caused by, cause, or are identical with physical things, events, and so on; and (*2*) particular questions about particular "mental" concepts—*intention, belief, knowledge, memory,* and so on—and their interrelations. Naturally, this distinction is not between unrelated parts of the subject. One's general view of the relation of mind and matter, to put it grandly, to some extent influences what will be said about particular concepts, and much more seriously, accounts given of concepts directly affect what theories of mind can be entertained seriously.

II. SOME GENERAL CONSIDERATIONS ABOUT THE MIND/ BODY DISTINCTION

A. How to Pose the Question?

To ask "What is mind?" now seems droll and antiquated. Indeed, it already seemed so to Bertrand Russell's godparents, when they iterated

"What is matter? Never mind! What is mind? No matter!" (Russell was not amused.) It is the fashion in contemporary philosophical literature to ask instead, "What are mental states, processes and events?," which, it must be confessed, has an air of a little sophistication. An advantage is that there is no hidden assumption of a special agency, faculty, container or possessor of experiences, thoughts and perceptions. The disadvantage is that the sophistication is bogus. What is the sense of the word "mental." in "mental states, processes, etc."? "Conscious" is both too vague and too restrictive. None want to limit the "problem of mind" to questions about consciousness, and furthermore none can speak with clarity, honesty, and illumination about consciousness. No less seriously, it is not a foregone conclusion that there *are* states, processes, and events, be they mental, physical, or of any other kind. This last remark may seem preposterous to those unacquainted with developments (particularly those brought about by W.V.O. Quine, 1953, pp. 1–19) in thinking about ontological commitment. To put a central point of his all too briefly: the assertion that an individual is, say, colored, commits the speaker to the existence of the colored *individual,* but not to a thing called *color,* neither considered as a Platonic universal identical in many particulars, nor to the color-of-the-individual considered as an individual property-instance. The same point applies to "events." To say that a fox jumped is to commit oneself to the existence of a jumping *fox,* that is, an animal, but not to a thing called a *jumping,* that is, an event. The upshot of this? To pose the problem of mind as "What is the nature of mental events, states and processes?" is to risk asking an obscure question about nonentities. [I must remark that there is a great deal of controversy hidden by this sketch. Donald Davidson (1969; Martin, 1969) has outlined a number of strong reasons for taking events, processes, states, or—most comprehensively—property-instances, as basic individuals susceptible of description no less than objects, rather than regarding them as mere ontological shadows cast by syntax in the sunlight of objects.]

B. Behaviorism and Philosophical Problems about Mind

Since at least the 1930's it has become a commonplace for psychologists to say that the concept of mind is not worth repairing, and that instead we must ask "What is the minimum which must be postulated in order to explain the full diversity of human behavior?" Alas, this new conceptual invention was no more able than its predecessors to remove those fundamental disputes which apparently are unresolvable by any theoretically unprejudiced appeal to facts. The invention left entirely unclear both what was to be explained and what was to provide the explanation.

To use my own terms, there is both reductive and nonreductive behaviorism; nonreductive behaviorism accepts the legitimacy and necessity for a "personalist" manner of description of at least human and perhaps other animal behavior. By "personalist" descriptions, I mean predicates such as "is smiling," "is weeping," "is challenging," "is urging," "is voting," etc. If these are allowed, then there is almost no chance of a complete explanation of behavior which makes no use of personal or social terms. The "stimulus" conditions for "Why did he vote?" will have to be put in terms such as "Because the chairman put the question," and the "intervening variable" or "hypothetical construct" will be *his belief that the motion is supported by the reasons that* . . , and *his wish that* [whatever the motion proposes] be achieved. As with *reductive behaviorism,* these "beliefs" and "wishes" must be explained away by means of purely hypothetical statements relating stimulus and behavior statements. Reductive and nonreductive behaviorists agree in eliminating any postulate of real entities functioning between stimulus and behavior; they disagree about the terms necessary in the description of behavior and of its stimulus conditions. (Actually, the use of a mechanistic phase such as "stimulus condition" will raise the hackles of nonreductive behaviorists, who will maintain that such factors do not operate in the "blind way" implied by the use of terms such as "stimulus condition.")

Reductive behaviorism would replace all and only those descriptions unique to persons, by complexes, of terms none of which uniquely applies to persons. For fun, one can introduce various terms to indicate levels of reduction:

(a) Animalistic behaviorism, which would describe human behavior and stimuli in terms which apply equally to all animals, or higher subclasses of animals; the special feature of man's behavior would be handled by complex combinations of those terms.

(b) Biological behaviorism, which would describe human and animal behavior, and the stimuli of that behavior in terms which apply equally to any form of living organism whatsoever, and which pick out this and that species only by the complex combination of those basic terms.

In a similar and simple way you can define biochemical and physical reductivism.

Behaviorism does not help us leave behind basic theoretical disputes about the nature of men and mind, and this is because it leaves the field open to any number of levels of description of behavior and provides no procedure for deciding which to choose, nor any way of explaining why or how all descriptions of behavior are to be reduced to the descriptions of physics (to choose the most general theoretical terms we have). The same points apply to the terms used to describe the stimulus conditions for behavior and, therefore, to the intervening variables or hypothetical constructs which relate stimulus conditions to behavior.

In conclusion, although I scarcely need mention it, behaviorism, whether reductive or not, can say nothing adequate about the nature of a person's sensations, current conscious thoughts and perceptions. No one has even shown how these are to be accounted for in terms of actual behavior or capacities, propensities, or dispositions for various forms of behavior.

III. MAIN SOURCES OF PHILOSOPHICAL PROBLEMS ABOUT MIND

A. Certainty and Uncertainty

Descartes, Locke, Berkeley, and Hume treat what they call our "idea" of objects as things known prior to and more certainly than the objects of which they are ideas. Their problem then is why we should think that there are objects at all. With a little forcing, Kant's treatment of the problem of knowledge also can be made to fit this pattern.

It is very hard now to see why their problems seemed real. Even if it is true that I am more *certain* that there appear to be two shoe-shaped brown patches than that I have shoes on and, even if it is true that there would appear to be two shoe-shaped brown patches on what appear to be the end of my legs even if there were no shoes and no legs there at all, still it is a far cry from all of this to say that when (as we should ordinarily say) I look at an object, I really know only that there are shoe and leg-shaped colored patches.

And even if it were true that "really" I know no more than that, still it is another far cry from such a conclusion to assert that my visual experiences are the basis from which, if I know at all, I know how the external world is. Further, even if it were true that my visual impressions constitute the basis from which I know about physical objects and affairs, and that always I know more certainly that I have visual impressions than that objects exist as suggested by those impressions I do *not* know that the suggested objects exist. Finally, it is to fly in the face of reason for anyone to argue that since what he knows most directly and certainly is his own sense impressions, he has no good reason to believe in physical objects. I defend that charge thus:

Where, in some sense mode, it plainly appears to be that p, then unless there is adequate and independent reason not to believe that p, then it is purely and simply irrational not to believe that p. What of the problem raised by the clause "unless we have reason *not* to believe that p"? Where "p" is the kind of proposition which must be empirically based, any reason *not* to believe that p can itself arise only from relying on the senses. Hence, to reject the ordinary presumption that if it appears that p, then it is thereby reasonable to believe that p, is to reject all reason to *doubt* what plainly appears to be the case.

It may be objected that this will make no headway against the skepticism inbuilt in the thinking of the empiricists, since their conception of an *idea of sense* is not that of a *sense–impression,* i.e., for someone to have a sense–impression is for it to appear to him that there is some physical object or state of affairs. In contrast, the classical empiricists' *idea of sense* is a private *object,* surrogate for a physical object, known by an internal mental perception considered as a ghostly counterpart of ordinary physical processes of perception. But, apart from doubts about this commonly accepted interpretation of the classical empiricists (Locke, Berkeley, Hume, Mill, and, at times, Russell), we can simply ask why anyone should *believe* in ideas or in mental "perception" as so conceived. Surely what is undeniable is that it does appear to us that there are chairs and tables, trees and fields, animals and people. If it is in any way a matter of conjecture and theory that there are these chairs and tables, trees and fields, certainly it is no less a conjecture or matter of theory that there are private mental objects of perception called chair-like ideas, table-like ideas, and so on. If this point requires emphasis or support, it can be given by the following: if there are private objects of perception, then certainly there are nonphysical properties, and certainly *that* is a matter of theory.

B. The Occurrence of Various Forms of Illusion and Delusion

When a mirage of an oasis is seen, there is no oasis where there appears to be one. Yet we seem forced to say either that *something* is seen—not a physical oasis, therefore some nonphysical surrogate; or else that something just like seeing an oasis occurs—therefore the experience of "just like" seeing must be distinguished from our successful visual acquaintance with a physical object.

Various rejoinders may be made: the most conservative of scientific commonsense is that fundamentally *light* is observed—what is in common between veridical perception and illusions is the objective light-ray pattern stimulating the eye. Though this is the most conservative among the various alarming alternatives, it is, nevertheless, highly paradoxical. In what sense do we *see* light? That it is light which stimulates the experience of sight does not prove that it is light which is *seen,* any more than the fact that it is nerve impulses from the retina to the brain which stimulate the experience of sight proves that the nerve impulses are seen.

The case of pure hallucination raises the question of the nature of the experience of seeing (as divorced from being informed by sight of an external or public object). Here, presumably, the experience of seeing involves only a central process, and there can be no question of postulating a physical stimulus as the object of sight. In hallucination an object can be "seen" just as vividly and clearly as when vision actually occurs. If one says on that basis that *some* object is seen, then in the nature of the case it is not the physical object. That merely appears to be present. The only conclusion then seems to be: a nonphysical object is seen. Call this the claim of perceptual surrogates.

Apart from the repugnance of this conclusion to anyone with a desire to create a unified scientific world view, it is very mysterious. What is the nature of this nonphysical object? To say that it is nonphysical is to say what it is *not.* We are still in the dark concerning what it *is.* Further, *how* is it seen; by what mechanism of sight? So far as we understand vision, we see by turning our eye toward something. This inner process of seeing a nonphysical object in appearance like a physical object is entirely hidden from us.

It may be suggested that the nonphysical surrogate is not seen, but "apprehended" without mediation of any perceptual process. Apart from the further darkness and obscurity of this suggestion, it forsakes the only intellectual advantage of the theory of illusion under present consideration. This advantage may be expressed as follows: since it is a necessary truth that in optical illusion or hallucination it may seem to the subject just as if he is seeing something, the person who suffers illusion or hallucination wants to say he sees *something* and the "nonphysical" object theory postulated something to satisfy this wish. The more "sophisticated" version in which this surrogate object of vision is merely "apprehended" removes this sole theoretical advantage and offers nothing in return.

Another objection can be pressed against the claim of perceptual surrogates. What if a person has a vivid hallucination of something rough? Consider anew the theory which would say that *something* is *seen* in a hallucination. Can we say also that he must feel something?; a nonphysical something which *is* rough? If something is rough there must be a surface texture strong enough to offer some degree of resistance to other objects moved across the surface. So it makes no sense to suggest that in a purely hallucinatory case, a nonphysical rough object is perceived. Since the intellectual reaction to vivid hallucination—that there must be *something* perceived—cannot lead universally to correct results, and since also it leads to considerable intellectual embarrassment even in the case of sight, there is the best reason to look for some better analysis of the nature of perceptual experience, considered as divorced from the physical objects of perception.

There has been a contemporary revival of interest in the notion of intentionality. By way of rough introduction, the idea of an "intentional" object is the idea of something thought of or perceived, even if an actual thing does not exist to be thought of or perceived. Some philosophers think that this notion can give us an adequate understanding of what to say about the question "In being hallucinated, does a man thereby perceive anything?" Unhappily, there is great fundamental confusion about *what* is properly said to be intentional. Sometimes it is perception itself, sometimes the perceptual experience and sometimes the beliefs or thoughts made on the basis of perception, and sometimes it is the linguistic expression of these perceptions and thoughts (Anscombe, 1965).

On the only clear explanation, intentionality is predicated of linguistic contexts created by various "mental" verbs. To give an example: On the following two grounds people say that "hopes for" creates an intentional context for phrases which otherwise would be classified as being definitely referring.

(i) Suppose that a person hopes for what does really exist, as when a child, looking at an ice cream, hopes for it. Now suppose that the ice cream is the worst-tasting food in the shop, due to an impurity in its manufacture. It does not follow that the child hopes for the worst-tasting food in the shop. Thus "hoping for" creates a context for occurrences of phrases following "for" different from that created by the extensional "looks at." To see this, reflect on the following example:

> If the child looks at an ice cream, and the ice cream is the worst-tasting food
> in the shop, it follows that he is looking at the worst-tasting food in the shop.

It is customary terminology in the philosophy of language and mind to say that verbs such as "looks at" create referentially *transparent* contexts, whereas verbs such as "hopes for" create referentially *opaque* contexts. The notion of referential opacity is central to the contemporary concept of intentionality.

(ii) The other central notion of intentionality is what I shall call *referential irrelevance*. This trait can be illustrated by the previous example: "hopes for." Suppose, now, that the child thinks he sees an ice cream in a shop window, but he is deceived by a trick of light. He hopes for the ice cream in the window; there is no ice cream in the window to hope for. He cannot *look at* an ice cream if there is no ice cream to look at; at most he can fancy he looks at one. This is to say that intentional verbs such as "hopes for" require no "real" object, by way of contrast with extensional verbs such as "looks at," "shoots" (though "shoots at" is intentional), "touches" (compare the intentional "feels for"), "separates," and "electrifies."

There is a strange tension between these two criteria of intentionality. If the phrase of referring form following the intentional verb does not really refer *at all* (one condition for intentionality), then the truth of the whole proposition containing an intentional verb followed by a phrase of referring form cannot be related to the *manner* of reference achieved by that phrase. What does not refer at all cannot refer in any manner!

Though fatal to some common accounts of intentionality, this objection can be met by rejecting at least one of the conditions for intentionality. But even with that done, there is obscurity in the notion of intentionality if it is to be attributed to mental *states or processes,* rather than to "mental" *verbs.* Naturally, unless there is a nonphysical property of mental *entities* rather than of mentalistic *language,* we have no basis for assertion of a unique and nonphysical mental attribute, inconsistent with a general scientific world view. So, either "intentional" is used obscurely, or it does not commit us to the existence of a nonphysical property.

The notion of intentionality neither explains anything, nor does the so-called phenomenon of intentionality (that one may have a mental attitude to what does not exist) by itself prove that there is anything nonphysical in mental attitudes. Some have gone so far as to define the mental/physical distinction as the intentional/nonintentional distinction. This is wrong because some mental states (e.g., bodily sensations) are not intentional. Further, it is wrong because it is easy to construct physical analogies to the mental kind of intentionality. Think of a machine which stamps out dimes from a bar of metal; the supply of metal runs out, it is no longer really punching out dimes; still it is going through the same machine process of punching out dimes—it is dime-punching, rather than nickel or quarter-punching which it goes on doing. (I owe this example to Ian Hunt of Flinders University.)

IV. PHYSICALISM

The theory I call physicalism is often dubbed "materialism," but that is an unhappy title. A materialist need not be a physicalist, that is, he may not believe that all properties of matter are physical. Further, a person might be a physicalist without being a materialist; he might believe that the basic physical elements were fields or relations between featureless points, or point masses, charges, etc. Such a theorist is scarcely a materialist, since for him physical *material* no less than mental "material" is spoken of only in unreduced everyday speech.

The following principal objections are commonly brought against this doctrine of central-state physicalism, which I explain as follows: something is physical *only if* it is located in space and time and, if observable or detectable at all, is in principle observable or detectable in the same way by more than one observer. An adequate account of a concept will enable us to say "Something is physical *if and only if* . . . ." There is, unfortunately, no agreed way of completing the account. Some will add to the above partial definition: ". . . and is capable of being integrated into basic physical theory."

This account is useful for disputes about the mental/physical distinction. It reduces the problem to that of explaining all mental phenomena in terms of neurophysiological (and other physiological) conditions, assuming, of course, that the relevance of the environment is always to be explained via the effect of environment on those various kinds of physiological conditions. Yet the account is, in some respects, begging the question. According to that account, if some event such as, say, the breaking of a vase, had no *cause* at all, then since that event could not be explained in terms of any theory, it would have to be classified as nonphysical. Certainly, an event must have effects, if it is to be observable or detectable, but it does not seem that it *must* have a cause, in order to be physical.

The other main defect of the proposed completion of the account of what is physical is that it leaves unclear what it is for something to be explained within a theory. If something is fully *explained* by a theory is it, necessarily, described truly only by the terms of that theory? There is no short answer and certainly a discussion of the matter lies outside the scope of this contribution.

The other main completion for an account of what is physical, is that it should be fully describable by use of terms lying solely within the limits of some physical theory—most stringently, those of basic physics. The most obvious objection to the suggestion is that, at most, only the behavior of the fundamental particles can be fully *described* in the terms of basic physics. Water can be splashing, rippling, frothing, and so on. No doubt all of these conditions of water can exist only because of the nature of the basic components of water, yet this scientific fact does not help explain how descriptions of water are reducible to those of submicroscopic particles. If even such a simple reduction is hard to comprehend, how is the reduction of "He is thinking happily of his expected holiday" to be reduced to descriptions of his brain processes?

A distinction is commonly drawn between two types of physicalism which I shall call "subject" and "predicate" physicalism. Subject physicalism, the more easily defended theory, has it that both mental and physical descriptions are predicated of the same thing: if we say that a man is healthy, the subject of the description is the same as that of more crudely physical characterizations such as "weighs ten stone."

If we say that some event in him is that of being a powerful feeling, then according to subject physicalism the subject of that description, too, will have to be a physical process probably in some part of the brain. But it is not thereby claimed that the "feeling" characterization is reducible to any one of the physical, chemical, biochemical, physiological or neurophysiological predicates. Predicate physicalism claims all that subject physicalism does, but asserts also the reducibility of all mental predicates to physical ones. This implausible but exciting theory has received elaborate defense recently by Armstrong (1969) in *A Materialist Theory of Mind*. It is impossible to sketch the outline of his conceptual contentions here. Very crudely, his line of approach is this: the only communicable and therefore intelligible content of mental descriptions must be expressed in terms of the publicly observable causes and effects of the mental processes; the mental entity is described always and only as a bare *"that which* has certain observable causes and behavioral effects." The scientific hypothesis about mental processes, then, is: the "that which" is always a physiological "that."

Briefly put, one main objection to Armstrong's treatment of mental concepts is that it fails to account for the meaning of many descriptions of mental events. To use a point made by C. B. Martin: certainly if a pain is a burning sensation, then it may well be the sort of pain caused by burning or stabbing; however, it is not therefore merely something of the sort "sensation caused by burning." Burning might well have caused an entirely different sensation; similarly, burning sensations might well have had quite different causes, such as cutting. The physicalist's general contention that the content of descriptions of one's mental life is public and communicable is impossible to deny without a kind of paradox. However, we have yet to discover an explanation of how the content is communicated and what it is.

V. RELIGION AND MIND

Many of those who believe in a distinction of mental and physical objects or events, do so for religious reasons. Naturally, those who do, if they have intellectual standards, will protest that I put their cart before the horse. They will claim to hold religious views on account of *independent* reasons for believing in a distinction of mind or soul, and body, for believing in God, and so on. All that I can insist, in that case, is that the distinction between mind and body as used in a religious connection need not be considered as a separate religious issue at all, but is prior to it.

Nevertheless, there *are* reasons for the mind/body distinction which proceed uniquely from religious hypotheses. The following would be a typical example: "God, being perfect or even just good, would not be so wasteful of what is valuable, to allow a human being simply to die. What a person is, and what he has made of himself must, in some mysterious way, be preserved by him."

This is a general weakness in all arguments which proceed from the postulate of God's goodness or perfection. There are very many ills and defects in this poor world which can be explained only by reference to God's unknown and mysterious overall plan. In consequence, for God's own mysterious reasons, what we might expect in the light of His goodness might not always be done by Him. Besides this general objection to *any* inference proceeding from God's goodness, we must remember that God is supposed to be omnipotent, so that He can make good any loss of what is valuable without any loss to Himself. Most importantly, something valuable *is* lost in death—the body itself. Who can love (or deeply hate, for that matter) and still think that nothing of value is lost when the body dies and decays? So here is a particular example of the form of argument that God would not permit what is valuable to be lost, and that argument has a false conclusion. Hence, either the premise of God's goodness must be rejected or else the form of inference from it must be accepted as fallacious. The religious believer cannot deny the premise and so he must accept the invalidity of his argument from God's goodness or perfection to the preservation of the souls of men.

Of course, the soul is also supposed to be important in order to make it possible that something of the human person should represent him and account for his deeds at judgment day. It is thought to be unjust that an evil man should die and never be punished for his sins, or a good man never be rewarded for his virue. Apart from the widely questioned theory of justice and desert implied in this doctrine, it simply will not do. It fails to take account of a kingpin of theology—God's omnipotence. There is nothing to stop God punishing or rewarding a man before he dies, or keeping him alive in the usual bodily state. If it is thought that eternal reward and punishment can be merited, then God could keep the whole person alive, and not merely a poor remnant called the soul. The

world would fill up? God can effortlessly expand it, or effortlessly trans-
port people, at the time they would have died, to another planet. Therefore the alleged need for a soul can be viewed as just one more puzzle
about God's omnipotence. Neither life everlasting, nor reward and punishment, nor the preservation of something valuable and created requires
any division of body and soul.

VI. FREE WILL

The title is quaint enough to raise a smile. "Free wheel" I might have
said; it's what the mind does when it considers matters under such headings; it's what a person would do, in all probability, if there existed and
he possessed what is supposed to be named by the title; certainly it is
what I do, in all directions, when I wonder if I have any.

Can we ask, more soberly: "Am I responsible for my actions?" Another
absurdity! They are not *my actions* if I am not.

"Can I *act* then?" Let me see. (What is there, but to try and find out?)
I am writing. So I act; I cannot escape it—escaping it is, necessarily, not
escaping it. (If, if p then not p, then not p.) Suppose that someone meets
these commonsense stone-walling tactics with: "But, perhaps, *acting* is
not as we conventionally think it to be. Is what we call 'acting' *really*
the exercise of responsible choice; is it *really* voluntary? Perhaps, unknown
to the 'agent,' what he does is determined by causes, so that he *could*
have done nothing but what he did. No arty-smarty metareflection on the
writing or thought about freedom answers that."

Let us ask, then: "Can I do other than I do now?" I move my finger
one way. Could I have moved it in another? I do so now. But could I
have done so when I moved it in the first way? What reason could I have
to think otherwise?

If there is a complete set of causes for my action, then nothing other
than my action could have occurred. And if nothing other than my action
could have *occurred,* could I have *done* anything different? The answer
to that question is far from obvious. Certainly it is not obvious that the
answer is "No!" Of a car standing in a garage it may be true that, given
all the physical conditions at the time, nothing could have happened but
that the car stand there. But this does not imply that the car could not
have gone at 100 mph, since a thing may have a *capacity* even when
conditions for the exercise of that capacity do not obtain. If that were
not possible, we should have no need for the idea of a capacity. Someone
might feel like saying "But *in the garage,* a car can scarcely do 100 mph."

That is, if we generalize the point, if a thing is not doing X, then this is because some cause necessary for that action is absent; hence, *while* that factor is absent, the thing cannot do X. In general terms, that can sound the merest statement of a scientist's belief in determinism. But look back to the car in the garage. Of course it cannot do 100 mph, while in the garage. But that does not imply that the car in the garage cannot do 100 mph.

Another point strikes me. It is easy to be puzzled about what it means to say that a person is free to do other than he does, and to wonder if this idea can ever be made clear. But is it any easier to explain what it means to say that if there is a complete set of causal conditions for an event, then nothing else could have happened?

Does it just mean that the event which occurred was caused? In that case, why exactly should it be thought that we are not responsible for what we do? Because if an action is caused, it is predictable, and if predictable, then we do not really have the freedom to choose differently. But that is not correct. If a person is predictably honest, does it *follow* that he does not choose freely to act honestly? Does the mere consistency in a pattern of chosen acts secretly undermine their freedom and his responsibility? And, incidentally, it does not follow that what has complete causal conditions is therefore completely predictable. As is well known, the process of predicting certain events may affect the conditions which cause them.

In brief, the existence of freedom to act and to choose one way or another is beyond question; there is no reason to think that in order to be free there must be some uncaused events. Hence, the existence of human freedom does not force us to look outside the physical order for an explanation of it. People differ from machines in that their actions are influenced by their perceptions, desires, beliefs, etc. The problem of freedom in a physicalist's conception of man then resolves into the question whether perception, desires, beliefs, etc., are simply physical processes and states.

VII. DESCRIBING, REPORTING, AND EXPRESSING ONE'S THOUGHTS AND FEELINGS

I conclude this sketch of philosophical questions about the "mind" by calling to attention some facts about describing one's own sensations. These facts are among those which explain why there is a feeling of strangeness about mental states and events, a feeling which persists when a person concentrates on his own inner life and attempts to describe it precisely.

One model of honesty (about yourself) is this: You notice certain feelings; you decide it appropriate to let another person know what they are; you understand what your words will mean to the other; choosing, then, the correct words in relation to your knowledge of the other person's understanding, you report and describe those feelings to him.

There are deficiencies in this, if taken as a general account. It seems to cope quite well with at least such matters as sincerely describing physical pain, and other sensations. But in speaking of the emotions, for instance, the conception of honesty as involving a simple correspondence between what already exists and is felt, and the statement of its existence, is inadequate. There are many reasons for this, and I suggest the following two as an introduction to the problem.

One reason is that to describe your own emotion to another is also to express it, as well as to express many other emotions and feelings, fears, and beliefs. (This is no less the case when you describe your sensations just to yourself. And also such soliloquies are part of our method of leading, developing and defending some among our many conflicting and diverse tendencies to think and feel.) This expression of emotion—feeling and thought—is part of what creates between people an emotional attachment or revulsion. Someone is dishonest if he says something which helps to bring about an attachment when he does not intend to be attached, even if he feels what he says. So honesty cannot just be "saying what you actually feel." Equally, even though to say something which creates revulsion when you desire to attract must give a false impression, yet the alternative of hiring the thought whose expression creates revulsion, also is not straightforward.

The second reason is this: to some extent at least, what emotions we have is within our control. This sounds ridiculous to some. They have a romantic novelist's image of strong men swept along by passion, sweeping weaker little things in turn off their feet. It is, of course, undeniable that we can be caught unawares by emotion. Hate, joy, disgust, lust, or tenderness can surprise a person. But this no more proves that the existence of emotions lies beyond one's control than the occurrence of involuntary movement of the limbs proves that one's limbs are never really under one's control. I concede a difference between control of the limbs and control of the emotions. In the case of emotion, there is nothing like simply moving one's finger at will. What sort of bodily control is it, which is an analogy with emotional control? (I notice a nuisance. The phrase "emotional control," as commonly used, refers to the control of behavioral expression of emotions. I want to consider the control of emotion itself, allowing, naturally, that this can be achieved to some extent through control of bodily expression.) Also, is there *any* kind of emotional control which is an analogy with bodily control? What are some examples?

A man becomes annoyed with someone's behavior. He feels his anger rising. How does he control it? It seems that there are three main ways. He can intellectualize; he can try to convince himself that the cause of his anger is trivial, for instance. By forcing his attention onto something else he can distract himself from the situation or from his emotion. Alternatively, he can give vent to his feeling in some relatively milder way—anything which acts as negative rather than positive feedback. There seems to be a close analogy between this set of possibilities and a corresponding set for controlling behavior.

Suppose cramp begins to grip one's leg. One might *just* try to relax. Alternatively, one might in some indirect way try to relax—for example, one might concentrate attention on relaxing other parts of the body which are still fully under one's control. Or, one might directly flex and move the leg, forcing against the constriction.

Just because emotion, to take one example, can be directly or indirectly under some degree of voluntary control, and our saying one thing or another about ourselves and our current mental states is a means both of defining, making more definite and real, and of *directing* the current state in one direction or another—just because of all these obvious and well-known things, we can flounder when we wish simply to describe our mental states as they are "in themselves." Then our mental life seems elusive and to lack solidity. We escape from this feeling by the *expression,* not the "more careful" *description* of our mental life. When we shout in anger, cry in pain, or simply converse without premeditation or constraint, then the absence of an attempt to describe ourselves permits the uncluttered communication of what we think or feel.

References

Anscombe, G. E. M. The intentionality of sensation. In R. J. Butler (Ed.), *Analytical philosophy*. Ser. II. Oxford: Blackwell, 1965. Pp. 158–181.

Armstrong, D. M. *A materialist theory of mind*. London: Routledge & Kegan Paul, 1969.

Davidson, D. On events and event descriptions. In J. Margolis (Ed.), *Fact and existence*. Oxford, Blackwell, 1969. Pp. 74–84.

Martin, C. B. Unpublished paper.

Martin, R. M. In J. Margolis (Ed.), *Fact and existence*. Oxford, Blackwell, 1969. Pp. 63–74.

Quine, W. V. O. *From a logical point of view*. Cambridge, Massachusetts: Harvard Univ. Press, 1953.

Part II

Historical Background of Contemporary Perception

Chapter 5

THE PROBLEM OF PERCEPTUAL STRUCTURE

MICHAEL WERTHEIMER

I. INTRODUCTION

For most intelligent laymen, there is a feeling of surprise in the recognition that there may be such a thing as a problem of perceptual structure. Do our senses not give us straightforward, usually reasonably accurate information about the world around us and about the things in it? Why bother to raise a question of "perceptual structure" at all? Can't we just act in a commonsense way, and take it for granted, as we do almost all the time anyway, that our sensory and perceptual apparatus simply serves its intended function by leading to an adequate awareness of things as and where they actually are?

Indeed, it is hard to see that there is any problem until one begins to look at how such an awareness might be mediated. Consider, for example, the visual system. Light impinges upon various objects in the environment, and is selectively reflected to the eyes. There an image is focused upon the retinas at the back of the eyes, and, depending upon the sensitivities of the particular visual cells involved and the particular pattern of light energies falling on the retinal surface, certain chemical processes occur in some cells and not in others. The chemical breakdown in turn leads to neural impulses in certain tiny fibers deep in the retina, which induce nerve impulses in second order and third order neurons; the message that leaves each eye is an intricate pattern of impulses traveling along particular fibers of the optic nerve. These impulses, reaching various centers above and behind the eyes, in turn activate other neurons, culminating in nervous activity in a number of places in the brain, including a major lobe at the back of the head, the occipital lobe.

It has been known for many decades that neural activity is basically all or none in character. That is, a neuron either is actively firing or it is not. An impulse goes down a neuron, or it does not.

What does all this mean about the question of perceptual structure? It means this: the nicely segregated, organized, and meaningful environment, and the clearly differentiated objects within it, get broken up by our receptor system and the nervous system into nothing but a series of certain cells which are active and others which are not, with some cells perhaps more active than others. What has happened to the roundness of the clockface? What has happened to the rectangularity and solidity of the buildings in our visual world? Where is the unity of the tree? How come my hand is perceptually differentiable from the surface of the table upon which it rests? All of the rich information about perceptual structure which we take for granted has somehow dissolved into a series of yes or no electrical blips moving along some tiny, poorly insulated fibers.

The problem of perceptual structure, then, comes down to the question of how the nervous system can reconstruct the real world of objects of various sizes, qualities, and shapes in various spatial relationships to each other, from the mosaic pattern of sensory and neural activity which must mediate our ability to develop such an awareness. In a mosaic, one piece of glass doesn't say to the observer, "I belong with this other one that's just above me and to the left, but do not belong to the one that's below me and to the right." Nor do various parts of the mosaic tell the observer that they belong together to form a unit which happens to look like a horse, while other bits of glass are to be organized together so as to be perceived as a sword. In the same way, a nerve impulse along one fiber, activated perhaps by the reflection from one brilliant piece of glass which the artist intended as part of the horse has no way of conveying to the observer that its message should be sorted out as belonging together with particular other messages in the optic nerve at the time, and not with still a different set.

This problem, the question of unit formation, is only one of many that are part of the general problem of perceptual structure. Other questions include such things as the following: Why does my friend not seem to shrink as he walks away from me, in accord with the shrinking of his image on my retina? Why does the wheel of a car continue to look reasonably round as it passes me, even though the image on my retina is first a tall thin ellipse, then gradually becomes more circular, then becomes more elliptical again, until it becomes a vertical line and then vanishes? How can I tell that one car, while I am driving in traffic, is next to but slightly in front of another car? Why do a 6 and a 9 not look almost identical, when they really are often just about the same shape, but one turned upside down relative to the other? Why does the vanilla ice cream in the bowl in front of me not look darker than the black topped road outside the window, when it is reflecting a smaller amount of light per unit of retinal area into my eye than the road is? Why does the upper right hand corner of this page appear to belong to the rest of the page and with the book, rather than being organized as part of the table on which it is lying, or as whatever else happens to be the visual background of the page at the moment that you are looking at it?

If you stop to think about how chaotic the experienced world would be if perceptual structure did not exist, you can begin to realize its extra-ordinarily fundamental nature. How can we adapt to a world unless we know something about the objects in it, and their properties? How could we ever hope to learn anything about reality, if our perception of reality were totally unstructured? Motivation, learning, thinking, problem-solving, indeed virtually all psychological functions are predicated upon our ability to have a reasonably veridical conception of the world around us and of ourselves in it. If perception were not structured, were not richly organized, no other psychological processes could occur. Structured perception is a necessary condition for virtually any kind of effective organismic function.

The ubiquity of organization, and the fundamental nature of perceptual structure, has not by any means always been recognized. This is, perhaps, not so surprising, if we consider how much we take for granted in everyday life the naïve idea that somehow our brains just automatically manage to recreate a reasonably accurate image of the world "out there" because of the effective functioning of our perceptual systems. In this chapter, we shall briefly examine the history of the problem of perceptual structure, beginning with its recognition in a somewhat rudimentary form by Aristotle, then mentioning some attempts to solve the problem essentially by ignoring it, leading to recognition that ignoring the problem does not make it go away, and on to a number of proposed solutions. During the nineteenth century, and early in the twentieth, attempts were made to solve it by using a mechanism of association, or by positing new elements that were, in effect, identical with the structural aspects of perception. The Gestalt revolution early in the twentieth century suggested a very different ap-proach, which made structure rather than elements primary. During the

second half of the twentieth century, some major new insights have provided the seeds of a quantitative and a physiological solution to the
problem.

II. RECOGNITION OF THE PROBLEM

While a clear acknowledgment of the existence of a problem of perceptual structure did not really occur until early in the twentieth century, at
least a vague awareness of it had existed in some form since the beginnings
of recorded philosophical thought. Aristotle (ca. 330 B.C., 1954) was by
no means the first, but there are glimmerings in his doctrine of form and
matter. He realized that it is possible to analyze the world according to
levels of organization, with the higher levels serving in effect as organizing
principles for the lower. Precisely how this organization takes place, and
what the physiological mechanisms behind it might be, were issues to which
Aristotle did not devote his deliberations.

Aristotle did not consider form and matter fixed, but, rather, thought
that they depend upon the level of analysis. Matter, Aristotle argues, is the
constituents, the elements, making up the form, while form is the inclusive
totality whose subparts are matter. Thus, marble can be considered as
matter relative to the form of a pillar, and conversely in relation to the
marble, the pillar is the form. At the same time, however, the pillar is
matter to the building, the building is matter to the city, and so on, with the
higher level always being the form and the lower the matter. Every level
of analysis, or object, is then both form and matter: form to the lower,
matter to the higher. While this implies an infinite reducibility on the one
hand and infinite possibilities of organization on the other, Aristotle put an
end to the upper levels. The highest form he considered akin to God. God,
then, is form to all things, matter to none, and therefore in a sense provides
meaning, structure, and organization to the matter of all the world.

Aristotle's conception of everything as infinitely reducible, by a successive ever finer analysis of form and matter, did not deal with the question
of how the matter interacts in particular ways in order to achieve the next
level of form, nor the question of the specification of particular aspects of
matter. This question was not to be addressed until the Gestalt psychologists, early in the twentieth century, made the distinction between "natural" and "arbitrary" parts; "natural" parts are directly responsive to the
structure of an object while "arbitrary" parts ignore it. This was later to
become one of the major objections of the Gestalt school to the elementism
of the prevalent associationistic views which have been so ubiquitous on
the philosophical and psychological scene since the early eighteenth century.

During the so-called Dark Ages there was relatively little philosophical speculation about the kinds of problems raised by the Greeks before the birth of Christ and then resurrected, sometimes in forms similar to those 2000 years earlier, by the thinkers of the Renaissance and by the subsequent Western philosophers. The problem of perceptual structure was not, of course, the only one to suffer from neglect during those years; it was only one of many which suffered from the decline in scientific and empirical thinking during this period.

III. SOLVING THE PROBLEM BY IGNORING IT

During the Dark Ages the problem was ignored in the sense that thinkers were devoting their attention to other matters, largely theological ones. But early in the history of what has since been called the era of modern philosophy, a major school, British empiricism, with a strong emphasis on association, in effect acted as though it were solving the problem, but at the same time really skirted it. Late in the seventeenth century, John Locke, in his attempt to answer the fundamental question of how we obtain knowledge, decided that ultimately all knowledge must come from experience (Locke, 1700). Experience comes in the form of particular ideas, and the idea is the fundamental unit or element of mind. These elements are tied together in groups because we experience them concomitantly; this was an early, quite clear assertion of the need for a principle of association (although Aristotle too, several thousand years earlier, had already addressed the question of how one idea may lead to another, and had formulated some seminal laws of association). Such things as the shape, weight, taste, etc., of particular objects, including their basic meaning, are experienced because of association, because of our prior experience with the object. Thus the principle of association was, for Locke and his immediate followers, the key to the understanding of how experience is organized into meaningful structures. But this analysis never could explain why we experience objects as segregated units in the first place.

Other British empiricists, like David Hume (1739–1740) and James Mill (1829), continued and purified the Lockeian approach. Association was the key concept in Hume's philosophy even more than it had been in Locke's. The associationist philosophy reached its culmination, however, in James Mill, a strict elementist, who conceived of the mind as constituted solely of sensations and ideas, held together by association. Any mental whole, including any percept, is simply the sum total of the compounded, that is, associated, elements. The elements are sensations and ideas, the latter being replicas of previous sensations.

The associationist philosophers wrote as though they assumed that sensations and their compounding by association could, in effect, account for the entirety of what occurs in mental life. They were unaware that the arbitrary hooking up of elements cannot account for why we perceive structured, segregated, differentiated objects in a meaningful world. It is in this sense that the associationist solution was a matter of solving the problem by ignoring it.

IV. RECOGNITION THAT IGNORING THE PROBLEM DOESN'T MAKE IT GO AWAY

Benedict Spinoza, born the same year as John Locke, has also had a profound impact upon subsequent Western philosophy. His approach was entirely different from that of the British empiricists, and quite alien to a fundamentally associationistic orientation. While he too speculated upon metaphysics and epistemology, let us touch here only very briefly on his concern with the problem of perceptual structure itself.

Spinoza recognized the problem far more clearly than Aristotle had. Yet, even though he was aware of the problem, his solution did not fully satisfy him. He formulated the issue by examining the question of how a circle was to be defined. "If a circle be defined," he wrote, "as a figure, such that all straight lines drawn from the center to the circumference are equal, everyone can see that such a definition does not in the least explain the essence of the circle, but solely one of its properties" (Spinoza, 1677; 1956). But although this quotation makes it clear that Spinoza did indeed sense the problem, his proposal that the circle be defined as "the figure described by any line whereof one end is fixed and the other free" still does not capture the "essence of the circle," in the structural sense of the essence having to do with what could perhaps be called the law of constant, closed curvature of the circumference.

Geometry itself has not managed to achieve anything much more than this attempt of Spinoza's; the piecemeal approach seems almost inevitably to lose the structural core of "circleness," whatever that may be and however it may be defined. Clearly, a circle has at least two immediate, outstanding whole-qualities: continuous constant curvature at each point on the circumference, and fully symmetrical closedness. But how such immediately perceived, salient characteristics of the circle as a perceptual whole are to be described or analyzed or, for that matter, where they come from in perception in the first place, still remained unclear. Later suggestions, which we will take up shortly, were to add another element, like "circleness" to the other elemental "sensations" the "compound" of which is the circle; von Ehrenfels (1890), of the Graz school, and his colleagues Meinong and Schumann, were to make this proposal late in the nineteenth and early in the twentieth century.

James Mill's son, John Stuart Mill (1869), espoused an associationism which was, in a sense, diametrically opposed to that of his father. While, like his father, he was convinced that association is the primary law of mind, he preferred the term "mental chemistry" for the compounding of ideas. Complex ideas are not just the sum total of the constituent ideas, but ideas in effect melt and coalesce with each other, forming wholes. The compound of several elements can have properties which are entirely new—as, for example, the wetness of water is not deducible from the properties of the elements composing it. Here was a clear recognition, in the middle of the nineteenth century, that association in the sense of a simple adding together of inert bits and pieces does not account for perceptual structure and organization.

The founding father of experimental psychology, Wilhelm Wundt (1874), a little later in the nineteenth century, was also steeped in the empiricistic associationist tradition. While he tried to be a strict elementist as much as possible, he felt compelled to formulate a principle of "creative synthesis," a process whereby mental contents, which are compounded of elements, are worked upon by the mind. Mental activity results in creative, unifying combinations of mental elements; the result of the creative synthesis is different from the simple sum of the elements making it up. Here Wundt essentially acknowledged John Stuart Mill's argument, and at least indirectly acknowledged that the associationist solution to the problem does not actually solve it.

It is interesting to note, incidentally, that a much more modern elementist, the famous learning theorist Clark L. Hull (1942), saw the need for what can be seen as a close parallel to Wundt's principle of creative synthesis within his own objective, behavioristically oriented stimulus–response psychology in the 1940's. He formulated a theorem on afferent neural interaction, which at least acknowledged the fact that somewhere between the punctiform stimulation of the receptors and the organized nature of the response something must happen which breaks the undifferentiated mosaic up into meaningful perceptual objects to which it is possible for the organism to respond.

V. A PROPOSED SOLUTION: A NEW ELEMENT

In 1890 Christian von Ehrenfels insisted in a very influential paper that the preceding and contemporaneous psychology of Wilhelm Wundt, while it was a thorough-going elementism, had neglected a very important element: the form quality, or Gestaltqualität. Ehrenfels' colleagues, Meinong (1891), Schumann (1900a, 1900b), and Cornelius (1892, 1893), later elaborated on his approach. His principle was an extension of John Stuart Mill's mental chemistry, and a clear recognition that an analysis into sensory "elements" may be such that the essence of a perceptual whole is eluded. A square is not just the sum total of four equal lines plus four right angles; this leaves out the most important aspect of the square, its "squareness." A form quality, then, for von Ehrenfels, was an element over and above the elements composing a whole. A melody played in a given key is not just the sum of the notes, but is, in addition, their total configuration. If you change the relations among the elements, the whole changes. On the other hand, you can transpose the melody, that is, put it into a different key and thus change all the elements, and yet still retain the melody itself, the Gestaltqualität, as long as the relations among the individual elements or notes remain the same. For von Ehrenfels, dependence upon relations among elements and transposability were the essential properties of the proposed new elements, the form qualities. Thus form qualities included, in addition to such things as melodies, properties like triangularity, roundness, squareness, pointedness, shapeliness, etc.

Friedrich Schumann (1900a, b), in an experimental study published early in the present century, showed how subtle these added elements or form qualities could be. If you take a square and rotate it by 90 degrees, you end up with a second figure that is identical in virtually every respect with the first. The "elements" of the four equal sides and the four right angles remain unchanged, as does also the superordinate element of "squareness." On the other hand, though, if you rotate it through only 45 degrees, the superordinate element changes in a rather striking way. The square has been transformed into a diamond. The relations among the "elements" remain unchanged; it is the relationship of the entire configuration to the gravitational dimension that has been altered. This fact alone is enough to produce a phenomenally quite new percept. While the square looks as though it is resting solidly and substantially on one quite stable side, the diamond is a much more delicate figure, balanced precariously upon one point.

The Graz School, then, accepted the premise of reductionism and elementism that was taken for granted by most psychologists late in the nineteenth century, and that had prevailed in the associationism of the British empiricists and, indeed, had been indigenous to much Western thinking at least since the days of Aristotle. While it recognized that a pure associationistic elementism, based upon preconceived sensory "elements," was unable to confront the problem of where perceptual organization came from, it proposed to solve the problem of perceptual structure by postulating a new, higher order, set of elements.

VI. ANOTHER PROPOSED SOLUTION: EMPIRISM

The popularity of learning as an explanatory notion is not peculiar to twentieth century American psychology. Another offshoot of elementistic reductionism, as implicit in associationism, and to some extent parallel to the superordinate element approach, was the proposal, fully consistent with preceding associationism, that our awareness of perceptual structure is simply due to learning. This idea was almost explicit in John Locke's, David Hume's, and James Mill's formulations, and was then made central to the perceptual doctrine of the great nineteenth century man of science, Hermann von Helmholtz (1856–1866, 1878). In a slightly modified form, this doctrine carried on into the middle of the twentieth century in the form of the transactionalist position.

Helmholtz suggested that every perceptual act is an act of unconscious inference. On the basis of our prior experience, we organize any current sensory input into categories with which we are familiar, and our past experience translates sensory cues into the perception of familiar, real objects in particular spatial relation to one another. This view, empirism, is still very widely held; it maintains that everything in our experience is due to past experience. Its continuing popularity may be due to its consistency with the prevalent reductionistic elementism that has characterized most Western thinking since Aristotelian days.

Around the middle of the twentieth century, the American transactionalist school represented a kind of modern Helmholtzian approach. Such men as Cantril (1950), Ittelson and Kilpatrick (1952), and Ames (1949) developed this highly influential school, largely with the help of an ingenious series of demonstrations. The basic tenet of the position is that we see what we are used to seeing; our perceptions are consistent with our expectations, and our expectations are built up on the basis of an intricate, rich, never-ending series of transactions with our environment. Thus, for example, we are accustomed to seeing rectangular rather than trapezoidal windows. For years, we have been accustomed to rooms that are not complex, irregular, three-dimensional quadrilaterals, but are, instead, reasonably straightforward boxes with edges that are horizontal and vertical. Thus, as in one of the more famous of the transactionalist demonstrations, if an artificial room is constructed which, to an eye placed at an appropriate point, looks normal, but which is constructed so as to be rather dramatically distorted, so that the right-hand far corner of the room is actually much closer to the observer's eye than the left-hand far corner of the room, people in this room can seem to take on strange sizes. A person standing in the far right corner will look much larger than a person standing in the far left corner, since he is really much closer to the observer. Since the image cast by the room upon the retina of the observer is no different from that cast by a normal room, the observer's preceding transactions with his environment lead him to conclude, in this case erroneously, that the room is a normal rectangular one, and consequently the person in the right corner looks like a giant while the one in the left corner looks like a dwarf. Our expectations determine our perceptions: we expect rectangular rooms, and therefore we see them, whenever the sensory input is consistent with such an interpretation. Past experience and expectations, therefore, are the prime determinants of the nature of perceptual structure.

Later critics have, of course, pointed to the anomaly of the position, since the presumed tendency for us to perceive things as we are accustomed to, produces illusions. In the distorted room, for example, we perceive things that are very different from what we are accustomed to (such as people whose stature is very distorted); in fact, it has been maintained that the ingenious transactionalist demonstrations disprove the very position that they were intended to support, since the illusions produce percepts which are highly inconsistent with past experience and expectation.

Be that as it may, the transactionalist position is a relatively modern version of the earlier empiristic solution to the problem of perceptual structure. It says that we see particular perceptual objects as units with particular properties and particular spatial relationships purely on the basis of past experience. Quite aside from the possibility that the transactionalist demonstrations may in effect disprove the position itself, there is another question which arises with any pure learning approach to the solution of the problem of perceptual structure. This is the question of where unit formation comes from in the first place. Learning could account for the fact that we see as a unit something which we perceived as a unit before; but how do we ever perceive it as a unit in the first place? No principle of learning seems to be able to help much here.

VII. TURNING THE PROBLEM RIGHT SIDE UP

As we indicated a few pages ago, the philosopher Benedict Spinoza was at least aware of the problem, even though he did not find a satisfactory solution. A little over a century later, the great philosopher Immanuel Kant

(1781) provided a radically new view of the issue, one which, in principle, was to be elaborated early in the twentieth century by the Gestalt psychologists.

Aware of how radical his thought was, Kant compared himself to Copernicus, in reversing the order of things: where pre-Copernican views had been geocentric, Copernicus developed the heliocentric conception of the universe, so that the sun rather than the earth is at the center of things. Comparably, Kant argued that perceptions do not give us our concepts, but instead our percepts are given to us according to our concepts—according to our intrinsic inborn ways of perceiving the world. These inborn molds, filters, or "categories," as Kant called them, include cause and effect, time and space; because of our physiological and epistemological nature, we cannot perceive the world other than in causal, spatial, and temporal terms. It is foreordained that we perceive the world according to innate principles or categories; the categories—not learning—are responsible for the organization and structure of our perceptions.

The organization of perception, then, is not something which develops gradually with experience out of a compounding of prior elements; instead, perception is organized from the start, and the extraction of elements is something which becomes possible only with sophisticated adult philosophical analysis. Organized wholes, not elemental sensations, are epistemologically and experientially prior. The problem of perceptual structure, then, is not the one of how organized, segregated units arise in our experience, but rather the opposite one of how the organized, segregated world of perception can analytically be reduced to its elemental sensations or to its natural subparts. This was, indeed, a radical reversal of the traditional elementaristic, associationistic reductionism which had been taken for granted by almost all pre-Kantian philosophers.

The Kantian formulation did not really influence psychological thought very substantially until a modified version of it was formulated early in the twentieth century by the Gestalt psychologists. In the meantime, von Ehrenfels' proposal of a new element of form quality played a kind of transitional role between Wundtian elementism and the Gestalt approach.

The early Gestalt writers (Koffka, 1935; Köhler, 1929; Wertheimer, 1923, 1933) characterized preceding thinking as "from below up," while they suggested that a more appropriate way of looking at things is "from above down." It is the organization of the whole which determines the nature of the parts; the properties of parts depend upon the relation of the parts to the whole. Rather than beginning with a series of arbitrary elements and trying to synthesize the whole out of them, it is much more appropriate, they argued, to determine the characteristics of the whole and then to analyze—that is, to see what the parts have to be in order for the whole to have the properties it does. Part qualities depend upon the place, role, and function of each part in the whole. This principle of relational determination was central in most of the Gestalt work.

Ehrenfels had said that the whole is more than the sum of its parts; the Gestalt psychologists went beyond this, and held that the whole is different from the sum of its parts. The whole quality is not just one more added element. The qualities of the whole determine the characteristics of the parts; what a part has to be is determined by its relationship to the whole. Max Wertheimer suggested the "law of prägnanz," which held that the organization of any whole is as good as the prevailing conditions allow.

This formulation involved the same radical reorientation that the Kantian proposal did. The nature of the parts is determined by the whole rather than vice versa; therefore analysis must go from above down rather than below up. One should not begin with elements and try to synthesize the whole from them, but study the whole to see what its natural parts are. Furthermore, the parts of a whole are not neutral and inert, but structurally intimately related to one another. That parts of a whole are not indifferent to one another was illustrated, for example, by a soap bubble: change of one part results in a dramatic change in the entire configuration.

The Gestalt approach to the problem of perceptual structure was most forcefully developed in a 1923 paper by Max Wertheimer on the organization of perception. In it he argued for a nonempiristic view of how percepts arise out of the punctiform activity of neural elements on the receptor surface. Those parts of the perceptual field are organized together, are perceived as belonging together or as forming a unit, which are similar and close to each other, which move together or constitute a "good" form.

Buttressing the Gestalt analysis were a series of powerful demonstrations and arguments against what the Gestalt psychologists called the "mosaic" or "constancy" hypothesis. This hypothesis, implicit in most earlier writings about perception, took it for granted that experience is related in a one to one fashion with the detailed mosaic input of the stimulus. Hence, a particular stimulation of a particular part of the retina should always result in the same percept. That this is not so was demonstrated dramatically and repeatedly with experiments on the perceptual constancies (which showed that a percept can remain the same even though the physical stimulus undergoes major changes) and on perceptual contrast effects (which show that the percept of a given local part of the stimulus field can change radically, depending upon surrounding stimulation, even if the local stimulus remains unaltered). Many influential experiments were conducted in these areas, and with what the Gestalt psychologists rechristened the "Ehrenfels qualities," as well as with "dependent part qualities," the qualities that parts of a whole have by virtue of their place, role, and function within the whole (for example, a particular note in a chord may sound quite different, depending upon the rest of the chord: a middle C as part of a C tonic chord sounds quite different from that same middle C played as part of an A minor chord or as part of a D seventh chord).

New but rather vague concepts were proposed, such as that of the "homotype," to try to handle some of the intricate relational aspects of perceptual structure. Parts which are, from a piecemeal point of view, quite different, may serve the same perceptual function ("be homotypically identical") in different wholes. For example, in building a bridge out of three blocks, the height of the two uprights is homotypic, but their color is not; there is also a homotypic relationship between the distance separating the two uprights and the length of the crosspiece, but the material out of which the blocks are made is not homotypic (Wertheimer, 1933).

The success of the Gestalt attempt to turn the problem right side up was evidenced, among other things, by the recognition of D. O. Hebb (1949). His influential neuropsychological theory was tinged by the elementistic, associationistic tradition; yet he recognized that there are certain fundamental perceptual properties which are not dependent upon learning. He acknowledged that all percepts have a "primitive unity" which is immediately given and is not substantially affected by experience. Whatever the physiological origin of such unit formation, Hebb acknowledged that differentiated perceptual structure is a product of the primitive operation of the sensory and perceptual apparatus itself.

Perception functions so as to yield an awareness of distinct perceptual units; the Gestalt principles of the organization of perception provide a description of how such units come about. Perceptual structure is not the product of sensory elements tied together by association, but is, instead, the immediate product of the operation of the perceptual apparatus itself.

VIII. BEGINNINGS OF A QUANTITATIVE SOLUTION

While the Gestalt formulation radically reoriented the problem of perceptual structure from the approach of preceding philosophical and psychological elementism, it still left much of the problem quite unclear, including the quantitative and physiological details of how perceptual structure arises and develops. It was not until the middle of the twentieth century that some real progress was made on these aspects of the problem.

The concepts of information theory, emerging from telephony and electrical engineering, provided a contentless metric that proved to be very promising for the solution of a wide variety of transmissional and structural problems. Using the definitions of information theory for such terms as uncertainty, redundancy, and information, Fred Attneave (1954) suggested that an array which contains a great deal of uncertainty (or information) is disorganized or chaotic, and, conversely, the more redundancy an array contains (i.e., the less information or uncertainty it has), the more structured or organized it is. Thus measurement of the amount of information technically contained in a stimulus provided a way to begin measuring how structured or organized a configuration is.

Hochberg and McAlister (1953) extended this reasoning to an attempt to quantify the Gestalt law of prägnanz; the idea that the organization is as "good" as the prevailing conditions allow becomes less vague when translated into the formulation that in ambiguous situations (and almost all perceptual situations contain ambiguity), in which a particular stimulus input could potentially be perceived in many different ways, that organization will be perceived which contains the least information. In the 1960's Wendell Garner carried this work further, undertaking a detailed quantitative analysis of the concept of structure within an information theoretical framework (Garner, 1962). The problem of unit formation becomes much less mysterious when couched in the terms of information theory.

IX. BEGINNINGS OF A PHYSIOLOGICAL SOLUTION

Two different recent thrusts have made inroads into the question of the physiological mediation of perceptual structure. One technique, represented by the work of Evans and Piggins (1963), is the method of the stabilized retinal image. A microprojector is attached to a contact lens, which has been placed on the eye, or some other technique is used to stabilize the image. However much the eye moves, then, the stimulus covers exactly the same place on the retina. Thus, a line projected in this way, for example, will continually stimulate precisely the same group of receptors. Under such conditions, the receptors soon stop firing impulses, and the line disappears as a whole. If more complicated patterns are projected, various meaningful parts of them disappear and reappear. This nonrandom disappearance is such that parts which have a good organization, according to the Gestalt laws, succeed one another. Well organized and meaningful figures tend to persist the longest. The afferent and cognitive system seems to be arranged in such a way that it responds not to the punctiform mosaic of stimulation of particular cells by particular wavelengths and brightnesses, but instead responds to complex units and natural subparts of these units.

The other approach, used with great success by Hubel and Wiesel (1962), implants microelectrodes in the visual brain of experimental animals, and records activity in individual cortical neurons as a function of differential stimulation of the eye. They discovered early in the 1960's that certain cells in the visual brain do not respond to brightness or wavelength as such, but rather to complex stimulus characteristics such as the angle of a line and its direction of motion. Thus a given unit in the brain might fire if a short line, rotated 45 degrees from the horizontal, is moved in a vertical direction, but not if it moves in a horizontal direction, or, conversely, might respond to such a line but not to a horizontal one moved vertically. This demonstrates that, at least at higher levels of the nervous system, neural organization is not according to the presumed stimulus elements of the sensationalists, the empirists, or the associationists, but rather according to a conception which recognizes the primacy of complex structure in the perceptual process itself.

X. SUMMARY AND CONCLUSION

The fact that perceptual structure, which is taken for granted in everyday life, actually constitutes a problem because perception is mediated by a neural and physiological process which, in effect, breaks it down, already began to be recognized by the Greeks of the time of Aristotle. The problem was essentially sidestepped by the early modern philosophers of the associationist tradition, such as Locke, Hume, and James Mill, but there was at the same time an uneasy recognition that ignoring the problem does not make it go away, in the writings of Benedict Spinoza, John Stuart Mill, and then later of Wundt and Hull.

Two unsuccessful solutions were suggested and became quite popular, until the Gestalt revolution radically reoriented the way in which the problem was viewed. Empirism, in the formulations of Helmholtz in the nineteenth century and the transactionalists in the twentieth, suggested that our awareness of perceptual organization is fundamentally a matter of learning. The Gestalt quality approach of Ehrenfels, Meinong, Cornelius, and Schumann proposed that organization is essentially another element added to the sensory elements composing a percept.

Gestalt psychology, preceded by the philosopher Kant, asserted that structures, rather than sensory elements, are primary in a percept. This approach turned out to be consistent with a formulation based upon information theoretical concepts, and with later findings with the technique of the stabilized retinal image and microelectrode recordings from the visual brain. These quantitative and physiological approaches, already very successful, are also very promising with regard to further progress in the understanding of the problem of perceptual structure, which is so basic in perception and organismic adaptation.

References

Ames, A. *Nature and origin of perceptions.* (Preliminary laboratory manual.) Hanover, New Hampshire: Hanover Institute, 1949.

Aristotle *De anima.* (Ca. 330 B.C.) (Transl. by K. Foster & S. Humphries.) New Haven, Connecticut: Yale Univ. Press, 1954.

Attneave, F. Some informational aspects of visual perception. *Psychological Review,* 1954, **61,** 183–198.

Cantril, H. *The "why" of man's experience.* New York: Macmillan, 1950.

Cornelius, H. Über Verschmelzung und Analyse. *Vierteljahrschrift fuer Wissenschaftliche Philosophie,* 1892, **16,** 404–446.

Cornelius, H. Über Verschmelzung und Analyse. *Vierteljahrschrift fuer Wissenschaftliche Philosophie,* 1893, **17,** 3–75.

Evans, C. R., & Piggins, D. J. A comparison of the behavior of geometrical shapes when viewed under conditions of steady fixation, and with apparatus for producing a stabilized retinal image. *British Journal of Physiological Optics,* 1963, **20,** 1–13.

Garner, W. R. *Uncertainty and structure as psychological concepts.* New York: Wiley, 1962.

Hebb, D. O. *The organization of behavior: A neuropsychological theory.* New York: Wiley, 1949.

Hochberg, J. E., & McAlister, E. A quantitative approach to figural "goodness." *Journal of Experimental Psychology,* 1953, **46,** 361–364.

Hubel, D. H. & Wiesel, T. N. Receptive fields, binocular interaction and functional architecture in the cat's visual cortex. *Journal of Physiology,* 1962, **160,** 106–154.

Hull, C. L. *Principles of behavior.* New York: Appleton, 1942.

Hume, D. *A treatise on human nature.* London: 1739–1740.

Ittelson, W. H., & Kilpatrick, F. P. Experiments in perception. *Scientific American,* 1952, **185,** 50–55.

Kant, I. *Critique of pure reason.* 1781. (Transl. by N. K. Smith) New York: St. Martin's Press, 1965.

Koffka, K. *Principles of gestalt psychology.* New York: Harcourt, 1935.

Köhler, W. *Gestalt psychology.* New York: Boni & Liveright, 1929.

Locke, J. *An essay concerning human understanding.* (4th ed.) London: 1700.

Meinong, A. Zur Psychologie der Komplexionen und Relationen. *Zeitschrift fuer Psychologie,* 1891, **2,** 245–265.

Mill, J. *Analysis of the phenomena of the human mind.* London: 1829. (Edition with notes by J. S. Mill, 1869.)

Schumann, F. Beiträge zur Analyse der Gesichtswahrnehmungen. *Zeitschrift fuer Psychologie,* 1900, **23,** 1–32. (a)

Schumann, F. Beiträge zur Analyse der Gesichtswahrnehmungen. *Zeitschrift fuer Psychologie,* 1900, **24,** 1–33. (b)

Spinoza, B. *How to improve your mind.* (Transl. by R. H. M. Elwes) New York: The Wisdom Library, a Division of Philosophical Library, 1956. (Originally published: Amsterdam, 1677.)

von Ehrenfels, C. Über Gestaltqualitäten. *Vierteljahrschrift fuer Wissenschaftliche Philosophie,* 1890, **14,** 249–292.

von Helmholtz, H. *Handbuch der physiologischen Optik.* Leipzig: 1856–1866.

von Helmholtz, H. *Die Thatsachen in der Wahrnehmung.* Leipzig: 1878.

Wertheimer, M. Untersuchungen zur Lehre von der Gestalt. II. *Psychologische Forschung,* 1923, **4,** 301–350. (Transl. and abridged as Principles of perceptual organization. In D. C. Beardslee & M. Wertheimer (Eds.), *Readings in perception.* Princeton, New Jersey: Van Nostrand-Reinold, 1958. Pp. 115–135.)

Wertheimer, M. Zu dem Problem der Unterscheidung von Einzelinhalt und Teil. *Zeitschrift fuer Psychologie,* 1933, **129,** 353–357. (Transl. as On the problem of the distinction between arbitrary component and necessary part. Appendix 1. In M. Wertheimer (Ed.), *Productive thinking.* New York: Harper, 1959. Pp. 260–265.)

Wundt, W. *Grundzüge der physiologischen Psychologie.* (1st–6th eds.) Leipzig: 1874 and 1908–1911.

Chapter 6

ASSOCIATION (AND THE NATIVIST–EMPIRICIST AXIS)

*BRUCE EARHARD**

I. PHILOSOPHICAL BACKGROUND

Modern association theory is a by-product of the introspective stance assumed by British empiricist philosophers during the seventeenth and eighteenth centuries. Locke (1690), a leading proponent of that school, sought to ascertain "the original, certainty, and extent of human knowledge." Other philosophers such as Descartes (1701) had expressed similar objectives, but the British empiricists' approach was unique in that it was concerned not merely with what could be known, but with how that knowledge could be acquired. The British empiricists could find no evidence of any innate knowledge. Quite to the contrary, they were agreed that all

* Preparation of this report was facilitated by Grant APA-142 from the National Research Council of Canada.

knowledge originated in experience. The mind at birth, Locke argued, was a blank tablet. The empiricists disagreed among themselves, however, with respect to what constituted the basic elements of experience. Locke's view was that the basic data of experience were ideas produced by external objects acting upon our senses, and ideas which stemmed from the awareness of the mind of its own operations. Berkeley (1713) contended that Locke had assumed too much, and that there was no evidence of an external world of objects, but only of ideas in the mind. Hume (1739) carried the argument to its logical conclusion and contended that we have impressions and ideas, and the assumption of either an external world or a mind is unwarranted.

For the purpose of the present chapter it is not important whether Locke, Berkeley, or Hume were correct in their assumptions about the basic data of experience. What we are concerned with is the device used by the empiricists to account for the development of knowledge from the given elements of experience. Obviously knowledge is something more than random sequences of impressions and ideas. To acquire knowledge we must make order out of this sensory and ideational chaos, and the empiricists introduced the principle of association to achieve this end.* They assumed that ideas which occurred contiguously, that were similar, or that contrasted with one another, would be associated. They assumed further that, as an associative network linking the various impressions and ideas encountered grew in size, the world would begin to acquire an orderliness and predictability originally absent. Associations thus served, in a very real sense, as the connective tissue of the mind. Our concern will be the application of association theory to perception. If broader coverage of general association theory is sought by the reader, Brett (1921) and Warren (1921) are worth consulting.

II. EMPIRICISM, ASSOCIATIONISM, AND PERCEPTION

A. Perception: A Learned Associative Process

The position taken by empiricists required that all the complexities of the adult mind develop as a result of experience. This means that those events we categorize as perceptual must be dependent upon experience, i.e., we must learn to see. The clearest demonstration of this attitude is provided in the answer given by both Locke (1690) and Berkeley (1709)

---

* This is not meant to imply that associationism originated with the British empiricists. It can be traced back to Aristotle and further (see Boring, 1957; Deese, 1965; Esper, 1964; Spearman, 1937).

to a question posed by Molineux (see Locke, 1690, p. 186) as to whether a man born blind, but capable of distinguishing between a sphere and a cube by touch, could distinguish between these objects by sight if the ability to see were granted to him. Locke, Berkeley, and Molineux himself agreed this would be impossible. For an empiricist it was necessary that such an individual have experience which permitted the association of ideas corresponding to visual sensations with appropriate ideas resulting from tactile sensations in order to enable him to make the discrimination.

B. Assumptions of Early Empiricists: What Is Given?

Empiricists maintained that experience was necessary to provide the associative structure that permits identification of objects, but even an empiricist had to assume some form of visual content to provide a nucleus about which an associative structure could be woven. Early empiricists were by no means agreed with respect to what should be assumed as given. A widely held but by no means universal assumption was that the visual field was in the first stage of vision composed of two-dimensional forms. Locke (1690), for example, assumed that a sphere would appear to an entirely naïve eye as a "flat circle, variously shadowed." Reid held a similar view noting that: "we perceive visible objects to have extension in two dimensions, to have visible figure and magnitude, and a certain angular distance from one another. These, I conceive, are the original perceptions of sight" (Reid, 1764, p. 331). Further description of this viewpoint with supporting arguments may be found in Hamilton (1865).

An alternative view reflecting a more extreme form of empiricism was that even simple two-dimensional form had to be acquired through experience, and the nature of the first visual experience was simply a variably colored and shaded but "formless" visual field. Such an approach is evident in sections of Berkeley's "Essay Toward a New Theory of Vision" (1709), in the writings of Brown (1820), Bain (1868), and J. S. Mill (1878). It is this latter viewpoint that has proven most durable and finds representation in modern associationist approaches to perception, e.g., Hebb (1949).

Although empiricists were divided on whether two-dimensional extension had to be learned, they were united in the belief that spatial depth, as well as size, distance, and position had to be learned by associative processes. In that two-dimensional form perception has tended to be assumed a necessary prerequisite for any account of size, distance, or positional relationships, attention here will be directed first toward explaining how those empiricists who held that two-dimensional form perception was not directly given in experience accounted for the acquisition of such percepts.

C. Associationism and the Acquisition of Form Perception

Given that color boundaries, and abrupt changes in luminosity are visible even to the untrained eye, how does the capacity to differentiate and recognize two-dimensional forms develop? Generally explanations have been based on the belief that, as the eye and hand are moved simultaneously over a boundary in the visual field, associations develop which link visual and muscular sensations from ocular movement with tactile sensations from the movement of the hand. Bain (1868), for example, saw the acquisition of simple form as the development of a unique physiological correlate representing the associative sequence of ocular and muscular sensations generated as the eye traced out the boundaries of the figure in the visual field.

Underlying such explanations is the assumption that the mind cannot apprehend the whole visual field simultaneously (see Brown, 1820; Stewart, 1854). To use an example of Stewart's, if the eye were fixed and a figure were somehow painted on the retina, it would appear to us that perception of the figure occurred instantaneously, but in this Stewart argues we would be mistaken because the visual field is a mosaic of separately discriminable or "minimally visible" points, only one of which can receive attention at a given time. How then can the act of perception appear instantaneous if it is in fact sequential? Stewart resolved this issue by arguing that individual acts of attention occur with such rapidity that we are deluded into believing perception is immediate. Other empiricists resolved the issue without recourse to attention. A simple, mechanical-compounding view of the sequential associative process such as that of J. Mill (1829) assumed that, with experience, events could spring up in "such close combination as not to be distinguishable." His son, J. S. Mill (1872, 1878) went further, and assumed a type of chemical fusion could occur such that individual impressions and ideas repeatedly associated could "melt and coalesce" into a new unitary idea and that impressions and ideas so fused would be no longer discriminable. In short, even a very complex percept so generated will have a unity and coherence that will persuade the naïve adult observer that no learning was ever involved in their formation. Obviously, this process is such that no form of introspective analysis will deliver up the elements so combined.

Modern applications of association theory to form perception have much in common with the older approaches described above. Hebb (1949), for example, places much emphasis on the importance of eye movements in the acquisition of form perception, and he views perception as a sequential process. Basically, Hebb assumes that repeated visual tracing of the boundaries of figures permits the development of cortical representations called cell assemblies for perceptual elements such as lines and angles, and that these cell assemblies must combine sequentially into "phase sequences" before even the simplest of visual forms can be identified. The associationist tradition is retained in more recent approaches to form perception such as those of Dodwell (1970) and Sutherland (1969). The main difference between these more recent approaches and those taken by the more traditional associationist viewpoint represented by Hebb is that recent theorists do not assume that associations take place between neural analogs representing each discriminably different point of a stimulus pattern. Instead such theorists seize upon the findings of sensory physiologists such as Hubel and Wiesel (1962) suggesting that the visual system is pre-wired to be selectively sensitive to the presence of certain features in stimulus patterns, and argue that it is the rules governing the combinations of features characteristic of different forms that are learned via associative principles, i.e., the visual system is assumed to involve multistage processing, and associative learning is carried out only after preliminary coding of sensory input has taken place.

Given that associative mechanisms have traditionally played an important role as connective principles in accounting for differentiation of two-dimensional form, the next question to be asked is how we come to perceive such forms as representations of objects in a world external to us.

D. Associationism and the Problem of Objective Reference

If Hume was correct, and all that we can justifiably assume about experience is that we have impressions and ideas, how are perceptions to be distinguished from sensations or from other kinds of mental processes such as thinking or reasoning? For the empiricist the answer must be that the properties associated with perceptual events make them unique. There was not a great deal of accord, however, with respect to which properties served to distinguish perceptual events. Reid (1764) took the commonsense view that perceptions differed from sensations because a perception carries with it the certainty that it was produced by an external object, but he took the rather unusual step of arguing that this certainty was given immediately without the necessity of associative learning. His followers thought otherwise. Brown (1820) argued that perception "is a sensation suggesting, by association, the notion of some extended and resisting substance." While Brown's view has strong intuitive appeal, the most insightful analysis of the problem of external reference for the psychologist remains that of J. S. Mill (1878). Mill maintained that perception is no more than an expectation acquired as a result of associative learning, or to use his own terminology, a belief in the "permanent possibility of sensation." Mill's view becomes clearer if it is realized that what we perceive when we open our eyes is not merely the information provided by immediate sensory experience. If we rest our eyes on an ice cube floating on the surface of a beverage, we see only that it is translucent and cubelike in visual form but we *expect* that it will be cold to the touch as well as slippery and hard. In short, the properties of many different sensory modalities have become associated with the visual correlate of ice. To glance at an ice cube is to expect or infer that it will have certain additional sensory consequences if examined, and that ice cubes will continue to have these properties tomorrow and long after we are dead. Thus, the expectation developed through associative learning that certain sensory experiences are inseparably linked generates our belief that an external world of objects exists and is responsible for our perceptual experience. This policy of defining perception as expectation remains evident in contemporary perception (e.g., Bruner, 1957; Hochberg, 1970).

E. Associationism and Relations: Size, Distance, and Depth

Locke (1690) contended that a sphere is a two-dimensional form "variously shaded" when first viewed by the inexperienced eye. How do we come to see the two-dimensional representation as a three-dimensional object of a fixed size and at a specifiable distance? Locke's view was that through interactions with the object we acquire the capacity to interpret the visual shading as the basis for inferring a third dimension of depth. While Locke's approach remains representative of the associative approach, it was Berkeley (1709) who was primarily responsible for developing associative interpretations of size and distance relationships.

Berkeley began with the assumption that distance and magnitude were not given directly in experience. He maintained that, to the naïve eye, "the remotest object as well as the nearest would all seem to be in his eye or rather in his mind" (p. 186). It was only when certain nonvisual kinds of experience were associated with visual sensations that size and distance could be apprehended. Touch played the most important role. The close connection between vision and touch was made evident in his contention that to say we see something at a distance means no more than the understanding that "having passed a certain distance to be measured by the motion of his body which is perceivable by touch we shall come to see such and such a tangible idea" (p. 188). He made it emphatically clear that the perception of distance was not possible until tactual experience in handling, and moving toward and away from objects in our visual field had taken place. It is as a result of such experience that we associate sensations resulting from a convergent movement of the eyes, the relative straining of the eyes, and blurring of vision, with the viewing of objects at different distances and thus become capable of immediately and accurately inferring distance.

Berkeley's emphasis on the importance of touch was just as evident in his treatment of size perception as in his treatment of distance. For Berkeley, there were two objects of perception each with its own size. First, there was a directly visible size associated with the two-dimensional retinal image, and second, there was a tangible magnitude perceived and measured by touch—associated with the object of sight only as a result of experience. The magnitude of the visual image can be used as a basis for inferring the size of an object in that, generally, objects which are large occupy a large segment of the visual field, but the visual image varies also as a function of distance, and, therefore, alone it is at best an equivocal sign of size. In fact, Berkeley argued, "we take little heed of the visual magnitude of objects." The main role of the visual image is to suggest, as a result of associative learning, the tangible magnitude that is acquired by touch. Other indicants of size are available. If the visual image is faint or confused in appearance, we learn to judge the object to be further away and necessarily larger in size.

More modern empiricists would place less emphasis on touch in accounting for the judgment of objective size (see Boring, 1942), and contemporary research raises doubts about the capacity of touch to influence vision in the manner described by Berkeley (Harris, 1965; Rock & Harris, 1967). Nevertheless, the theory remains a classic example of the associative analysis of a perceptual problem, and was viewed by Brett (1921) as the most significant contribution to psychology in the eighteenth century.

III. OPPOSITION AND ALTERNATIVES TO EMPIRICISM: THE RISE OF NATIVISM

Criticisms of the empiricist approach to perception generally assume two forms: (a) a direct assault on the adequacy with which associative learning serves as a mechanism to account for the development of the perceptual process, or (b) the argument that empiricism places too much emphasis on learning, i.e., it neglects the very substantial organization imposed by the receptive system which is native to the organism.

A. Opposition to Empiricism: Limitations of Associationism

Associationists such as Berkeley made the assumption that tactual impressions must be associated with visual impressions to permit perception of size and distance. A basic problem with such theories involves determining the consequences of the act of association. Berkeley viewed the connection between the immediate visual impression and the associated tactual impressions to be so close as to be analogous to the relationship existing between a word and its meaning, but he did not assume that visual and tactual components of experience fused into a unitary whole. This means that perception must be almost exclusively inferential in character and that experience does not alter the phenomenal world of visual appearances. But if this is true why does a building across the street appear to be *visually* more distant? Why does a sphere appear to be visually convex? Why is it not seen as a flat, variously colored circle which is known to have depth?

The adequacy of associative theories of perception was systematically debated by Bailey (1842) and J. S. Mill. An excellent description of this debate may be found in Pastore (1965, 1971). Bailey pointed out that if Berkeley was correct and visual and tactual impressions do not fuse, then we should be conscious of tactual impressions when we view objects at a distance. He argued that because we have no awareness of such impressions Berkeley must be wrong. The reaction of an empiricist to such a criticism is that because an idea is not discernable in consciousness, it does not mean such an idea was not present at an earlier time. Elements entering into an associate network often become less evident, or drop out of the sequence after repeated experience. Bailey's other questions about how nonvisual sensory experience could alter or augment visual perception was less readily answered, and this has remained a contentious issue. At the turn of the twentieth century, Gestalt theory strenuously opposed empiricist and association theory views that perception could be altered or augmented by experience (see Kohler, 1947; Zuckerman & Rock, 1957). At midcentury a fierce debate raged over whether perception could be altered by needs, values, familiarity, and other forms of experience (Allport, 1955), and the well-known disagreement between Gibson and Gibson (1955) and Postman (1955) is largely based on this issue.

One other criticism raised by Bailey was a source of serious concern to association theory. Bailey pointed out that the young of certain species of animals appear to have a highly developed perceptual capacity immediately after birth. This made recognition that innate processes might mediate perceptual behavior difficult to avoid.*

B. The Alternative to Empiricism: Nativism

The empiricists, Locke, Reid, and Hamilton, took the position that two-dimensional form perception was given prior to experience. Müller (1852) was the first to systematically try to extend nativist accounts of perception beyond this simple assumption by arguing that the spatial organization of two-dimensional space, i.e., the relative distance, position, and magnitude of two-dimensional retinal images are given also prior to experience. Just as we can apprehend the spatial locations of different impressions on the skin, he argued, we can apprehend directly the location of impressions on the retina. Thus the relative distance, position, and magnitude of images on the two-dimensional retinal surface must be directly perceptible. Touch and movement cause us to project this two-dimensional spatial surface outward, and as we acquire the capacity to judge absolute size and distance, three-dimensional perception is achieved.

Further ground was cut away from under the feet of empiricists by Hering (1861) who took the next logical step and argued that two- *and* three-dimensional spatial organizations were given prior to experience. He assumed each retinal point produced three different signs. Two of the signs served to signify the two-dimensional location of the retinal point and the third served to signify the depth of the object stimulating the retinal point. The depth sign was either positive or negative. As the distance of retinal points on the nasal side of the retina from the fovea increased the sign became increasingly positive. A similar relationship held for negative retinal points on the temporal side of the retina. To see how such a system works, it is only necessary to assume that light rays reflected from a distant object are brought to focus on the foveal area. Light rays reflected from still more distant objects will fall on the nasal or positive side of the retina and will be judged more distant. Light rays reflected from objects closer than the object on which the eyes are fixed will fall on the temporal or negative side of the retina, and be judged closer. Such a scheme would permit relative depth perception to occur without any prior experience. Learning would be necessary to apprehend absolute distance however.

---

* The widespread acceptance of Kant's philosophical view that space perception was not a consequence of experience but a necessary precondition for experience was also influential in encouraging the development of nativist views of space perception.

C. Empiricist Reactions to Nativism

The reaction of the empiricist to nativist views that the spatial location of objects was given directly by special retinal depth signs was to argue that such assumptions were unnecessary. All that need be assumed, they argued, was that each different retinal location gave rise to a discriminably different response. What the organism had to do was to learn the significance of these signs to achieve three-dimensional space perception (von Helmholtz, 1884).

Lotze (1886) was largely responsible for outlining the empiricist account of how the significance of retinal signs is learned. He noted that we move our eyes when any area of the retina is stimulated so that the stimulus falls upon the foveal area in order to take advantage of its greater resolving power. The depth of an object in the visual field is thus signified directly by the amount of ocular movement required to move a stimulus exciting any particular retinal location to the foveal area. Because each retinal point is assumed to have a distinct sign, we become capable, after a suitable degree of experience, of estimating the amount of muscular activity necessary to bring an impression to the foveal area without the necessity of actually making the ocular movement.

The empiricist approach underwent further development with von Helmholtz (1860) who entered into a long and often spirited controversy with Hering and other nativists. The details of their differences may be found in Sully (1878) and James (1890), or von Helmholtz (1860) and Hochberg (1962). By 1884, von Helmholtz regarded the battle as won and claimed, "that intuitive theories of vision . . . are really quite unnecessary. No fact has yet been discovered inconsistent with empirical theory" (von Helmholtz, 1884, p. 264). Von Helmholtz was premature in his judgment. The nativist–empiricist issue has yet to be resolved.

IV. NATIVISM AND EMPIRICISM: DATA

Nativists were obviously correct in their view that the physiological structure of the eye and the brain must in some measure predetermine the properties of visual experience. Empiricists would appear to be correct also in their position that the significance of what is given must be learned through associative learning. The difficulty always has been that there is no way of providing a definitive description of what is given. This situation has not changed. At best, we can merely indicate certain general kinds of data that have been viewed by both empiricists and nativists as having particular relevance to this issue.

A. Deprivation Studies

Studies in which animals or humans have been denied visual experience for a substantial portion of their lives constitute the oldest type of data relevant to the nativist–empiricist controversy. As early as 1728, Cheselden operated to restore the vision of a young boy denied normal visual experience since early childhood because of cataracts. Since then many cases of persons who have been born blind, or suffered blindness in early childhood, and later had their vision restored have been reported. These cases have been summarized by von Senden (1960). The interested reader may find an up-to-date summary of studies dealing with visual deprivation studies carried out on animals in Gibson (1969).

In general, both the human and the animal studies show that deprived S's have substantial difficulty in adjusting to the world of sight. This difficulty is not surprising in that previous dependence on nonvisual modes of behavior must be overcome and replaced by visual modes of behavior. Also deprivation may impair development of the visual system (Gibson, 1969; Hubel & Wiesel, 1963). These difficulties notwithstanding, there is no evidence of the primordial chaos or buzzing confusion that some empiricists have assumed.

B. Early Experience Studies

Speculations about the visual world of the young child appear to be second in popularity only to speculations about the visual capabilities of a man born blind who is suddenly endowed with sight. Recent experimentation suggests the visual abilities of the young child have been underestimated. Experimentation reported by Fanz (1967) suggests that newly born infants can "resolve, discriminate, and differentially attend to visual patterns" (p. 192). Studies by Bower (1966, 1967) have indicated that children no older than 2 months of age are able to discriminate form and possess a measure of shape constancy. More recently Bower (1971) has added further evidence indicating that children display at a very early age evidence of perceptual expectancies about the solidity and permanence of objects that have been assumed generally to emerge only after extensive experience involving associative integration of visual and tactile information (see Section II, D). Studies involving animals have reported similar findings. It has long been known that young chicks show very rapid perceptual motor development (see Pastore, 1971). Almost as soon as coordinated movement is possible visual targets can be localized. In fact, Fanz (1967) has reported evidence of a visual form preference among chicks within 2 days of birth. Clearly a much higher level of perceptual competence is evident in young children or animals than would be the case if perception was entirely dependent upon the development of perceptual learning.

C. Functional Physiological Studies

The most recent and by far the most impressive body of evidence favoring the view that there is a large measure of organization native to the visual system has been provided by the development of single cell recording techniques. Such techniques permit the physiologist to record directly from individual cells at different points in the visual system and to determine the area of the retina which when stimulated activates the cell selected for study. More important, it permits the physiologist to determine whether the cell is sensitive to any particular form of stimulus. A very large degree of selective sensitivity has been found. Recordings have been made of cells which respond selectively to appropriately oriented stationary bars and edges, to moving bars and edges, to directional movement, and to degree of binocular disparity (Barlow, Blakemore, & Pettigrew, 1967; Barlow & Hill, 1963; Hubel & Wiesel, 1962). In addition, there is evidence to indicate that a convergent hierarchical type of functional arrangement governs transmission of information from the receptor surface to the cortex (Hubel, 1963). Lastly, it has been found that recordings of single cells in the cortex of visually derived young kittens is similar to that observed in adult animals suggesting that the organization is not built up by experience (Hubel & Wiesel, 1963).

While these findings indicate a substantial measure of selective sensitivity is native to the visual system, it should be noted that of late evidence has emerged to suggest that experience may play an important role in shaping the character of the selective sensitivity observed. Blakemore and Cooper (1970) found that when they restricted the visual environment of young kittens exclusively to either vertical or horizontal striated patterns, these kittens had an extremely difficult time coping with linear stimuli perpendicular to the direction of original exposure. Recordings from single cells in the visual cortex revealed that these cells responded normally, but instead of finding the typically observed distribution of cells sensitive to lines in all varieties of orientation, they found virtually no cells sensitive to lines perpendicular to the orientation to which the kittens were exposed in rearing. This finding led Blakemore and Cooper to advance the suggestion that preferred orientation sensitivity of cells may change as a result of experience to match the probability of features in the visual environment.

Other investigators have reported similar findings. Hirsch and Spinelli (1970) have presented data indicating the importance of early experience in determining the selective sensitivity of cortical cells to linear orientation, and Shlaer (1971) has observed systematic compensatory shifts in the distribution of cortical cells sensitive to disparity as a result of rearing kittens under conditions of prism-induced disparity. Thus it seems possible that although there is a substantial degree of inherent sensitivity to environmental features such as contour orientation or disparity, the specificity of that sensitivity may be determined by very early experience.

V. EPILOGUE: WHAT IS LEARNED?

When the data described above are weighed, the conclusion that the visual system has a much higher level of inherent organization than empiricists have been wont to assume in the past seems unavoidable. The old questions about what is learned, and whether what is learned alters our phenomenal visual experience remain unsettled, however. Some contemporary theorists take the position that what is learned are the rules that describe the features (lines, edges, orientation, extent, etc.) isolated by prewired detection mechanisms and that these rules determine what is seen (Sutherland, 1969). Others conclude that what is seen is influenced by the application of inferential rules operating at the level of the proximal stimulus (Rock, 1970). Still others see the development of rules or schemes as crucial for the certain aspect of perception but are doubtful about the degree to which visual appearances can be altered by experience (Hochberg, 1968). Whether association theory can account for the development of the rules or schemas emphasized by current theory remains to be seen. Association theory is presently in decided disfavor as an explanatory principle for the rules assumed to underlie the perception and apprehension of language (Dixon and Horton, 1968). Further, the importance of certain biological constraints which limit the traditionally assumed generality of the associative process is only now being recognized (Seligman & Hager, 1972). What does seem to be certain is that attempts to account for perceptual operations exclusively in terms of associative processes belong to the past. Associative mechanisms appear to be increasingly regarded as connective principles of secondary importance. The main emphasis in current theorizing is concentrated on inherent physiological mechanisms which appear responsible for analyzing and transforming visual input at different stages in the visual system.

References

Allport, F. H. *Theories of perception and the concept of structure.* New York: Wiley, 1955.

Bailey, S. *Review of Berkeley's theory of vision; designed to show the unsoundness of that celebrated speculation.* London: Ridgway, 1842.

Bain, A. *The senses and the intellect.* (3rd ed.) New York: Longmans, Green, 1868.

Barlow, H. B., Blakemore, C., & Pettigrew, J. D. The neural mechanism of binocular depth perception. *Journal of Physiology (London),* 1967, **193**, 327–342.

Barlow, H. B., & Hill, R. M. Selective sensitivity to direction of movement in ganglion cells of the rabbit retina. *Science,* 1963, **139**, 412–414.

Berkeley, G. Three dialogues between Hylas and Philonous, 1713. In T. V. Smith & M. Grene (Eds.), *From Descartes to Kant.* Chicago, Illinois: Univ. of Chicago Press, 1940. Pp. 523–617.

Berkeley, G. Essay toward a new theory of vision, 1709. In A. A. Luce & T. E. Jessop (Eds.), *The works of George Berkeley Bishop of Cloyne.* Vol. 1. Toronto: Nelson & Sons, 1948. Pp. 143–239.

Blakemore, C., & Cooper, G. F. Development of the brain depends on the visual environment. *Nature (London),* 1970, **228**, 477–478.

Boring, E. G. *Sensation and perception in the history of experimental psychology.* New York: Appleton, 1942.

Boring, E. G. *A history of experimental psychology.* New York: Appleton, 1957.

Bower, T. G. R. Slant and shape constancy in infants. *Science,* 1966, **151**, 832–834.

Bower, T. G. R. Phenomenal identity and form perception in an infant. *Perception & Psychophysics,* 1967, **2**, 74–76.

Bower, T. G. R. The object in the world of the infant. *Scientific American,* 1971, **225**, 30–38.

Brett, G. S. *A history of psychology.* Vol. 2. New York: Macmilian, 1921.

Brown, T. *Lectures on the philosophy of the human mind.* Vols. 1 & 2. Edinburgh: Tait, 1820.

Bruner, J. S. On perceptual readiness. *Psychological Review,* 1957, **64**, 123–152.

Deese, J. *The structure of associations in language and thought.* Baltimore, Maryland: Johns Hopkins Press, 1965.

Descartes, R. Selections from the rules for the direction of the understanding, 1701. In T. V. Smith & M. Grene (Eds.), *From Descartes to Kant.* Chicago, Illinois: Univ. of Chicago Press, 1940. Pp. 52–164.

Dixon, T. R., & Horton, D. L. (Eds.) *Verbal behavior and general behavior theory.* Englewood Cliffs, New Jersey: Prentice-Hall, 1968.

Dodwell, P. C. *Visual pattern recognition.* New York: Holt, 1970.

Esper, E. A. *A history of psychology.* Philadelphia, Pennsylvania: Saunders, 1964.

Fantz, R. L. Visual perception and experience in early infancy: A look at the hidden side of behavior development. In H. W. Stevenson, E. H. Hess, & H. L. Rheingold (Eds.), *Early behavior, comparative and developmental approaches.* New York: Wiley, 1967. Pp. 181–224.

Gibson, E. J. *Principles of perceptual learning and development.* New York: Appleton, 1969.

Gibson, J. J., & Gibson, E. J. Perceptual learning: Differentiation or enrichment? *Psychological Review,* 1955, **62**, 32–41.

Hamilton, W. *Lectures on metaphysics.* (3rd ed.) Vol. 2. London: Blackwood, 1865.

Harris, C. J. Perceptual adaptation to inverted, reversed, and displaced vision. *Psychological Review*, 1965, **72**, 419–444.

Hebb, D. O. *Organization of behavior*. New York: Wiley, 1949.

Hering, E. *Beitrage zur physiologie*. Heft 1. Leipzig: Engelmann, 1861.

Hirsch, H. V. B., & Spinelli, D. N. Visual experience modifies distribution of horizontally and vertically oriented receptive fields in cats. *Science*, 1970, **168**, 869–871.

Hochberg, J. Nativism and empiricism in perception. In L. Postman (Ed.), *Psychology in the making*. New York: Knopf, 1962. Pp. 255–330.

Hochberg, J. In the mind's eye. In R. N. Haber (Ed.), *Contemporary theory and research in visual perception*. New York: Holt, 1968. Pp. 309–331.

Hochberg, J. Attention, organization and consciousness. In D. L. Mostofsky (Ed.), *Attention: Contemporary theory and analysis*. New York: Appleton, 1970. Pp. 99–124.

Hubel, D. H. The visual cortex of the brain. *Scientific American*, 1963, **209**, 54–62.

Hubel, D. H., & Wiesel, T. N. Receptive fields, binocular interaction and the functional architecture in the cat's visual cortex. *Journal of Physiology (London)*, 1962, **160**, 106–154.

Hubel, D. H., & Wiesel, T. N. Receptive fields of cells in striate cortex of very young, visually inexperienced kittens. *Journal of Neurophysiology*, 1963, **26**, 994–1002.

Hume, D. A treatise on human nature, 1739. In *Philosophical works*. Vol. 1. Boston: Little, Brown & Co. 1854.

James, W. *Principles of psychology*, Vol. 2. New York: Holt, 1890.

Kohler, W. *Gestalt psychology*. New York: Liveright, 1947.

Locke, J. *An essay concerning human understanding*. 1690. 2 vols. (Ed. by A. C. Fraser from the 4th ed.) London & New York: Oxford Univ. Press (Clarendon), 1894.

Lotze, R. H. *Outlines of psychology: Dictated portions of the lectures*. (Transl. by G. T. Ladd, Ed.) Boston, Massachusetts: Ginn, 1886.

Mill, J. *Analysis of the phenomena of the human mind*. 1829. Vol. 1. (Ed. by J. S. Mill from the 2nd ed.) New York: Kelley, 1967.

Mill, J. S. *A system of logic*. (8th ed.) New York: Longmans & Green, 1872.

Mill, J. S. *An examination of Sir William Hamilton's philosophy*. (5th ed.) New York: Longmans, Green, 1878.

Müller, J. *Elements of physiology*. (Transl. by W. Baly) New York: Leavitt, 1852.

Pastore, N. Samuel Bailey's critique of Berkeley's theory of vision. *Journal of the History of Behavioral Science*, 1965, **1**, 321–337.

Pastore, N. *Selective history of theories of visual perception*. New York: Oxford, 1971.

Postman, L. Association theory and perceptual learning. *Psychological Review*, 1955, **62**, 438–446.

Reid, T. An inquiry into the human mind, 1764. In *Philosophical works*. (8th ed.) Hildesheim: Olms, 1967. P. 331.

Rock, I. Perception from the standpoint of psychology. *Research Publications, Association for Research in Nervous and Mental Disease*, 1970, **48**, 1–11.

Rock, I., & Harris, C. J. Vision and touch. *Scientific American*, 1967, **216**, 96–104.

Seligman, M. E. P. & Hager, J. (Eds.) *Biological boundaries of learning*. New York: Appelton, 1972.

Shlaer, R. Shift in binocular disparity causes compensatory change in the cortical structure of kittens. *Science,* 1971, **173**, 638–641.

Spearman, C. *Psychology down the ages.* Vol. 2. New York: Macmillan, 1937.

Stewart, D. In W. Hamilton (Ed.), *Collected works of Dugald Stewart.* Vol. 2. Edinburgh: Constable, 1854. P. 142.

Sully, J. The question of visual perception in Germany (II). *Mind,* 1878, **3**, 167–195.

Sutherland, N. S. Outlines of a theory of visual pattern recognition in animals and man. In R. M. Gilbert & N. S. Sutherland (Eds.), *Animal discrimination learning.* New York: Academic Press, 1969. Pp. 385–411.

von Helmholtz, H. *Physiological optics.* 1860. Vol. 3. (3rd ed.) (Transl. by J. P. C. Southall, Ed.) New York: Dover, 1962.

von Helmholtz, H. *Popular lectures on scientific subjects.* (Transl. by E. Athinson.) New York: Longmans, Green, 1884.

von Senden, M. *Space and sight.* (Transl. by P. Heath) London: Methuen, 1960.

Warren, H. C. *A history of association psychology.* London: Constable, 1921.

Zuckerman, C. B., & Rock, I. A reappraisal of the role of past experience and innate organizing processes in visual perception. *Psychological Bulletin,* 1957, **54**, 269–296.

Chapter 7

CONSCIOUSNESS, PERCEPTION, AND ACTION

WOLFGANG METZGER

I. THE CONCEPTS OF CONSCIOUSNESS, PERCEPTION, AND STIMULUS

This section on the historical background of contemporary perception research briefly surveys the development of scientific opinion about the role that judgment and action of the subject play in the constitution of percepts or of conscious phenomena. It is impossible to follow up the history of those three concepts through the millenia. Some arbitrariness in limiting the period that will be taken into consideration is unavoidable. Perhaps it is suitable to take as terminus a quo the time about the eighteensixties when, among others, Fechner, von Helmholtz, Wundt, and Hering began to make psychology an empirical science.

A. Consciousness

Consciousness was then understood in a narrower sense than it is today; it included only the subjective side: proprioception—as consciousness of the self or ego with its feelings, tendencies, and bodily states—plus representation—ideas, images, opinions, beliefs, convictions, dreams. In other words, consciousness in this sense is the object of *introspection* in the strict sense of the word. Ewald Hering (1861–1864, 1925) was the first to distinguish clearly between percept and physical object and to consider as part of consciousness the external world, too. This is the meaning of his contention that the things and events we find in our surroundings are but percepts; this implies the acknowledgment of the fact that these are found—not created—by the subject (Gibson, 1966). And if so, they must substantially be the product of organic processes that can be induced and modified but not replaced by activities of the subject. Hering's view was not adopted more generally in perceptual theory until much later. But the difficulties of correct application are still noticeable even in recent psychology publications.

In summary, at the moment it seems suitable to define consciousness as the sum total of what a subject experiences; in everyday language it distinguishes a waking man from a man in dreamless sleep.

B. Perception

Obviously, perception is an essential part of consciousness; it is that part which consists of stubborn facts and insofar constitutes reality as experienced (cf. Metzger, 1968, pp. 8–47). This function of perception depends on the activity of receptors that are affected by processes from the physical world. Perception, then, can be defined as the result of processing information that consists of stimulations of receptors under conditions which in every case are partially due to the subject's own activity. The question of this chapter can therefore be restated as follows: To what degree have bodily or mental activities of the subject, not including autonomous organic processes, been supposed to contribute to this information processing in the course of the development of experimental psychology?

C. The Concept of Stimulus

In order to answer the question stated above, we need a clear concept of stimulus. The term stimulus is defined here—in agreement with Hering—as physical or chemical influence from outside on a receptor element by which the state of this element is altered (excited) in such a way that nervous processes are aroused that are conducted to the central nervous system. In the case of a reflex, a motor activity follows immediately; in the case of perception, peculiar central processes are initiated that are correlated with conscious phenomena, percepts, things, events, or situations in the phenomenal world of the subject.

If more than one receptor element is stimulated simultaneously, we speak of "configurations" or "distributions" of stimuli; and if the time dimension enters we speak of sequences of stimulus distributions or of spatiotemporal configurations of stimuli. Obviously alterations of receptors can also be caused by other parts of the organism itself.

Stimulation from outside may be caused by (1) physical changes in the environment while the state of the organism, except the receptors, remains constant; (2) a change of the state of the organism with regard to the environment; or (3) both. [Of course it is logically admitted to call a configuration of stimuli or a sequence of such or certain features of them "a stimulus," if this is done explicitly, as, e.g., when J. J. Gibson (1952) speaks of "gradients" as stimuli for depth phenomena.]

As is obvious, the meaning of the term stimulus, as used here, is equivalent to what has been called "proximal" stimulus by Koffka (1935) and many succeeding authors. But we prefer to say simply "stimulus" because we are not going to use the term "distant" or "distal" stimulus as being equivocal. On the one hand it means a physical object insofar as it serves as a source of (e.g., visual) stimulation in the proper sense, on the other hand, particularly in behavioristic discussion, it signifies a percept (a *Sehding* in the sense of Hering) which, as caused by stimulation of receptors, cannot at the same time be the cause of that stimulation (cf. Gibson, 1966, p. 28). Neither do we call "stimuli" the valences of percepts by which activities of the subject are induced or controlled.

In behavioristic discussion, the concept of stimulus fluctuates between these three meanings of physical object or event, of affection of a receptor, and of valence of a percept (cf. Metzger, 1968, pp. 297–299). Taken strictly, the term stimulus is serviceable in theory of perception only if it signifies an intermediate link in the causal chain leading from object to percept. In this sense the term will be further used in this chapter. In doing so, we are in full agreement with Hering's view.

II. JUDGMENT HYPOTHESES

The view that prevailed in the half century up to the beginning of the first World War was not that of Hering but was one which had been proposed by the great H. von Helmholtz in the first edition of his *Treatise on Physiological Optics* (1860, 1866, 1925, pp. 4–5): the theory of judgment (*Urteilstheorie*).

A. Survey of Hypotheses

In his theory, von Helmholtz starts from the explicit statement that it is invariably the *nervous stimulations* (we should say excitations) *that are perceived directly,* but never the objects themselves. But there are *mental activities* that enable us to form *an idea as to the possible causes* of the observed actions on the senses (with this formulation, von Helmholtz takes up an idea that had been uttered by A. Schopenhauer in 1818).

The results of these activities are equivalent to a conclusion or inference from analogy, and this is what he calls them. Visual illusions and other deviations from the geometry of stimulus configurations were then interpreted as *erroneous interpretations* of stimuli (*Urteilstäuschungen*). Von Helmholtz does not ignore the fact that these processes differ from free acts of conscious thought in several regards: (1) they are instantaneous; (2) they are unconscious and, as Wolfgang Köhler (1913) adds, occupied with unconscious material; (3) they can, as von Helmholtz already sees, not be corrected by the perceiver by better knowledge. (4) There is one more fundamental difference between those supposed unconscious processes and conscious thought that was not yet known to von Helmholtz and Köhler: conscious inferential thinking becomes more difficult, the more complicated the situation which is to be interpreted grows; contrariwise the most unequivocal and irresistible tridimensional effects are observed just in those two-dimensional spatiotemporal configurations of stimuli which are much too complicated for drawing clear inferences from them.

B. Criticisms

The first criticism of von Helmholtz's judgment theory came from Wolfgang Köhler (1913). As he points out, the unconscious inferences supposed by Helmholtz are but a stopgap for all those phenomena (1) which are not in line with expectations derived from some known features of stimulation and (2) for which there exist no simple objective explanations, as is the case, for instance, for mixture and contrast of colors. The assumption of unconscious inferences is indispensable only as long as lateral interactions between simultaneous excitations are considered as impossible (*Konstanz-Annahme*). The assumption of lateral interactions—which play an important role in modern electrophysiology—was already made by

Hering (1905) in his theory of color contrast, but first recognized in its bearing and formulated explicitly (under the name *Querfunktionen*) by Wertheimer (1912); it was one of the fundamental theses of Gestalt theory from its beginning.

C. Renewals

As more concrete ideas about direct interaction were developed, the theory of unconscious judgment disappeared from the discussion of perception. But still in 1917 J. Pikler based his theory of binocular depth perception on comparisons made by the subject between the two retinal images of the object. And after an interval of about 40 years the theory of unconscious judgments about unconscious material had a kind of renaissance in some theories of monocular depth perception and of visual illusions (e.g., Gregory, 1963, 1967; Tausch, 1954, 1955, 1962) but was refuted again by Zanforlin (1967), Fisher (1968), and Metzger, Vukovich-Voth, and Koch (1970).

Another temptation to relapse into Helmholtzian speculations is to be found in the representation of decision theory by Swets, Tanner, and Birdsall (1964). The progress they made in psychophysics by adding the viewpoint of choice of criterion to the concept of sensitivity is impressive. But when they try to apply the clear concept of decision as an undeniable activity of the subject in the borderline situation of a threshold exposure to perception in general they face the danger of slipping into obsolete pseudo theories, as in situations where (1) as while looking at a human face or a landscape, the subject should be required to make thousands of decisions at one and the same moment, decisions which (2) are never noticed by him—in contrast to the decisions required in threshold observations—and which (3) are not necessary, because—to use the metaphor introduced by themselves—the cards lay open on the table (Swets *et al.,* 1964, pp. 54–55).

A late aftereffect of von Helmholtz's theory is present day's laboratory slang and is frequently found in serious publications—according to which we "perceive," "compare," and "judge" *stimuli.*

III. ACT HYPOTHESES

A. Brentano's Criticism

While judgment theory was in vogue among experimental psychologists, *act psychology* was proclaimed by Franz Brentano (1874). An act, according to him and his (mostly philosophical) followers is merely a mental activity by which not objective reality (or the subject's objective relations to it) but only percepts and images are affected. Instances are attending, analyzing, picking out, laying stress on. Of course there is no sharp borderline between these mental activities and bodily exploring activities as fixating, scanning, reading, counting, searching in the perceptive field. Brentano contends that psychology should rather occupy itself with perceiving instead of percepts, with attending instead of the objects and effects of attention, and so forth. *Objects* of perception in his opinion belong to the realm of physics. With this statement he falls back behind Hering's distinction between physical and perceptive worlds. But he gave the first discussion of the possibility of a psychology in which the subject's *actions* play a dominant role.

B. Attention Theories

Not much later we find a theory of perception based explicitly on acts of the subject: G. E. Müller's *Komplextheorie* or theory of "collective attention" (1904, 1923), followed by B. Petermann's theory of attention-direction (1929, 1931), which deviates slightly from the former. Petermann explicitly describes the idea underlying his attempt to overcome a psychology to which the subject while perceiving is but a passive "battlefield of stimuli." According to Müller, unit formation in perception is the outcome of collective acts of attention. As is known, there are equivocal stimulus situations, under which such acts can be successful to a certain degree in discontinuous structures with a limited number of "elements." But in order to generalize, both authors were compelled to introduce "cues" or criteria for the action of attention, and give them finally such a decisive role that the question arises whether it is useful to intercalate a hypothetical factor x called attention instead of assuming that these "cues" or criteria are actually factors that immediately determine the unit formations in question, and often in a way opposite to active collective intentions of the subject (Bühler, 1913; Köhler, 1926).

In all these attempts, instead of studying experimentally the effects of observable acts of attending on perception, attention is made a magical principle that can do everything and explains nothing.

Also, if it is doubted whether it is of much use to assume hypothetical acts as fundamental factors in perception, this doubt does not in the least refer to the importance of mental activities that can actually be observed and controlled by the subject (cf. Duncker, 1935).

IV. THE ROLE OF BODILY ACTIVITIES

What does bodily action with respect to overt behavior contribute to perception? I would like to note here that general statements, sometimes rather elaborate, according to which some kind of behavior *must* be at the basis of perception, or even, that a person's world *must* be created by himself, will not be discussed here. The presentation will be restricted to a survey of observations and assumptions about the importance of specific kinds of bodily activity for concrete features of perception.

A. Tracing Movements of the Eye

The earliest assumption of this type is W. Wundt's eye-movement hypothesis of seen shape. This is the first of many "motor-copy hypotheses," which hold "that objects in the world are reflected in perception by action, that is, by responses which trace them or embody them in such a way as to recreate their form or structure" (Gibson, 1966). The assumption that eye movements trace the outlines of seen objects was renewed by Piaget in the 1940's by stating that the concept of such an object is the sum total of the movements made before by the subject in the endeavor to recognize it. This view is still held by Soviet psychologists, e.g., Zinchenko (1966).

What is the value of it? In order to explain what they are expected to, any deviations of the tracks of eye movements must not exceed the threshold for visual form. As Stratton (1902) has shown, their actual deviations are astonishingly far beyond this threshold. That means that visual shape perception cannot be based on them. Hereby Wundt's hypothesis—and Piaget's and Zinchenko's as well—has definitely been disproved.

Actually in consequence of the peculiar construction of the motor apparatus of the eye, tracing outlines by eye movements is objectively impossible. *Voluntary* eye movements are without exception jumping from one fixation point to the next. Vision occurs only during the phases of rest at these points, not because the eye is blind while jumping but because stimulus configurations are displaced on the retina so rapidly that all contours are completely blurred and no image can result. That means that simultaneous stimulation of relatively large areas of the retina must be the basis of visual form perception; in other words we have to attribute a much greater role to passive reception than is customarily done among psychologists these days. Besides, why shouldn't we? How should a landscape be perceived in the night during a lightning of a tenth of a second? And by what kind of eye movements should a human face be recognized?

B. Hand Movements in Haptic Perception

What about the role of hand movements in haptic perception? These movements are much more striking to an outward observer than are eye movements. Moreover to the movements of the touching hand there are no such restrictions as to voluntary movements of the eyes. So the motor copy hypothesis has more chances here. Piaget (cf. Aebli, 1963) reports that his eye-movement theory is inferred by him from observations on haptic perception of children, in which it was shown that geometric figures were recognized by tracing their edges with the fingers. This statement seems to be generally accepted. But observation cannot have been very exact in these experiments. New experiments of the author (unpublished) of the same kind had no such unambiguous results: there were too many movements that did not coincide with edges and nevertheless recognition occurred. Decisive observations were made by Bürklen (1917), who was blind himself, about reading braille by blind men. As his records of finger movements show, their paths have no relation to the distribution of the braille points but correlate exclusively (1) with practice of reader, approaching a straight track along the line in the most skilled readers, and (2) with the age of the copy, more directly with the distinctness of the symbols, which gradually diminishes by frequent use and finally requires very complicated rubbing movements on every single symbol.

In clear braille, symbols or dotted figures (circle, cross, angle, etc.) which are not much larger than these, it can easily be observed that in order to get a clear image, it is sufficient to make one single straight rubbing movement in any direction with the tip of the finger on them. This means that even hand movements need not be motor copies. They can, but need not be motor copies and we do not yet know whether other than tracing movements are sometimes more effective.

C. Actual Functions of Hand and Eye Movements While Recognizing an Object

If tracing is not the essential function of the movements of the touching hand, what is its actual use? There are at least three effects of moving the touching limb which are indispensable for its efficiency:

1. Calling forth qualities of the material: roughness by rubbing, hardness by pressing, elasticity by bending, etc.

2. Extending the area to be explored beyond that of the finger tips; in vision looking around in a new room or walking about in a large new building or in a city seen for the first time corresponds to this.

3. Slowing down adaptation of receptors, so that sensory structures do not fade so quickly. Hand movements fulfill this task by shifting "stimuli," i.e., singularities of a surface in a manner that ever new sensory elements are subjected to increased pressure and continuous on-and-off-effects are released, so that the configuration of excitations does not fade. This phenomenon has long been known in tactile perception: a belt or braces are only felt for a few seconds after being put on. Then they disappear to be perceived again for some moments only when slightly shifted off their proper place.

That similar conditions prevail in vision was found only recently. On closer consideration it had always been astonishing that the fading of visual structures as predicted by Hering's color theory occurred so slowly and was never complete (Metzger, 1940, 1968, p. 169). The hidden factor responsible for this has meanwhile been found and studied by Ditchburn and Ginsborg (1952), Pritchard, Heron, and Hebb (1960), and by many others in their investigations of fixed retinal images. It consists of minute eye movements of different types by which the continuous "reviving" shift on the retina of the visual structures is brought about. This means that the decisive factor in vision is exactly the same as in touch, except that in vision the movements are subliminal and therefore do their work unconsciously.

A similar role of *supraliminal* eye movements intensifying the effect of disparity has been found in binocular depth perception (Metzger, 1953, pp. 293–295).

4. If these three conditions are fulfilled, the haptic apprehension of specific form can take place. But if tracing plays only an incidental role, how does it actually come about? As unpublished experimental findings suggest, there is a complicated interaction between finger movements in rubbing and grasping on the one side and shift of configuration of singularities of the object on the surface of the moving fingers on the other side, shifts that are simultaneous with and opposite to the active movement. And, as can immediately be observed, there exists (just like in eye movements) a kind of constancy of localization of these singularities, active movements of fingers and shifts of stimulation on their surface paralyzing each other (cf. von Holst & Mittelstaedt, 1950). This way, the moving fingers do not find "elements" that are "combined" by them, but rather "spots" of something that is supposed to be more extended and to contain more of them with stable relations among each other from the beginning.

In this respect touching and visual scanning prove to be closely related. In scanning, the fixation point is successively displaced to the spots that are of most interest in the moment. By this shift of fixation, the stimulation coming from the corresponding spots of the physical object is brought to the most differentiated and sensitive parts of the retina. As already mentioned, in scanning the eye jumps more or less systematically from one point to the other of a whole that in visual space already exists owing to the continuous simultaneous stimulation of the entire retina.

The function of scanning, then, is not to gather "elements" scattered around in the visual field in order to "combine" them to larger units only afterward. Rather the regard wanders around from spot to spot of larger units that are given beforehand, though in a preliminary and more or less molar way, in order to clarify and specify local details of them. The classical instance is the difference between merely "seeing" a printed line from a distance and "reading" it. In the first case, the line represents itself as a sequence of longer and shorter blocks of indeterminate letters with intervals between them. In the second, the individual letters are singled out and the specific structure of every word is recognized so that its meaning can be understood.

But it must be stressed that visual scanning does not only serve to "know more details" but may release far-reaching restructuring processes: two-dimensional designs the retinal image of which exceeds the macula and, in consequence of this, can in a given moment be seen quite clearly only within an area that corresponds to the macula, may undergo a reorganization with regard to *unit formation* (Metzger, 1953, p. 88) or to *depth distribution* (Hochberg, 1966, pp. 18–26), if fixation happens to fall on spots of the object that are decisive in these points of view.

These findings must not be overvalued. Scanning is *not* indispensable in every case of unit formation or of depth distribution, but only under the condition mentioned above. If, e.g., as in most of Wertheimer's (1923) or Kopfermann's (1930) demonstrations, the image of the design does not exceed the macula, or if the decisive parts are of greater magnitude and do not require the recognition of such minute details, visual organization does *not* depend on scanning.

D. Effects on Seeing and Hearing of Gross Bodily Movements

On the other hand, there are bodily movements quite different from scanning that can influence visual and acoustic organization in a decisive way.

1. One of the most effective factors of monocular depth perception is the deformation of the retinal image of solid bodies if these rotate with an axis not identical with the line of vision (Metzger, 1935, pp. 195–260). This deformation of the retinal image occurs just as well if the observer moves by the object, as if the object rotates in front of him (as, apparently,

in the movies). The first case is traditionally called "motion parallax," but can be treated adequately only in connection with the second. But there is one fundamental difference. If there are no other factors (as, e.g., illumination) cooperating with deformation of image, the depth effect is ambiguous with moving *object* (second case): spatial inversion is likely to occur. This is not the case if the deformation of image is due to movement of the *subject*. In case of inversion of apparent depth in relation to objective depth, every motion of the subject is accompanied by an illusory rotation of the object with an angular velocity twice as high as his, while if apparent depth corresponds to the objective, all concomitant illusory movements disappear (Ittelson, 1960; Klix, 1962; Metzger, 1935; Tschermak-Seysenegg, 1939).

2. A similar minimizing tendency of the perceptive system underlies our faculty to discriminate between sounds that come from above or below, and from the front or from the backside. A specific mechanism is only provided for the discrimination between left and right. This is the distance of the two ears. But without additional mechanisms, the distinction in the other two dimensions is possible by simply turning the head. If apparent direction of sound is inverse to the real one, the sound appears to move in the direction of the head's movement, and this again, by geometric reasons, with double angular speed. If apparent and objective direction coincide, these concomitant illusory movements disappear and the source of sound appears to be resting in its surroundings, as it really does, no matter how the subject moves (Wallach, 1939).

E. Subject's Activities Contributing to Perception: A Survey

Besides these bodily movements increasing the efficacy of structural responses of higher senses, there is quite a number of conscious and subconscious activities supporting, improving, refining, optimizing sensory functions (cf. Zaporozhets & Gibson, 1966 passim; Sokolov, 1967, pp. 61–93). The space available allows a survey which is not much more detailed than a table of contents.

There are bodily activities by which:

1. Receptors are exposed to stimulation by certain objects (as looking about, bending to a key-hole, grasping something etc.)

2. The area accessible to receptors is enlarged (as wandering about in order to survey, groping in the dark, etc.)

3. Stimulus configurations are shifted to the most sensitive parts of a receptor (fixation reaction that shifts stimuli to the fovea centralis, bringing objects to the fingertips or to the tip of tongue)

4. State of receptors is optimized (as in accommodation, convergence, retinal adaptation, modification of width of pupil etc.)

5. Outer conditions of perception are improved (as in moving the watch toward the ear, putting on or taking off eyeglasses, turning on a light, twinkling, snuffing, sucking, moistening and lifting up a finger in order to feel the direction of subliminal air draught, leaving and reentering a room in order to recognize a smell, stopping one's breath in order to hear faint noise, shutting the window in order to understand one's partner, etc.)

6. Local adaptation and fading are slowed down (cf. above, Section IV, C, ¶ 3)

7. Exploratory movements in the strict sense of the word (as touching and scanning, including tracing; but cf. above, Section IV, C, ¶ 4)

8. Voluntary movements that are intended to be observed themselves as a means of building up or restoring visual-kinesthetic coordination (Held, 1966; and Smith & Smith, 1966)

9. Accompanying music by abortive conducting or dancing movements

10. Active performance of music or recitation of poetry; active reproduction of handwriting in order to facilitate empathy

11. Operations with objects which serve the purpose of knowing them better (as matching, arranging, copying, memorizing, building up out of given parts; cf. Zaporozhets & Gibson, 1966, passim)

12. Searching for principles of organization of a given material (Katona, 1940). As this survey shows, subject's action in perception above all supports the "receiving" function of receptors, and does by no means serve the purpose of "creating" anything, as some of us believe. This is the task of poets and artists. By the way, we ought to be content with this. For should freedom of subjective creation of the perceptive world surpass a very limited range, incessant paranoid misunderstandings between all of us would be the unavoidable consequence, and communication and cooperation would be impossible.

References

Aebli, H. *Psychologische Didaktik*. Stuttgart: Klett, 1963.

Brentano, F. *Psychologie vom empirischen Standpunkt*. 2 vols. Leipzig: Meiner, 1874.

Bühler, K. *Die Gestaltwahrnehmungen I*. Stuttgart: Spemann, 1913.

Bürklen, K. Das Tastlesen der Blindenschrift. *Zeitschrift für Angewandte Psychologie*, Beiheft 16, Leipzig 1917.

Ditchburn, R. W., & Ginsborg, B. L. Vision with a stabilized retinal image. *Nature* (*London*), 1952, **170**, 36–37.

Duncker, K. *Zur Psychologie des produktiven Denkens*. Berlin & New York: Springer-Verlag, 1935.

Fisher, G. H. *The frameworks for perceptual localization.* London: Newcastle upon Tyne, 1968.

Gibson, E. J., Perceptual development and the reduction of uncertainty. In A. V. Zaporozhets & J. J. Gibson (Eds.), *Symposium perception and action.* Moscow: 1966. Pp. 7–17.

Gibson, J. J. The relation between visual and postural determinants of the phenomenal vertical. *Psychological Review,* 1952, **59,** 370–375.

Gibson, J. J. *The senses considered as perceptual systems.* Boston, Massachusetts: Houghton, 1966.

Gregory, R. L. Distortion of visual space as inappropriate constancy scaling. *Nature (London),* 1963, **199,** 678–680.

Gregory, R. L. Comments on the inappropriate constancy scaling theory of the illusions and its implications. *Quarterly Journal of Experimental Psychology,* 1967, **19,** 219–223.

Held, R. Plasticity in sensorimotor coordination. In A. V Zaporozhets & J. J. Gibson (*Symposium perception and action.* Moscow: 1966. Pp. 27–34.

Hering, E. *Beiträge zur Physiologie.* Leipzig: W. Engelmann, 1861–1964.

Hering, E. *Grundzüge der Lehre vom Lichtsinn.* Berlin, J. Springer 1905. (2nd ed.: 1920.) Also in A. Graefe-Saemisch (Ed.), *Handbuch der gesamten Augenheilkunde* (2nd ed.) Vol. III. Berlin: 1925. Ch. XII, pp. 1–294.

Hochberg, J. Reading pictures and text: What is learning in perceptual development? In A. V. Zaporozhets & J. J. Gibson (Eds.), *Symposium perception and action.* Moscow: 1966. Pp. 18–26.

Ittelson, W. H. *Visual space perception.* Berlin & New York: Springer-Verlag, 1960.

Katona, G. *Organizing and memorizing: Studies in the psychology of learning and teaching.* New York: Columbia Univ. Press, 1940.

Klix, F. *Elementaranalysen zur Psychophysik der Raumwahrnehmung.* Berlin: VEB Deutscher Verlag der Wissenschaften, 1962.

Koffka, K. *Principles of Gestalt psychology.* New York: Harcourt, 1935.

Köhler, W. Über unbemerkte Empfindungen und Urteilstäuschungen. *Zeitschrift fuer Psychologie,* 1913, **66,** 51–80.

Köhler, W. Zur Komplextheorie. *Psychologische Forschung,* 1926, **8,** 236–243.

Kopfermann, H. Psychologische Untersuchungen über die Wirkung zweidimensionaler Darstellung körperlicher Gebilde. *Psychologische Forschung,* 1930, **13,** 293–364.

Metzger, W. Tiefenerscheinungen in optischen Bewegungsfeldern. *Psychologische Forschung,* 1935, **20,** 195–260.

Metzger, W. Zur anschaulichen Repräsentation von Rotationsvorgängen und ihrer Deutung durch Gestaltkreislehre und Gestalttheorie. *Zeitschrift fuer Sinnesphysiologie,* 1940, **68,** 261–279.

Metzger, W. *Gesetze des Sehens* (2nd ed.) Frankfurt am Main: Kramer, 1953.

Metzger, W. *Psychologie. Die Entwicklung ihrer Grundannahmen seit der Einführung des Experiments.* 1940 (4th ed.) Darmstadt: Steinkopff, 1968.

Metzger, W., Vukovich-Voth, O., & Koch, I. Über optisch-haptische Maßtäuschungen an dreidimensionalen Gegenständen. *Psychologische Beiträge,* 1970, **12,** 329–366.

Müller, G. E. Die Gesichtspunkte und die Tatsachen der psychophysischen Methodik. In L. Asher & K. Spiro (Eds.), *Ergebnisse der Physiologie,* 1903, Jahrgang II, Abtheilung II, 1904. Pp. 267–516.

Müller, G. E. *Komplextheorie und Gestalttheorie.* Göttingen: Vandenhoek & Ruprecht, 1923.

Petermann, B. *Die Wertheimer-Koffka-Köhlersche Gestalttheorie und das Gestaltproblem.* Leipzig: Barth, 1929.

Petermann, B. *Das Gestaltproblem in der Psychologie im Licht analytischer Besinnung.* Leipzig: Barth, 1931.

Pikler, J. *Sinnesphysiologische Untersuchungen.* Leipzig: Barth, 1917.

Pritchard, R. M., Heron, W., & Hebb, D. O. Visual perception approached by the method of stabilized retinal images. *Canadian Journal of Psychology,* 1960, **14,** 67–77.

Schopenhauer, A. *Die Welt als Wille und Vorstellung* (1st ed.) 1818. (6th ed.: Leipzig: Brockhaus, 1887.)

Smith, O. W., & Smith, P. C. Response produced visual stimuli vs. non-RPVS for distance judgements in natural and unnatural units by children and adults. In A. V. Zaporozhets, & J. J. Gibson (Eds.), *Symposium perception and action.* Moscow: 1966. Pp. 101–109.

Sokolov, E. N. Die reflektorischen Grundlagen der Wahrnehmung. In H. Hiebsch (Ed.), *Ergebnisse der sowjetischen Psychologie.* Berlin: Akademie-Verlag, 1967. Pp. 61–93.

Stratton, G. M. Eye movements and the aesthetics of visual form. *Philosophische Studien (Wundt),* 1902, **20,** 336–359.

Swets, J. A., Tanner, W. P., Jr., & Birdsall, T. G. Decision processes in perception. In J. A. Swets (Ed.), *Signal detection and recognition by human observers.* New York: Wiley, 1964. Pp. 3–57.

Tausch, R. Optische Täuschungen als artifizielle Effekte der Gestaltprozesse von Größen- und Formkonstanz in der natürlichen Raumwahrnehmung. *Psychologische Forschung,* 1954, **24,** 299–348.

Tausch, R. Nichtbewußte (sogenannte unbewußte) Vorgänge bei der optischen Größenwahrnehmung von Gegenständen. *Psychologische Forschung,* 1955, **25,** 28–64.

Tschermak-Seysenegg, A. Über Parallaktoskopie. *Pfluegers Archiv fuer die Gesamte Physiologie des Menschen und der Tiere,* 1939, **241,** 455–469.

Tausch, R. Empirische Untersuchungen im Hinblick auf ganzheits- und gestaltpsychologische Wahrnehmungserklärungen. *Zeitschrift fuer Psychologie,* 1962, **166,** 26–61.

von Helmholtz, H. In J. P. C. Southhall (Ed.), *Treatise on physiological optics.* (Engl. transl. of 3rd German ed.) 1909/1911. (Reprint of the 1925 ed.: New York, Dover, 1962.)

von Holst, E., & Mittelstaedt, H. Das Reafferenzprinzip, *Naturwissenschaften,* 1950, **37,** 464–476.

Wallach, H. On sound localization. *Journal of the Acoustic Society of America,* 1939, **10,** 270–274.

Wertheimer, M. Experimentelle Studien über das Sehen von Bewegungen. *Zeitschrift fuer Psychologie,* 1912, **61,** 161–265.

Wertheimer, M. Untersuchungen zur Lehre von der Gestalt. *Psychologische Forschung,* 1923, **4,** 301–350.

Zanforlin, M. Some observations on Gregory's theory of perceptual illusions. *Quarterly Journal of Experimental Psychology,* 1967, **19,** 193–197.

Zaporozhets, A. V., & Gibson, J. J. (Eds.) *Symposium perception and action.* Moscow: 1966.

Zinchenko, V. P. Perceptions as actions. In A. V. Zaporozhets & J. J. Gibson (Eds.), *Symposium perception and action.* Moscow: 1966. Pp. 64–73.

Chapter 8

ATTENTION

D. E. BERLYNE*

"To the question, 'What is attention?'," wrote Groos in 1896 (p. 210), "there is not only no generally recognized answer, but the different attempts at a solution even diverge in the most disturbing manner." Forty-one years later, Spearman (1937, p. 133) felt that the growing prominence of the "faculty" of attention "would appear to have been achieved at the price of calling down upon its builders the curse of Babel . . . . For the word 'attention' quickly came to be associated . . . with a diversity of meanings that have the appearance of being more chaotic even than those of the term 'intelligence'." If these two authors had been writing at the beginning of the 1970's, they would have found even more grounds for their doleful observations. The difficulties are compounded by the fact that contemporary writers on attention, like the work gang of the original Tower of Babel, often fail to realize that they are speaking different languages.

* The preparation of this paper was facilitated by research grant APB-73 from the National Research Council of Canada.

Most of us probably first came across attention as a source of trouble in school. A teacher is sure that all the information necessary for answering a particular question or performing well at a particular task has been made available to the pupil and that his native endowments are adequate. Consequently, his defective performance can only be due to a lack of something called "attention." Whatever it is, it is supposed to be under voluntary control, which affords her the satisfaction of moral condemnation and exempts her from looking for ways to improve her own communicative skills. Psychologists also have sometimes treated vicissitudes of "attention" as an escape hatch through which they can save themselves when a stimulus fails to affect behavior as expected.

For both the teacher and the psychologist, the word "attention" refers to processes or conditions within the organism that determine how effective a particular stimulus will be. But already, several distinctions (see Berlyne, 1960, 1969, 1970) are possible that are not always carefully made.

There are a number of different ways in which the effectiveness of external stimuli can vary, and they can be controlled by distinct factors. First, the degree to which the external environment as a whole influences behavior can fluctuate. A subject's overt actions can reflect variations in what is going on around him with greater or lesser precision. In the language of information theory, the rate of total information transmission between sensory and motor processes can go up or down. There are, as we say, increases or decreases in his overall level of *"attentiveness," "alertness,"* or *"vigilance."* Secondly, there can be fluctuations in the degree to which control over behavior is distributed among features of the environment. The *distribution* can be *concentrated* or *diffuse.* Behavior may be exquisitely sensitive to events in a small region of the environment or affected in a rough and general way by what is occurring at widely scattered points. Granted the well-known limited capacity of the nervous system for transmitting information, the information contained in overt behavior may virtually exhaust the information content of one source of stimulation or draw incompletely on the information contents of several sources. Lastly, and in contrast to these two so-called *intensive* aspects of attention, there are *selective* or *directive* aspects. Many stimulus elements, present simultaneously, generally compete for control over behavior or, in other words, for occupation of the nervous system's limited information-transmitting capacity. Events inside the organism may grant predominant influence to one property of a stimulus object, causing other properties of the same object to be ignored. When this is so, we may properly speak of "abstraction." Alternatively, they may place behavior under the control of stimuli belonging to one region of space rather than another or impinging on one region of the sensory surfaces rather than another. Subjects exposed to concurrent auditory messages (see Moray, 1969) can pick sequences of sounds characterized by a particular pitch spectrum, language, or subject matter out of a hubbub and respond selectively to them.

Furthermore, there are several senses in which one stimulus can be more "effective" than another that accompanies it. It may be a matter of degree of influence on responses that are performed while, or just after, the stimulus is present. Alternatively, we might be thinking of the role of the stimulus in learning. When learning occurs, a response becomes more (or less) strongly associated with certain features of the situation in which the learning experience took place. In other words, the performance of the response becomes more (or less) likely when a situation including such features is encountered in future. Some of the stimuli that are present are likely to acquire greater increments (or decrements) of association with the response than others. Finally, when a human subject has been exposed to a large number of stimuli at once, some will have impressed themselves on his memory more strongly than others, so that he can more easily specify them verbally or in some other symbolic fashion after they have been withdrawn. So, in correspondence with these three possibilities, we must be prepared to distinguish *attention in performance, attention in learning,* and *attention in remembering.* It may well be that these three kinds of attention depend on the same determining factors and the same neurophysiological processes. It seems plausible that the stimuli that become most strongly associated with a learned response should be those that exerted the fullest control over behavior at the time of learning. These, it may well be supposed, will also be the ones most readily remembered on some future occasion. But these assumptions are by no means logically necessary. They require experimental verification, which they have not yet received in anything like sufficient measure.

The foregoing discussion concerns, of course, the role of attentional factors in the study of behavior. For the prebehaviorist philosophical or experimental psychologist (as so often for the layman today), attention was something that increased the vividness or clarity of the sensation induced by a perceived event or of some other conscious experience. It was (and frequently still is) assumed that the events most conspicuously represented in consciousness will dominate behavior, learning, and remembering. The general validity of this assumption has been called in question by theories (e.g., psychoanalysis) that lay great stress on unconscious determinants of behavior, as well as by theories (e.g., James, 1884; Taylor, 1962) holding that conscious experiences depend on bodily movements rather than the other way round. Nevertheless, the behavioral manifestations of attention are commonly taken to include those of awareness, e.g., ability to describe a stimulus verbally.

I. THE PREBEHAVIORIST PERIOD

A. Philosophical Beginnings

Spearman (1937, Ch. VII) has traced the etymological origins of the term "attention" back to classical antiquity. Among several Greek and Latin expressions meaning "to direct the mind" was *animum attendere,* which had connotations of "tension" or "stretching." The noun phrase *attentio animi* appeared first in the writings of Cicero, and, in the course of succeeding centuries, the word *attentio* came to be used alone, with *"animi"* understood and omitted.

Writers with a special interest in attention have often argued that it must occupy a central place in psychological theory. In Titchener's (1908, p. 173) characteristically portentous words, "The doctrine of attention is the nerve of the whole psychological system, and . . . as men judge of it, so shall they be judged before the general tribunal of psychology."

This tribunal must, however, have spent much of its time in a censorious mood, since gross neglect of attention has been a recurrent failing. It received only rare and fleeting mention from the originators of modern philosophy. Descartes (1649, XLIII) related it, like most mental processes, to movements of the pineal body acting on the animal spirits: "Thus when one wishes to arrest one's attention so as to consider one object for a certain length of time, this volition keeps the gland tilted towards one side during that time." Locke (1690, II, 19) acknowledged that "The mind employs itself about (ideas) with several degrees of attention."

The first extended treatment of attention seems to have been that of Malebranche (1674). He accepted Descartes's (1637, 1644) designation of clarity and distinctiveness as the touchstones of evident truth but asserted (Sect. VI) that "attention is necessary for conserving evidence in our knowledge." It alone can prevent ideas from being confused and imperfect. The seeker after truth must therefore avoid strong sensations and passions that can distract him. Malebranche recommended detailed procedures for cultivating attention, with the study of geometry as a prime element.

A little later, Leibnitz (1765) introduced the concept of "apperception," which was destined for a prominent but variegated position in the psychology of the eighteenth and nineteenth centuries. Noting that many of the events stimulating our sense organs can evidently affect us without our being conscious of them (e.g., the sound of a mill wheel of which we are unaware until it stops, the sound of a single drop of water contributing to the roar of the sea), he characterized them as productive only of "miniature perceptions." If we are to become conscious of an event, an additional process called "apperception" is needed. He was apparently influenced by the French word *s'appercevoir* (to notice) and its Latin predecessor, *appercipere*. Leibnitz's disciple, Wolff (1732, 1734), maintained that "In order for the mind to become conscious of perceived objects, and therefore for the act of apperception, attention is required" (1734, p. 25). He was therefore moved to grant attention a key position in what was the first modern attempt to construct a systematic psychology.

Herbart (1824–1825) followed Leibnitz in believing that ideas can exist in the mind without being conscious, although he attributed this primarily to inhibition from competing ideas. He likewise said that an idea had to be "apperceived" if it is to achieve representation in the "field of consciousness," but he emphasized the dependence of apperception on the establishment of harmonious links between newly received ideas and others that are already contained within the mind. One of Herbart's minor writings (1822) consists of an elaborate algebraic model of attention, using the highly unusual combination for the psychologist (though not for the physicist who has read Newton) of Latin and differential calculus. "He is said to be attentive," wrote Herbart in his defining statement, "whose mind is so disposed that it can receive an addition to its ideas: those who do not perceive obvious things are, on the other hand, lacking in attention."

One further line of argument led deviously toward some of the first experimental attacks on attention. Locke (1690) had mentioned "sensation" and "reflection" as the two mental processes through which all knowledge is acquired. By reflection, he meant the "power by which the mind turns inward and observes its own actions and operations." Reid (1785), the leader of the Scottish Spiritualist school, which insisted on the unitary, active nature of mind, identified reflection with a voluntary act of attention. His successors, Stewart (1792) and Brown (1820), denied that we can attend to more than one thing at once. The point can actually be traced back to Hobbes (1655, Ch. 25, ¶6): "While the sense organs are occupied with one object, they cannot simultaneously be moved by another so that an image of both arises. There cannot therefore be two images of two objects but one put together from the action of both."

Sir William Hamilton (1859) stoutly disputed this view. "The doctrine that the mind can attend to, or be conscious of, only a single object at a time would," he maintained (p. 175) "in fact involve the conclusion that all comparison and discrimination are impossible . . . ." He was therefore led to raise the question of what came later to be called the "span of attention." "Supposing that the mind is not limited to the simultaneous consideration of a single object, a question arises, How many objects can it embrace at once?" (p. 176). He proposed the experiment of throwing a handful of marbles on to the floor and ascertaining how many of them can be apprehended as a unit.

B. Early Introspective Experimental Psychology

Wundt (1874, II, 235–236) described attention as an "inner activity," causing ideas to be present in consciousness to differing degrees. Consciousness contained inner equivalents of the restricted focus (*Blickpunkt*) and more extensive visual field (*Blickfeld*) of the eye. Perception meant entry into the inner field, whereas entry into the inner focus was apperception. Apperception binds several sensations together into a unitary idea. However, the focus of attention, unlike that of the eye, can narrow or widen, "whereby its brightness alternatively increases and decreases."

Titchener (1908) repudiated this view, with its overtones of Continental European Rationalism and Spiritualism, in favor of a position more in keeping with the Empiricist–Associationist tradition. For him, attention was simply an "intensive attribute" of a conscious experience, equated with "sensible clearness."

Thus, the very essence of attention was embroiled in vehement controversy, and the polemic flames were fed by many a ponderous disquisition on the question of whether attention was active or passive and on the distinctions between voluntary and involuntary attention and between concentrated and diffuse attention. Arguments were sometimes based on systematic introspective experiments and sometimes on facts about conscious experience that were supposed to be evident to everyone. Among the leading contributions of this sort were those of Müller (1873), Pilzecker (1889), Ribot (1889), James (1890), and Pillsbury (1906).

C. Other Early Experimental Approaches

Apart from the minute scrutinies of subjective experience to which the pioneers of experimental psychology were so partial, several lines of investigation of observable behavior soon brought experimental psychologists face to face with attentional problems.

1. SPAN OF ATTENTION (SPAN OF APPREHENSION)

Jevons (1871) followed up Hamilton's suggestion for an experiment on attention. He threw sets of black beans into a round box and examined his own ability to estimate their number "by a single mental act" without counting. This task, which has more recently come to be known as "subitizing," could be studied in a better controlled manner once the tachistoscope came into use. Cattell (1885) was apparently the first of several experimenters who used this instrument to manipulate duration of exposure in span experiments, so as to prevent a change in fixation.

2. PERCEPTUAL FLUCTUATIONS

Hume (1739) had noted how faint stimuli fluctuate between perceptibility and imperceptibility. This phenomenon was studied a little more systematically by von Urbantchitsch (1875), who observed that, if a watch were held so far away that its tick could barely be heard, the sound would alternately disappear and reemerge. The current techniques of experimental psychology were first applied to this phenomenon by N. Lange (1888), who ascribed it to "periodical fluctuations of sensory attention," which he believed to be "the cause of all other periodicities in consciousness."

McDougall (1905) introduced another technique, in which there was more emphasis on the output or response side and the stimuli to which the subject had to respond were well above the absolute threshold. The subject had to mark irregularly scattered dots on a moving tape with a stylus. Although the task was devised as a means of measuring "mental fatigue," it was described as one "demanding for its execution a continued maximal voluntary concentration of attention." This research was pursued further by Philpott (1932), who used a variety of procedures requiring response to a protracted and rapid succession of stimuli, regarded the oscillations in output as manifestations of changes in attention (1934), and devised a mathematical model to fit them. This approach can be regarded as the inception of research on the intensive aspects of attention or "attentiveness." Procedures of this kind are still widely used to monitor attentional capacities (e.g., the Continuous Performance Test introduced by Rosvold et al., 1956) under the influence of neurological disorders, sleep deprivation, drugs, etc.

The binocular rivalry that occurs when different visual patterns are presented to the two eyes in a stereoscope was yet another kind of perceptual fluctuation on which experiments were carried out quite early

(Breese, 1899). Since the subject sees material in the two visual fields in turn, it is natural to consider the direction of attention to be changing from one moment to the next. But this phenomenon is distinguished from most forms of visual attention by its low susceptibility to voluntary control.

3. REACTION-TIME EXPERIMENTS

The so-called complication experiment, which grew out of the difficulties that astronomers had faced in recording transit times of stars, was introduced by von Tschisch (1885) in Wundt's laboratory. Subjects had to watch a moving pointer and specify its location when a sound or some other nonvisual stimulus occurred. It was regularly found that, although two stimulus events of differing modalities might be simultaneous, one was likely to be registered in consciousness before the other. James (1890) conjectured that this might be due to concentration of attention on each of the two stimuli in turn. The link with attention received some corroboration in the experimental work of Angell and Pierce (1892), subsequently followed up by others.

Attentional factors also obtruded themselves in the more usual kind of reaction-time experiment. Exner (1882) argued that, in the simple reaction-time situation, the most important psychological work goes on before the stimulus is received. "While one is awaiting the stimulus with tense attention, one feels an indescribable something going on in the sensorium (brain), which prepares for the quickest possible reaction." The nervous system is mobilized for the response by *"Bahnung"* (literally "making of a pathway"). L. Lange (1888) reported that simple reaction time was markedly shorter when subjects directed their attention toward the bodily movement to be performed (the muscular reaction) than when they attended predominantly to the stimulus to be received (the sensorial reaction). The generality of this finding was soon disputed, especially when Cattell's (1893) work indicated the importance of individual differences, but the influence of the subject's "attitude" or "preparatory set" while he was awaiting the stimulus was repeatedly confirmed as research continued.

4. SET

Although concurrent views had been coming from quarters remote from the laboratory (e.g., Freud), experimental psychologists learned from the Würzburg school of the early twentieth century that responses (overt or covert) depend jointly on the external stimulus and other, internal factors. The Würzburgers recognized varieties of internal determinants to which they gave names like "task" (*Aufgabe*), "determining tendency," and "idea of goal." But the word "set" came into use among English-speaking psychologists to refer to all such phenomena comprehensively. It has certainly had a confusing variety of connotations (see Gibson, 1941). It was applied generally to what would later have been classed as "motivational" or "mediating" processes or "intervening variables."

One of the most famous Würzburg experiments launched the investigation of attention in remembering. Külpe (1904) exposed subjects to a display of nonsense syllables and told different groups that they would be asked to recall, respectively, the actual syllables, their spatial arrangement, their color, and their number. All subjects were, however, subsequently questioned about all four attributes. They were then able to supply markedly more accurate information about the attribute that had figured in their instructions than about the other three. This experiment has some grave imperfections according to the norms of modern experimental design. Since all subjects were told what they would have to remember before the display was presented, it is impossible to tell whether the results depended on some selective process working during perception or on one operating on memory traces after the stimulus material had been withdrawn. Apart from that, no attempt was made to counterbalance the order in which recall of the different attributes was called for. However, Chapman (1932), as well as a succession of later experimenters, have verified that information about what is to be remembered facilitates recall more effectively when it precedes exposure of stimuli than when it comes between exposure and recall.

II. THE INTERWAR PERIOD

A. Behaviorism and Early Neobehaviorism

Attention is not to be found among the mental phenomena that Watson (1919, 1924) felt obliged to reinterpret in behavioristic terms. When they considered attention at all, the early behaviorists and those close to them were partial to the view that had been vigorously propounded by Ribot (1889), namely that attention can be identified with the postural and other motor processes that facilitate reception of stimuli. As Holt (1915, p. 178) wrote, "The volitional element in behavioristic attention will be the process whereby the *body* assumes and exercises an adjustment or motor set such that its activities are some function of an object; are focused on the object." Dashiell (1928, p. 285) discussed "attending as a form of posturing." Mowrer (1938) studied effects of forewarning and expectancy on reaction time, response amplitude, and other phenomena. He connected these effects with what he called "preparatory set," which he equated a little later with "attention" (1939). He was moved away from the predominant behaviorist bias by evidence (Mowrer, Rayman, & Bliss, 1940) that the mechanism of preparatory set is central rather than peripheral. However, this later concept developed, through that of "anticipatory tension," into Mowrer's theory of anxiety as a secondary drive, which led him into topics less germane to attention.

In general, the learning theorists of the 1930's gave selective aspects of attention rather short shrift as by-products of cardinal principles of behavior. Tolman and Brunswik (1935) spoke of the need for an organism to develop "an adequate reception system that will tend to select reliable cues," i.e., cues that will point the way to gratifications and away from punishments. Tolman, Hall, and Bretnall (1932) offered the "law of emphasis," stating that an "accent or emphasis" on the correct response or on a stimulus indicative of the correct response will facilitate learning. Thus, the problems of attention in performance and of attention in learning received some cursory acknowledgment, but only glaringly incomplete intimations of the determinants of attention were given; all the examples discussed referred to food, electric shocks, or bells. Hull's (1943) sixteenth postulate stated that, when two or more incompatible responses are mobilized at once, the response that is momentarily strongest will be performed. Incompatible responses can be associated with one and the same stimulus or with different stimuli that are present simultaneously. Hull thus made the outcome of stimulus competition depend mainly on the responses corresponding to the stimuli and on the effectiveness of previous learning in which these responses had figured. He acknowledged (p. 209), however, that particularly intense stimuli or stimuli conditioned to strong autonomic or "emotional" reactions might become associated with responses more readily than others and thus outweigh others in the control of behavior.

B. The Gestalt School

Perception, including its subjective aspects, was the primary focus of interest for the Gestalt psychologists, who might therefore have been expected to take the problems of attention very seriously. But they actually gave them only scanty consideration. This was apparently because of their belief that the way the world appears to us, and the behavior that results from how it is perceived, are determined by forces inherent in perceptual structures and in the patterns of electrochemical activity that they set up in the brain. These forces sort things out among themselves and gravitate toward a form of organization that best reconciles their divergent claims. In the resultant organization, some portions of the perceptual field may well be more vivid and prominent than others. For example, the Gestalt psychologists attached great importance to the "figure–ground" phenomenon first studied by Rubin (1915); the portion of the perceptual field defined as figure tends to dominate both the perceptual experience and behavior. Rubin actually read a paper entitled "On the nonexistence of attention" at a meeting held in Jena in 1926.

The notion of attention as a meddlesome extraneous agent that intrusively selects among perceptual units would have been decidedly at odds with the Gestalt position. Koffka (1935), however, made something of a concession in that direction. He associated a voluntary effort of attention with "a force starting within the Ego and being directed towards an object" (p. 358). Defined in this way, attention is capable of "adding energy to the particular field part [that] will increase its articulation, if it is not articulated as well as it might be" (p. 206). This did not, however, mean recognizing attention as something extrinsic to the perceptual field, since the "Ego" (p. 319) "behaves like any other segregated object in the field."

C. Other Currents

While the two dominant schools of experimental psychology were neglecting attention for their different reasons, cognate concepts were undergoing development elsewhere. Freud's works (e.g., Freud, 1900) contain numerous brief references to attention. From the psychoanalytic point of view, attention was a form of cathexis or investment of energy, which could be directed either to inner mental content, such as thoughts and memories, to internal bodily sensations, or to external stimuli associated with gratification. Because "libidinal energy" is limited in amount, cathexis on one object must mean a diminution of interest in other objects.

In the 1930's, Piaget (1947) was working out his notion of "centering" or disproportionate, and therefore maladaptive, concentration of attention on what happens to be brought into temporary or idiosyncratic prominence by a person's present location and condition. In Piaget's view, intellectual development is in large part a progressive surmounting of misleading "centerings"—including the "egocentrism" that marks early social interaction, the perceptual centerings or fixations that give rise to visual illusions, and the intellectual centerings that give undue weight to certain items of evidence with the result that other items of equal importance are debarred from influencing judgment and behavior.

III. THE POSTWAR PERIOD

Since the end of the Second World War, there has been a distinct revival of research and theoretical discussion relating to attentional processes. Several distinct areas of experimentation and theorizing can be distinguished, but they have so far achieved little convergence. All of them stem from phenomena that were either newly discovered or began to receive methodical investigation at the beginning of the 1950's.

A. Neurophysiological Developments

1. INTENSIVE ASPECTS

After the introduction of human electroencephalography by Berger (1929), a great variety of external stimuli and internal ideational processes was found to induce the replacement of alpha waves, generally characteristic of a waking but relaxed state, by the fast, irregular, low-amplitude "desynchronization" or "arousal" pattern. These conditions were evidently ones that can be expected to put the organism into a "mobilized," "alerted," or "attentive" state. Later work singled out the brain-stem reticular formation as the principal brain structure controlling such changes in electrocortical activity (Moruzzi & Magoun, 1949). It was subsequently discovered that activation of the reticular formation can also heighten skeletal muscular activity and produce the vegetative changes, dependent on the autonomic nervous system, that had long been recognized as bodily accompaniments of "emotion." All these processes came to be regarded as indices of an overall "arousal level" (Duffy, 1957, 1962; Malmo, 1957, 1959; Berlyne, 1960). More recently, research has focused on evoked potentials and contingent negative variations as electrophysiological correlates of attention bearing some relation to arousal level (see Tecce, 1970, 1972).

There is evidence that fluctuations in arousal level have pervasive sensory, as well as cortical, vegetative, and motor effects. In particular, there are indications that a rise in arousal means an increase in the organism's capacity to take in and process information from the external environment. In other words, it means increased attentiveness. However, it seems likely that the actual relation between attentiveness (identifiable with transmission of information from the stimulus situation as a whole to the organism's motor equipment) is curvilinearly related to arousal, since the upper extremes of arousal are reached in states of frenzy or mania, which are notoriously characterized by obliviousness of important events in the external world.

There are also believed to be correlations between arousal and the concentration-diffusion dimension of attention. Easterbrook (1959) reviewed evidence that "emotion" decreases the range of cues utilized for the guidance of behavior. Solley (1969) has confirmed this with a diversity of arousal-raising treatments. On the other hand, there have been experiments showing a widening of the range of attention with a rise in arousal (Solley & Thetford, 1967; Solso, Johnson, & Schatz, 1968). Perhaps here again there is a curvilinear function such that the range of attention reaches a maximum with moderately high arousal. It is also possible, as suggested by Solley and by analogies with Pavlov's notions of irradiation and concentration, that phases of expansion and contraction occur in succession.

2. SELECTIVE ASPECTS

Pavlov's (1927) group discovered several phenomena, and postulated several principles of brain functioning, that seem unmistakably relevant to selective attention. It was found in his laboratory that any unexpected or unprecedented stimulus is likely to induce the "orientation reflex," resulting in bodily movements directing sense organs toward the source of stimulation. At the same time, there is an interruption of response to other stimuli that may be present, including "external inhibition" of conditioned salivation when it would otherwise have been evoked by a conditioned stimulus. These phenomena were linked with "negative induction," the tendency for a strong focus of excitation in one region of the cerebral cortex to generate inhibition in neighboring regions and consequently to weaken responses controlled by those regions. Another notion of considerable influence in the U.S.S.R. was that of the "dominant," introduced by Ukhtomski (1923), one of the leaders of the St. Petersburg School of physiologists. A dominant is an area of enhanced excitability in the cerebral cortex, which tends to draw to itself excitation from the most varied sources and concurrently transmits inhibition to other areas.

In the West, Hebb (1949) pleaded for greater recognition of the importance of attention, using this term to mean the "central facilitation of a perceptual activity" (p. 102), particularly by a neural process corresponding to an "expectancy." He indicated that such a phenomenon was compatible with existing neurophysiological knowledge, e.g., evidence of extensive convergence among cortical fibers and of the need for approximately simultaneous impulses from several presynaptic neurons to discharge a postsynaptic neuron. Hebb's view of attention was certainly a limited one and echoed what had been said before, e.g., by Mowrer (1938) about "preparatory set." Nevertheless, his voice was extremely influential. Shortly afterwards, accumulating information about the brain made selective attention appear even more intelligible and more consequential. It became apparent that centrifugal fibers terminating in sense organs and at various points along afferent pathways can inhibit or facilitate conduction of sensory information (see Livingston, 1959), that inhibition of competing processes in the brain is essential if a prepotent course of action is to be executed effectively (Beritov, 1961; Milner, 1957), that diffuse excitation from the reticular activating system (as well as localized processes corresponding to specific expectations) can alter the excitability of cortical neurons and thus collaborate with afferent impulses in determining when they will fire.

A series of experiments by Hernández-Péon (1966) and collaborators showed how visual and auditory evoked potentials could be attenuated by the presence of some extraneous stimulus that could be expected to capture attention (e.g., the sight of a rat or the smell of fish for the cat, instructions to solve arithmetical problems for human subjects). Similar effects were produced by direct stimulation of the reticular arousal system. The interpretation of these findings has stirred up quite heated controversy (Desmedt & Mechelse, 1958; Horn, 1965; Worden, 1966). But they encouraged the growing use of evoked potentials, D. C. shifts, and microelectrode recording, as well as progressively subtler techniques for analyzing EEG waves, to measure the attention-catching powers of particular stimuli (Evans & Mulholland, 1969).

Pavlov's concept of the "orientation reflex" took on a new lease of considerably transformed life at the beginning of the 1950's, when the kinds of stimuli that bring out this reflex were found to produce a wide gamut of physiological changes, including temporary lowering of sensory thresholds and various electrocortical, somatic, and autonomic changes indicative of a short-lasting rise in arousal (Robinson & Gantt, 1947; Sokolov, 1958). Pavlov's original descriptions of the postural adjustments associated with the orientation reaction focused on selective aspects. The later phase emphasized fluctuations in overall attentiveness or receptivity to information coming from the whole environment. As conceived by recent investigators, this reaction can entail selection only among stimuli received in succession rather than among simultaneous and competing stimuli. However, Soviet psychologists (notably Zaporozhets, 1960) have tended to regard the orientation reaction as an objective equivalent of attention, or even awareness, with reference to quite complex discriminative and intellectual functions, such as those of interest to educationists.

B. Exploratory Behavior

A great mass of experimental work (see Berlyne, 1960, 1963, 1966) has been devoted to the exploratory responses through which animals and human beings seek exposure to particular forms of stimulation. These responses include receptor-adjusting responses such as eye movements and head movements, locomotion, and manipulation of objects under inspection. The power of a stimulus object to attract exploration depends on many factors but especially on such attributes as novelty, surprisingness, complexity, and ambiguity, which have close links with the information–theoretic concepts of "uncertainty" and "information content." When an organism's exploratory behavior brings its receptors into contact with a particular source of stimulation, its behavior is generally placed under the control of that source and withdrawn from the influence of other sources. For this reason, exploratory responses are not uncommonly connected, or even equated, with attention. Nevertheless, they are best regarded as adjuncts and aids to attention. They effect a selection among possible sources of stimulation before the sense organs are excited, determining what will or will not be perceived and with what degree of intensity and clarity. But they must be distinguished from other filtering processes that evidently come into play in the peripheral and central parts of the nervous system after receptors have been stimulated.

C. Classical Conditioning with Compound Conditioned Stimuli

The investigation of attention in learning was initiated in Pavlov's laboratory. Two simultaneous conditioned stimuli, belonging to different modalities, were presented simultaneously before the appearance of food. When the two components of the compound were later presented separately, one but not the other was generally found to have acquired the power to elicit conditioned salivation. As Pavlov (1927) put it, the "stronger" stimulus "overshadowed" the other. It has been confirmed by plenty of later experiments, both Russian (see Razran, 1965, 1971) and Western (see Baker, 1968), that a conditioned response originally associated with a compound will be evoked to differing degrees by the compound and by its various components.

More recent work has brought out the importance of the informative properties of a conditioned stimulus element, i.e., properties such as have been found to affect exploratory behavior and other attentional phenomena. Kamin (1968) has somewhat modified the usual compound-stimulus–conditioning technique, first establishing a conditioned fear response to one conditioned stimulus, then pairing the original conditioned stimulus with a second one as well as with the unconditioned stimulus (electric shock), and finally presenting the second conditioned stimulus alone. His findings led him to the general conclusion that a response will become conditioned to a particular stimulus (so that the animal can be said to "notice" or "attend to" the stimulus in this sense) only if the occurrence of the shock after the stimulus is "surprising." Rescorla and Wagner (1972) have likewise built a quite elaborate, experimentally suported theory of classical conditioning around the principle that "organisms only learn when events violate their expectations" (p. 75). The related discovery (Egger & Miller, 1962) that a stimulus will acquire secondary reinforcing properties only if it provides nonredundant information about the imminence of a reward has deeply affected subsequent research on secondary or conditioned reward value (see Hendry, 1969).

D. Discrimination Learning

From the 1930's, two diametrically opposed theories divided investigators of discrimination learning. The "continuity theory," presented by Spence (1936) and accepted by Hull (1943), held that, if an animal has been rewarded after approaching a particular stimulus object, "all stimulus components affecting the subject's sensorium at the initiation of this approach response receive an increment in their association to this approach response." Otherwise their associations will undergo a decrement. Krechevsky (1932) and Lashley (1938, 1942) argued for a "noncontinuity theory," holding that a definite attribute of the stimulus is "abstracted" or "attended to" and forms a basis of the reaction at any one time, but that control over behavior will be shifted rather abruptly to a different stimulus attribute if the first attribute turns out to be an unreliable pointer to reward. These two extreme positions do not, of course, exhaust all plausible possibilities, and Mackintosh (1965) has reviewed evidence that an animal may "attend to" (in the sense of having a learned response attached to) several stimulus attributes but to differing extents. Restle (1955), Trabasso and Bower (1968), Lovejoy (1968), and Sutherland and Mackintosh (1971) have extended noncontinuity theory in the form of mathematical models. On the other hand, the continuity line of thinking still has its advocates (e.g., Kendler, Basden, & Bruckner, 1970).

Spence (1937) acknowledged the importance of "responses which lead to the reception of the appropriate aspects of the total environmental complex on the animal's sensorium." He was referring to eye movements and other receptor-adjusting responses, and, beginning with Wyckoff's (1952) work, there has been much study of "observing responses," i.e., manipulatory acts that cause discriminative cues to appear. It became clear, however, that overt responses do not suffice to determine which stimulus attributes will dominate attention in learning. For example, the direction of the eyes cannot very well select among color, shape, and size. Existing preconceptions were challenged with particular severity by experiments on "reversal learning," showing reliably greater transfer when positive and negative cues, representing different values of one variable, were interchanged than when the variable or attribute on which the subject had learned to base his response became irrelevant and an altogether different one had to take control (Kendler & Kendler, 1962; Lawrence, 1949). Talk of "implicit mediational responses," "acquired distinctiveness of cues," etc., thus became current.

E. Vigilance

The experimental study of fluctuations in performance when subjects have to watch out for, and respond appropriately to, stimuli of particular kinds for prolonged periods can be traced back to the work of McDougall, which has already been mentioned. A great expansion in this line of research (Buckner & McGrath, 1963; Davies & Tune, 1970; Mackworth, 1950) was prompted in large part by practical problems encountered in military and industrial situations, such as keeping watch over a radar screen or over a number of dials. The degree of success at such tasks can be used as a sensitive measure of attentiveness, and the word "vigilance," which was introduced by Head (1926) to refer to an attribute of neural functioning, has become the usual label for this kind of experiment. In the Soviet Union, a great deal of experimental research on the time course of oscillations in attentiveness and in concentration on the stimuli pertinent to a task has been prompted by pedagogical problems (see Dobrynin, 1959; Endovitskaia, 1964). Training procedures for improving the attention capacities of schoolchildren have also been devised.

F. Selective Attention in Performance

1. EXPERIMENTAL APPROACHES

Berlyne (1950, 1951a) introduced a free-choice technique to identify factors determining the outcome of competition among several stimuli for control over behavior. Subjects were exposed on each of a succession of trials to several simultaneous visual stimuli (spots of light), each of which had a corresponding key-pressing response, and had to respond to any one (but no more than one) of the stimuli that were present. This technique was resumed by McDonnell (1968, 1970; see Berlyne, 1969, 1970) with tachistoscopic exposure to preclude intervention of eye movements. The power of a stimulus to attract attention was found to depend, among other things, on its luminous intensity, contrast with the background, and novelty. Subsequent experiments (Berlyne, 1971) have confirmed that the tendency to attend to a novel color is not due to chromatic retinal adaptation and that the effect is stimulus-specific rather than stimulus-response-specific.

Later experiments (see Moray, 1969, Ch. 5) have investigated visual selection with verbal responses. Much more work has, however, been done with selective hearing (see Broadbent, 1958; Moray, 1969; Treisman, 1969; Kahneman, 1973). Beginning with experiments by Cherry (1953) and Poulton (1953), subjects have generally been exposed simultaneously to two or more verbal messages, distinguished by presentation to different ears, by sex of speaker, content, language, or acoustical characteristics, with or without preliminary instructions to attend to one of them. They have more often than not been required to repeat or answer questions about what they have heard. Performance must then reflect the vagaries of short-term memory as well as those of attention. This difficulty has sometimes been obviated by having subjects respond to verbal stimuli while they are being received, e.g., by "shadowing" (uttering words as they are heard) or by some manual reaction. Furthermore, the use of verbal material must introduce processes peculiar to reception and understanding of speech. Attempts are likewise being made to overcome this limitation by using tones as stimuli (Moray, 1969, Ch. 10).

2. Theories of Selective Attention

Berlyne related findings about selective attention to Hull's (1943, 1949) behavior theory. He invoked "stimulus-intensity dynamism" to explain the effects of intensity (Berlyne, 1950) and "conditioned inhibition" to explain those of novelty (Berlyne, 1951a) although later work (Berlyne, 1957) showed the inadequacy of this latter suggestion. Subsequently (Berlyne, 1951b), it was argued that attention could be identified as the "momentary effective reaction potential" (i.e., momentary response strength) of a "perceptual response," which intervenes between receipt of an external stimulus and selection of a motor response. Stripped of its Hullian trappings, this view implied a filter through which all stimuli must pass, most of them leaving it with diminished potency.

Broadbent (1953) first attributed attentional phenomena, such as vigilance decrements and shifts in selective attention, as well as other inhibitory phenomena, to a principle of stimulus weakening (rather than response weakening), which had much in common with Glanzer's (1953) notion of "stimulus satiation." A few years later, Broadbent (1957) introduced his influential mechanical model, postulating a "filter" that allowed only one of several simultaneously arriving signals to pass through to the higher reaches of the central nervous system. There was also a short-term memory store, where signals could be kept waiting for a few seconds so that several arriving together might be processed in turn.

Treisman's (1960) theory took account of evidence that information about overall properties of a rejected message may be registered, that a rejected message may suddenly capture attention if it contains an item of special significance for the subject (e.g., a person hearing his own name, a mother hearing a baby crying), and that the discriminability of a stimulus often depends on its conditioned probability given the context. She replaced Broadbent's all-or-none filter with an attenuating mechanism, which allowed signals outside the focus of attention to proceed further in a weakened form. After the attenuating filter came a "dictionary" mechanism, in which the meaning of each signal was analyzed so that its importance and conditional probability could be assessed.

Deutsch and Deutsch (1963) maintained that the facts could be better explained by the one-stage assumption that every signal reaches the pattern-recognizing structures of the brain with a strength depending on its importance. The strongest signal will then "switch in further processes, such as motor output, memory storage, and whatever else it may be that leads to awareness," provided that it does not fall below a minimum strength that varies inversely with level of arousal.

A rather different approach has been taken by Neisser (1967), who recognizes that we can attend to our own thoughts, as well as to external stimulus events. For him, attention works through "analysis by synthesis." It amounts to matching stimulus sequences with processes that the subject can construct (e.g., inner speech, abstract structures identifiable with meaning).

Moray (1969) has built on Kristofferson's (1967) all-or-none gating model. Such a notion will, he hopes, cover both the facts explained by other theories and some additional facts, particularly concerning temporal properties of attention. He assumes that attention is confined to one "channel" or stimulus sequence at a particular moment but can switch over to another channel. Such a shift takes up a certain "switching time," during which nothing can be processed. A shift will occur if the activity level or importance of the accepted channel goes down far enough or that of a rejected channel goes up. Alternatively, attention may switch over to a rejected channel periodically for very brief periods, which will suffice to monitor its "crude physical characteristics" but not to absorb its full content.

Finally, Kahneman (1973) suggests that, in an initial stage of perceptual analysis, units are formed out of incoming stimulation, after which certain units are selected for varying degrees of more detailed processing. The effectiveness of selection depends on the ease with which units can be formed, and the effectiveness of rejection of irrelevant stimuli depends on how much processing capacity is demanded by the primary task.

References

Angell, J. R., & Pierce, A. H. Experimental research on the phenomena of attention. *American Journal of Psychology,* 1892, **4**, 528–541.

Baker, T. W. Properties of compound conditioned stimuli and their components. *Psychological Bulletin,* 1968, **70**, 611–625.

Berger, H. Über das Elektrenkephalogramm des Menschen. *Archiv fuer Psychiatrie und Nervenkrankheiten,* 1929, **87**, 527–570.

Beritov, I. S. *Nervnye mekhanizmy povedeniia vysshikh pozvonochnykh zhivotnykh.* Moscow: Academy of Sciences of USSR, 1961. [*Neural mechanisms of higher vetebrate behavior.* Boston, Massachusetts: Little, Brown, 1965]

Berlyne, D. E. Stimulus intensity and attention in relation to learning theory. *Quarterly Journal of Experimental Psychology,* 1950, **2**, 71–75.

Berlyne, D. E. Attention to change. *British Journal of Psychology,* 1951, **42**, 269–275. (a)

Berlyne, D. E. Attention, perception and behavior theory. *Psychological Review,* 1951, **58**, 137–146. (b)

Berlyne, D. E. Attention to change, conditioned inhibition ($_sI_R$) and stimulus satiation. *British Journal of Psychology,* 1957, **48**, 138–140.

Berlyne, D. E. *Conflict, arousal and curiosity.* New York: McGraw-Hill, 1960.

Berlyne, D. E. Motivational problems raised by exploratory and epistemic behavior. In S. Koch (Ed.), *Psychology—A study of a science.* Vol. 5. New York: McGraw-Hill, 1963. Pp. 284–364.

Berlyne, D. E. Curiosity and exploration. *Science,* 1966, **153**, 25–33.

Berlyne, D. E. The development of the concept of attention in psychology. In C. R. Evans & T. Mulholland (Eds.), *Attention and neurophysiology.* London: Butterworth, 1969. Pp. 1–26.

Berlyne, D. E. Attention as a problem in behavior theory. In D. Mostofsky (Ed.), *Attention: Contemporary theories and analyses.* New York: Appleton, 1970. Pp. 25–49.

Berlyne, D. E. Novelty and attention: Controls for retinal adaptation and for stimulus-response specificity. *Psychonomic Science,* 1971, **25**, 349–351.

Breese, B. B. On inhibition. *Psychological Monographs,* 1899, **3**, No. 1.

Broadbent, D. E. Classical conditioning and human watch-keeping. *Psychological Review,* 1953, **60**, 331–339.

Broadbent, D. E. A mechanical model for human attention and immediate memory. *Psychological Review,* 1957, **64**, 205–215.

Broadbent, D. E. *Perception and communication.* Oxford: Pergamon, 1958.

Brown, T. *Lectures on the philosophy of the human mind.* Edinburgh: Tait, 1820.

Buckner, D. M., & McGrath, J. J. (Eds.) *Vigilance: A symposium.* New York: McGraw-Hill, 1963.

Cattell, J. McK. The inertia of the eye and brain. *Brain,* 1885, **8**, 295–312.

Cattell, J. McK. Aufmerksamkeit und Reaction. *Philosophische Studien (Wundt),* 1893, **8**, 403–406.

Chapman, D. W. Relative effects of determinate and indeterminate aufgaben. *American Journal of Psychology,* 1932, **44**, 163–174.

Cherry, C. Some experiments on the reception of speech with one and with two ears. *Journal of the Acoustical Society of America,* 1953, **25**, 975–979.

Dashiell, J. F. *Fundamentals of general psychology.* Boston, Massachusetts: Houghton, 1928.

Davies, D. R., & Tune, G. S. *Human vigilance performance.* London: Staples, 1970.

Descartes, R. *Discours de la méthode.* Leyden: Maine, 1637.

Descartes, R. *Principia Philosophiae.* Amsterdam: Elzevier, 1644.

Descartes, R. *Les passions de l'âme.* Paris: Le Gras, 1649.

Desmedt, J. E., & Mechelse, K. Suppression of acoustic input by thalamic stimulation. *Proceedings of the Society for Experimental Biology and Medicine,* 1958, **99**, 772–775.

Deutsch, J. A., & Deutsch, D. Attention: Some theoretical considerations. *Psychological Review,* 1963, **70**, 80–90.

Dobrynin, N. F. [Basic problems of the psychology of attention] In B. G. Ananiev *et al.* (Eds.), *Psikhologicheskaia nauka v SSSR.* Vol. 1. Moscow: Academy of Pedagogical Sciences, 1959. [*Psychological Science in the USSR.* Washington, D. C.: U. S. Joint Publications Research Service, 1961]

Duffy, E. The psychological significance of the concept of "arousal" or "activation." *Psychological Review,* 1957, **64**, 265–275.

Duffy, E. *Activation and behavior.* New York: Wiley, 1962.

Easterbrook, J. A. The effect of emotion on cue utilization and the organization of behavior. *Psychological Review,* 1959, **66**, 183–201.

Egger, M. D., & Miller, N. E. Secondary reinforcement in rats as a function of information value and reliability of the stimulus. *Journal of Experimental Psychology,* 1962, **64**, 97–104.

Endovitskaia, T. V. [The development of attention.] In A. V. Zaporozhets & D. B. Elkonin (Eds.), *Psikhologiia detei doshkol'nogo vozrasta.* [*The psychology of pre-school children*] Moscow: Prosveshchenie, 1964. Pp. 72–93.

Evans, C. R., & Mulholland, T. (Eds.) *Attention and neurophysiology.* London: Butterworth, 1969.

Exner, S. Zur Kenntniss von der Wechselwirkung der Erregungen im Centralnervensystem. *Archiv fuer die gesamte Physiologie des Menschen und der Tiere,* 1882, **28**, 487–506.

Freud, S. *Die Traumdeutung.* Vienna: Deuticke, 1900. [*The interpretation of dreams*]. In A. A. Brill (Ed.), *Selected works of Sigmund Freud.* New York: Modern Library, 1938]

Gibson, J. J. A critical review of the concept of set in contemporary experimental psychology. *Psychological Bulletin,* 1941, **38**, 781–817.

Glanzer, M. Stimulus satiation: An explanation of spontaneous alternation and related phenomena. *Psychological Review,* 1953, **60**, 257–268.

Groos, K. *Die Spiele der Thiere.* Jena: Fischer, 1896.

Hamilton, W. *Lectures on Metaphysics and Logic.* Vol. 1. *Metaphysics.* Edinburgh & London: Blackwood, 1859.

Head, H. *Aphasia and kindred disorders of speech.* New York: Macmillan, 1926.

Hebb, D. O. *The organization of behavior.* New York: Wiley, 1949.

Hendry, D. P. (Ed.) *Conditioned reinforcement.* Homewood, Illinois: Dorsey, 1969.

Herbart, J. F. *De attentionis mensura causisque primariis.* Königsberg: Borntraeger, 1822.

Herbart, J. F. *Psychologie als Wissenschaft neu gegründet auf Erfahrung, Metaphysik und Mathematik.* Königsberg: Unzer, 1824–1825.

Hernández-Peón, R. Physiological mechanisms in attention. In R. W. Russell (Ed.), *Frontiers in physiological psychology.* New York: Academic Press, 1966. Pp. 121–147.

Hobbes, T. *Elementorum philosophiae sectio prima de corpore.* London: Crook, 1655.

Holt, E. B. *The Freudian wish and its place in ethics.* New York: Holt, 1915.

Horn, G. Physiological and psychological aspects of selective perception. In D. S. Lehrman, R. A. Hinde, & E. Shaw (Eds.), *Advances in the study of behavior.* Vol. 1. New York: Academic Press, 1965. Pp. 155–215.

Hull, C. L. *Principles of behavior.* New York: Appleton, 1943.

Hull, C. L. Stimulus-intensity dynamism (V) and stimulus generalization. *Psychological Review,* 1949, **56**, 67–76.

Hume, D. *A treatise of human nature.* London: Moon, 1739.

James, W. What is emotion? *Mind,* 1884, **9**, 188–204.

James, W. *Principles of psychology.* New York: Holt, 1890.

Jevons, W. S. The power of numerical discrimination. *Nature (London),* 1871, **3**, 281–282.

Kahneman, D. *Attention and effort.* Englewood Cliffs, N. J.: Prentice-Hall, 1973.

Kamin, L. J. "Attention-like" processes in classical conditioning. In M. R. Jones (Ed.), *Miami symposium on the prediction of behavior.* Coral Gables, Florida: Univ. of Miami Press, 1968. Pp. 9–31.

Kendler, H. H., & Kendler, T. S. Vertical and horizontal processes in problem solving. *Psychological Review,* 1962, **69**, 1–16.

Kendler, T. S., Basden, B. H., & Bruckner, J. B. Dimensional dominance and continuity. *Journal of Experimental Psychology,* 1970, **83**, 309–318.

Koffka, K. *Principles of Gestalt psychology.* New York: Harcourt, 1935.

Krechevsky, I. Z. "Hypotheses" in rats. *Psychological Review,* 1932, **39**, 516–532.

Kristofferson, A. Attention and psychophysical time. In A. Sanders (Ed.), *Attention and performance.* Amsterdam: North-Holland Publ., 1967. Pp. 93–100.

Külpe, O. Versuche über Abstraktion. *Bericht uber den Kongress fuer experimentelle Psychologie,* 1904, **1**, 56–68.

Lange, L. Neue Experimente über den Vorgang der einfachen Reaction auf Sinneseindrücke. *Philosophischen Studien (Wundt),* 1888, **4**, 479–510.

Lange, N. Beiträge zur Theorie der sinnlichen Aufmerksamkeit und der activen Apperception. *Philosophische Studien (Wundt),* 1888, **4**, 390–422.

Lashley, K. S. The mechanism of vision. XV. Preliminary studies of the rat's capacity for detailed vision. *Journal of General Psychology,* 1938, **18**, 123–193.

Lashley, K. S. An examination of the "continuity theory" as applied to discriminative learning. *Journal of General Psychology,* 1942, **26**, 241–265.

Lawrence, D. H. Acquired distinctiveness of cues. I. Transfer between discrimination on the basis of familiarity with the stimulus. *Journal of Experimental Psychology,* 1949, **39**, 770–784.

Leibnitz, G. W. Nouveaux essais sur l'entendement humain. In R. E. Raspe (Ed.), *Oeuvres philosophiques de feu M. Leibnitz.* Amsterdam & Leipzig: Schreuder, 1765.

Livingston, R. B. Central control of receptors and sensory transmission systems. In Amer. Physiol. Soc., J. Field (Ed.), *Handbook of physiology.* Sect. 1. *Neurophysiology.* Vol. I. Baltimore, Maryland: Williams & Wilkins, 1959, Pp. 741–760.

Locke, J. *Essay concerning human understanding.* London: Basset, 1690.

Lovejoy, E. P. *Attention in discrimination learning.* San Francisco: Holden-Day, 1968.

McDonnell, P. M. Effects of intensity, contrast and novelty on selective attention and choice reaction-time. Unpublished Ph.D. thesis, University of Toronto, 1968.

McDonnell, P. M. The role of albedo and contrast in a test of selective attention. *Perception and Psychophysics,* 1970, **8,** 270–272.

McDougall, W. A new method for the study of concurrent mental operations and of mental fatigue. *British Journal of Psychology,* 1905, **1,** 435–445.

Mackintosh, N. J. Selective attention in animal discrimination learning. *Psychological Bulletin,* 1965, **64,** 124–150.

Mackworth, N. H. *Researches in the measurement of human performance.* London: HM Stationery Office, 1950.

Malebranche, N. *De la recherche de la vérité.* Paris: Pralard, 1674.

Malmo, R. B. Anxiety and behavioral arousal. *Psychological Review,* 1957, **64,** 276–287.

Malmo, R. B. Activation: A neuropsychological dimension. *Psychological Review,* 1959, **66,** 367–386.

Milner, P. M. The cell assembly: Mark II. *Psychological Review,* 1957, **64,** 242–252.

Moray, N. *Attention: Selective processes in vision and hearing.* London: Hutchinson, 1969.

Moruzzi, G., & Magoun, H. W. Brain stem reticular formation and activation of the EEG. *Electroencephalography and Clinical Neurophysiology,* 1949, **1,** 455–473.

Mowrer, O. H. Preparatory set (expectancy): A determinant in motivation and learning. *Psychological Review,* 1938, **45,** 62–91.

Mowrer, O. H. A stimulus-response analysis of anxiety and its role as a reinforcing agent. *Psychological Review,* 1939, **46,** 553–565.

Mowrer, O. H., Rayman, N. N., & Bliss, E. L. Preparatory set (expectancy)—an experimental demonstration of its "central" locus. *Journal of Experimental Psychology,* 1940, **26,** 357–372.

Müller, G. W. *Zur Theorie der sinnlichen Aufmerksamkeit.* Doctoral dissertation, George Augustus University, Göttingen, 1873.

Neisser, U. *Cognitive psychology.* New York: Appleton, 1967.

Pavlov, I. P. *Conditioned reflexes.* London & New York: Oxford Univ. Press, 1927.

Philpott, S. J. F. Fluctuations in human output. *British Journal of Psychology,* 1932, (Monogr. Suppl. 17).

Philpott, S. J. F. A theoretical curve of fluctuations of attention. *British Journal of Psychology,* 1934, **25,** 221–255.

Piaget, J. *La psychologie de l'intelligence.* Paris: Colin, 1947. [*The psychology of intelligence.* New York: Harcourt, 1950].

Pillsbury, W. B. *L'attention.* Paris: Doin, 1906. [*Attention.* New York: Macmillan, 1908]

Pilzecker, A. *Die Lehre der sinnlichen Aufmerksamkeit.* Doctoral dissertation, George Augustus University, Göttingen, 1889.

Poulton, E. C. Two channel listening. *Journal of Experimental Psychology,* 1953, **46,** 91–96.

Razran, G. Empirical codifications and specific theoretical implications of compound-stimulus conditioning: Perception. In W. F. Prokasy (Ed.), *Classical conditioning.* New York: Appleton, 1965. Pp. 215–233.

Razran, G. *Mind in evolution: An East-West synthesis.* Boston, Massachusetts: Houghton, 1971.

Reid, T. *Essays on the intellectual powers of man.* Edinburgh: Bell, 1785.

Rescorla, R. A. & Wagner, A. R. A theory of Pavlovian conditioning: Variations in the effectiveness of reinforcement and nonreinforcement. In A. H. Black & W. F. Prokasy (Eds.) *Classical conditioning II: Current theory and research.* New York: Appleton, 1972.

Restle, F. A theory of discrimination learning. *Psychological Review,* 1955, **62**, 11–19.

Ribot, T. *La psychologie de l'attention.* Paris: Alcan, 1889. [*The psychology of attention.* Chicago, Illinois: Open Court, 1890]

Robinson, J., & Gantt, W. H. The orienting reflex (questioning reaction): Cardiac, respiratory, salivary and motor components. *Bulletin of the Johns Hopkins Hospital,* 1947, **80**, 231–253.

Rosvold, H. E., Mirsky, A. F., Sarason, I., Bramsome, D. E., & Beck, L. H. A continuous performance test of brain damage. *Journal of Consulting Psychology,* 1956, **20**, 343–350.

Rubin, E. *Synsoplevede figurer: Studien i psykologisk analyse.* Copenhagen: Gyldendal, 1915. [*Visuell wahrgenommene Figuren: Studien in psychologischer Analyse.* Copenhagen: Gyldendal, 1921]

Sokolov, E. N. *Vospriiate i uslovny refleks.* Moscow: Univ. of Moscow Press, 1958. [*Perception and the conditioned reflex.* Oxford: Pergamon, 1964]

Solley, C. M. Effects of stress on perceptual attention. In B. P. Rourke (Ed.), *Explorations in the psychology of stress and anxiety.* Don Mills, Ontario: Longmans, 1969. Pp. 1–14.

Solley, C. M., & Thetford, P. E. Skin potential responses and the span of attention. *Psychophysiology,* 1967, **3**, 397–402.

Solso, R. L., Johnson, J. E., & Schatz, G. C. Perceptual perimeters and generalized drive. *Psychonomic Science,* 1968, **13**, 71–72.

Spearman, C. E. *Psychology down the ages.* New York: Macmillan, 1937.

Spence, K. W. The nature of discrimination learning in animals. *Psychological Review,* 1936, **43**, 427–449.

Spence, K. W. The differential response in animals to stimuli varying within a single dimension. *Psychological Review,* 1937, **44**, 430–444.

Stewart, D. *Elements of the philosophy of the human mind.* London: Strahan & Cadell, 1792.

Sutherland, N. S., & Mackintosh, N. J. *Mechanisms of animal discrimination learning.* New York: Academic Press, 1971.

Taylor, J. G. *The behavioral basis of perception.* New Haven, Connecticut: Yale Univ. Press, 1962.

Tecce, J. J. Attention and evoked potentials in man. In D. Mostofsky (Ed.), *Attention: Contemporary theory and analysis.* New York: Appleton, 1970. Pp. 331–365.

Tecce, J. J. Contingent negative variation (CNV) and psychological processes in man. *Psychological Bulletin,* 1972, **77**, 77–108.

Titchener, E. B. *Lectures on the elementary psychology of feeling and attention.* New York: Macmillan, 1908.

Tolman, E. C., & Brunswik, E. The organism and the causal texture of the environment. *Psychological Review,* 1935, **42**, 43–77.

Tolman, E. C., Hall, C. S., & Bretnall, E. P. A disproof of the law of effect and a substitution of the laws of emphasis, motivation and disruption. *Journal of Experimental Psychology,* 1932, **15**, 601–614.

Trabasso, T., & Bower, G. H. *Attention in learning: Theory and research.* New York: Wiley, 1968.

Treisman, A. M. Contextual cues in selective listening. *Quarterly Journal of Experimental Psychology,* 1960, **12**, 242–248.

Treisman, A. M. Strategies and models of selective attention. *Psychological Review,* 1969, **76**, 282–299.

Ukhtomski, A. A. [The dominant as a working principle of neural centres.] *Russky fiziologichesky zhurnal,* 1923, **6**, 31–45. [Reprinted with later relevant papers in *Dominanta (The dominant).* Moscow & Leningrad: Nauka, 1966.]

von Tschisch, W. Uber die Zeitverhältnisse der Apperception einfacher und zusammengesetzter Vorstellungen, untersucht mit Hülfe der Complications-methode. *Philosophische Studien (Wundt),* 1885, **2**, 603–634.

von Urbantchitsch, V. Über eine Eigenthümlichkeit der Schallempfindungen geringster Intensität. *Zentralblatt fuer die medizinischen Wissenschaften,* 1875, **13**, 625–628.

Watson, J. B. *Psychology from the standpoint of a behaviorist.* Philadelphia, Pennsylvania: Lippincott, 1919.

Watson, J. B. *Behaviorism.* New York: Norton, 1924.

Wolff, C. *Psychologia empirica.* Frankfort & Leipzig: Renger, 1732.

Wolff, C. *Psychologia rationalis.* Frankfort & Leipzig: Renger, 1734.

Worden, F. G. Attention and auditory electrophysiology. In E. Stellar & J. M. Sprague (Eds.), *Progress in physiological psychology.* Vol. 1. New York: Academic Press, 1966. Pp. 45–114.

Wundt, W. *Grundzüge der physiologischen Psychologie.* Leipzig: Engelmann, 1874.

Wyckoff, L. B. The role of observing responses in discrimination learning. Part I. *Psychological Review,* 1952, **59**, 431–442.

Zaporozhets, A. V. *Razvitie proizvol'nykh dvizhenii. [The development of voluntary movements]* Moscow: Academy of Pedagogical Sciences, 1960.

Chapter 9

COGNITION AND KNOWLEDGE: PSYCHOLOGICAL EPISTEMOLOGY

JOSEPH R. ROYCE'†

I. INTRODUCTION AND OVERVIEW

The question is "How do we know?" That is, what is the nature of the knowing process and how do we discriminate between knowing and not knowing? How do we know we're not merely hoping or wishing, for example, rather than knowing? And if we accept people's verbal reports when they see red, or when they report illusory movement of a stationary pinpoint of light (i.e., autokinesis), how come we doubt their veracity when they report they've sighted pink elephants or unidentified flying objects? And how come the earth was once flat, but now we "know" it is round? And why did we drop Ptolemy for Copernicus, Newton for Einstein, etc.,

* A modified version of my Presidential Address, Division of Philosophical Psychology, American Psychological Association. Presented at the 1970 Annual Meeting in Miami Beach, Florida. Royce & Tennessen, *Inquiries into a psychological theory of knowledge* (in preparation) will contain the original version.

† Partially supported by Canada Council Grants (68-0138, 69-0358, S70-0544) on Knowing. The author would also like to acknowledge the indirect assistance received from all Center participants, especially staff colleagues L. von Bertalanffy, W. W. Rozeboom, H. Tennessen, T. Weckowicz, and K. V. Wilson, as well as direct critical feedback received from the Knowing Project Group, namely Harold Coward, Owen Egan, Frank Kessel, Jack Lewis, Leo Mos, and John Peyton. I particularly wish to acknowledge the contribution of Owen Egan in the development of the section on cognitive structure. He researched the relevant literature on this topic and prepared initial drafts of several segments of the text.

ad infinitum? And why are the truths and insights of one discipline of knowledge in conflict, or at least not in harmony, with the awarenesses of neighboring disciplines? And how come the bastions of knowledge can be so shifty—for example, the humanities dominating our conception of reality in the Middle Ages, and hardly able to survive in the science-dominated twentieth century?

There are, of course, no satisfactory answers to these questions, although partial insights are available. My own bias is that epistemic questions such as these will continue as philosophic perennials regardless of whatever "progress" we might make in providing answers. Why? Because the question of knowledge is inextricably bound up with the question of reality and meaning. Because what and how we know lie behind our world views and because "epistemic styles" are key manifestations of what we are.

The conceptual basis for my own involvement in problems of epistemology was initiated via an interdisciplinary book under the title *The Encapsulated Man* (Royce, 1964), the major point being that men of differing world views reflect limited or encapsulated images of reality as a function of their psychoepistemological profiles. Subsequent conceptual analysis (e.g., Royce, 1970b; Royce & Rozeboom, 1972; Royce & Tennessen, in preparation*), and empirical research (e.g., Royce, 1970a; Royce & Smith, 1964; Smith, Royce, Ayers & Jones, 1967) resulted in the conclusion that there are three valid ways of knowing: empiricism, rationalism, and metaphorism. These three "isms" have been regarded as basic because of their direct dependence upon various cognitive processes on the one hand, and their epistemological testability on the other hand.

As I got deeper into the problem, and as the decade of the sixties unfolded, it became increasingly apparent that the psychological study of epistemology might not be the "irrelevant" philosophic side trip it looked like in the midfifties. Rather, it can now be viewed as one of many manifestations of a paradigm shift toward a more cognitive psychology, as well as a greater willingness on the part of contemporary psychology to form alliances with philosophy (Royce, 1965 a,b, 1970b). In short, it has become increasingly apparent that a new interdisciplinary field, epistemological psychology, is emerging. In this connection, it is significant that one of America's leading philosophers has recently put forward a view which is not typical of traditional philosophy. His position is that empirical knowledge of how we, in fact, "know" will at least provide a viable alternative to the usual rational reconstructions of the philosopher. Thus, in a paper entitled "Epistemology Naturalized," Quine (1969, and reprinted in Royce

* Royce, J. R., & Tennessen, H. *Inquiries into a psychological theory of knowledge.*

& Rozeboom, 1972) elaborates the case for epistemology becoming a chapter heading in the book of psychology. Most psychologists will agree with Quine's appraisal of the problem, and furthermore, they seem to be ready to tackle it. Thus, my approach is to focus on *processes of knowing* rather than on a theory of knowledge per se.

Theories of knowledge are, of course, the major concern of epistemology and, as such, they represent one of the cornerstones of philosophy. However, no existing theory is capable of accommodating all knowledge claims, nor is it possible to placate proponents of alternative theoretical positions. In short, detailed analysis of epistemic issues per se is properly left to the philosophers. But, since the topic is knowing, it is clear that the psychologist, despite his disclaimer as philosopher, cannot continue to get away with his usual gambit, namely, psychologism, or regarding cognition as synonymous with knowing. A theory of knowledge demands that something be said about "knowability" in addition to the "knower." By "knowability" I mean the grounds or criterion for a truth claim—that is, the issue of epistemic justifiability. Thus, while the approach to be presented in this chapter differs from the usual philosophic effort in that the focus of attention is on cognitive functioning, it is consistent with the philosophic approach in requiring epistemological criteria. This means that philosophic issues will be alluded to, although they will not be adequately developed in the text.

Let me initiate the exposition by reference to Fig. 1, where the key problems of knowing are indicated down the center of the diagram. In this figure it is suggested that knowing involves several modes—that knowing in the arts, for example, is not the same as knowing in the sciences. How might they differ? They might differ both psychologically and philosophically. On the philosophic side there may be different truth criteria. Does it make sense, for example, to demand empirical repeatability in evaluating truth claims in literature? And psychologically one might expect differential involvement of the cognitive processes. Symbolizing, for example, may be more crucial, or be of a different order, in the creation of artistic products, than in the creation of mathematical or logical-deductive systems. If it can be shown that there are different ways of knowing, then it seems reasonable to anticipate that people will combine these in different preference orders, and that such epistemological hierarchies might at least partially account for differences in *Weltanschauung*. The philosophic analysis of *Weltanschauung* is elaborated in terms of reality image, and the psychological counterpart is elaborated under the rubric of cognitive structure (see Fig. 1).

This double aspect analysis also provides the basis for a working definition of knowledge, namely, those cognitions of an organism's cognitive

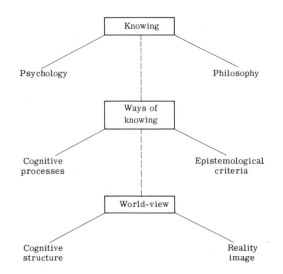

FIG. 1.   Psychological and philosophical aspects of the problem of knowing.

structure (psychological perspective) which are epistemologically justifiable (philosophical perspective).*

II. THREE WAYS OF KNOWING

The essence of my thesis can be summarized by reference to Figure 2. The implication is that each of the three isms represents a legitimate approach to reality, but that different criteria for knowing are involved. Rationalism, for example, is primarily dependent upon logical consistency. That is, this approach says we will accept something as true if it is logically consistent, and we will reject something as false if it is illogical. Empiricism says we know to the extent we perceive correctly, and metaphorism says that knowledge is dependent upon the degree to which symbolic cognitions lead to universal rather than idiosyncratic awarenesses. While each of these cognitive processes may lead to error, the implication is that each is also capable of leading to truth. The possibilities of perceptual error, for example, are readily apparent. The errors of the thinking process are probably more subtle, but I have been led to believe that they have plagued the

* While it is beyond the scope of this paper to offer detailed analyses of philosophic issues, minimal semantic clarification requires my indicating that the term justifiable is used in an "open" sense; that is, not limited to any one approach such as physicalism or "justified true belief." Additional definitions, such as cognitive structure and cognition, will be clarified in subsequent sections of the text.

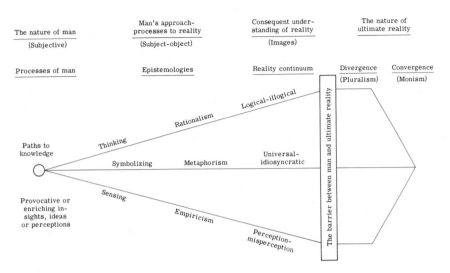

FIG. 2. The basic paths to knowledge (modified version of Royce, 1964, p. 12).

efforts of the logicians and mathematicians. And the errors of symbolizing are even more elusive, primarily because of the sheer difficulty of providing an adequate articulation of metaphoric knowing (e.g., the problem of what symbols "mean"; what qualifies as "universal"?). Furthermore, it should be apparent that none of the psychological processes operates independently of the others. That is, one does not think independently of sensory inputs and the process of symbol formation; nor do we perceive independently of thinking. In short, although the correspondences indicated in Fig. 2 are oversimplified for purposes of analysis and exposition, they represent the best fit between a given cognitive class and its parallel epistemological criterion.

Although psychologists have just begun the task of evolving an adequate cognitive psychology, it is incumbent upon me to at least indicate what I am alluding to when I employ such terms as thinking, perceiving, and symbolizing. Tentative working definitions of these terms follow.*

Thinking: Cognitive processes which focus on concepts—their formation, elaboration, and functional significance to the organism; more deductive

---

* These conceptions have emerged out of a literature review on epistemological psychology (Royce & Tennessen, *Inquiries into a psychological theory of knowledge,* in preparation) which is currently in progress. This review is being conducted by a research team at the Center on a Canada Council Grant (68-0138) allocated to the author. Since the project is not yet complete, further modifications of these definitions are likely.

than inductive; focus is on the logical consequences of information currently available to the organism.

Perceiving: Cognitive processes which focus on observables—sensory inputs and their "meaning"; more inductive than deductive; focus is on the processing of sensory information.

Symbolizing: Cognitive processes which focus on the formation of symbols—"constructed productions" offered as representations of reality; analogical rather than deductive or inductive; focus is on the processing of "new-formation" (i.e., internally generated forms) rather than "in-formation."

Although the conceptual portion of this section leans heavily on Chapter 2 of *The Encapsulated Man* (Royce, 1964), the original version has been modified somewhat. In particular, a fourth way of knowing, authoritarianism, has been dropped on grounds of not being primary, either as psychological process or in terms of truth criterion, and intuitionism has been replaced by metaphorism. My present stance is that intuition is a valid cognitive class, but that it does not have a parallel valid epistemology. Therefore, it is not shown as an independent way of knowing in Fig. 2.

In terms of cognitive process it is hypothesized that intuition is actively involved in all three epistemologies, although probably more so in symbolizing than in thinking and perceiving. This guess is based primarily on the greater involvement of unconscious processes in symbolizing than is the case for either thinking or perceiving. Numerous sources indicate that intuition is involved in the three modes of knowing. For example, see Hammond (1966) and Westcott (1968) for its relevance to thinking, Werner and Kaplan (1963), and Westcott (1968) for its relevance to perceiving, and Werner and Kaplan (1963), and Jung (1964) for its relevance to symbolizing. Also, see Polanyi (1958, 1967) and Coward (1969) for their relevance to knowing in general.

But how shall we deal with intuition as a way of knowing per se? Let us adopt the suggestion of Hammond (1966) and Westcott (1968) that this mode of cognizing has something to do with short-circuiting the solutions to problems (not just logical or problem solving tasks). That is, "intuitive" persons reach decisions on the basis of a relatively small amount of information. Furthermore, "good intuitions" are frequently right. Let us grant this, but follow with the epistemological question "On what criterial grounds are intuitions correct?" So far as I can see, none that intuitionism per se can put forward. In my judgment what happens when an intuition turns out to be correct is that it receives confirmation from some other epistemic source. For example, if a scientist, on the basis of the inadequate information available to him prior to July 1969, had "intuited" that there is no life on the moon, we could now say (i.e., since the successful moon landing) that this notion has been confirmed. But notice that the confirmatory basis is not from within "intuitionism," but rather, from subsequent empirical evidence, with such evidence subject to the usual epistemological requirements of empirical claims. Similarly, I am arguing that other kinds of intuitive claims would receive their confirmation or disconfirmation from the epistemic requirements of rationalism and metaphorism. This confounding of psychological process with epistemological justification (i.e., psychologism) is the most ubiquitous error I have encountered in my efforts to understand the nature of knowing. And this error is a particularly easy one to make in the case of intuition because of the confounding effects which accompany its involvement in all three epistemologies. In summary, my view is that *intuition* is a valid mode of cognition, but that *intuitionism* per se is not a valid epistemology because of its failure to provide epistemic justification.

In Fig. 2 I have attempted to show the relationships between man, the knower, and the nature of reality via three ways of knowing. The two columns to the extreme right are separated from the other three columns by a barrier between man and ultimate reality. That which is epistemologically untestable lies to the right of this barrier and constitutes unknowable ultimate reality (for more on this, see Royce, 1964). That which is testable by some criterion for knowing lies to the left of the epistemological barrier and leads to "reality images" which are "true" or "real." Despite the efforts of great thinkers to somehow circumvent the epistemological limits involved, the only valid assessments open to finite man necessarily lie to the left of the barrier. Such efforts to find truth have presumably been going on since man first made his appearance in the universe, and they have slowly evolved to the current special disciplines of knowledge such as history, literature, and biology.* By definition, such specialties provide a

---

* I view the various special disciplines as further differentiations or subcategories of Cassirer's symbolic forms. According to Cassirer, all knowledge manifests itself in one symbolic form or another. The earliest such form was the myth, followed by certain primitive art forms, such as the dance and ritualistic drama, and primitive scientific forms, such as early astronomy and astrology, and simple number systems, such as Roman numerals. One of Cassirer's major theses is that in the course of cultural evolution there has been increasing elaboration of these early manifestations of knowledge. With the increase in elaboration over the centuries there has also been a corresponding differentiation, culminating in the multitude of arts and sciences which are the essence of twentieth century culture. For various historical and other reasons, these have been codified into special disciplines which we can think of as a more differentiated taxonomy of symbolic forms. It is in this sense that I would argue for beginning any analysis of knowing with its products—namely knowledge. And I have adopted Cassirer's approach as the most adequate basis for such an analysis because his philosophy of symbolic forms (Cassirer, 1953, 1955, 1957) deals with the full spectrum of knowledge.

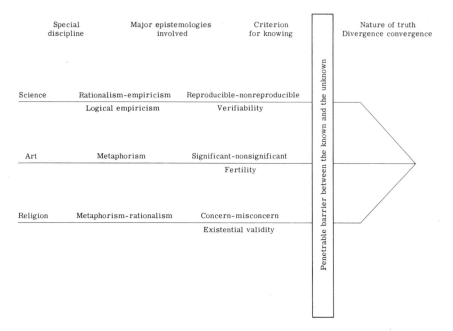

FIG. 3. Representative special disciplines of knowledge (modified version of Royce, 1964, p. 20).

highly selective view of reality, and lead to divergent world views. The psycho-epistemological basis for this state of affairs is depicted in Fig. 3. For present purposes I suggest we ignore the right half† of this figure and focus on the left hand portion. It is understood that all three epistemologies are involved in each of the three representative disciplines of knowledge, but it is also clear that each discipline gives greater credence to one or more of them. The scientist, for example, "thinks," "symbolizes," and "perceives" as scientist, but he maximizes the rational and empirical ways of knowing

---

† In seminar and lecture presentations of this material I have been asked why I include the right hand section of the diagram, particularly since it deals with unknowable reality. The major reason is for the sake of completeness. For example, much of the metaphysical history of philosophy is alluded to via the right hand portion of Fig. 2. A second reason is that omitting presentation of that portion of the diagram invariably leads to questions about ultimate reality. Psychologically, I have come to think of reality projections to the right of the epistemic barrier as a kind of cosmic Rorschach test. Ontologically, I see no way to circumvent, pole vault, go under, or through the barrier, and I hereby issue a challenge to any man or other being to demonstrate that this can be done (e.g., some mystics and/or drug takers have made such claims, but, so far as I know, such claims have not been successfully demonstrated).

and minimizes metaphoric symbolizing as final judge. Conversely, the artist, who also invokes his entire cognitive repertoire, maximizes the symbolizing process at the expense of the thinking and perceptual processes. There are, of course, wide variations in the possible combinations of epistemological profiles; this brief exposition should be taken as relative and typical rather than as absolute and general.

While my own epistemological hierarchy places rationalism at the apex, I also experience strong empirical pressures. Thus, I have initiated a long-range series of investigations on the adequacy of the above-mentioned theoretical formulation. Although studies to date represent only a beginning, they fortunately tend to confirm my intuitive-rational speculations. I will now briefly summarize these findings.

Our approach was to construct an inventory, the psycho-epistemological profile (Royce, 1970a; Royce & Smith, 1964; Smith et al., 1967), as a way to assess a person's epistemological hierarchy. This standardized test consists of 90 items, 30 for each of three scales designated as rationalism, empiricism, and metaphorism. The inventory has now been through five revisions, several administrations to selected and unselected samples, and several item analyses and weighting schemes. A partial summary of specific findings to date is as follows:

1. It is possible to assess a person's epistemological hierarchy by way of an inventory known as the psycho-epistemological profile (P.E.P.).

2. It is estimated that the test-retest reliability coefficients of the three scales of the P.E.P. are around 0.80–0.90.

3. There is evidence that the inventory is valid in the sense that it can discriminate between contrasting groups. For example, the data summarized in Table 1 show that empiricism is the dominant characteristic of the chemistry-biology group, that metaphorism is the highest in the music-

TABLE I

GROUP MEANS ON EMPIRICAL, METAPHORIC, AND RATIONAL SCALES
OF THE PSYCHO-EPISTEMOLOGICAL PROFILE
(Revised Experimental Form II)

Group	Group mean		
	Empirical scale	Metaphoric scale	Rational scale
Chemistry-biology $n = 48$	1.223	1.141	1.337
Music-drama $n = 50$	1.102	1.489	1.203
Mathematics-physics $n = 44$	1.162	1.142	1.452

drama sample, and that rationalism is highest for the mathematics-theoretical physics group. This empirical confirmation of theoretical expectations is most encouraging because of the overall consistency of the data. Normative comparisons (i.e., when one compares scale performances *between* groups) turn out as predicted in all cases, and ipsative comparisons (i.e., when one compares scale performance *within* groups) turn out as predicted in all cases except one (i.e., the average scale score for the chemistry-biology group is 1.337 on the rational scale and 1.223 on the empirical scale). All but one (mathematics-physics = 1.142 *versus* chemistry-biology = 1.141 on the metaphoric scale) of the nine possible "t" tests are significant beyond the 5% level.

Now that minimal test construction requirements for reliability and validity have been met, we are extending the application of the P.E.P. to a wide variety of empirical problems (e.g., see Royce, 1970a) such as cultural (e.g., East *versus* West) and subcultural (e.g., "the two cultures") differences, and we are exploring the conceptual relationships to cognitive style and value commitments (such as the six values in the Allport, Vernon, Lindzey Study of Values).

Interrelationships among the various theoretical approaches to epistemological psychology are presently under investigation and will be elaborated in detail in a forthcoming volume (Royce & Tennessen, in preparation*). The volume in question includes a critical analysis of the relevant literature on perception, thinking, symbolizing, intuiting, and developmental psychology. Thus, all I can do in the present context is offer a brief summary.

One facet of the current remarriage (Royce, 1964, 1965b) of philosophy and psychology is the emergence of the interdisciplinary subject of epistemological psychology. Major influences to this development from philosophy include the contributions of Wallraff (1961), Hamlyn (1957), and Armstrong (1961) to perception, the work of Kuhn (1962), Feyerabend (1962), and Hanson (1966) on the importance of the theoretical paradigm in science, and the underrated contributions of Cassirer (1953, 1955, 1957) and Langer (1949), whose comprehensive and penetrating system is actually a psychologically oriented theory of how the mind symbolizes or transforms inputs into knowledge outputs. In addition, we have the more traditional philosophy of science concern of contributors such as Feigl (1956) and Scriven (1969), both of whom, however, have made sympathetic efforts to deal explicitly with psychology. And finally, we must note the contributions of Polanyi (1958) who, although he deals with the total enterprise of science, makes his most important contributions in elaborating on the nature of intuition (i.e., tacit knowing).

---

* Royce, J. R., & Tennessen, H. *Inquiries into a psychological theory of knowledge.*

Major influences from psychology include the general commentary on relationships between philosophy and psychology provided by such writers as Koch (1964), Rozeboom (1970), and Turner (1965), Brunswik (1956) and Gibson (1966) in perception, Piaget (1952) and Bruner (1956) on thinking, and Werner and Kaplan (1963) and Jung (1964) on symbolizing. We also must take note of Westcott's (1968) contribution to our understanding of intuition, Kelly's (1963) notion of personal constructs, Campbell's (1959) development of what he calls evolutionary epistemology, and Berlyne's (1960) exploration of the role of motivation in epistemic behavior. In addition, there are various statements put forth in defense of a humanistic psychology, most of which are not adequate in terms of epistemological issues (Royce, 1972).

However, the works which impinge most directly on my own efforts are those of the sociologist Sorokin (1941) and the neuropsychologist Pribram (1972). All three of us appear to have independently developed the same three-process system, with my approach focused on the psychological level, Sorokin focused on the cultural level (sensate, idealistic, and ideational societies) and Pribram looking for the neural basis of induction, deduction, and abduction.

III. COGNITIVE STRUCTURE*

I will define *cognitive structure as a multidimensional, organized subsystem of processes (which subsume perceiving, thinking, symbolizing) by means of which an organism produces cognitions.* The focus of this conception is on the underlying organization of cognitive processes—the basic dimensions of cognition, how each process works, and interrelationships

* There is considerable semantic confusion concerning the usage of the term cognitive structure. However, the most frequent usages can be categorized under two descriptions: the structure of cognitive processes and the organization of cognitions. In an effort to minimize further semantic and conceptual confusion we think it is important to make a distinction between these categories. We suggest, therefore, that the term cognitive structure be used in the former case, and world view (see p. 167) in the latter case. To see that these are quite different concepts one need only observe that identical cognitions can be arrived at by different processes. For example, one says "I can remember that x, see that x, infer that x, etc." In the case of one's world view we are concerned with the way cognitions are organized and in the case of cognitive structure we are concerned with how they were arrived at (i.e., the process of seeing, or inferring, or remembering, etc.). The present account of cognitive structure, although more explicit than most comparable statements, is necessarily highly compressed. A more complete elaboration of the nature of cognitive structure is presently in progress.

between processes. Note that cognitive structure does not deal with cognitions per se, but rather with how cognitions come into being. Nor does it deal with all possible psychological phenomena. Further clarification on these points will be provided after we have elaborated on the nature of cognitive structure by taking a closer look at the major segments of the definition.

First, I've claimed that cognitive structure is *multidimensional*. In view of the fantastic quantity and variety of information the human organism can, in fact, cope with, it almost seems axiomatic that the underlying cognitive system must be multidimensional. This claim is, of course, well documented in the empirical literature, particularly as a result of factor analytic findings. The message from this research has been abundantly clear, namely, that concepts such as intelligence and perception, which were originally treated as univariate dimensions are, in fact, conceptual complexes which must be broken down into their component parts. Thus, the multispace model of factor analysis is explicitly adopted here, as it allows us to look at the complete range of processable information on the one hand, but to reduce the underlying structure to the smallest number of nonredundant dimensions on the other hand. Guilford's (1967) structure-of-intellect model, an orthogonal, three-dimensional taxonomy of 120 factors, is the most complete, monolithic view offered to date. The three major axes of this periodic table of intellectual elements are contents, products, and operations. Each element of this cube is a hypothesized factor, 98 of which have been empirically confirmed. These factors occur at the intersections of the 4 by 5 by 6 matrix reproduced in Fig. 4. Because of the difference in chapter heading (i.e., intelligence rather than cognition), the essentially cognitive nature of Guilford's work may not be apparent. The most obvious points of contact are his 28 cognitive (read knowing) factors and his 24 memory factors. Furthermore, it seems reasonable to relate the 24 convergent factors to thinking, the 30 figural factors to perceiving, and some of the 24 divergent factors and the 30 symbolic factors with symbolizing. Thus, my suggestion is that each of the three ways of knowing constitutes a class of cognitive processes, and that each class is multidimensional.

Let me briefly illustrate by way of examples for each of the three ways of knowing. In the case of perception such factors as figural identification (ability to pick out patterns in confusing situations), spatial visualization (ability to imagine displacements of given configurations), a spatial relations factor (ability to recognize a configuration when displaced), and a factor of length and size estimation, etc. (see Pawlik, 1966), are relevant to accuracy in perception. Each of these factors is seen as a cognitive dimension or process—a way to make contact with invariants of the perceptual ecology. Thus, in the context of perception as a knowledge process

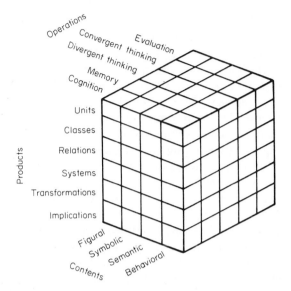

FIG. 4.   A cubical model representing the structure of intellect (Guilford, 1967).

our concern is that the factors of figural identification and size estimation, for example, reveal "real" objects, and "accurate" distances and sizes as opposed to mere appearances.

The most obvious examples of "thinking" dimensions in the deductive sense are subsumed under Guilford's convergent production category. About half of the 24 hypothesized factors have been empirically confirmed (especially those factors identified as convergent symbolic relations, convergent symbolic systems, convergent symbolic transformations, and convergent semantic implications). The epistemological significance of this work is that each of these factors is regarded as being capable of leading the cognizer to logically valid conclusions (i.e., the kind of reality which comes out of logical consistency).

Although the metaphoric approach has received relatively little attention by psychologists, it is highly probable that some symbolizing dimensions have already been identified. One place to look for these is at the crossroads of cognition and symbolic and divergent and symbolic in Guilford's structure of intellect model. Here we find, for example, three likely candidates which we can briefly describe as "getting at an organized pattern" (CSS or cognitive symbolic transformation), and "a fluency factor" (DSU or divergent symbolic units). Again, in the present context, the implication is that such symbolic-metaphoric awareness can convey relatively "universal" significance, thereby dealing with truth or reality.

Second, I have claimed that cognitive structure is an *organized system of processes* (*perceptual-conceptual-symbolic*). The problem here is to describe how the cognitive system is organized. This calls for specifying general principles, principles which "organize" a subsystem, such as perception, or/and the total structure of cognition. For example, the gestalt principle of *prägnanz* (the tendency of a perceptual system to become organized in terms of "good form," i.e., to maximize symmetry, balance, and simplicity), clearly appropriate for the subdomain of perception, may also apply to the areas of thinking and symbolizing. The organizing principle of redintegration, originally developed to account for memory and problem-solving phenomena, is also relevant to the perceptual and metaphoric modes of cognizing. The essence of this principle is that a complex, such as R (A,B, C, etc.), is redintegrated (i.e., reorganized) by the presentation of one of its elements (Horowitz & Prytulak, 1969; Rozeboom, 1970). Is this principle also relevant to metaphoric cognizing? I suspect it is, because in all art forms the artist makes use of elements called themes or leit-motifs—these elements, which usually recur, set off or recapitulate the total symbolic product. Thus, redintegration, or some process like it, is hypothesized to be an "organizing principle" which will account for a significant segment of symbolizing, as well as segments of thinking and perceiving.

Perhaps the most general organizing principle identified to date, however, is Piaget's twin concept of assimilation-accommodation. This mechanism is a general coping process which determines when the organism will step out and modify existing cognitions in order to accommodate the new, or hold fast and assimilate the new input as part of the existing world view. Since the assimilation-accommodation process relates to the total world view, the suggestion is that all three subclasses or ways of knowing are governed by this principle, which means that various combinations of the dimensions of cognition (i.e., both within and between the three subcategories) come into play in accordance with it and other organizing principles.

But the most exciting prospect concerning the organization of cognitive dimensions also comes from the factor analytic literature. While Guilford's taxonomy is impressive in its coverage (Royce, 1968), his insistence on orthogonality flies in the face of overwhelming counterevidence (i.e., correlated first order factors and the identification of higher-order factors). In short, it is beginning to look as though some kind of hierarchical model, such as the one depicted in Fig. 5, will be required. Such a model is not only more consistent with the extant empirical literature, but the hierarchical arrangement is also more promising as a conceptual framework for accommodating principles of cognitive organization.*

---

* The reader is referred to a recent theoretical paper (Royce, 1973) for more

Third, I have stated that cognitive structure leads to *cognitions.* By *cognitions* I mean *those internal (i.e., neurologically coded) representations or mental phenomena (e.g., ideas, insights, percepts) which are products of cognitive processes (i.e., perceiving, thinking, and symbolizing).* This definition immediately raises the question "Representations of what?" In the most general terms it seems to be the case that cognitions can represent anything, ranging from a wild, highly autistic superstition or fantasy, to very prosaic, literal objects of the everyday world. However, in the present context, namely that of trying to understand the knowing process, cognitions are presumed to have something to do with reality (i.e., the world, "the way things are"). But a given percept or concept may or may not represent reality; that is, the mere having of an idea or a percept does not qualify as knowing. This means we must retain the distinction between cognizing and knowing, between perceiving as knowing and not knowing, symbolizing as knowing and not knowing, and thinking as knowing and not knowing. Thus, cognitions per se do not qualify as knowledge. However, cognitions combined with epistemic justification *can* lead to knowledge.

In both cases, however (the cases of cognition and knowing), internal representation is required. The point is that there must be some mechanism for mediating between inputs on the stimulus side and outputs on the response side of this stimulus-organism-response formulation. The fact that the organism is in the picture suggests that it would be empirically desirable, even if it is not logically necessary, to eventually spell out the nature of the implicit biological mechanisms. The sheer redundancy of information which can be processed by the average human suggests that some form of coding is crucial in the mediating machinery. Furthermore, this notion has received both heuristic and simulation demonstration support from the computer science theorists. The neuropsychologist who has addressed himself most directly to this issue is, in my judgment, Karl Pribram. In a paper addressed specifically to the neural basis of knowing (Pribram, 1972) he uses "consensually validated coded information" as his definition of knowledge. He then elaborates a hologram-like mechanism as the neural basis for coding, and marshals the neuropsychological evidence for three classes

details on the hierarchical nature of cognitive structure and to a book-in-progress (Royce J. R., & Buss, A. *A multi-factor theory of individuality.* In preparation.) for elaboration of organizing principles of the dimensions of cognitive structure. The complete theory goes beyond cognitive structure, including affective structure and style structure. Style structure is of particular significance in this context as there is good reason to conceptualize the three ways of knowing, rationalism, empiricism, and metaphorism, as epistemic styles. As such, these three theoretical constructs provide higher order linkages between specifiable dimensions of cognitive structure on the one hand and specifiable dimensions of affective structure on the other hand. Thus, their integrative role in the development of a world view (see pp. 167–173) and in the organization of personality is a potent one.

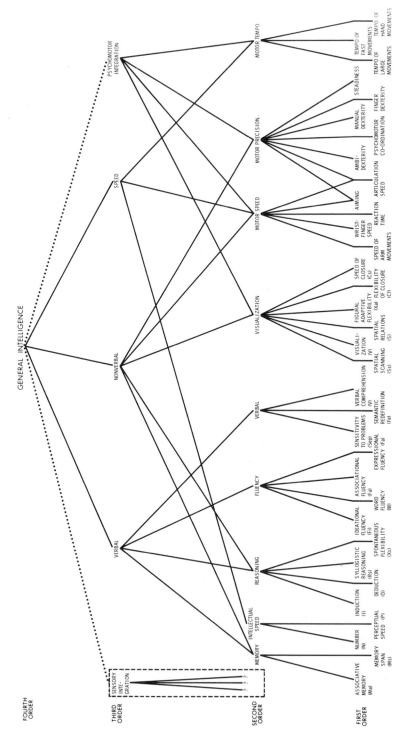

FIG. 5

of knowing: knowing what (images of events), knowing that (monitor images), and knowing how (images of achievement).

Finally, I claim that cognitive structure is *constructive*. Although this point is not stated explicitly, it is implicit throughout. The claim here is that cognizing allows for the development or construction of categories, concepts, or constructs which guide or control the way we view the world. Constructs emerge in a variety of ways,* and they have been variously classified. Bruner (1956), for example, describes three modes of codifying, Piaget (1952) focuses on developmental change on the one hand, and the similarity in construct formation between the child and the cultural evolution of scientific epistemology on the other hand. And George Kelly (1963) has evolved a "system of personal constructs" which he also sees as roughly comparable to scientific constructs. In short, the constructivist claim is a central theme in contemporary cognitive psychology and is, in fact, the core concept of a recent approach (Neisser, 1967) to a large segment of psychology.

At least two points are common to the constellation of "constructive" approaches. One is that some form of information theory provides the general conceptual framework. The other is that various mechanisms are postulated for dealing with information overload. The most frequent means for dealing with this is to require some kind of *code*, and a set of *rules*. Thus, we end up with a set of constructs which, in effect, are the elements of the code. The code, combined with a set of operational rules, constitutes a "representation" of "the way things are."

Relating this to the present context, we can view each of the three ways of knowing as an elaborate code, each with its own rules, devised in such a way that they are consistent with the epistemic justification for a given way of knowing. For example, the fundamental requirement in rationalism is that the rules lead to logical consistency. Departure from this requirement constitutes breaking the rules of that particular epistemic game, and it is simply not allowed (that is, the epistemic umpire will yell "false!"). In the

* No attempt will be made in this paper to deal with the nativism–empiricism issue involved in cognitive structure. The most obvious contrast in extant views is evident in the writings of Skinner (1957) and Chomsky (1959) on language. It is anticipated that work presently under way on another project (Royce, Canada Council) which is an attempt to provide a theoretical synthesis of our knowledge of "individuality" (Royce, 1973), will have a direct bearing on this issue. Our best guess at this juncture is that the personal constructs of cognitive structure are differentially affected by both genetic and environmental determinants, and that only empirical work will clarify the details.

FIG. 5. Hierarchical structure of cognition (modified from Royce, 1973).

case of metaphorism, the rules call for "meaningful symbolizing," and so an Ingmar Bergman, a Fellini, or an Edward Albee hits us with similes, analogies, and allegories which are pregnant with "universal" significance for the "human condition." In this case, since the focus is on "life" rather than logic, paradoxes and logical inconsistencies are not only permitted, they are encouraged by the rules of this epistemic game. The point is that the three ways of knowing are elaborate cognitive subsystems, *constructed* by the organism as ways to understand the various sub-segments of the totality we call "reality."

It was stated earlier that cognitive structure does not deal with all psychological phenomena. It does not deal with simple reflexes, for example, or releasers, and a variety of simple conditioning and learning phenomena. The point here is that, important as cognitive structure is for advancing our understanding of psychological events, it seems to be unwarranted to extend it to all of psychology. My position is that cognitive structure is an important segment of the total psychological structure, and that cognitions are a subset of mental phenomena. Let me clarify this stance by defining *mental structure as a multidimensional, organized subsystem of processes (subsumes cognitive structure) by means of which an organism manifests mental phenomena,* where mental phenomena refer to internal (i.e., neurologically coded) representations, whether or not they are representative of reality. The point is that mental phenomena include the full range of internal events, such as wishes, desires, beliefs, fantasies, dreams, illusions, delusions, hallucinations, etc., as well as ideas, insights, and percepts. Parallel to previous definitions, I will define *psychological structure as a multidimensional, organized system of processes (subsumes mental structure) by means of which an organism manifests behaviour and mental phenomena.* It should be apparent from these definitions that we are describing a general system and its subsystem, and that a given structure is nested or embedded within a more inclusive structure (see Fig. 6A). This means, for example, that cognitions (e.g., percepts, ideas, insights; see Fig. 6B) evolve primarily from cognitive structure but that such cognitions

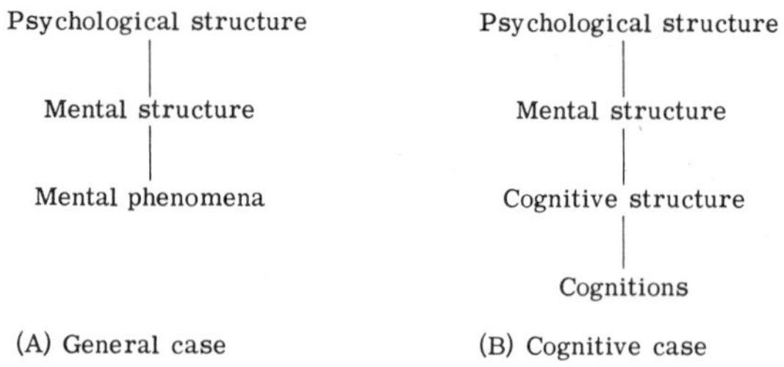

FIG. 6.   The hierarchical embeddedness of cognitive structure.

are also influenced by the underlying mental structure, which, in turn, is influenced by the organism's total psychological structure.

IV. TOWARD A PSYCHOLOGY AND PHILOSOPHY OF THE WELTANSCHAUUNG

Let us assume that this multidimensional, representational, constructivist, interacting-with-the-environment conception of cognitive structure is a reasonable first approximation of how the organism processes information. What might be the relationship between the cognitions which emerge from cognitive structure and the variety of epistemologically testable reality? The answer to this question requires explication of the concept of reality image or world view. I will, therefore, define *world view as an organism's organized set of personal cognitions which constitutes a model or image of reality (i.e., "the way things are")*. It is implied that personal cognitions* are directly based on cognitive structure, and indirectly based on mental and psychological structures. It is further implied that world views tend to be "encapsulated" (Royce, 1964), i.e., less than the totality of reality. The precise form encapsulation takes depends upon one's psycho-epistemological profile; that is, whether rationalism, empiricism, or metaphorism is at the apex of one's epistemological hierarchy. If rationalism, for example, is dominant, this means the resulting world view is based on an essentially thinking cognitive structure (see Fig. 7A). And if we are considering a case of ultraempiricism, then we have an example of perceptual dominance (see Fig. 7B).† This means the resulting world-view is based primarily on the processes of perceiving, even though some cognitions of the total set emerge from the processes of thinking and symbolizing as well.‡

The strong constructivist element in cognition highlights the traditional subject-object issue of epistemology and raises the question of the "truth"

* Personal cognitions are concepts, constructs, or categories; more specifically, that subset of cognitions which tends to unify or systematize reality for a given person.

† It would not be unreasonable to regard such epistemological profiles as varieties of epistemic style, where that term implies both temperament and ability components. We have initiated several empirical investigations which may eventually throw some light on this question. Adequate conceptual analysis will also be required. The point in this context is to at least allude to the importance of the affective determinants of one's *Weltanschauung*.

‡ I have assumed it is clear that cognitive structure and the corresponding world view never fall into the "hypothetical pure types" just described but, rather, are composites of all three ways of knowing, and that individual epistemological and construct priorities depend upon one's psycho-epistemological profile.

Psychological structure	Psychological structure
|	|
Mental structure	Mental structure
|	|
Cognitive structure	Cognitive structure
|	|
Thinking cognitions	Perceptual cognitions
(A) Rational world-view	(B) Empirical world-view

FIG. 7.   Cognitive structure and epistemological hierarchies.

of a given world view. The problem here is: When we "know," how much is supplied by the subject, and how much is supplied by the object? I suggest the answer is that both subject and object are required, and further, that knowing ranges over the full spectrum of relative subject or object domination. But let me initiate the clarification of this issue by taking two extremes. First, let me take the extreme case of subject-dominated world view. Here we have the case of "pure" construction—cognition not constrained by object or other environmental inputs. Extreme cases of autism, such as might occur in schizophrenic or other types of psychosis, point up the obvious delusional possibilities (e.g., see Weckowicz, 1972). Epistemologically this forces us into the solipsistic bind, and psychologically it is maladaptive. In short, subjective constructions which completely ignore the object (i.e., the environment) or other external constraints (e.g., the logical consistency of mathematics) cannot qualify as knowing.

Now let us consider the case of complete object domination. In its ultimate extreme we would merely have an environment without sentient organisms. The universe would simply exist, and there would be no organism on hand to know this universe. Recent observations from space flights to the moon suggest that the situation on that sphere is such a microcosm.

We have now reaffirmed what seems to be the obvious starting point, namely, that knowledge only exists out of the interaction between subject and object (i.e., environment). What happens if we move the analysis closer to the center? Working in from the extremes, but still remaining peripheral, we can speak of partial subject or object dominance. This brings the epistemological issue into somewhat sharper focus. For we have now allowed for subject-object interaction and therefore the possibility of knowing, but notice that we have given up certainty. That is, the partial subject-dominant case is relatively inadequate in terms of epistemological testability and the partial object-dominant case provides us with a relatively impoverished world view (e.g., as in the case of a plant, an amoeba, a worm, or an infant).* As we move still closer to the center, we bring the subject-

* This point brings up the issue of whether it makes sense to attribute a world

object problem into its sharpest focus. For now we allow for a rich, constructivist, world view on the one hand, and the totality of the environment on the other hand. And the essence of the problem is that when this occurs there is an inescapable ambiguity surrounding what can be known. The point is that we cannot completely separate what is provided by the subject from what is given by the object. My answer to this dilemma is to accept ambiguity as the nature of the beast, but to add that increments in understanding should reduce the level of ambiguity, and that the key to increased understanding lies in the match between world views and epistemological criteria.

Why must there be ambiguity? Surely there is a world "out there" and we can know it. The problem is that, since we can only know via the psychobiological equipment we have, and since the process of knowing involves an active, constructivist knower, it is impossible to be certain of the extent to which the resultant world view represents "reality out there." Stated another way, it would be necessary to know the nature of reality in some ultimate sense in order to evaluate how well the world view in question approximates "the objective truth." On the other hand, since various organisms, utilizing the psychobiological equipment available to them, have successfully adapted to the world (Campbell, 1959, 1960), it is equally erroneous to conclude that knowledge of some sort is impossible (i.e., pure skepticism). Thus, ambiguity regarding "the truth" necessarily follows.

In my judgment, reduction in ambiguity can occur only by increasing our understanding of the cognitive and epistemological aspects of the knowing process. Such increase in understanding surely begins by showing the inadequacy of the two extreme positions that (1) no knowledge is possible, or (2) completely objective knowledge is possible. The first position, that of the complete skeptic, is rarely defended any more, and is probably not worth extended treatment in this context. The second position, however, has been seriously defended, particularly in the twentieth century, and

---

view to a lower organism. The definition of world view herein presented allows for this interpretation, as would Campbell's conception of knowledge (e.g., 1959, 1960). My guess on this point is as follows: as we descend phylogenetically the world views of lower organisms become increasingly impoverished. Furthermore, in general, infrahuman world views are probably dominated by the perceptual processes. The available evidence indicates that symbolizing is confined to *Homo sapiens,* but that thinking and concept formation occur in higher level species (e.g., mammals). It is doubtful that even simple concepts occur at the lower phylogenetic levels, but some forms of perceptual cognizing occur at all phylogenetic levels, including the simplest, single-celled animals, for even at these levels gross sensory discriminations (e.g., avoidance) are possible. Thus, in terms of species survival, natural selection, and the evolutionary process, it would appear that perceptual cognizing is the most primitive and fundamental of the three classes of cognition.

particularly as a result of the success of science. The fallacy in this position lies in being overimpressed by the power of scientific epistemology, combined with underplaying the extent to which the subject's (i.e., various scientists) personal constructions have entered into the "discovery" of scientific knowledge. Focus on the theoretical structure of science, in contrast to its apparently neutral, factual data, allows us to bring out this subjective contribution more clearly, for it is well established that the most creative aspects of science are required on the theory side, and further, scientific epistemology is forced to admit that, since several theoretical structures can accommodate the same set of observed data, it follows that no one theory can be proved to be true. Although logical positivism and operationalism may have misled us into believing completely objective knowledge is possible, recent developments have provided correctives to such an extreme posture. The writings of the scientific historian Kuhn (1962), and philosophers Hanson (1966) and Feyerabend (1962, 1963), for example, move away from the earlier empiricist stance and place more emphasis on conceptual paradigms and the rational basis of science. And in this connection Piaget (1957) offers the hypothesis that the development of concepts in children has parallels to the evolution of concepts in science. If this assumption is correct, the implication is that we can improve our understanding of the epistemology of science by investigations in genetic (i.e., developmental) epistemology.*

Analysis of the subjective in science has been pursued by various psychologists, including Maslow (1966), Rogers (1964), Koch (1961), and Royce (1964, 1965a), but it has received the most extensive treatment in the writings of Polanyi (1958), particularly under the rubric of "tacit knowing." Tacit knowledge is "knowledge of an approaching discovery" (Polanyi, 1967). Such knowledge is informal, anticipatory, and highly imaginative, and, when sufficiently insightful, it can provide the conceptual framework for a scientific revolution (Kuhn, 1962). The positive aspect of Polanyi's contribution is to break down the myth of the completely objective scientist. Stated in the context of the conceptual framework of this paper, we could say that Polanyi has demonstrated, via case studies from the history of science, that symbolizing and intuiting are involved in all facets of the scientific enterprise. For example, in an analysis of how mathematics advances he says,

> The manner in which the mathematician works his way towards discovery, by shifting his confidence from intuition to computation and back again from computation to intuition, while never releasing his hold on either of the two,

---

* Philosophers, however, refer to such claims as the genetic fallacy, meaning that knowledge of how a truth claim evolves has nothing to do with its validity.

represents in miniature the whole range of operations by which articulation disciplines and expands the reasoning powers of man. This alternation is asymmetrical, for a formal step can be valid only by virtue of our tacit confirmation of it. Moreover, a symbolic formalism is itself but an embodiment of our antecedent unformalized powers—an instrument skillfully contrived by our inarticulate selves for the purpose of relying on it as our external guide. The interpretation of primitive terms and axioms is therefore predominantly inarticulate, and so is the process of their expansion and reinterpretation which underlies the progress of mathematics. The alternation between the intuitive and the formal depends on tacit affirmations, both at the beginning and at the end of each chain of formal reasoning (Polanyi, 1958, p. 131).

The weakness of Polanyi's position lies in his failure to offer an adequate statement of how the subjectivity of symbolizing and intuiting relate to scientific truth criteria. My answer to this issue is that these cognitive processes are clearly involved in doing science, but that, in principle, they are not primary for that discipline. What is primary are the cognitive processes of thinking and perceiving and their corresponding epistemologies of rationalism and empiricism. In short, while it is clear that subjectivity is a significant part of scientific *cognition,* to the extent that such subjectivity is openly or surreptitiously carried over to the *epistemological side,* it contaminates the search for scientific truth.

But now that we have thrown doubt on the idea of objective knowledge, it is pertinent to ask in what sense it is answerable in the affirmative. The affirmative answer receives greatest support from the epistemological side— on the grounds of a variety of confirmability criteria such as the verifiability principle, empirical repeatability, and correspondence between theoretical structure and observed data. The weakness in this position stems from the *cognitive* side, namely, that in spite of various epistemological justifications, the cognitions which emerge from the underlying cognitive structure can simply be wrong (e.g., notions of a flat earth, ether). However, we might get some help here from that portion of the psychological literature on perception which deals with the question of veridicality. Here I am thinking, for example, of research on the senses per se (i.e., relatively free of constructivist transformations) and of the extensive research on illusions. However, even more relevant is the research on the perceptual constancies and other invariants of the environment. The point is that findings of this kind might give us leverage on the problem of a reality "out there," not in the sense of veridicality, or what's "really out there," but in the sense of picking up what we might think of as "functional veridicality." The suggestion here is that, as so often happens with intractable problems, we may be asking the wrong question. In short, instead of asking how the subject can "know" the real object, perhaps it is more appropriate to ask in what way the object is "real" to the subject. When put in this way, the "probabilistic functionalism" of Brunswik, and the "ecological invariants" of Gibson's perceptual systems provide us with powerful linkages to "reality out there." For Gibson is saying that there are aspects of the ecology the organism can detect, and I am suggesting that regardless of its "objective reality," the fact that these are perceived as ecological invariants means there is some kind of linkage between "internal order" or "world view" and "external order" or "the object," and that it is this linkage to ecological invariance which provides reality. Note, however, Brunswik's (1963) warning that there is inherent ambiguity in this process for the simple reason that the human operator is, in fact, a fallible organism, and not a physics-like precision machine.

Now let us rejoin subject and object in the process of knowing. What we have is a cognitive structure, an organized system of processes coming into contact with some aspect of the environment (internal or external) which, for purposes of simplification, we will refer to as the object (a thing, a person, one's self). This new input is decoded in accordance with the existing hierarchy of personal constructs or cognitions (i.e., one's world view), followed by subsequent transformations including feedback and feedforward* loops (Pribram, 1971), which eventuates in an output. Several recent experiments on this output-input loop have considerable relevance in this context. Piaget (1954) has elaborated at some length on the necessity for motor output in order for true knowing to occur in the young child. Festinger, Bamber, Burnham, and Ono (1967), Held (1964), and others have taken a similar stance on the importance of motor output for perception. And various other investigators, Gyr (1969, 1972) and Platt (1961) for example, have elaborated on the importance of these feedback loops as part of the knowing process. The point is that the subject's personal constructions act directly upon the environment, and that this step, combined with subsequent feedback, is essential for knowing. From the epistemological point of view what is important here is that this efference-reafference mechanism (which apparently is literally motoric in the developing child, and becomes less overt or more vicarious in later development) provides a way for internal cognitions to be checked against the environment. More

---

* The mechanism of feedforward refers to the internal "control," sensitizing, or selection of sensory inputs. The evidence is that feedforward is primarily a function of cortical association areas (Pribram, 1971). The most convincing demonstration of what is implied here is Pribram's electroencephalographic evidence indicating a monkey's "intention" to press the left or right lever in a specified task *before* making the response. Although not the same, the voluminous "new look" evidence on central (e.g., motivational) determinants of perception, is also relevant in this context. In short, there can be little doubt of the importance of inside-out or constructionist determinants of perception and cognition in addition to the more obvious outside-in determinants.

specifically, I am arguing that confirming feedback from the environment increases the probability that the world view in question is an adequate representation or image of reality. Conversely, to the extent there is disconfirming feedback, changes in world view are required.

The relevance of the previously described three ways of knowing should now be apparent, for each of these provides processes (i.e., how the components of thinking, perceiving, or symbolizing are organized) of one's cognitive structure on the one hand, and the epistemological rules (i.e., logical-illogical, perception-misperception, universality-idiosyncrasy) for positive or negative feedback from the environment on the other hand. That is, in "pure," empirical knowing perceptual cognitions of a world view are checked against the epistemic rules for accurate perception (e.g., yes, that is a chair). "Pure" rational knowing involves checking thinking cognitions of a world view against the epistemic rules for logical thinking (e.g., yes, that deduction follows within this particular logical system). And metaphoric knowing involves checking symbolizing constructs of a world view against the epistemological requirements of universality (e.g., yes, Mr. X's play, written 500 years ago, and still produced in various parts of the world, meets the criterion of universality). In short, world views are validated, or we "know," when there is some kind of isomorphism between personal cognitions and structurable segments (not just "thingy") of the world.

References

Armstrong, D. M. *Perception and the physical world.* London: Routledge & Kegan Paul, 1961.

Berlyne, D. *Conflict, arousal and curiosity.* New York: McGraw-Hill, 1960.

Bruner, J. S., Goodnow, J. J., & Austin, G. A. *A study of thinking.* New York: Wiley, 1956.

Brunswik, E. *Perception and the representative design of psychological experiments.* Berkeley: Univ. of California Press, 1956.

Brunswik, E. Organismic achievement and environmental probability. *Psychological Review,* 1963, **50**, 255–272.

Campbell, D. T. Methodological suggestions from a comparative psychology of knowing processes. *Inquiry,* 1959, **2**, 152–182.

Campbell, D. T. Blind variation and selective retention in creative thought as in other knowledge processes. *Psychological Review,* 1960, **67**, 380–400.

Cassirer, E. *The philosophy of symbolic forms.* Vols. 1, 2, & 3. New Haven, Connecticut: Yale Univ. Press, 1953, 1955, and 1957.

Chomsky, N. Review of B. F. Skinner, *Verbal behavior. Language,* 1959, **35**, 26–58.

Coward, H. Symbolizing and intuiting processes in metaphorism. Unpublished M. A. thesis, University of Alberta, 1969.

Feigl, H. Some major issues and developments in the philosophy of science of logical empiricism. In H. Feigl and M. Scriven (Eds.), *Foundations of science and the concepts of psychology and psychoanalysis.* Minneapolis: Univ. of Minnesota Press, 1956. Pp. 3–37.

Festinger, L., Bamber, D., Burnham, C. A., & Ono, H. Efference and the conscious experience of perception. *Journal of Experimental Psychology, Monograph,* 1967, **74,** 1–37.

Feyerabend, P. K. Explanation, reduction and empiricism. In H. Feigl & G. Maxwell (Eds.), *Minnesota studies in the philosophy of science.* Vol. 3. Minneapolis: Univ. of Minnesota Press, 1962. Pp. 28–97.

Feyerabend, P. K. How to be a good empiricist—a plea for tolerance in matters epistemological. In B. Baumrin (Ed.), *Philosophy of science: The Delaware seminar.* Vol. 2. New York: Wiley (Interscience), 1963. Pp. 3–40.

Gibson, J. J. *The senses considered as perceptual systems.* Boston, Massachusetts: Houghton, 1966.

Guilford, J. P. *The nature of human intelligence.* New York: McGraw-Hill, 1967.

Gyr, J. W. Is there direct visual perception? Unpublished manuscript, The Center for Advanced Study in Theoretical Psychology, University of Alberta, 1969.

Gyr, J. W. Perception as reafference and related issues in cognition and epistemology. In J. R. Royce & W. W. Rozeboom (Eds.), *The psychology of knowing.* New York: Gordon and Breach, 1972. Pp. 267–279.

Hamlyn, D. W. *The psychology of perception.* London: Routledge & Kegan Paul, 1957.

Hammond, K. R. Probabilistic functionalism. In K. R. Hammond (Ed.), *The psychology of Egon Brunswik.* New York: Holt, 1966. Pp. 15–80.

Hanson, N. R. *Patterns of discovery.* London & New York: Cambridge Univ. Press, 1966.

Held, R. The role of movement in the origin and maintenance of visual perception. *Proceedings of the 17th International Congress of Psychology.* Amsterdam: North-Holland, 1964.

Horowitz, L. M., & Prytulak, L. S. Redintegrative memory. *Psychological Review,* 1969, **76,** 519–531.

Jung C. G. *Man and his symbols.* London: Aldus Books Ltd., 1964.

Kelly, G. A. *A theory of personality.* New York: Norton, 1963.

Koch, S. Psychological science versus the science-humanism antinomy: Intimations on a significant science of man. *American Psychologist,* 1961, **16,** 629–639.

Koch, S. Psychology and emerging conceptions of knowledge as unitary. In T. Wann (Ed.), *Behaviorism and phenomenology.* Chicago, Illinois: Univ. of Chicago Press, 1964. Pp. 1–41.

Kuhn, T. S. *The structure of scientific revolutions.* Chicago, Illinois: Univ. of Chicago Press, 1962.

Langer, S. K. *Philosophy in a new key.* New York: Mentor Books, 1949.

Maslow, A. H. *The psychology of science: A reconnaissance.* New York: Harper, 1966.

May, R. The origins and significance of the existential movement in psychology. In R. May, E. Angel, & H. F. Ellenberger (eds.), *Existence.* New York: Basic Books, 1958. Pp. 3–36.

Neisser, U. *Cognitive psychology.* New York: Appleton, 1967.

Pawlik, K. Concepts and calculations in human cognitive abilities. In R. B. Cattell (Ed.), *Handbook of multivariate experimental psychology.* Chicago, Illinois: Rand McNally, 1966. Pp. 535–562.

Piaget, J. *The origins of intelligence in children.* New York: International Universities Press, 1952.

Piaget, J. *The construction of reality in children.* New York: Basic Books, 1954.

Piaget, J. The child and modern physics. *Scientific American,* 1957, **196**, 46–51.

Platt, J. R. Functional geometry and the determination of pattern in mosaic receptors. *General Systems,* 1961, **7**, 103–119.

Polanyi, M. *Personal knowledge.* Chicago, Illinois: Univ. of Chicago Press, 1958.

Polanyi, M. *The tacit dimension.* New York: Doubleday, 1967.

Pribram, K. H. *Languages of the brain.* Englewood Cliffs, New Jersey: Prentice-Hall, 1971.

Pribram, K. H. Neurological notes on knowing. In J. R. Royce & W. W. Rozeboom (Eds.), *The psychology of knowing.* New York: Gordon & Breach, 1972. Pp. 449–462.

Quine, W. V. O. *Ontological relativity and other essays.* New York: Columbia Univ. Press, 1969.

Rogers, C. R. Toward a science of the person. In T. W. Wann (Ed.), *Behaviorism and phenomenology.* Chicago, Illinois: Univ. of Chicago Press, 1964. Pp. 109–132.

Royce, J. R. *The encapsulated man: An interdisciplinary essay on the search for meaning.* Princeton, New Jersey: Van Nostrand-Reinhold, 1964.

Royce, J. R. (Ed.) *Psychology and the symbol: An interdisciplinary symposium.* New York: Random House, 1965. (a)

Royce, J. R. Pebble picking vs. boulder building. *Psychological Reports,* 1965, **16**, 447–450. (b)

Royce, J. R. Metaphoric knowledge and humanistic psychology. In J. F. T. Bugental (Ed.), *Challenges of humanistic psychology.* New York: McGraw-Hill, 1967. Pp. 20–28.

Royce, J. R. A model of the mind. Book review of J. P. Guilford's, *The nature of human intelligence. Science,* 1968, **162**, 990–991.

Royce, J. R. Test manual for the psycho-epistemological profile (P.E.P.). Unpublished manuscript, The Center for Advanced Study in Theoretical Psychology, University of Alberta, 1970. (a)

Royce, J. R. (Ed.) *Toward unification in psychology.* Toronto: Univ. of Toronto Press, 1970. (b)

Royce, J. R. On conceptual confusion in humanistic psychology. *Contemporary Psychology,* 1972, **17**, 704–705.

Royce, J. R. The conceptual framework for a multi-factor theory of individuality. In J. R. Royce (Ed.), *Multivariate analysis and psychological theory.* London: Academic Press, 1973. Pp. 305–381.

Royce, J. R., & Rozeboom, W. W. (Eds.) *The psychology of knowing.* New York: Gordon & Breach, 1972.

Royce, J. R., & Smith, W. A. S. A note on the development of the psycho-epistemological profile (P.E.P.). *Psychological Reports,* 1964, **14**, 297–298.

Rozeboom, W. W. The art of metascience, or, what should a psychological theory be? In J. R. Royce (Ed.), *Toward unification in psychology.* Toronto: Univ. of Toronto Press, 1970. Pp. 53–163.

Scriven, M. Psychology without a paradigm. In L. Breger (Ed.), *Clinical-cognitive psychology: Models and integrations.* Englewood Cliffs, New Jersey: Prentice-Hall, 1969. Pp. 9–24.

Skinner, B. F. *Verbal behavior.* New York: Appleton, 1957.

Smith, W. A. S., Royce, J. R., Ayers, D., & Jones, B. The development of an inventory to measure ways of knowing. *Psychological Reports,* 1967, **21**, 529–535.

Sorokin, P. A. *The crisis of our age.* New York: Dutton, 1941.

Turner, M. B. *Philosophy and the science of behavior.* New York: Appleton, 1965.

Wallraff, C. F. *Philosophical theory and psychological fact.* Tucson: Univ. of Arizona Press, 1961.

Weckowicz, T. E. Depersonalization-derealization syndrome and perception: A contribution of psychopathology to epistemology. In J. R. Royce & W. W. Rozeboom (Eds.), *The psychology of knowing.* New York: Gordon & Breach, 1972. Pp. 429–444.

Werner, H., & Kaplan, B. *Symbol formation.* New York: Wiley, 1963.

Westcott, M. R. *The psychology of intuition.* New York: Holt, 1968.

Part III

Contemporary Views of Perception

A. Modern Classical Tradition (*Chaps. 10–11*)

B. Current Psychological Emphases (*Chaps. 12–20*)

Chapter 10

ORGANIZATION AND THE GESTALT TRADITION

JULIAN HOCHBERG

The problems of perceptual organization comprise various examples of the general fact that we cannot predict how subjects will respond to patterns of stimulation from what we know about their sensory responses to local measures on the proximal stimulation. In visual perception, this means the following: we can analyze the stimulus display into a set of the smallest discriminable points or homogeneous patches; we can then determine how the appearance of each such point varies lawfully as we change its physical characteristics (i.e., the spectral distribution and time course of the photic energy within its boundaries); and we can try, with some success, to explain those lawful variations in physiological terms that are not inconsistent with our current beliefs about neuroanatomy. We might go a step further, and try to treat the appearances of such points or patches of color as elementary *units of experience* in this sense: that the appearance of any scene of objects and events is simply the sum of the appearances that would be experienced if each patch into which the scene can be divided were viewed separately. This attempt (called *structuralism* or, more pejoratively, *atomism*) does not work, in general, for two reasons. First, the appearance of any part of the display may be changed significantly by changes elsewhere in the stimulus display. Second, any normal scene has apparent properties (e.g., depth, shape) that go beyond the apparent properties of points or small homogeneous patches (e.g., color, direction, and extension). In general, the phenomena that appear to depend on the configuration of all (or some sizable subset) of the stimulus pattern, rather than on the local values of the individual points of stimulation, will be called the phenomena of perceptual organization. The traditional explanation of these phenomena was that they consist of the observer's tactual and kinesthetic memories of the previous occasions in which those particular patterns of visual sensations had been accompanied by touch and action in the world of objects.

The major categories of such phenomena include the following: facts of figure–ground organization; the transposition phenomena; the constancies; the geometric illusions; the figural aftereffects; the invariances or couplings. We shall define these while discussing Gestalt theory, which was an attempt to displace structuralism on the grounds that the latter could not adequately deal with such phenomena. Gestalt theory, however, as it was originally developed, has not provided an adequate explanatory or predictive account of perceptual organization, either, so that we will also discuss subsequent attempts to deal with the same phenomena.

I. THE GESTALT APPROACH TO THE PROBLEM OF ORGANIZATION

In opposition to structuralist theory, which takes local sensory experiences and specific nerve energies as its psychological and physiological units, respectively, Gestalt theory assumed that the nervous system responds as a whole to the entire pattern of proximal stimulation acting on its receptors. Many if not all of the perceived properties of objects were presumed to derive directly from the fundamental nature of the physiological processes that are set into action by the sensory stimulation, rather than from the observer's learning of environmental contingencies. These underlying physiological processes were conceived of as a mutually interacting set of forces produced in the visual nervous system by the entire pattern of stimulation, not as a mosaic of specific nerve energies. The structures and attributes of perceptual experience—e.g., apparent motion (Wertheimer, 1912), spatial configuration, and location (Köhler & Wallach, 1944), object quality or "figure density" (Köhler, 1920), solidity and tridimensionality (Koffka, 1935; Köhler, 1940; Köhler & Emery, 1947)— presumably reflect those of the electrochemical events in the brain field.

That is, perception and cortical processes are *isomorphic:* the two are topologically, if not metrically, the same in their configuration, so that the factors that determine the spatial and temporal organization of the cortical processes thereby determine the organization of perception, as well. These "field forces" therefore assume central importance, serving the conceptual function for Gestalt theory that *specific nerve energies* served for idealized structuralist theory.

To the Gestaltists the structuralist model is reminiscent of a telegraph exchange, and they wish us to think instead of the distribution of stresses in a system of soap bubbles, or of the interacting electrical fields produced by a complex network of conductors and charged bodies. The characteristics of a perceived object depend on the characteristics of the equilibrium state reached by these interacting forces and, therefore, on the entire pattern of stimulation produced by that object, rather than on local responses to individual parts of the stimulation that the object projects to the eye (Koffka, 1935; Köhler, 1920).

But if what we perceive depends on the form of the entire stimulus pattern, and on the configuration of neural processes that result from that pattern of stimulation, how can we proceed to analyze our perceptual experience and to undertake any lawful generalization? Each change in stimulation anywhere within the visual field should produce a new configuration of forces, with what would seem to be unpredictable consequences. We need *some* units of analysis, else all we are left with is a useless but serious set of objections to the structuralist position.

A. Possible Tools of Gestalt Analysis

Gestalt theory does offer two possible sets of analytic tools, namely the *figure–ground phenomenon* and so-called *laws of organization,* both of which are directly relevant to the perception of object properties.

1. FIGURE–GROUND PHENOMENA

In order to perceive the shape of the image that falls on a given region of the retina, it is not enough that all of the receptors in that region receive photic stimulation that is above threshold, nor is it enough that there be a brightness difference sufficient to produce a perceptible contour. In addition, that region must be perceived as *figure,* if it is to have a perceptible shape. In Fig. 1a, for example, the contour *i* divides the visual field, giving shape to one side *or* to the other but not both, at any point along the contour. Ideally, one sees *either* a vase (Fig. 1b) or a pair of faces (Fig. 1c). (Of course, other alternatives are also possible, but the ones shown at 1b

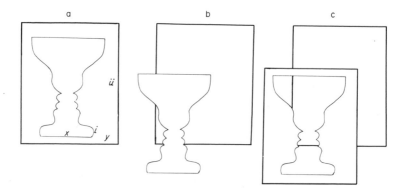

FIG. 1. In (a) the visual field is divided by contour *i*. At any point along the contour shape is given to one side or the other but not to both. What is seen ideally is either a vase as in (b) or a pair of faces as in (c).

and 1c are probably the most salient.) Introspectively, whenever the vase is figure, the region marked *x* seems to have a surface which extends out to the very edge of the contour, *i*, and no further; whereas the region marked *y* then has no definite terminus, other than the outer frame, *ii*, and seems to extend behind the contour *i* to some indefinite distance. When *y* becomes figure, the relationship at the edge reverses, and now *x* seems to become indefinite in extent, and formless. I.e., "shape" belongs only to the region that is figure, not to the ground. In order to perceive a given object at all, the perceptual field must be organized so that that object is the figure— hence the possibility of rendering objects invisible by the technique of camouflage (Metzger, 1953).

These descriptions comprise a deliberately casual and unanalytic kind of observation. We shall see that both the precision and the generality (Section I, B, 4 and 5) must be questioned. But the gross facts of camouflage and protective coloration in animals, and the Gestaltists' many demonstrations (Koffka, 1935; Metzger, 1953; Wertheimer, 1923) attest that this figure–ground distinction must be taken seriously in any attempt to account for the visual perception of objects. The figure–ground phenomenon has, however, been given a much more important place than that, in *Gestaltist*-type theories: the figure–ground phenomenon is asserted to characterize psychological processes in general (e.g., hearing, thinking, personality organization), not merely the perception of shapes. For this reason the study of drawings (e.g., Figs. 1–3) is presumably of great importance to many areas of psychology (cf. Asch, 1968), as well as to the study of visual perception. (We shall see later that if this presumption is true at all, it is probably true in a very different sense than was meant by Gestalt theory.)

Let us temporarily assume that figure and ground are clear-cut, non-overlapping sets of visual experience. Then there is a sense in which figures appear to have several of the characteristics of irreducible elements, in the Gestalt system. For example, the various attributes of figure and ground that we have described are presumably tied to each other, inasmuch as they are merely different consequences of a single brain process that underlies figure information: thus, the figure is more "dense" (or more thing-like) than the ground, shows a higher difference-threshold for test probes, and has more definite shape, in Köhler's physiological theory (Koffka, 1935; Köhler, 1920) because that is the way in which direct current flow is distributed in the optic cortex. Furthermore, a figure is indivisible in this sense: the function that each part of a figure plays is presumably determined by the whole configuration, not by the local characteristics of the part. The part doesn't exist except for the whole that gives it meaning. Note the very different roles played by the parts labeled a in Fig. 2q,r. (We shall see that figures can indeed be dissected into components, despite these demonstrations and assertions, and that the attempt at such dissection is generally instructive.)

Unfortunately, although the "brain processes" are presumably the fundamental agents in this approach, Gestalt theory has really offered no explanation of these hypothetical processes, other than an assertion that the figure–ground distinction characterizes the overall organization of the underlying brain processes. We have to look elsewhere if we are to tell what will be figure, in the perceptual response to any given stimulus display, and what will be ground. The so-called laws of organization offer some help to that end.

2. Laws of Organization

These "laws" are essentially only rules (largely untested) that predict which alternative area in an ambiguous pattern will be seen as figure. Four examples should suffice to illustrate how these rules are demonstrated: (1) Fig. 2c–e,g, suggest that we tend to perceive those shapes in which the lines or dots in the pattern function as the fewest separate (noncontinuous) contours or edges; this is called the "law of good continuation." (2) Where dots or small patches can be seen as the outline of more than one object, their proximity determines which sets are perceived as lying on a single line or contour ("law of proximity," Fig. 2c,h–j). (3) Where one shape is more symmetrical than another, it is the more symmetrical

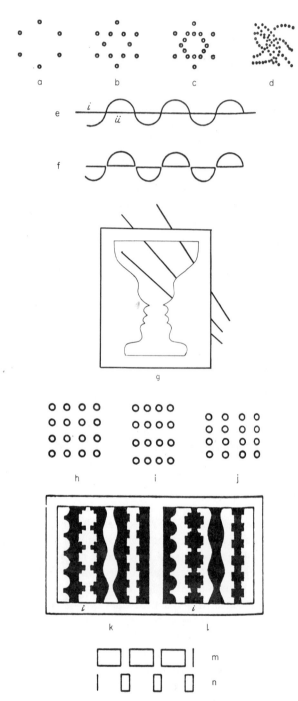

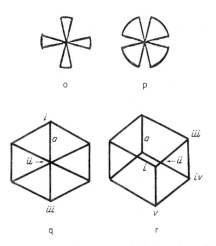

Fɪɢ. 2. Points, contours, lines and edges depicting various Gestalt laws of organization. See text for details.

(e.g., *i* in Fig. 2k,l) that is perceived (this is called the "law of symmetry"). (4) Where one shape is closed, and the other is open, or encloses the first, it is the former that is perceived (Fig. 2m,n).

The list of organizational laws, discovered and illustrated by such methods, is quite long (cf. Musatti, 1931; Woodworth, 1938) so that several of them are at work in any pattern that we may attempt to analyze. For example, in Fig. 2e, *good continuation* overcomes *closedness* (the latter should lead us to perceive the semidisks as figures, as at Fig. 2f). In Fig. 2q, *good continuation* and *symmetry* both lead us to see a two-dimensional object: e.g., one would have to break the continuous line *i–iii* into lines *i–ii* and *ii–iii* in order to see Fig. 2q as a cube; to the contrary, in Fig. 2r, we would have to break the continuous edge, *i–iii*, at *ii*, in order to see it as a flat object, and we would also thus have to break up the four square and symmetrical sides (e.g., side *i–iii–iv–v*) into four asymmetrical trapezoids, two triangles, and a small square (Hochberg & Brooks, 1960; Hochberg & McAlister, 1953; Kopfermann, 1930).

We should note that, in the Gestalt approach, an object's three-dimensionalty (and the apparent depth of space) are considered to be a direct consequence of the organizational process, rather than being due to the accretion of nonvisual kinesthetic imagery (which as we saw was the structuralist explanation).

The demonstrations that exemplify the laws of organization appear to me to be both important and convincing. But they remain simply demonstrations. Moreover, even were they better established, it would still be difficult or impossible to use them for analytic or for predictive purposes, for the following reasons.

Several organizational "laws" acting in concert or in conflict will usually apply to any given pattern. We need quantitative measurement of each factor, and quantitative statement of the relative strengths of the factors, if we are to predict what the result of any given combination will be. There have been several attempts to replace these casual and qualitative statements with more objective and quantitative ones, a task which requires appropriate measures of both stimulation and response.

a. STIMULUS MEASURES. Organization presumably depends on configuration, which is multidimensional and which defies a measure that is at once simple and general. Some of the laws of organization (e.g., proximity) can be tested with relatively simple physical measures (Goldhamer, 1934; Graham, 1929; Hochberg & Hardy, 1960; Hochberg & Silverstein, 1956; Künnapas, 1957; Oyama, 1960; Oyama & Torii, 1955; Rush, 1937); others, such as symmetry, are difficult to state and test; still others, like *simplicity* or *goodness,* have no obvious measures that suggest themselves. Information measures (Attneave, 1954, 1955, 1957, 1959), measures relating perimeter and area (Attneave, 1957; Bitterman, Krauskopf, & Hochberg, 1954; Hochberg, Gleitman, & MacBride, 1948; Stenson, 1966); and measures of angular and linear complexity (Hochberg & Brooks, 1960; Hochberg & McAlister, 1953; Vitz & Todd, 1971) have been used as independent variables. But whether we adopt any given stimulus measure should depend on whether it predicts figural organization, and that in turn depends on having adequate response measures.

b. RESPONSE MEASURES. The following measures seem reasonably close to the question of how strong the tendency is to see one figure–ground organization rather than another: relative duration with which subjects report seeing each alternative, during the spontaneous reversals that characterize ambiguous figures (i.e., figures of *multistable organization;* Attneave, 1971; Figs. 1 and 2; cf. Goldhamer, 1934; Graham, 1929); the proportion of stimulus presentations on which subjects report seeing each alternative (Hochberg & McAlister, 1953); subjects' ratings of the relative salience or prominence of each alternative (Hochberg & Brooks, 1960).

There are a set of procedures which are less immediately directed toward answering the question of what determines which area will be figure and which will be ground. They derive from the following logic. Gestaltist writers had occasionally posited two sets of determinants of organization: the *restraining* (or *external*) forces, that keep the apparent location of any point or contour in correspondence with its place in the proximal stimulus pattern, and the *internal organizing forces* (or *cohesive forces*), that lead to the redistribution of contours within the overall configuration (Brown & Voth, 1937; Koffka, 1935; Orbison, 1939). This distinction is abandoned in later theories (cf. Köhler, 1940, 1958; Köhler & Wallach, 1944), as I read them, but it seemed to account for various observations to the effect that as the restraining forces were weakened by *impoverishing* the proximal stimulation, the effects of the organizing forces increase. "Impoverishment" means, in essence, anything that interferes with good seeing, e.g., short tachistoscopic exposures; peripheral presentation; low luminance levels. By impoverishment of the stimulus, therefore, the working of the organizing forces could presumably be revealed.* The most complete impoverishment would be achieved, of course, by the complete removal of the stimulus pattern; this would leave the memory trace completely at the mercy of—and thereby make it a pure expression of—the forces of organization. Experiments on stimulus impoverishment have not given results consistent with Gestaltist expectations (Casperson, 1950; Helson & Fehrer, 1932).† The general pattern of results, especially those obtained in experiments on tachistoscopic recognition (Pierce, 1963) and on memory for form (Carmichael, Hogan, & Walter, 1932; Hanawalt & Demarest, 1939; Postman, 1954; Riley, 1962), is explained better by theories about how the subjects encode the stimulus than by theories about brain fields. These experiments have led into other fruitful lines of inquiry: how subjects' responses to a pattern depend on the set to which the subject infers the pattern to belong and on the distinctions that he is called on to make, rather than on the pattern alone (Garner, 1962, 1966; Garner & Clement, 1963; Hake, Rodwan, & Weintraub, 1966; Handel & Garner, 1965; Imai & Garner, 1965); the fine structure of search and short-term storage (cf. Neisser, 1967; Sperling, 1967); and inquiries into the mechanisms by which set, attention, and learning affect perceptual response (Egeth, 1967; Neisser, 1967; Hochberg, 1970; Haber, 1966). A strong challenge to the entire concept of organization, in these lines of research, places the burden of explaining the organizational phenomena on *response bias;* this is most explicit in the "verbal loop" hypothesis to the effect that

* This logic was later applied in attempts to measure and identify the motivational factors in perception. This is clear in the autism studies of Murphy and his colleagues (Schafer & Murphy, 1943; cf. Solley & Murphy, 1960), and the "New Look" research of Bruner and his colleagues (Bruner, 1951; Bruner & Postman, 1949).

† In retrospect, one may well question why they should have been expected to do so. If we attribute the phenomena of organization to the steady-state interactions of fields produced by brain currents that themselves result from sensory stimulation, it is not clear that anything like the same phenomena should occur in the absence of the sensory stimulation.

the subjects' recognition performance and errors are better predicted from the verbal responses into which the subjects encode the stimulus pattern, than from any measures taken on the stimulus pattern itself, or from any hypothetical brain processes (Glanzer & Clark, 1963a, 1963b, 1964; Glanzer, Taub, & Murphy, 1968). It is not clear how such a principle would predict the organizational phenomena demonstrated in Figs. 1 and 2, however, whereas models that assume encoding in terms of features of the stimulus pattern may be able to handle both of these classes of phenomena (Vitz & Todd, 1971).

In any case, the attempts to measure the efficacy of various Gestalt laws have at best met with only modest success. But then a Gestaltist would not really expect each "law" to act as an independent determinant of figural organization: after all, each is only a particular manifestation of the underlying process, namely, the overall distribution of biophysical events in the visual system. There have been a few attempts made to formulate unified principles of organization, and such attempt continue from various viewpoints (Attneave, 1954, 1972; Garner, 1962, 1966; Hochberg & Brooks, 1960; Hochberg & McAlister, 1953; Vitz & Todd, 1969, 1971), but they are still only tentative and programmatic.

These "laws of organization" are the closest things to analytic tools offered by Gestalt theory. They do appear to deal directly with at least some object properties. And they presumably offer us information about brain function.* But these "laws," and the Gestalt approach to the problems of perceptual organization, have certain severe inadequacies that it is profitable, rather than merely destructive, to survey.

B. Inadequacies of the Gestalt Approach to Organization

1. The "laws" are not *determinants:* i.e., by voluntary effort, the observer can alter and reverse figure and ground in some way that is not taken into account at all by a "brain-field" explanation of figural organization.

---

* After all, were we to take the idea of isomorphism seriously, the laws of organization should tell us a great deal about the nature of the underling cortical processes. Very little has actually been attempted in this line, however, and what has been done was based mostly on phenomena other than the laws of organization: the phenomena of apparent movement (Brown & Voth, 1937; Wertheimer, 1912); certain classes of geometrical illusions (Orbison, 1939; Sickles, 1942); and most heavily studied, the "figural aftereffects" (Köhler & Wallach, 1944; for reviews, cf. Day, Pollack, & Segrim, 1959; Ganz, 1966b; Hochberg, 1971a; McEwen, 1958; Spitz, 1958). And the brain-field models do not in general fare better than alternative explanations of those phenomena to which they have been applied (cf. Ganz, 1966a, 1966b; see Section IIB).

2. The laws of organization leave untouched several major aspects of perceptual organization, even though Gestalt theorists (cf. Koffka, 1935) invoked those very phenomena to illustrate the inadequacies of structuralist psychology. These omissions include such critical phenomena as the Constancies,* the illusions,† and the transposition phenomena.‡

All of these must clearly be dealt with by any theory of perceptual organization, and in fact the last phenomenon—transposition—is often referred to by non-Gestaltist theoreticians as "the" Gestalt problem.

3. No explanation has been offered to account for the phenomena of figural organization, whether in two or in three dimensions (and a physiological model of the latter in terms of brain currents would be particularly difficult to formulate; cf. Hochberg, 1962a). Nor has any explanation been offered to account for the laws of organization, even were we to stipulate their efficacy. The physiological models that have been offered have been silent on these issues, even though the "isomorphic brain processes" are presumably the bases of perceptual phenomena, and even though figural organization and grouping, and the laws which appear to effect them, have been central to Gestalt argument and inquiry. (A single exception to this point is Köhler's attempt (1920, 1940) to account for figures' greater apparent "density," and for figure–ground reversal, in terms of cortical current flows.)

4. It is not clear in what sense a figure is a single unit, i.e., a single mutually dependent structure or "gestalt." Consider the kinds of inconsistent pictures in Figs. 3c–f: They show that parts of figures act as "local depth cues" (Hochberg, 1968). These features determine whether a contour is perceived as the edge of one surface or another (Fig. 3f), or as one dihedral or another (3c,d), and seem in these examples to be effective only when they are looked at with the fovea (the high-acuity region at the center of eye). It is hard to see how any overall simplicity factor, or "minimum principle," could accommodate to the fact that Figs. 3c and d look tridimensional, and to the fact that the left hand side of Fig. 3e is reversible.

5. This raises a major point that has been almost completely ignored by Gestalt theory: the various parts of any pattern or object usually all

---

* E.g., that objects tend to appear to retain their distal physical characteristics of size, shape, reflectance, etc., even though the measured proximal stimulus that was thought to be the carrier of that information changes with changes in viewpoint of the observer or with changes in illumination, etc.

† E.g., that the same proximal stimulus characteristic can produce a different appearance, depending on its context, as do the identical lengths i and ii in Fig. 3.

‡ E.g., that an object is perceived as being of identical shape, even though it falls on very different sets of receptors (as when it is displaced laterally, in the retinal image, when either eye or object moves).

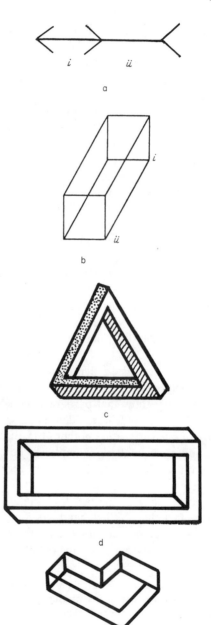

FIG. 3

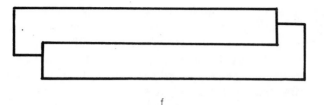

f

FIG. 3. Several major aspects of perceptual organization involving such phenomena as illusions (a and b) and inconsistent pictures (c–f) have been left untouched by the Gestalt laws of organization. In order that it be seen clearly, an object must be viewed foveally in many successive glimpses of its *locally* consistent parts. When finally seen as a single entity an object may be perceived as inconsistent or even "impossible." This shows (c–f) that a single perceived object arises from the integration of these successive glimpses, a fact that was not seriously addressed by Gestalt theory.

have to be viewed by the fovea in a succession of multiple glimpses. That is, the different regions must each fall in turn on the same place in the eye, if they are to be seen with full clarity.* But the fact that our perception of single figures requires us to integrate successive glimpses into a single perceived object, as dramatically demonstrated by Fig. 3c–f, was not seriously addressed.

* Gestaltists did consider the related problem of transposition, e.g., that the shape of some stimulus often appears unchanged (at least to casual observation) even when the pattern stimulates different parts of the retina. Normally, such change in stimulation with constant configuration occurs because either the pattern or the eye has moved. Theorists attempting to specify or simulate the visual nervous system have often taken this ability (the ability to respond in the same way to the same configuration) as *the* Gestalt problem, and various models have been devised with this constraint in mind (Deutsch, 1955; Dodwell, 1961, 1964; Lashley, 1942; Uhr, 1963). To the Gestaltists, the phenomenon demonstrated that the *configuration* is as much (or more) of an adequate stimulus for the visual system to respond to, as were the local patches of color, and their specific nerve energies, in the Structuralist account of the perceptual process. This is not much of an explanation, of course. But it is not clear how much there really is that we need to explain, at this level (cf. Hake, 1957, pp. 70–79; Hochberg, 1971a, pp. 449–552). Familiar patterns may simply evoke the same response when they stimulate different locations on the eye, as a result of training to make the same internal responses to the pattern in each location; there is evidence that at least some locus-specific shape recognition occurs (Wallach & Austin, 1954). And unfamiliar patterns, that have never before been seen in their entirety, may nevertheless be composed of features that are themselves familiar to a wide range of retinal locations. Furthermore, receptive fields "tuned" to respond in the same way to a given feature, regardless of its location within some relatively wide region, may further contribute to this ability to respond similarly to the same pattern in different locations, without requiring us to postulate the existence of machinery capable of transposition in a general sense.

Other catalogs of inadequacies in the Gestaltists' attempts to define and explain perceptual organization can of course be composed, and the reader is referred to Petermann (1932), for additional critical analyses. But the problems to which Gestalt theory was addressed remain central ones in any attempts to understand our perception of the world of things and objects (as contrasted with attempts to understand the responses to isolated sensory processes, to which most atheoretical study is addressed). We cannot leave the problems of perceptual organization, therefore, without considering how other attempts to deal with them continue and modify the Gestaltists' enterprise.

II. OTHER APPROACHES TO PERCEPTUAL ORGANIZATION

We have noted in passing that there are approaches to the problems of figural organization and grouping that do not depend on the idea of iso-morphic brain fields (e.g., the various "informational" approaches, the verbal encoding hypothesis, etc.). All of these are subject to most of the inadequacies of the Gestalt approach. In particular, they do not explain why the figure–ground and grouping phenomena occur; they do not encom-pass the other organizational phenomena (e.g., size-distance couplings, illusions); they do not deal with the effects of attention, except as a sep-arate and often unexplained influence.

Several other attempts to deal with perceptual organization are less subject to the list of objections given above (Section I,B). We can do no more, here, than to survey what can be retained of the Gestalt proposals, and to sketch possible alternatives for extending them.

A. What Remains of the Gestalt Contribution

To the Gestaltists, the phenomena of perceptual organization were all to be explained by reference to the underlying brain processes. Such explanation was only undertaken in detail, using a *figural current* model (Section I,A,1), to explain the two-dimentional visual figural aftereffects (which are changes in the apparent shape of some stimulus pattern, changes that occur after prolonged viewing of an inspection pattern; see Köhler and Wallach, 1944), and figural "density" (i.e., that the figure appears more "thing-like" and substantial than does the ground; see Köhler, 1920; Köhler & Wallach, 1944).* And this model would be

---

* Explanation of certain illusions of movement and shape were also made in terms of hypothetical "restraining" and "cohesive" forces (Brown & Voth, 1937; Orbison,

incapable of handling the laws of organization, the facts of three-dimensional appearance and reversible perspective, the illusions, transposition, constancies and the couplings; in fact, it can only make predictions based on retinal patterns and on distortions of these (Hochberg & Bitterman, 1951; Prentice, 1950; cf. however, Story, 1959). What is left of the specific Gestalt contribution, then, are the "facts" of figure–ground organization (i.e., observations about shape-recognition, and associated qualitative phenomena) and the "laws of organization" (i.e., a set of loose prescriptions about the way in which figure–ground segregation will occur), and no way of explaining the nature of the former nor the efficacy of the latter.

Additionally, Gestalt theory introduced some terminological changes that may be of value. For example, Helmholtz' "unconscious inference" was somewhat revised and rephrased as a set of *invariances*. Thus, instead of asserting that distance is taken into account in forming an "unconscious conclusion" about size, Koffka proposes only that a coupling exists between perceived size and perceived distance, e.g., that for a given visual angle, the ratio of apparent size to apparent distance is constant (cf. Koffka, 1935, p. 195). An isomorphic model with which to explain why perceived distance affects perceived size, however, is not available. And in fact, no adequate isomorphic model for dealing with tridimensional percepts has been devised (cf. Section I,B,3, above).

Perhaps it will be possible to construct a new form of isomorphism in terms of a hypothetical (or mental) "processing space," without trying to identify a concrete set of physiological processes that are counterparts to the things that we see in the world of experience. The interrelationships or couplings between the properties of the objects that we perceive; the effects that various inconsistencies or assymmetries in the picture of a regular object (e.g., a cube) have on its apparent extension into the third dimension (Attneave & Frost, 1969); the time that it takes to perform different kinds or amounts of mental spatial manipulation (Shepard and Metzler, 1971): measures like these may enable us to define a medium within which those perceived objects may be said to "exist" in analog form. But we do not know the limits on interobject and intraobject consistency (see Fig. 3c–e; Hochberg, 1968, 1970), and in any case this "new isomorphism" leaves the other organizational phenomena (e.g., figure–ground segregation, transposition; illusions, successive integration, selective attention) totally unexplained.

1939), without any specific physiological reference for these. Like the figural-current model, these explanations cannot be extended beyond the phenomena of two-dimensional appearance.

Perhaps we need not seek a single explanation for all (nor even for any) of the phenomena of perceptual organization (Hochberg, 1968). Perhaps a host of separate mechanisms and effects comprise the body of organizational phenomena, and perhaps there remains no core process to explain after these are taken into account.

B. On the Possibility That There Are No General Principles of Organization

The figural aftereffects, for example, were viewed by Köhler as being a fairly direct expression of (and evidence for) the isomorphic direct-current flows that he presumed to underlie figure (and object) perception (Köhler & Wallach, 1944). But their explanation may well lie in relatively local mechanisms like afterimage-persistence and lateral inhibition (Ganz, 1965, 1966a,b), and, in any case, the figural aftereffects do not relate in any way to the other organizational phenomena (e.g., to size/distance couplings, to laws of organization; to shape transposition; to illusions*), as they should if they reflected the single isomorphic process presumably underlying all these phenomena.

The illusions, in their turn, have had a multitude of particular and general theories offered to explain them (see, Hochberg, 1971a; Woodworth, 1938). The perspective theory and its variants (e.g., that perceived size is "corrected" to take distance into account, automatically and sometimes erroneously, whenever the "cues" to distance are present, whether or not any experience of distance is reported, and whether or not there really is any distance present) are presently receiving much popular attention, although they are by no means new (Thiéry, 1896; Tolman & Brunswik, 1935). Many of the illusions can be explained in such terms (Gillam, 1971; Gregory, 1963; Klix, 1963; Tausch, 1954). The adequacy both of the formulations and of the evidence for the perspective theories remain in question (Hotopf, 1966; Jahoda, 1966; Virsu, 1967; Zanforlin, 1967). But in any case, we should note that these explanations of the illusions are really only appeals to some version of the couplings (e.g., to size/distance invariance), and the latter are themselves a set of phenomena to be explained, not an explanatory mechanism.

As far as the size-distance coupling is concerned, there is still some

---

* Except for (a) an attempt to show that the decrement in the Müller-Lyer illusion is due to the operation of differential figural aftereffects generated by the pattern (Köhler & Fishback, 1950), without attempting to explain the illusion itself; and (b) an attempt to explain figure–ground reversal (Köhler, 1940), without attempting to explain figural organization or perspective reversal.

question about whether there really is a phenomenon that can be used to explain the illusions, and that itself needs explanation. Gibson (1959) has proposed that the coupling may occur because of the organization of the stimulus display and not because of any internal organizational process. Thus, the same stimulus array may provide one stimulus for distance (e.g., position in the texture-density gradient of the ground plane) and another stimulus for size (e.g., amount of texture-density gradient occluded). Presumably we learn (either ontogenetically or phylogenetically) which feature or variable of stimulation is invariantly related to any object-characteristics, like *size* or *distance,* that are important to us. Thus, amount-of-texture-gradient-occluded is invariantly related to object size (Gibson, 1959); ratio-of-local-luminance-to-surround-luminance is invariably related to object color or reflectance (cf. Wallach, 1948); and size constancy and color constancy will *normally* be achieved if our perceptions of size and of lightness are determined by the first and second of those variables, respectively. In ecologically unlikely environments (e.g., on a ground plane whose texture size increases with distance from the observer), perception will be nonveridical. But in any case, the organization is in the world, not in the observer: because the *stimulus* variables are normally coupled to each other by the physics of the situation, the perceptual responses to them will also be coupled—without any necessity for attributing the interresponse coupling to any organization inside the observer's nervous system. By this analysis, the only organization that our visual systems need is the ability to extract the relevant "higher-order variables" of stimulation, and some of this can be accomplished very simply indeed. For example, lateral interaction between a darker region and an adjacent brighter one might well account for most examples of lightness constancy (Hering, 1874, 1964; cf. Hochberg, 1971a). But we should remember that there appears to be at least some degree of inter-response coupling *even when there is no stimulus coupling at all;* for example, in the Sanford pattern of Fig. 3b, that end appears smaller which appears nearer, and when the perspective reverses, so does the ratio of the ends' apparent sizes. Similarly, a coupling between apparent rotation-direction and apparent size is obtained in the "Ames window" illusions, in situations in which the factors in Gibson's analysis should actually work against the occurrence of both the illusion and the coupling (Ames, 1951; Graham, 1963; cf. Hochberg, 1971b). And an explanation of coupling in terms of stimulus organization, even if it were not challenged by the Sanford effect and by the Ames Window, would still leave the other organizational phenomena (illusions and figural organization) to be explained by other mechanisms.

On the other hand, an attempt to explain the size-distance coupling does lead us to a possible explanatory system (and even some explanatory mechanisms) that may be able to subsume most of the organizational phenomena, without either involving us with the isomorphic brain field hypothesis on which many Gestaltists hoped to rest their explanations, or leaving us to face the array of objections and inadequacies that we noted above (Section I,B)

C. "Unconscious Conclusions," Readiness, and Organization

There is a long history of formulations to the effect that perceptions reflect the probabilities with which situations occur in the environment (Brunswik, 1934, 1952, 1956; James, 1890; von Helmholtz, 1925). As with the *minimum principle* that comprised the most succinct Gestalt attempt to summarize the phenomena of organization (Attneave, 1972; Hochberg, 1967; Koffka, 1935; Werner & Wapner, 1952), many heuristic examples with intuitive appeal can be brought to support this *ecological-probability principle,* and plausible explanatory mechanisms suggest themselves readily. Potentially, all of the organizational phenomena can be incorporated within such an explanatory system, at least at the level of heuristic example. Consider von Helmholtz' general proposal (1925) about illusions (and about perception in general).

> Thus it happens, that when the modes of stimulation of the organs of sense are unusual, incorrect ideas of objects are apt to be formed. . . . The psychic activities that lead us to infer that there in front of us at a certain place there is a certain object of a certain character, are generally not conscious activities, but unconscious ones. In their result they are equivalent to a *conclusion.* . . . [An astronomer's conclusions] are based on a conscious knowledge of the laws of optics. In the ordinary acts of vision this knowledge of optics is lacking. Still it may be permissible to speak of the psychic acts of ordinary perception as *unconscious conclusions* [p. 4] . . . . When . . . the right-hand portions of the retinas of the two eyes have been stimulated, our usual experience, repeated a million times all through life, has been that a luminous object was . . . on our left, we had to lift the hand toward the left to hide the light or to grasp the luminous object. Thus . . . the essential . . . office of a conclusion has been performed . . . simply, of course, by the unconscious processes of association of ideas going on in the dark background of our memory [p. 26].

The general principle with which to predict what we will perceive in any case is therefore that "such objects are always inspired as being present in the field of vision as would have to be there in order to produce the same impression on the nervous mechanism, the eyes being used under ordinary normal conditions" (p. 2).

Several features of the explanation are noteworthy: (1) Both the illusions and the adaptive mechanisms (the constancies) are attributed to the same mechanisms. And this list can easily be extended to include both figure–ground segregation and the "laws of organization," as we shall see shortly. (2) The rule or "conclusion" is retained because it is more often right than wrong. The inappropriate applications of the rule (e.g., illusions and figural organization), where they occur, must therefore tell us something both about the world and about the normal functioning of the organism. (3) Because any organizational phenomenon reflects some regularity in the world, it may be served by more than one process, and by very different processes. At the very least, it now appears reasonable to break the "constancies" apart into quite different kinds of mechanism, with that of lightness constancy (and brightness contrast) served predominantly by peripheral processes (e.g., lateral mechanisms). (4) To von Helmholtz, the rules are learned by "association of ideas," within the lifetime of the individual. But evolution, of course, might provide phylogenetic bases for adjustment to the world by "prewiring" the nervous system. This is most plausible in the case of lightness constancy (via lateral inhibition), but surely more complex prewirings are also possible. (5) Von Helmholtz (and most empiricists, even those of more recent vintage) were atomistic both in their units of analysis, and in their picture of the action of the nervous system. But we need not necessarily be atomistic in order to accept either the ecological-probability hypothesis, empiricism, or both. We now know that the sensory system contains neural structures of fairly sizable extent (cf. Riggs, 1971); there may be others that are even larger in extent and in generality (e.g., structures that are responsive to retina-wide gradients, to binocular disparities, etc.); and persuasive arguments have been made (Hebb, 1949, 1966) that repeated experience with any environment that contains stimulus regularities will result in the formation of structures in the central nervous system that respond as a unit to those oft-repeated features and variables.* In fact, von Helmholtz' own formulation of "unconscious inference" is more in the nature of a predictive rule to be applied by the organism, than like an accretion of associated atomistic elements (1925, p. 4), and although he asserts his *belief* that the rule really reduces to such accretion (1925, p. 26), we can drop this baggage with no discernible loss. And with this, a major distinction between his proposal and the Gestaltists' aims disappears. It must be remembered that, *formally,* the Gestalt thesis was not a nativist one, but only an antiatomistic one (Koffka, 1935, pp. 423–614; Köhler, 1960; cf. Asch, 1968; Hochberg, 1962a). (6) Perceptual organization reflects the ways in which the regularities of our environment (and of our own anatomy) *structure* the

---

* And in fact, that will even respond to objects whose features are only partially present, if the appropriate present or preceding context are provided (Hebb, 1949).

incoming stimulation, according to this approach. That is, the external and internal regularities introduce redundancies, i.e., correlations between one feature (or variable) of stimulation and another. For example, as an object approaches, many correlated changes occur in proximal stimulation: the object subtends a larger angle in the visual field; it requires an increase in the lens' accommodation and in the two eyes' convergence; it occludes other objects; it is shifted more by any parallax that occurs; etc. These changes in stimulation are not independent of one another but are constrained by the physics of the environment and by the physiology of the sensorimotor system.

In what form are these stimulus constraints reflected? The classical formulation, to which von Helmholtz subscribed, was, of course, that sensations accompany stimulation, and that any frequent stimulus correlation would be reflected in a correlation between the memories (images) of these sensations. But we should remember that, to Helmholtz, sensations were not necessarily (or even ordinarily) consciously observable (von Helmholtz, 1925, pp. 25–28), and that the term included "sensations of innervation," i.e., included *the efferent commands issued to the muscles*. So the ecological constraints may be mirrored in packets of sensations, they may be mirrored in packets of efferent commands, or mirrored in some combination of these.

How can we separate these possibilities? Introspective analyses of memory images and of perceptual organizations will not serve to dissect this question further, nor would any theory except the most naive form of structuralism lead us to expect otherwise. As our long and unsuccessful experience with the study of imagery per se has shown us, subjects' introspections about the strength and detail of their imagery is of little value in predicting how they will perform on objective tests of imagery. The latter are tasks that are designed to test the function that imagery serves in solving some assigned problem, and to assess the structure or dimensionality of the imagery used, i.e., whether it seems to be most like visual, auditory, kinesthetic, etc., information.* Analysis of the function to be served by perceptual organization, and of the nature of the information represented in such organization, are the only tools we have available.

---

* The absence of agreement between introspective and objective measures of imagery, and the harsh disagreements between investigators concerning the introspective content of imagery (Titchener, 1909; cf. Woodworth, 1938, pp. 782–790), have served as grounds for disregarding the concept of image (Brunswick, 1952). But this concept filled certain theoretical functions in the structuralist explanations of mental process; these functions still remain to be filled; and the concept has thus returned to fashion, in open guise (Neisser, 1970; Segal, 1971) as well as in trivial concealment (cf. Skinner, 1953, pp. 273ff).

D. Perceptual Organization in Function and Structure

As for the function that is served by perceptual organization, there is a traditional and continuing emphasis on its predictive function, and on the importance that that function gives it in the guidance of behavior (James, 1890; Miller, Galanter, & Pribram, 1960; Taylor, 1962; von Helmholtz, 1925). And such prediction must be particularly important in the guidance of perceptual behavior (e.g., in guiding the eye movements and the head movements by which the world is scanned) for these reasons: (a) it prepares the oculomotor system for the adjustments that will be needed to fixate any part of the visual world; (b) it allows the sensorimotor system to make effective selection of where information will be sought, i.e., it permits the viewer to fixate only those features that are needed to test (or to form) some expectancy (Hochberg, 1968); (c) by restricting the rate of incoming information to that which is needed to test an existing structure of expectations, it enables the viewer to encode and remember what would otherwise comprise an unmanageable number of separate inputs (Hochberg, 1968, 1970).

The most explicit model that seems to fit these functions is an analysis-by-synthesis view of listening to speech and reading text. As it does when applied to those perceptual tasks, an analysis-by-synthesis model applied to object-perception has the very considerable advantage of incorporating the processes of selective attention and of short-term memory right into the machinery of perception itself (Hochberg, 1970, 1973), thus dealing with the problem raised in Section I,B,1, above. And, as in the case of speech perception, it is tempting to attribute the perceptual organization of any stimulus pattern to the structure of behaviors with which the organism (and particularly its visuomotor system) is ready to respond to that pattern. This is not an eye-movement theory (nor a motor theory) of perception: organization cannot be reduced to actual eye movements, inasmuch as perception of shape, size, and distance does occur even when effective eye movements cannot be made during the stimulus presentation (Boring, 1942; Dove, 1841; Ogle & Reiher, 1962), but organization *can* be identified with the *structure of the programs of the efferent commands that would be needed to perform the oculomotor behaviors that are normally appropriate to a given stimulus pattern.* That is, we can try to identify the "plans" (Miller *et al.*, 1960) or "maps" that guide behavior directly with the readinesses to emit those behaviors. This seems both economical and non-mentalistic, and is one of the more specific meanings that we can provide to the term "expectancy," as long as we are concerned only with direction. At first glance, the qualification seems to be a minor one; all views after all, can be completely specified in terms of color and direction, and there is an old and still vigorous theory to the effect that the consciousness of direction and of two-dimensional shape *is* the set of efferent readinesses to execute whatever saccades are needed to bring each discernible point to the fovea of the eye (Festinger, Ono, Burnham, & Bamber, 1967; Lotze, 1852).

The explicitness of this model drops considerably when we consider color, or when we attempt to explain perceptual organization instead of mere apparent direction. The model can be extended, as we shall see, to explain the organizational phenomena in terms of multiple efferent readinesses, but when the model becomes more than one saccade "deep," its explicitness departs rapidly. And in any case, expectancy-testing does not in any sense *demand* a motor-plan model. For example, in Hebb's descriptive neural model, which was a deliberate and highly influential attempt to combine the best features of Gestalt and structuralist approaches, we perceive stimulus objects only when the corresponding neural processes (the processes that would be elicited by some focal features of the object's stimulus pattern) have already been "primed" by preceding or simultaneous context. This sort of *sensory-expectancy model* is much like analysis-by-synthesis in its major features, and perhaps only research on perceptual learning in early infancy could separate the two approaches in their present descriptive forms.

When we turn to the question of organizational structure both models can claim good prospects, at our present level of ignorance. As with attempts to study imagery objectively (to which, as we have seen, the problem is closely related), various methods can be devised to assess the nature of the perceptual structure: For example the subject can be required to perform tasks that would be expected to vary in one way if a specific dimension of structure is available to the subject, and not plausibly otherwise (cf. Attneave & Frost, 1969; Wallach & O'Connell, 1953; Shepard and Metzler, 1971, discussed above). Basically, such studies attempt to show that the subjects' responses to a stimulus are predicted more simply in terms of some hypothetical mediating response, or in terms of some object that is not really before him, than it can be predicted (or explained) in terms of the stimulus that is objectively presented to him (Hochberg, 1956). (Thus, in the verbal loop hypothesis discussed in Section I,A, 2(b), above, visual perceptual organization is asserted to be isomorphic to the subject's verbal mediating responses to the stimulus pattern, rather than to the stimulus pattern itself.) In effect, von Helmholtz's proposal was, as we saw, that perception is better predicted from the object that would *normally* produce the stimulus pattern that confronts the eye, in any given case, than it can be predicted from the stimulus pattern considered by itself. But Helmholtz's proposal may explain and predict perceptual organization more powerfully if we can amend it to take the following considerations into account.

In most of the classes of organizational phenomena that we have discussed, it may be argued that what is perceived is more directly isomorphic to the oculomotor behaviors that would be appropriate to the ecologically probable object than it is to the obvious measures of either the proximal or the distal stimuli, or to the various attempts at explicit brain field models. For example, it has long been noted that figures are "object-like" (Rubin, 1915, 1921). But we can be considerably more specific than that: the figure–ground properties are a good qualitative fit to what we would expect if the visuomotor system were prepared to treat peripherally viewed lines as though they were surface edges (Hochberg, 1962b, 1970, 1971a)*: For example, depth adjustments (convergence, etc.) are slower than saccades. Before it makes any saccade, the visuomotor system must therefore "decide" which of the two areas that are bounded by any line that falls in peripheral vision is a surface of definite points which can be fixated and viewed clearly without the necessity of making a further depth adjustment. This might be what it means to say that a given region is "figure." In contradistinction, the area to the other side of the line is treated as though it lies at a different distance than that for which the visuomotor system happens to be adjusted, and as though it would require the system to make a depth adjustment before any point that is fixated on it will be clearly visible. Moreover, the area is indefinite in shape because what is visible from one position may be hidden from another view by the near surface's edge, as a function of binocular and/or head-movement parallax. This may be what it means to say that a given region is "ground." Thus, figure–ground segregation may express visuomotor decisions to the effect that one surface occludes another. *And many of the laws of organization may simply be good cues as to which way occlusion or interposition occurs.*

For example, *good continuation* (Fig. 2e,r) is an indication that two segments of line bound the same surface edge, inasmuch as the likelihood is very low that any two objects' edges (e.g., *i–ii* and *ii– iii* in Fig. 2q,r) will line up within the limits of vernier acuity, which is extremely keen (Riggs, 1971).

---

*And if the visuomotor system were also prepared to treat peripherally-viewed groups of dots whose differentially distributed densities produce regions of different average luminance (e.g., when "smeared" by peripheral vision) as though they were surface-edges: consistent with this explanation of the grouping phenomena demonstrated in Fig. 2 is the recent finding by Beck and Ambler (1972) that grouping was improved when subjects were prevented from directing their attention to peripherally presented stimulus patterns.

Attempts have been made to explain many of the illusions in terms of eye movements or eye-movement readiness (cf. Coren & Festinger, 1967; Woodworth, 1938), and in terms of some form of size-distance coupling (Gregory, 1963, 1967; Tausch, 1954; Thiéry, 1896; Tolman & Brunswick, 1935), or both. Although the success of such attempts is not conclusive (Virsu, 1967; Zanforlin, 1967; cf. Hochberg, 1971a), they make the task of explaining the size-distance coupling seem doubly challenging. Gestalt theory makes no predictions about the couplings, whereas the kind of amended ecological-probability model that we have just discussed may be able to explain the size-distance and slant-shape couplings. Assume, first, that an object's perceived extent is some ratio of the saccade that will span the object, as numerator, to the depth adjustment of the visual system, as denominator: For example, assume that *apparent size = saccade angle/ cot convergence angle*. Assume, second, that when one part (i) of a pattern like Fig. 3b is fixated, the visuomotor system is prepared to make either of two mutually exclusive depth adjustments in fixating some other part (ii), and that the sets of these readinesses comprise the two alternative perceived orientations that such reversible-perspective figures evoke. The relative apparent sizes of *i* and *ii* will then vary whenever the preceived orientation reverses.

As modified, then Helmholtz's ecological-probability rule can thus, at least grossly and qualitatively, encompass size-distance couplings, all of the illusions, figural organization—in fact, those phenomena not attributable to specific factors like lateral inhibition (cf. Section II,B). But this leaves a great many questions unanswered and raises a host of new ones.

First, as to mechanisms: we have suggested that the phenomena of perceptual organization are more similar to the sets of oculomotor behaviors that would be appropriate to the ecologically probable objects whose characteristic features are presented in a given proximal stimulus pattern than they are either to the objects themselves or to any hypothetical brain fields. As a first test of this suggestion, the organizational phenomena must be examined for detailed adherence to the specific parameters that characterize the behaviors in question. But we surely cannot rest here: an appeal to behavioral readinesses imposes some responsibility to demonstrate that they exist as claimed. Overt eye movements were absolutely ruled out as explanations of shape perception and of depth perception by the fact, which we noted before, that both shape and depth can be recognized tachistoscopically. The direct-current brain processes hypothesized by Gestalt theory were not absolutely ruled out by the cortical short-circuiting experiments (Lashley, Chow, & Semmes, 1951; Sperry, Miner, & Myers, 1955), which showed that bits of gold foil and wire, placed on and in the visual cortex, failed to have any noticeable effect on monkeys' perceptual behaviors (cf. Köhler, 1965); but those experiments did indeed make the brain field models much less plausible. Similarly, the postulated oculomotor readinesses should be overtly demonstrable under suitable conditions,* else they too lose meaning and plausibility as explanatory constructs, even if they cannot be completely ruled out.

Other new problems are raised by this class of model,† and many of the old questions, left unanswered by brain-field isomorphism, remain unanswered still.‡ And in addition to the host of both new and old general questions that confront the new explanations of organization, there is the vastly larger number of specific questions that are needed to flesh those explanations in concrete and usable form.

III. IN SUMMARY AND ASSESSMENT

Gestalt theorists consolidated, defined, and called attention to a number of organizational phenomena that depend on the configuration of the stimulus, rather than on its particular point-by-point values. They proposed that (a) all or most of these phenomena were to be attributed to a single explanatory mechanism; (b) that the mechanism of "atomistic association" that structuralist theory had inherited from traditional philosophical psychology, and from nineteenth-century conceptions of physiological process, was invalid; (c) that a valid explanation of these phenomena was not to be reached by gaining further knowledge along the paths then laid out; and (d) that these phenomena reflected (were isomorphic to) electrical field processes in the brain.

---

* E.g., when the observer changes fixation from *i* to *ii* in Fig. *3b,* we would expect some identifiable and appropriate depth-adjustments to be initiated, depth-adjustments that would be different as a function of which tridimensional orientation is being perceived. Perhaps with *monocular* presentation of the figure, the latencies of binocular convergence and divergence would differ from each other as a function of figure's preceived three dimensional orientation.

† E.g., what are the acquisition rules for the schemas or structures of expectancies? How many movements "deep" are perceptuomotor plans (i.e., what is their span in time and space)? To what degree are the various readinesses that reflect the same ecological probabilities mutually coupled (e.g., do the "secondary" or pictorial depth cues indeed contribute to the same "schematic map" or program of readinesses as do accommodation, convergence, or parallax)?

‡ E.g., which organizational phenomena reflect the same level of causal process, and which ones do not (and must therefore be separated from each other in trying to formulate general explanatory mechanisms)? Which of the organizational phenomena require all parts of the pattern simultaneously present in the visual field, and which can also occur with successive input?

The field theory of brain function cannot really be maintained today. In practice, however, the brain field theory contributed little to the prediction or explanation of figure–ground segregation, or to the laws of organization which comprise the heart of the Gestalt contribution; and it contributed even less to the prediction and explanation of the other areas of perceptual organization (e.g., coupling, selective attention, illusions, transposition). Rejecting the Gestalt brain field model, however, does little to solve the problems to which the Gestaltists called attention, and whose disputed existence really comprise the bulk of our knowledge of object and event perception. (And, because we cannot return to structuralism, the problems of organization will continue to hold the center of the stage.) Alternatives to the Gestalt brain model, and to the Gestalist definition of what the problems of organization really are, have been formulated, and others are clearly possible to devise. These alternatives may be more or less satisfying as general explanations at present, depending on individual predilection, but they are as yet no better grounded in widespread and concrete fact or in specific theoretical explication than was Gestalt theory. It is not true, as has often been asserted, that Gestalt theory is tautological or a "nonexplanation": such statements are merely declarations of different theoretical or metatheoretical tastes. Although Gestalt theory remains vague in its predictions; although there are important organizational phenomena, such as the "invariances," that it really fails to consider; although it does not even explain the phenomena of figural organization that comprise its most visible argument; and although its early speculations about brain processes are clearly naive in terms of our present knowledge of brain structure and function—nevertheless, many of its demonstrations offer what appear to be both the potential foundations of a useful and applicable science of perception, and an insight into the nature of psychological and physiological process. The alternative approaches to the problems of organization may lie closer to the individual scientist's preferences, but they are at present either equally vague, or even narrower in the range of phenomena with which they deal. The Gestalt explanation of perceptual organization must be regarded as a first stage in an evolving formulation of both problem and solution, neither a closed issue nor a successful theory.

References

Ames, A. Visual perception and the rotating trapezoidal window. *Psychological Monographs,* 1951 (65, Whole No. 324).

Asch, S. Gestalt theory. In D. L. Sills (Ed.), *International encyclopedia of the social sciences.* New York: Macmillan, 1968. Pp. 158–175.

Attneave, F. Some informational aspects of visual perception. *Psychological Review,* 1954, **61,** 183–193.

Attneave, F. Symmetry, information and memory for patterns. *American Journal of Psychology*, 1955, **68**, 209–222.

Attneave, F. Physical determinants of the judged complexity of shapes. *Journal of Experimental Psychology*, 1957, **53**, 221–227.

Attneave, F. *Applications of information theory to psychology*. New York: Holt, 1959.

Attneave, F. Multistability in perception. *Scientific American*, 1971, **225**, 62–71.

Attneave, F. Representation of physical space. In A. W. Melton & E. Martin (Eds.), *Coding processes in human memory*. Washington, D.C.: V. H. Winston & Sons, 1972. Pp. 283–306.

Attneave, F., & Frost, R. The discrimination of perceived tridimensional orientation by minimum criteria. *Perception and Psychophysics*, 1969, **6**, 391–396.

Beck, J., & Ambler, B. Discriminability of differences in line-slope and in line-arrangement as a function of mask delay. *Perception and Psychophysics*, 1972, **12**, 33–38.

Bitterman, M. E., Krauskopf, J., & Hochberg, J. E. Threshold for visual form: A diffusion model. *American Journal of Psychology*, 1954, **67**, 205–219.

Boring, E. G. *Sensation and perception in the history of experimental psychology*. New York: Appleton, 1942.

Brown, J. F., & Voth A. C. The path of seen movement as a function of the vector field. *American Journal of Psychology*, 1937, **49**, 543–563.

Bruner, J. S. Personality dynamics and the process of perceiving. In R. R. Blake & Q. V. Ramsey (Eds.), *Perception: an approach to personality*. New York: Ronald Press, 1951. Pp. 121–147.

Bruner, J. S., & Postman, L. Perception cognition, and behavior. *Journal of Personality*, 1949, **18**, 14–31.

Brunswik, E. *Wahrnehmung und Gegenstandswelt: Grundlegung einer Psychologie vom Gegenstand her*. Leipzig: Deuticke, 1934.

Brunswik, E. The conceptual framework of psychology. In O. Neurath, R. Carnap, & C. Morris (Eds.), *International encyclopedia of Unified Science*. Vol. 1, No. 10, Chicago, Illinois Univ. of Chicago Press, 1952. Pp. 1–102.

Brunswik, E. *Perception and the representation design of psychological experiments*. (2nd ed.) Berkeley: Univ. of California Press, 1956.

Carmichael, L., Hogan, H. P., & Walter, A. A. An experimental study of the effect of language on the reproduction of visually perceived form. *Journal of Experimental Psychology*, 1932, **15**, 73–86.

Casperson, R. C. The visual discrimination of geometric forms. *Journal of Experimental Psychology*, 1950, **40**, 668–681.

Coren, S., & Festinger, L. An alternative view of the "Gibson normalization effect." *Perception and Psychophysics*, 1967, **2**, 621–626.

Day, R. H., Pollack, R. H., & Segrim, G. N. Figural after-effects: A critical review. *Australian Journal of Psychology*, 1959, **11**, 15–45.

Deutsch, J. A. A theory of shape recognition. *British Journal of Psychology*, 1955, **46**, 30–37.

Dodwell, P. C. Coding and learning in shape discrimination. *Psychological Review*, 1961, **68**, 373–382.

Dodwell, P. C. A coupling system for coding and learning shape discrimination. *Psychological Review*, 1964, **71**, 148–159.

Dove, H. W. Die Combination der Eindruke beider Ohren und beider Augen zu einem Eindruck. *Berliner Preussiche Akademie Wissenschaften*, 1841, 251–252.

Cited in Osgood, *Method and theory in experimental psychology.* London & New York: Oxford Univ. Press, 1953. P. 270.

Egeth, H. Selective attention. *Psychological Bulletin,* 1967, **67,** 41–57.

Festinger, L., Ono, H., Burnham, C. A., & Bamber, D. Efference and the conscious experience of perception. *Journal of Experimental Psychology, Monograph,* 1967 (Whole No. 637).

Ganz, L. Lateral inhibition and the location of visual contours: An analysis of figural aftereffects. *Vision Research,* 1965, **4,** 465–481.

Ganz, L. Is the figural aftereffect an aftereffect? *Psychological Bulletin,* 1966, **66,** 151–165. (a)

Ganz, L. The mechanism of figural aftereffect. *Psychological Review,* 1966, **73,** 128–150. (b)

Garner, W. R. *Uncertainty and structure as psychological concepts.* New York: Wiley, 1962.

Garner, W. R. To perceive is to know. *American Psychologist,* 1966, **21,** 11–19.

Garner, W. R., & Clement, D. E. Goodness of pattern and pattern uncertainty. *Journal of Verbal Learning and Verbal Behavior,* 1963, **2,** 446–452.

Gibson, J. J. Perception as a function of stimulation. In S. Koch (Ed.), *Psychology: A study of a science.* Vol. 1. New York: McGraw Hill, 1959. Pp. 456–501.

Gillam, B. A depth processing theory of the Poggendorf illusion. *Perception and Psychophysics,* 1971, **10,** 211–216.

Glanzer, M., & Clark, W. H. Accuracy of perceptual recall. An analysis of organization. *Journal of Verbal Learning and Verbal Behavior,* 1963, **1,** 289–299. (a)

Glanzer, M., & Clark W. H. The verbal loop hypothesis: Binary numbers. *Journal of Verbal Learning and Verbal Behavior,* 1963, **2,** 301–309. (b)

Glanzer, M., & Clark, W. H. The verbal loop hypothesis: Conventional figures. *American Journal of Psychology,* 1964, **77,** 621–626.

Glanzer, M., Taub, T., & Murphy R. An evaluation of three theories of figural organization. *American Journal of Psychology,* 1968, **81,** 53–66.

Goldhamer, H. The influence of area, position and brightness in the visual perception of a reversible configuration. *American Journal of Psychology,* 1934, **46,** 189–206.

Graham, C. A. Area, color and brightness difference in a reversible configuration. *Journal of General Psychology,* 1929, **2,** 470–481.

Graham, C. H. On some aspects of real and apparent visual movement. *Journal of the Optical Society of America,* 1963, **53,** 1019–1025.

Gregory, R. L. Distortion of visual space as inappropriate constancy scaling. *Nature (London),* 1963, **199,** 678–680.

Gregory, R. L. Comments on the inappropriate constancy scaling theory of the illusions and its implications. *Quarterly Journal of Experimental Psychology,* 1967, **19,** 291–323.

Haber, R. N. Nature of the effect of set on perception. *Psychological Review,* 1966, **73,** 335–351.

Hake, H. W. Contributions of psychology to the study of pattern vision. WADC Technical Report No. 57-621, Project No. 7192-71598, 1957, Wright Air Development Center, Aero Med. Lab.

Hake, H. W., Rodwan, A., & Weintraub, D. Noise reduction in perception. In K. R. Hammond (Ed.), *The psychology of Egon Brunswik,* New York: Holt, 1966. Pp. 277–316.

Hanawalt, N. G., & Demarest, I. H. The effect of verbal suggestion in the recall period upon the reproduction of visually perceived forms. *Journal of Experimental Psychology,* 1939, **25,** 159–174.

Handel, S., & Garner, W. R. The structure of visual pattern associates and pattern goodness. *Perception and Psychophysics,* 1965, **1,** 33–38.

Hebb, D. O. *The organization of behavior.* New York: Wiley, 1949.

Hebb, D. O. *A textbook of psychology.* (2nd ed.) Philadelphia, Pennsylvania: Saunders, 1966.

Helson, H., & Fehrer, E. V. The role of form in perception. *American Journal of Psychology,* 1932, **44,** 79–102.

Hering, E. Zur Lehre vom Lichtsinn. *Wiener Akademie der Wissenschaften. Mathematische-Naturwissenschaftlichte Klasse Sitzungsberichte,* 1874, **69,** 85–104.

Hering, E. Outlines of a theory of the light sense. (L. M. Hurvich & D. Jameson, translators) Cambridge, Massachusetts: Harvard Univ. Press, 1964.

Hochberg, J. Perception: Toward the recovery of a definition. *Psychological Review,* 1956, **63,** 400–405.

Hochberg, J. Effects of the Gestalt revolution: The Cornell symposium on perception. *Psychological Review,* 1957, **64,** 78–84.

Hochberg, J. Nativism and empiricism in perception. In L. Postman (Ed.), *Psychology in the making.* New York: Knopf, 1962. Pp. 255–330. (a)

Hochberg, J. The psychophysics of pictorial perception. *A-V Communication Review,* 1962, **10,** 22–54. (b)

Hochberg, J. In the mind's eye. In R. N. Haber (Ed.), *Contemporary theory and research in visual perception.* New York: Holt, 1968. Pp. 309–331.

Hochberg, J. Attention, organization and consciousness. In D. L. Mostofsky (Ed.), *Attention: Contemporary theory and analysis.* New York: Appleton, 1970. Pp. 99–124.

Hochberg, J. Color and shape. In J. W. Kling & L. A. Riggs (Eds.), *Woodworth and Schlosberg's experimental psychology.* New York: Holt, 1971. Ch. 12, pp. 395–474. (a)

Hochberg, J. Space and movement. In J. W. Kling & L. A. Riggs (Eds.), *Woodworth and Schlosberg's experimental psychology.* New York: Holt, 1971. Ch. 13, pp. 475–550. (b)

Hochberg, J. The representation of things and people. In E. H. Gombrich, J. Hochberg, & M. Black. *Art, perception and reality.* Baltimore, Maryland: Johns Hopkins Press. 1972. Pp. 47–94.

Hochberg, J., & Bitterman, M. E. Figural after-effects as a function of the retinal size of the inspection figure. *American Journal of Psychology,* 1951, **64,** 99–102.

Hochberg, J., & Brooks, V. The psychophysics of form: Reversible-perspective drawings of spatial objects. *American Journal of Psychology,* 1960, **73,** 337–354.

Hochberg, J., Gleitman, H., & MacBride, P. D. Visual thresholds as a function of simplicity of form. Proceedings of the 28th Annual Meeting of the Western Psychological Assoc. *American Psychologist,* 1948, **3,** 341–342. (Abstract)

Hochberg, J., & Hardy, D. Brightness and proximity factors in grouping. *Perceptual & Motor Skills,* 1960, **10,** 22.

Hochberg, J., & McAlister, E. A quantitative approach to figural "goodness." *Journal of Experimental Psychology,* 1953, **46,** 361–364.

Hochberg, J., & Silverstein, A. A quantitative index of stimulus similarity: Proximity vs. differences in brightness. *American Journal of Psychology,* 1956, **69,** 456–459.

Hotopf, W. H. N. The size-constancy theory of visual illusions. *British Journal of Psychology,* 1966, **57,** 307–318.

Imai, S., & Garner, W. R. Discriminability and preference for attributes in free and constrained classification. *Journal of Experimental Psychology,* 1965, **69,** 596–608.

Jahoda, G. Geometric illusions and environment: A study in Ghana. *British Journal of Psychology,* 1966, **57,** 193–199.

James, W. *Principles of psychology.* New York: Holt, 1890.

Klix, F. *Elementarenanalysen zur Psychophysik der Raumwahrnehmung.* Berlin: VEB Deutscher-Verlag der Wissenschaften, 1962.

Koffka, K. *Principles of Gestalt psychology.* New York: Harcourt, 1935.

Köhler, W. *Die physischen Gestalten in Ruhe und im stationären Zustand.* Braunschweig: Vieweg, 1920.

Köhler, W. *Dynamics in psychology.* New York: Liveright, 1940.

Köhler, W. The present situation in brain psychology. *American Psychologist,* 1958, **13,** 150–154.

Köhler, W. The mind-body problem. In S. Hook (Ed.), *Dimensions of mind.* New York: New York Univ. Press, 1960. Pp. 3–23.

Köhler, W. Unsolved problems in the field of figural after-effects. *Psychological Record,* 1965, **15,** 63–83.

Köhler, W., & Emery, D. A. Figural after-effects in the third dimension of visual space. *American Journal of Psychology,* 1947, **60,** 159–201.

Köhler, W., & Fishback, J. The destruction of the Muller-Lyer illusion in repeated trials: (1) An examination of two theories; (2) Satiation patterns and memory traces. *Journal of Experimental Psychology,* 1950, **40,** 267–281 and 398–410.

Köhler, W., & Wallach, H. Figural after-effects: An investigation of visual processes. *Proceedings of the American Philosophical Society,* 1944, **88,** 269–357.

Kopfermann, H. Psychologische Untersuchungen über die Wirkung Zwei dimensionälar Darstellungen körperlicher Gebilde. *Psychologische Forschung,* 1930, **13,** 293–364. Cited in K. Koffka, *Principles of Gestalt psychology.* New York: Harcourt, 1935. Pp. 184ff.

Künnapas, T. Experiments on figural dominance. *Journal of Experimental Psychology,* 1957, **53,** 31–39.

Lashley, K. S. The problem of cerebral organization in vision. In H. Klüver (Ed.), *Visual mechanisms. Biological symposium.* Vol. 7. Lancaster, Pa.: J. Cattell, 1942. Pp. 301–322.

Lashley, K. S., Chow, K. L., & Semmes, J. An examination of the electrical field theory of cerebral integration. *Psychological Review,* 1951, **58,** 123–136.

Lotze, R. H. *Medicinische Psychologie, oder Physiologie der Seele.* Leipzig, 1852. In R. J. Herrnstein & E. G. Boring (Eds.), *A source book in the history of psychology.* Cambridge, Massachusetts: Harvard Univ. Press, 1965. Pp. 135–140

McEwen, P. Figural after-effects. *British Journal of Psychology,* 1958, **31,** (Monogr. Suppl.).

Metzger, W. *Gesetze des Sehens.* Frankfort am Main: Kramer, 1953.

Miller, G. A., Galanter, E., & Pribram, K. *Plans and the structure of behavior.* New York: Holt, 1960.

Musatti, C. L. Forma e Assimilazione. *Archivio Italiano di Psicologia,* 1931, **9,** 65–156. Cited in R. S. Woodworth, *Experimental psychology.* New York: Holt, 1938.

Neisser, U. *Cognitive psychology.* New York: Appleton, 1967.

Neisser, U. Visual imagery as process and as experience. In J. S. Antrobus (Ed.), *Cognition and affect.* Boston, Massachusetts: Little, Brown, 1970. Pp. 159–178.

Ogle, K., & Reiher, L. Stereoscopic depth perception from after-images. *Vision Research,* 1962, **2,** 439–447.

Orbison, W. D. Shape as a function of the vector field. *American Journal of Psychology,* 1939, **52,** 31–45.

Osgood, C. *Method and theory in experimental psychology.* London & New York: Oxford Univ. Press, 1953.

Oyama, T. Figure-ground dominance as a function of sector angle, brightness, hue, and orientation. *Journal of Experimental Psychology,* 1960, **60,** 299–305.

Oyama, T., & Torii, S. Experimental studies of figure-ground reversal. I. The effects of area, voluntary control and prolonged observation in the continuous presentation. *Japanese Journal of Psychology,* 1955, **26,** 178–188 (English summary, Pp. 217–218).

Petermann, B. *The Gestalt theory and the problem of configuration.* New York: Harcourt, 1932.

Pierce, J. Determinants of threshold for form. *Psychological Bulletin,* 1963, **60,** 391–407.

Postman, L. Learned principles of organization in memory. *Psychological Monographs,* 1954, **68,** (3, Whole No. 374).

Prentice, W. C. H. The relation of distance in the apparent size of figural after-effects. *American Journal of Psychology,* 1950, **63,** 589–593.

Riggs, L. Vision. In J. W. Kling & L. Riggs (Eds.), *Woodworth and Schlosberg's experimental psychology.* (3rd ed.) New York: Holt, 1971. Ch. 9, pp. 273–314.

Riley, D. A. Memory for form. In L. Postman (Ed.), *Psychology in the making.* New York: Knopf, 1962. Ch. 7, pp. 402–465.

Rubin, E. *Synoplevede Figurer.* Copenhagen: Gyldendalske, 1915.

Rubin, E. *Visuell wahrgenommene Figuren.* Copenhagen: Gyldendalske, 1921.

Rush, G. P. Visual grouping in relation to age. *Archives of Psychology, New York,* 1937, 31, 5–95.

Schafer, R., & Murphy, G. The role of autism in a visual figure-ground relationship. *Journal of Experimental Psychology,* 1943, **32,** 335–343.

Segal, S. J. (Ed.) *Imagery: Current cognitive approaches.* New York: Academic Press, 1971.

Shepard, R. N., & Metzler, J. Mental rotation of three-dimensional objects. *Science* 1971, **171,** 701–703.

Sickles, W. R. Experimental evidence for the electrical character of visual fields derived from quantitative analysis of the Ponzo illusion. *Journal of Experimental Psychology,* 1942, **30,** 84–91.

Skinner, B. F. *Science and human behavior.* New York: Macmillan, 1953; New York: Free Press, 1965.

Solley, C. M., & Murphy G. *Development of the perceptual world.* New York: Basic Books, 1960.

Sperling, G. A. Successive approximations to a model for short-term memory. In A. F. Sanders (Ed.), *Attention and performance.* Amsterdam: North-Holland Publ., 1967. Pp. 285–292.

Sperry, R. W., Miner, N., & Myers, R. E. Visual pattern perception following subpial slicing and tantalum wire implantations in the visual cortex. *Journal of Comparative and Physiological Psychology,* 1955, **48,** 50–58.

Spitz, H. H. The present status of the Köhler-Wallach theory of satiation. *Psychological Bulletin,* 1958, **55,** 1–28.

Stenson, H. H. The physical factor structure of random forms and their judged complexity. *Perception and Psychophysics,* 1966, **1,** 303–310.

Story, A. Figural after-effects as a function of the perceived characteristics of the inspection figure. *American Journal of Psychology,* 1959, **72,** 46–56.

Tausch, R. Optische Täuschungen als artifizielle Effekte der Gestaltungsprozesse von Grössen und Formenkonstanz in der naturlichen Raumwahrnehmung. *Psychologische Forschung,* 1954, **24,** 299–348.

Taylor, J. G. *The behavioral basis of perception.* New Haven, Connecticut: Yale Univ. Press, 1962.

Thiéry, A. Ueber geometrischoptische Täuschungen. *Philosophisches Studien (Wundt),* 1896, **12,** 67–126.

Titchener, E. B. *Lectures on the experimental psychology of the thought processes.* New York: Macmillan, 1909.

Tolman, E. C., & Brunswik, E. The organism and the causal texture of the environment. *Psychological Review,* 1935, **42,** 43–77.

Uhr, L. L. "Pattern recognition" computers as models for form perception. *Psychological Bulletin,* 1963, **60,** 40–73.

Virsu, G. Contrast and confluxion as components in geometric illusions. *Quarterly Journal of Experimental Psychology,* 1967, **19,** 198–207.

Vitz, P. C., & Todd, T. C. A coded element model of the perceptual processing of sequential stimuli. *Psychological Review,* 1969, **76,** 433–449.

Vitz, P. C., & Todd, T. C. A model of the perception of simple geometric figures. *Psychological Review,* 1971, **78,** 207–228.

von Helmholtz, H. *Helmholtz's physiological optics.* Transl. from the 3rd German ed. (1909–1911) by J. P. C. Southall (Ed.) Rochester, New York: Opt. Soc. Amer., 1925.

Wallach, H. Brightness constancy and the nature of achromatic colors. *Journal of Experimental Psychology,* 1948, **38,** 310–324.

Wallach, H., & Austin, P. Recognition and the localization of visual traces. *American Journal Psychology,* 1954, **57,** 338–340.

Wallach, H., & O'Connell, D. The kinetic depth effect. *Journal of Experimental Psychology,* 1953, **45,** 205–217.

Werner, H., & Wapner, S. Toward a general theory of perception. *Psychological Review,* 1952, **59,** 324–338.

Wertheimer, M. Experimentelle Studien über das Sehen von Bewegung. *Zeitschrift fuer Psychologie,* 1912, **61,** 161–265.

Wertheimer, M. Untersuchungen zur Lehre von der Gestalt. II. *Psychologische Forschung,* 1923, **4,** 301–350.

Woodworth, R. S. *Experimental psychology.* New York: Holt, 1938.

Zanforlin, M. Some observations of Gregory's illusions. *Quarterly Journal of Experimental Psychology,* 1967, **29,** 193–197.

Chapter 11

THE LEARNING TRADITION

WM. W. ROZEBOOM

By the "learning tradition" we may understand those historical con-
tinuities of psychological research and theory which have expressly sought
to describe, systematize, and explain how past experience influences present behavior. Not included are studies in which learning principles are
presupposed as an adjunct to accounting for something else. The "tradition" actually comprises several lines of development which arose more or
less independently about a century ago and have largely preserved their
distinctive identities to this day. None of these have explicitly addressed
perceptual issues. In fact, learning theory has been home ground for
psychology's behaviorist turn against uncritical acceptance of mentalistic
concepts, and in frequent moments of extremity has been wont to repudi-
ate all internal processes alleged by common sense to mediate between stim-

ulation and behavior. Even so, any sector of psychology in which stimulus reception is a critical factor must perforce reckon with perceptual issues in one guise or another. In this review, I shall (1) chart the main channels along which learning theory has developed, (2) sketch the logic of its inherent perceptual concerns, and (3) note the more salient points at which these concerns have surfaced.

I. THE HISTORICAL STRUCTURE OF LEARNING THEORY

Modern approaches to learning have a fourfold origin in the late nineteenth century dawn of scientific psychology, corresponding to the still familiar labels "acquisition of skills," "verbal learning and memory," "classical (Pavlovian) conditioning," and "instrumental (operant) conditioning." The last two, in an uneasy union ("conditioning theory") eventually dominated by the latter, soon gave rise to behavior theory, most importantly of the Hullian, Tolmanian, and Skinnerian varieties. On the fringe of these main traditions lies work on concept formation and naturalistic/comparative accounts of animal behavior, while within recent times mathematical modeling has established a distinctive albeit still actively evolving outlook on learning issues.

A. Acquisition of Skills

As understood by ordinary language, "learning" is what one gets from education, namely, cognitive knowledge and skills (cf. any standard dictionary). Technical psychology has never seriously studied the acquisition of knowledge, though educational and phenomenalistic psychologists have toyed with it, and the current renaissance of cognitive psychology should soon alleviate this deficiency. On the other hand, the very earliest stirrings of learning research addressed the manner in which practice improves proficiency at a skillful task. Observations on transfer of training across body regions date back to the 1850's (Woodworth, 1938, p. 181), while Bryan and Harter's (1897) classic study of telegraphic-skill learning established the definitive character of this tradition. Subsequent decades saw a flurry of studies on a variety of sensorimotor skills, settling down by the 1940's to an emphasis on tracking tasks and other complex eye/hand coordinations. (For access to the history of this movement, see Fitts, 1964; Irion, 1966.) What most distinguishes "skills acquisition" from other learning traditions is the ordinary language holism of its conceptual paradigms: The dependent variable is a person's *ability* to achieve a difficult goal, as measured by the merit of his success at this on occasions when he is presumably trying to excel. And learning of an ability is construed to occur simply through *practice,* that is, by repeated doings of the relevant actions. This tradition has thus remained tied to the ordinary language view of complex psychological functioning as a purposeful flexing of mental muscles, strengthened through exercise. Technical research on skills quickly recognized that these are integrations of manifold subprocesses, and has sought to identify significant parameters of practice (notably, in its temporal pacing, intertask and part/whole transfer efficiencies, and, most recently, fine details of outcome feedback; see Bilodeau, 1969). But the specific mechanisms responsible for skillful performance have remained largely tenuous conjecture built on theoretical ideas developed elsewhere in learning theory.

B. Verbal Learning and Memory

Since the main dependent variable in Ebbinghaus's (1885) monumental creation of the verbal learning tradition was accuracy of recall, i.e., success at a memory task, he could easily have construed his results in terms that would have pioneered the learning of abilities. Or, with greater emphasis upon the cognitive aspects of memory, he might have founded an experimental psychology of knowledge. Instead, Ebbinghaus's familiarity with classical philosophic analyses of mental events induced him to view memory as a sequence of ideational elements evocatively linked by associations. The recall task he invented, serial reproduction of nonsense-syllable lists, was admirably suited to this interpretation. And when Calkins' (1894) paired-associates modification of the technique apparently gave direct experimental access to the strengths of individual item bonds, research on the acquisition and loss of rote verbal associations was off and running in a narrow-gauge rut whose nineteenth century outlook endured without essential modification until the late 1950's. Unlike the other main learning traditions, however, verbal learning has recently undergone a profound metamorphosis in keeping with psychology's new cognitive turn. Concerns for information storage, meaning, imagery, linguistic structure, and their like have become ascendant, and the long regency of elementwise associations as the area's key explanatory mechanism has nearly run its course. (See especially Tulving & Donaldson, 1972.) Having never really abandoned human mental life to begin with (except to rename ideas "words" and then conflate the afferent, central, and efferent embodiments of these), the verbal learning tradition needed only a fresh look at where it had been all along to find itself in the vanguard of psychology's return to the inner organism.

214 WM. W. ROZEBOOM

C. Classical (Pavlovian) Conditioning and Instrumental (Operant) Conditioning

Under these labels I mean to contrast not so much empirical stimulus-pairing versus response-rewarding conditioning paradigms as the distinctive, persistent outlooks on learning theory which have respectively emphasized these particular training procedures. The origins of classical conditioning in the work of Pavlov, Bechterev, and their father-figure Sechenov needs no recounting here (see Kimble, 1961, Ch. 1; Razran, 1965a). What is perhaps not so evident from latter-day integrative surveys of learning is the distance—both conceptual and historical—between this and the instrumental conditioning tradition initiated by Thorndike (1898) and later powerfully enhanced by Skinner (1938). Classical conditioning is the legacy of psychology's medical/physiological root and has been persistently physiotropic in stance. Stimuli and responses are paradigmatically conceived as proximal events, i.e., minimally patterned bursts of action in localized regions of the organism's sensorimotor surface,* and its main explanatory construct relating input to output is the reflex arc construed as neural pathway (Sherrington, 1906).

In contrast, the instrumental conditioning tradition arose in naturalistic accounts of animal behavior, notably the inspiration of Thorndike's early work by Morgan's (1894) attempted deanthropomorphizing of animal psychology), and has consistently maintained the "distal focus" (Brunswik, 1952) dictated by this origin. Paradigmatically, its stimuli are molar features of the organsm's external surround. Responses are molar changes in his environment or his relation thereto defined indifferently as to how he brings these about. And those states of the organism held responsible for S–R regularities are conceived functionally in terms of what they do rather than what they may physiologically be. As part of the behaviorist movement's general decline, instrumental conditioning has of late shown more than a trace of senescence. But in its day it had greater integrative breadth than perhaps any other sector of research psychology, investigating not merely the parameters of behavior modification through reward and punishment but also the determinants of stimulus properties other than response evocation, notably drive and reinforcement effects. Often its concern was less for learning as such than for disclosing the nature of what gets learned (cf. the varieties of "latent learning" and "transposition" experiments). In contrast, though classical conditioning has pointed toward an intriguing intricacy of detail (see Razran, 1957), it has never really *gone* anywhere except at the

---

* It is clear from Razran (1965b) that this verges upon caricature. Even so, *qua* caricature, I think it is fair enough.

hands of neurophysiologists whose studies of evocative relationships between activity patterns in localized brain regions, classically conditioned or otherwise, have begun to achieve impressive sophistication (e.g., John, 1967; Konorski, 1967; Pribram, 1971). As important as the latter development promises to be, it lies beyond the scope of this chapter.

D. Behavior Theory

Behavior theory has been the speculative phase of conditioning research, devising explanatory constructs and directions of inquiry for the latter's empirical work even while proposing to account for all organismic (or at least mammalian) behavior in those same terms. The earliest behavior theories, commencing with Watson (1914), had a classical conditioning orientation which persisted into Hull's (1943, Ch. 3) professed conception of stimulation as a pulse of energy transduced by a localized sense receptor. By the 1930's, however, the increasing dominance of empirical conditioning research by Thorndikian paradigms assimilated a similarly burgeoning awareness of motivational phenomena to produce the three great universal systems of Hull (1943, 1952), Skinner (1938, 1953), Tolman (1932, 1959), and their respective disciples. The universality of these resides in that each tried in its own distinctive way to formulate explicit principles according to which molar behavior is jointly determined by present stimulation, past experience, and motivational factors, thus covering in intent, if not necessarily in accurate detail, all primary categories of psychological events' ultimate sources other than constitutional determinants. Since much of the nomic force of Skinnerian theory is covert in its definitions of terms, the gross extent to which its implications outrun its data base, including implicit denial of many complex empirical phenomena alleged if poorly documented by commonsense psychology,* has remained largely invisible to its parti-

---

* For example, suppose in a Skinnerian variant of Type-3 latent learning (Mac-Corquodale & Meehl, 1954, p. 209) that (A) an organism o receives water reward for operant response R at a time when he is so water-satiated that no increment in his rate of R-emission then occurs. What will happen to o's R-rate if he now becomes motivated by (B_1) water deprivation or (B_2) frigid ambient temperature? According to the standard Skinnerian conception of "reinforcing stimulus," receipt of water is nonreinforcing to o in Phase A and should hence produce no increment in his R-rate under either B_1 or B_2. Even were the notion of reinforcer broadened to admit "latent" reinforcements, moreover, it would still remain to develop an account under which the latent reinforcement in Phase A might bring R under the control of water deprivation but not of temperature extremities. The important point here is not that the operant conditioning perspective is incapable of such conceptual development, but that its radical-empiricist profestations of scientific purity have to date been a mask for grotesquely overgeneralized oversimplifications.

sans. Such selective awareness, combined with the enormous technical power of operant research methodology, may well be why this special branch of the behavioristic tradition is still flourishing even if cultishly ingrown. Tolmanian expectancy theory, on the other hand, never really became respectable except as counterpoint to S–R theory, and faded from contention as S–R mediational mechanisms seemingly took over its distinctive predictions.* Meanwhile Hullian S–R theory grew with the yeoman assistance of Spence, Mowrer, Neal Miller, and numerous lesser lights to dominate not just behavior theory but virtually the whole of American psychology from the 1930's until its death around 1960 from attrition of dedication.†

Even as outline the foregoing does insufficient justice to the history of learning research. Comparative/naturalistic approaches to adaptive animal behavior, especially the Ethology movement (see Hess, 1962) and studies of animal intelligence (e.g., Maier & Schneirla, 1935), have exploited concepts and paradigms‡ not always readily assimilable to conditioning theory. Work on concept acquisition (classically Heidbreder, 1924, 1947; Hull, 1920; Vygotsky, 1934; for recent surveys, see Bourne, 1966; Pikas, 1966), though often interpreted in S–R terms, has had a sufficiently distinctive past and increasingly active present to warrant recognition as a minor tradition of its own. (Some might wish to make a similar claim for work on problem solving, but I would argue that the latter is not properly classified as "learning.") Though largely suppressed until quite recently by an inhospitable zeitgeist, a "trace" theory of memory importantly more powerful than association formation§ has been persistently voiced, albeit never effectively developed, by the Gestalt movement (see Koffka, 1935; Köhler, 1929).

*Tolmanian theory's fatal error was to remain so commonsensically intuitive for so long. By the time MacCorquodale and Meehl (1954) gave it a precision comparable to Hullian theory, the latter had already cornered the market among whatever psychologists had not already turned elsewhere for gratification for their cognitive yearnings.

† Although the failure of extant S–R theory to yield unequivocal predictions in specific applications (for reasons indicated in Section II) had become increasingly fretful to some, this should have been merely a goad to further development of this perspective. However, yearnings to get on with central mediators (proscribed by the S–R outlook though not by behavior theory in general) had been thwarted for too long. Inner events were elsewhere becoming respectable again, and although its creation in the late 1950's of incentive-motivation mechanisms (see Bolles, 1967, Ch. 12; Rozeboom, 1970, pp. 109–119 and 130–136) amply proved S–R theory to be still capable of major innovations, few any longer cared.

‡ E.g., delayed-response and double-alternation tasks.

§ Despite the burgeoning of trace notions in recent memory models, the formal differences between memory traces and associations still remain largely unappreciated. For a brief explication thereof, see Rozeboom (1969).

And most significant of all, the mathematical-models approach to learning born in 1950 as statistical learning theory (see Neimark & Estes, 1967) has increasingly come of age, most recently joining forces with fresh thinking in the verbal learning and concept formation traditions to mount the most progressive thrusts of current learning research (e.g., Norman, 1970). Even so, to the extent there exists an identifiable "learning" outlook in the history of psychology, it is characterized by the peripheralistic associationism embodied in the main traditions sketched above and epitomized by Hullian *S–R* theory.

II. PERCEPTUAL COMMITMENTS OF LEARNING THEORY

Psychology's behaviorist era expired in the late 1950's; we may choose 1960 as a convenient year from which to date the contemporary cognitive period. The visibility of perceptual concerns in learning theory depends greatly upon which side of this divide is examined. For insofar as some of behavioral research's old vitality has persisted to the present, its main post-1960 investment has been precisely in problems of "stimulus selection" which would have been taboo or at least *outré* previously. The vocabulary of perception is still rare in these studies, however, and even were it not one might well wonder what in the data justifies such talk. The foremost task of this chapter, therefore, is to indicate what, in a theory of learned behavior, can fairly be construed as a perceptual concern.

The variables which constitute a behavior system such as an environment-coupled organism can usefully be classified according to whether their values represent *states* or *process stages* (Rozeboom, 1965, p. 340ff). Process stages are the system's moment-to-moment fluctuating activities, notably stimulus reception, behavior, and the internal episodes such as perceiving and thinking whose variation as a function of input mediates the effect of stimulation upon concurrent behavior. In contrast, an organism's state properties—habits, preferences, and all others of the sort commonly thought of as "dispositions"—are relatively stable attributes which determine the parameters of the organism's process regularities at a given moment but are not themselves a function of input on that occasion even though they may well depend importantly upon the organism's past process history. For example, organism o's strength of Hullian habit ${}_{S_i}H_{R_j}$ at time t governs the probability or vigor with which o performs R_j at t in response to stimulus S_i, but is not affected by whether or not o is in fact stimulated by S_i at t even though an experience involving S_i at t will generaly modify o's subsequent ${}_{S_i}H_{R_j}$-strength.

Since "learning" comprises changes in an organism's state properties induced by experience (Rozeboom, 1965, p. 343), any account of learning perforce rests upon some view of what *are* the state variables which characterize real-life behavior systems—habits or expectancies, reflexes or rules, drives or wants, etc.—and by what deterministic or stochastic laws these control the organism's response to his environment. Such a theory may undertake perceptual commitments in two ways, one obvious and voluntary, the other neither.

The obvious way is to postulate a class of process variables, intervening causally between input and output, which are described in a way more like what common sense says about percepts than about memories, desires, or other central mediators distinguished from perception by classic mentalistic psychology. Since above all percepts are prima facie veridical inner representations of concurrent externality, a conjectured stage of central mediation is *manifestly perceptual* if it is described in terms of features $\{s_i\}$ which stand in some sort of logical correspondence to features $\{S_i\}$ of the organism's environment or his relation thereto and are such that when o's process activity contains s_i, it is highly probable that the corresponding external S_i, or another rather like it, is present in o's surround. For example, if S_i is the color *red,* the corresponding perceptual feature s_i might be described as "red-seeing," or "attending to red," or "detecting red," or more abstractly "s_{red}" in contrast to overt stimulus "S_{red}," and so on for various styles of notation or terminology in which an internal process is characterized in terms of an environmental feature considered to be its primary elicitor.

But what if one's learning theory does not acknowledge any mediational process meeting the above criterion—or even if it does, what empirical grounds could there be for such an $S–R$ heresy? It turns out that a special logical property of natural behavior systems induces a perceptual phase in any realistic theory thereof, namely, that so far as we have any reason to believe, *an organism's input receptivity is descriptively unbounded.* By this I mean that we cannot plausibly assume that any given description of o's environment at time t includes or entails all features thereof which have some effect on o at t. From this it follows, by an argument impractical to develop here,* that a theory which allows o's value of a state or process variable $\mathbf{X}$ to be partially (probabilistically) predictable at t from finite information about the input to o at t, even though $\mathbf{X}$'s stimulus determinants are descriptively unbounded, must conceive of the environment as affecting $\mathbf{X}$ through a class $\{S_i\}$ of potential stimulus features—call them *action units*

---

* See my "The logic of unboundedly reactive systems," in preparation.

with respect to **X** for *o* at *t*—which have the following properties: (*a*) The number of **X**-wise action units (i.e., stimulus features relevant to **X**) which can be simultaneously present to *o* at *t* has no fixed upper limit. (*b*) Each action unit S_i actually present to *o* at *t* generates a corresponding **X**-strength *tendency* (or distribution of tendencies over the alternative strengths possible for **X**) whose value for *o* at *t* is determined by the state parameters which modulate S_i's effect on **X**. (*c*) The actual strength (or probability distribution over alternative strengths) of **X** for *o* at *t* is a concatenation (i.e., quasi-additive function) of all the **X**-strength tendencies variously evoked by action units present to *o* at *t*.* If this abstract and highly compressed sketch of stimulus action is not immediately clear, no matter: the essential point is that a realistic behavior theory must treat the impinging environment as an indefinitely large set of stimulus components (though perhaps not logically simple ones—see Section III, J, below), each of which exacts its own behavioral influence independently of the other stimulus contributions to this. Moreover, the set of *all* environmental features conceivable by us as logically possible action units for a given organism will generally be much larger than for one reason or another it makes sense to admit as his actual action units. But if a behavior theory grants *o* fewer action units at *t* than are definable features of his environment, and especially if the theory allows the set of action units for *o* at *t* to be specified by parameters which are lawfully dependent upon antecedents of their own, it thereby adopts views on *stimulus selection* which are tantamount to a stand on perceptual issues.

Action-unit restrictions intrude into accounts of learning in two main ways. One is the theorist's presumptions, usually implicit, about what stimulus features could possibly be psychologically efficacious. For example, should we allow even in principle that the stimulus-object property of *being either-square-or-soft*, or *being non-red*, or *having remained motionless for the last 30 minutes*, or *having once been admired by a descendent of*

---

* This definition (more precisely, definition sketch) of "action unit" does not preclude the possibility that the distribution of **X**-tendency strengths generated by an action unit S_i is uniformly null as a result of null parameters in the $S_i \rightarrow$ **X** function. E.g., a stimulus feature S_i might be perceived by *o* at *t* even though, through insufficient prior conditioning of habits in which it is the stimulus term, S_i has no effect on *o*'s behavior at that time. It is also important to note that the set of action units for *o* at *t* relative to one system variable need not be the same as the action units for *o* at *t* relative to another. In particular, a stimulus feature which interacts with state property H_j to influence process **X** need not be all or part of an action unit for modifying H_j itself; while conversely, input features which affect H_j need not affect **X** at the process level. In somewhat different terms, this point has already been emphasized by Berlyne (1970, p. 31) and Lovejoy (1968, p. 15).

Benjamin Franklin can be an action unit for o at t? A priori intuitions on this score—which tend in practice to be unreasonably constrictive*—are obviated, however, by a second and more legitimate delimitation of action units, namely, by empirical diagnosis. For any general theory of how an organism's response to a present composite of action units is governed by his past experience with these or related stimulus features will inevitably fail dismally to account for the local input/output covariations observable within a brief period of a given organism's history unless the stimulus features admitted as action units for this particular o at this time are a select subset of those which must be acknowledged to account for behavior in other organisms or even in this same o at other times. Since the details of this point are rather complex, I will try to convey its essence through a brief, highly simplified example in the next three paragraphs which the reader may omit if preferred.

Suppose that our theory of learning postulates (a) that if stimulus feature S is an action unit for o at t, then for each possible behavior R, o has some strength (possibly zero) of a habit variable $S \rightarrow R$ such that occurrence of S in o's input at t interacts with $S{\rightarrow}R$ to produce an R-doing tendency whose strength is proportional to the strength of $S \rightarrow R$ for o at t; (b) that o's probability of actually doing R at t is an increasing symmetric function of all his variously aroused R-doing tendencies at t; and (c) that increases in o's $S{\rightarrow}R$ strength are caused by, and only by, experiences in which doing R while receiving S-featured input is followed by reward.† Consider, now, a set $\{T_{ij}\}$ of possible stimulation totalities which are identical in all respects except the size of a contained rectangle, the rectangle in T_{ij} being i inches tall and j inches wide. (For simplicity, I will speak as though each T_{ij} is nothing but this triangle.) For a given behavior R, we can estimate the probability of o's doing R at t in response to each T_{ij} by observing within a series of test trials commencing at t the proportion of T_{ij}-trials on which o does R.‡ If we give an o whose initial probability to R-doing is (for sim-

---

* Thus Taylor (1964, p. 131ff.) scoffs at a suggestion by Restle that the property, *having been reinforced on the last trial,* could in itself be a stimulus feature of the sort to which responses can be conditioned. But while it is indeed contrary to common sense that such properties are perceivable, this is more an intuitive acknowledgment that we do not in fact ordinarily perceive them than it is reason to hold that we cannot do so. Similarly, the failure of some psychologists to grant action-unit status to feature-absences is a demonstrable source of needlessly quirky theory (see Section III, J, below).

† Precise details of this learning principle, which when properly formulated subsumes extinction as well as acquisition, are not required here. The interested reader can find its specific Hullian version (which Hull himself never quite made completely explicit) in Rozeboom, 1970, p. 110ff.

‡ In practice, of course, empirical determination of response probabilities is nastily

plicity) the same to all the different rectangles $\{T_{ij}\}$ some experiences in which R is reinforced to a particular one of these, say $i = 4$, $j = 3$, what will be the shape of o's resultant R-response gradient over $\{T_{ij}\}$? According to our simplistic model, o's post-training probability of R-doing given stimulus totality T_{ij} should be an increasing function of the number of features common to a 4-inch by 3-inch and i-inch by j-inch rectangle which are action units for o at this time. Examples of such features by which training on T_{43} might transfer to other rectangles are (1) being 4 inches tall, (2) being 3 inches wide, (3) being both 4 inches tall and 3 inches wide, (4) having a height-to-width ratio of 1.25, (5) being at least 2 inches tall, (6) not being 5 inches wide, (7) etc. Each of these stimulus properties, if an action unit for o, contributes a distinctive R-tendency pattern to o's post-training response gradient over $\{T_{ij}\}$. Thus, if for simplicity we assume that tendency strengths come in just two grades, "some" versus "none," feature (1) as action unit contributes some R-evoking tendency to T_{ij} if $i = 4$ regardless of j, and none if $i \neq 4$; feature (2) contributes some R-tendency to T_{ij} just if $j = 3$; (3) contributes some only if both $i = 4$ and $j = 3$, i.e., only to the training stimulus; (4) contributes some to just those rectangles whose heights are 1.25 times their widths; and so on. According to the model, o's post-training R-doing probability gradient over $\{T_{ij}\}$ is a composite of these tendency patterns for just those training-stimulus features which are action units for o at this time; hence from our empirical determination of the former we can diagnose what the latter must be. For example, if $Pr(R|T_{ij})$ is equally low when $i \neq 4$ and $j \neq 3$, equally medium when $i = 4$ and $j \neq 3$ or $i \neq 4$ and $j = 3$, and high when $i = 4$ and $j = 3$, we can infer that the action units in T_{43} for o are (1), (2), and perhaps (3), whereas if $Pr(R|T_{ij})$ is high at $i = 4$ and $j = 3$, equally medium when $i = 1.25 \times j$ for $j \neq 3$, and equally low otherwise, our inference is that they are just (3) and (4).

In practice, diagnosing action units from pretraining/post-training response-surface comparisons, i.e., empirical generalization gradients, is usually complicated by inclusion in one's learning theory of some principle of *similarity induction*. According to such a principle, the more that two stimuli are alike, the more strongly does a state or process effect of one on o at t tend also to be produced by the other as well. (Some such principle is inescapable if the theory is to avoid unnatural discontinuities.) For example, a more realistic version of the present learning model would include one or both of the following postulates: $(G1)$ Reinforcement of re-

---

contaminated by the learning which occurs during the test trials. Except for a nod of appreciation to operant conditioning methodology for having vastly enhanced our technical prowess at such diagnoses, we may ignore such complications here.

sponse R to action unit S_i strengthens habit $S_j \to R$ by an amount which is an increasing function of the similarity between S_i and S_j. ($G2$) Stimulation by action unit S_i interacts with habit $S_j \to R$ to evoke an R-doing tendency which is an increasing function of both the strength of $S_j \to R$ and the similarity between S_i and S_j.* The notion of stimulus "similarity" is sufficiently vague that it readily becomes a theoretical construct characterized in part by organism-specific parameters (e.g., in Hullian theory, a *jnd* metric). So treated, "similarity" is a relation between input features as received rather than as presented and thus constitutes the theory's version of a *perceptual resemblance* factor.

Moreover, once one has acknowledged that a given feature of the environment may or may not be psychologically efficacious for a particular organism, little motive remains to require that action-unit status be all-or-none. Instead, a sophisticated behavior theory will admit a class of receptivity or "salience" parameters such that the effect of feature S_i upon system variable $\mathbf{X}$ for o at t is modulated by the degree of $\mathbf{X}$-wise salience S_i has for o at t. With empirical generalization gradients simultaneously reflecting both salience and similarity induction parameters, however, the former no longer afford *simple* diagnosis of the latter. For the degree of generalization between two stimulus complexes T_i and T_j can be due either to the salience of features which T_i and T_j have in common, to the perceptual resemblance between salient features wherein T_i and T_j differ, or to some combination of both. Considering the extensive redundancy between these two mechanisms, it is not surprising that studies of generalization seldom discriminate clearly between them.

In brief, then, a behavior theory which allows every one of the infinitely many logically distinguishable properties of an organism's environment to acquire stimulus control over his behavior in the fashion envisioned by its learning postulates would yield predictive absurdities. And once the theory admits as behaviorally consequential input only a parametrically adjustable portion of the organism's stimulus surround, it thereby acknowledges a reception selectivity which is tantamount to a perceptual stage of input processing even if perception in the strictest cognitive sense may be only a special case of this. The primary empirical phenomena which constrain a theory's treatment of input selection, moreover, are the patterns by which behavior established in one environment generalizes to another. Precisely

---

* Few accounts of stimulus generalization are articulate enough to distinguish similarity induction in learning from similarity induction in performance, i.e. type-$G1$ versus type-$G2$ inductions, or for that matter, generalization based on similarity induction from generalization due to shared action units. Hullian theory, however, was reasonably (though not completely) clear that "primary stimulus generalization" was a principle of type $G1$ rather than $G2$.

how generalization gradients are to be so interpreted depends greatly on the specifics of the theory in question. Even so, an important principle which obtains for all is that *if two complex stimulus alternatives* T_i *and* T_j *contain the same action units* (*i.e., features with nonzero salience*) *for o at t with respect to state or process variable* **X**, *then* T_i *and* T_j *are* **X**-*wise equivalent for o at t, i.e., it makes no difference for* **X** *which of the two o receives.* Conversely, if $\{T_i\}$ is a class of complex stimulus alternatives sharing a common property S, and all members of $\{T_i\}$ are **X**-wise equivalent for o at t, then it is likely that the only action units with respect to **X** for o at t contained in any member of $\{T_i\}$ are features entailed by S, especially if shifts in the **X**-effect of any one T_i generalizes completely to the others. The most explicit perceptual concerns of recent learning research have in fact centered upon just such equivalence classes.

III. LEARNING-THEORETIC ACKNOWLEDGMENTS OF PERCEPTION

Fragmentary and cryptic as they usually are, learning-theoretic encroachments upon perception do not submit to tidy organization or concisely comprehensive summary. My best efforts in this regard suggest the following gridwork of overlapping hits and near misses.

A. Perceptual Lip Service

Explicit acknowledgement of perceptual mediators by leading learning theorists has been largely vacuous, an occasional genuflection to this concept's stature elsewhere in psychology without, however, finding any distinctive role for it in the theorist's own system. Thus for Neal Miller (1959, p. 242ff.), percepts are just internal responses to which other responses can in turn be conditioned; and with a de-emphasis on centrality the same is true for Skinner (1953, pp. 140 and 275ff.). Guthrie (1959, p. 165ff.) insisted that learning theory must describe input in "perceptual terms" insomuch as only stimuli which are "meaningful" to the organism get conditioned to responses, but said nothing about the nature of such meaningfulness, how some stimuli get that way, or even how we diagnose this condition. For early Tolman (1932, p. 137), percepts were expectancies activated wholly by present input rather than through previously established means-ends-readinesses; later, Tolman (1959) spoke of perceptions merely as internal counterparts to external stimuli without equating them with expectancies or for that matter giving them any particular work to do, and suggested (1959, p. 114) that they can be detected by noting which changes in the organism's environment leaves his responding thereto undisrupted. This would amount to searching out equivalence classes of inputs, Tolman's assumption presumably being that the members of such an equivalence class would have their perceived features in common. It is important to appreciate, however, that two different stimulus configurations to which o has the same response probabilities are by no means certain to be perceptually alike to o; it is also possible that they have had the same past reinforcement contingencies for o despite a lack of shared perceptual features.

B. Sensory Integration

A more significant move to analyze perception, as a received phenomenon, in learning-theoretic terms lies in the proposal [e.g. Hilgard, 1948, p. 332; Sheffield, 1961 (quoted in Hilgard & Bower, 1966, p. 98ff.)] that perception consists in, or at least involves, evocation by a stimulus S of the total sensory complex previously aroused in o by a larger stimulus ensemble S^* containing S, the power of S to do this deriving from sensory-sensory associations acquired through past contiguity of the afferent processes respectively elicited by S and the other elements in S^*. Osgood (1957) has proposed a behavior-theoretically advanced version of this notion which melds not merely sensory components but efferent "meanings" as well, the latter being covert cue-producing responses ("representations") reliably elicited by the stimuli whose meanings they are. For Osgood, one perceives, say, an apple when some apple-produced cue (which one doesn't particularly matter) releases the whole congeries of multiple-modalitied sensations (visual, tactile, gustatory, etc.) and representational responses which have become evocatively interconnected through one's past sensorimotor transactions with apples. This of course merely updates a centuries-old tradition in mental philosophy (cf. Boring, 1942, pp. 5–9 and 14–18; Brett, 1965, esp. pp. 120 and 389), and has the considerable merit of providing for the thing-constancy and aura of expectations which seem to typify perception. There is, however, something amiss in seeking the essence of percepts in their manner of arousal rather than the character of the processes aroused. If, by experiential association, cue S evokes the same sensory or sensorimotor complex P previously aroused by a more inclusive stimulus compound S^*, it seems perverse to class P as perceptual when evoked by S but not by S^*. But if P is a percept even when evoked by a stimulus sufficient for this without learning (e.g., S^*), then sensory integration cannot be definitive thereof. And of course neither does the sensory-integration notion distinguish perception from mnemonic recall or other forms of postperceptual ideation. (Even so, see p. 236 below.)

C. Distal versus Proximal Stimulation

A learning theory which takes the organism's distal environment to be the initial stage of input can scarcely deny that events upon and within o's sensory surface ("proximal" stimulation) mediate the former's psychological import for o (see, e.g., Hull, 1943, Ch. 3). Several perceptual issues turn on this distal/proximal distinction. For one, do not the receptor processes evoked by o's distal environment qualify as "perceptual" by my first criterion in Section II, above? Prima facie, they fail at this through insufficient object-constancy, i.e., distal and proximal features do not seem to be even remotely in one-one correspondence (cf. variation in the retinal outline projected by an object of fixed shape). Actually, there is reason to think that o's perceiving of a distal feature S must be mediated by a distinctive proximal-stimulus *pattern* whose presence/absence correlates with the environmental presence/absence of S at least as highly as does occurrence/nonoccurrence of a central percept of S (cf. Gibson, 1950; also see Rozeboom, 1972a, p. 324, on rotation of axes in Brunswikian proximal-cue space). However, the learning literature has never seriously contemplated the stimulus potential of proximal patterns. Instead, there has been a historically persistent behavior-theoretic tension over the proper locusing of stimuli: Should input be defined in environmental terms, as comes most naturally to empirical studies of learning, or in terms of physiologist-approved sensory signals which, though causally closer to output, show negligible correlations with response measures when they are empirically accessible at all. The "generic" conception of stimulus so well stated by Skinner (1938, p. 33ff.) has by now fairly well carried the day, namely, that a "stimulus," properly construed, is a class of input events whose members (which can be at any distality distance from o) are interchangeable for o in their demonstrable effect on an appropriately defined response variable —in short, whatever stimulus descriptions yield the tidiest empirical regularities.* For a behavior theory which seeks to identify its stimuli in this way, the defining feature of such an equivalence class is prima facie

---

* Skinner's treatment of this matter, which I have heavily compressed and paraphrased, is essential reading for anyone seriously interested in the logic of "stimulus" and "response" concepts. Unfortunately, Skinner does not make very clear what are to be taken as the "events"—distal versus proximal, repeatable configurations versus dated occurrences (cf. MacCorquodale & Meehl, 1954, p. 220), stimulation totalities versus augmentable complexes—which compose these classes.

an action unit in the sense discussed above, and hence an implicit diagnosis by that theory of what the organism perceives. But which input features are "stimuli" for *o* at *t* is then an empirical fact about *o* at *t,* not just an arbitrary choice of units by the theorist, a fact which raises the important questions (*a*) Why is *o* at *t* responsive to this particular set of input features rather than to some alternative set?, and (*b*) When these stimuli are distal, what mechanism can produce so profound an equivalence among the diverse proximal input manifolds through which the distal feature alternatively exerts its effect? These are puzzles which learning theory has as yet scarcely considered, much less solved.

D. Orienting Behavior

When distal events are taken to be the first stage of input, *o*'s generalization patterns at *t* are due at least in part to parameters of *o*'s sensory-surface functioning. An obvious case in point is sensory capacity: whatever the objective differences between two environments, they must belong to the same equivalence class for any organism whose receptors cannot react differentially to them. For learning researchers (unlike comparative psychologists), individual differences in sensory capacity have been mainly a nuisance complication which help explain why certain promising experiments came to grief with the subjects used. Neither has learning theory paid much attention to transient reception changes of the satiation sort, probably because learning data tend to average out such effects. An appreciable body of conditioning literature has, however, recognized that organisms have an important degree of efferent control over their own sensory function. Most of this material, under the title "orienting reflex" or "orienting reaction," is Pavlovian (e.g., Lynn, 1966; Sokolov, 1963; Voronin *et al.*, 1958); but the instrumental conditioning and mathematical model traditions have also given heed to learned "observing responses" (e.g., Atkinson, 1961; Wyckoff, 1952; Zeiler & Wyckoff, 1961) whose only direct reinforcement is a stimulus change affording increased accuracy of a subsequent discrimination response. As most recent writers on the topic have noted, orientation reactions and their reception-modifying kin (see Lynn, 1966, p. 6ff.) subsume a multiplicity of mechanisms, of which Pavlov's original "investigatory reflex," positioning the sense organs to maximize pickup from a novel stimulus, is merely one. The major issues which weave through these seem to me to be the following: (*a*) *Receptor positioning versus receptor tuning.* Most easily comprehended of orienting behaviors are movements which affect the environment's receptor impingements. However, there is also increasing evidence (Sokolov, 1963; see also

Bruner, 1957) that the receptor's reaction to that impingement is itself under some central control. Whatever may be the nature of this still-obscure tuning process, it is surely similar enough to more central perceptual mechanisms that an adequate theory of the former will do much to clarify the latter as well. (*b*) *Feature specificity.* The behavioral import of orienting reactions to an environment T lies in how these affect the salience and similarity-induction parameters of T's assorted features for o at t. When distal features S_i and S_j of T are spatially well separated or emphasize different sense modalities (e.g., an object's color and temperature), orientations which enhance reception of one generally degrade it for the other. But to what extent can orientations accomplish such differential selectivity when S_i and S_j act simultaneously upon the same receptors? Is there, for example, any way for positioning to help o perceive a rectangle in terms of shape and size rather than height and width, e.g., *squat and small* versus *moderately wide but very short*? And while poor orientation can obviously blur the input difference between, say, two complex tones, to what extent and in what way following optimal ear placement might orientation further decrease the similarity between the percepts aroused by these?* The point here is that while orienting behavior clearly provides for sharpening or attenuating reception from stimulus *regions,* its contribution to specific *feature* selection is problematic. (*c*) *Perceptual preconditions of orientation.* The very operation of an orienting reaction generally requires some perceptual processing of the preorientation input. Thus a Pavlovian investigatory reflex requires registering some input feature as "unfamiliar" and, if the resulting orientation is to be properly directed, locating it within a spatial reference frame. When explanations of perceptual phenomena are sought in orienting behavior, there is a good chance that the account presupposes much of what it professes to explain.

E. Vigilance

The term "vigilance" alludes to whatever is involved in the human performance decrements generally found to occur with increasing duration of

---

* I speak of "similarity between percepts" rather than "perceived similarity" because in principle these are quite different things. Perceived similarity between distal features is perception of a supposedly objective relation between these which may or may not be closely correlated with the similarity between the internal representations of those features. Hence an adjustment which decreases the similarity between percepts need not alter how similar the corresponding external features are perceived to be. Insufficient appreciation of this distinction is, I think, an important contributor to the confusion which widely persists on the difference between generalization and discrimination (see p. 230, below).

effort on repetitive sensory tasks such as signal monitoring (see Buchner & McGrath, 1963; Davies & Tune, 1970; Mackworth, 1968). The topic is at best marginal to this chapter, for it has entered learning theory only as a minor consideration in the skills-acquisition tradition. Even so, it deserves passing mention in that insofar as vigilance is to be analyzed "in terms of emission of observing responses" (Jerison & Pickett, 1963, p. 219), it points up the prospect that orienting behavior is but an executive phase of a more complex, centrally integrated system for self-regulation of input. Moreover, the concepts of "expectancy" and "habituation" (Sections III, F, G) have figured prominently in discussions of vigilance, albeit more as presuppositions than as targets of analysis. The perceptual issues of orienting behavior cited above are equally relevant to vigilance theory.

F. Expectancy

Theoretical controversies in perception and learning find an important intersection, though with rather different emphases, in the concept of "expectancy." For perception theory, expectancies have been problematic mainly in regard to how they may help enrich bare sensory givens into full-bodied percepts (see "sensory integration," above) and bias reception sensitivity to specific input features. Learning theorists, on the other hand, have worried whether such blatantly mentalistic entities as expectancies, i.e., central "ideas" of stimuli previously contingent in experience upon their present elicitors,* could be countenanced by an objective science of psychology. The main behaviorist sponsor of expectancies was of course Tolman (1932, 1959), whose theorizing however remained unconscionably intuitive until MacCorquodale and Meehl (1954) toughened it for him far too late in the day to reclaim its fair share of behavior-theoretic respect. Meanwhile, Hullian S–R partisans had (a) engaged Tolmanian theory in a series of inconclusive "latent learning" contests (see MacCorquodale & Meehl, 1954, pp. 199–213); (b) argued in some quarters that the theoretical point at issue was empirically vacuous (Kendler, 1952); and (c) conjectured mediation-response mechanisms to explain purported phenomena of the expectancy sort. [The inconsistency between moves (b) and (c) does not seem to have occasioned much embarrassment.] I have discussed the logic of S–R expectancy surrogates at some length elsewhere (Rozeboom, 1970, pp. 103–109, 118–123, and 130–136). Their trick is to replace an

---

* The additional refinements of commonsense expectancies, specifically, as anticipations of the future in contrast to other varieties of ideation, have never been recognized by behavior theory, nor to my knowledge by modern perceptual theory, either.

unmediated sensory-sensory association $s_i \rightarrow s_j$, where s_i and s_j are the respective ideational correlates of external stimuli S_i and S_j, with an S–R association $S_i \rightarrow r_j$ in which r_j is a hypothesized mediation response productive of sensory feedback s_j' more or less functionally equivalent to S_j. Although these S–R expectancy surrogates work very badly if at all, and there never has been the slightest evidence to favor them over ideational expectancies, hard-core behavior theory eventually (post-1950) came to tolerate any and all speculations about internal arousal sequences so long as these feigned a mediation-response embodiment. Unfortunately, there has been little empirical effort to determine in detail how expectancies operate, even though behavioral paradigms for doing so with quantitative precision now exist (Rozeboom, 1958). In humans, these show that expectancies can indeed occur in considerable strength, but also that neither S–S nor S–R associations adequately characterize their nature (Rozeboom, 1967). Thus the ebb of behavior-theoretic resistance to expectancies should not be taken as uncritical support for traditional views thereof.

G. Habituation and Inhibition

An extraordinarily pervasive phenomenon at all organizational levels from firing of single neurones to linguistic and existentialistic meaning (cf. semantic satiation and *ennui*) is that exercising a psychological function creates a temporary decrement in the ease with which that process can be reactivated, such decrements being to some extent cumulative under repetitive arousal (Thompson & Spencer, 1966; also see Ratner, 1970; Razran, 1971 Ch. 3). Moreover, the considerable duration of such habituation in some instances (notably, investigatory responses and defense reactions) and the ease with which it can often be set aside (disinhibition) by a shift in context strongly suggests that habituation is not just an inherent fatigue of the process activated, but also involves some extrinsic suppressive control which can be conditioned to and modified by other processes. Few topics in learning theory have had such a schizoid history as this one. Pavlov (1927, 1928) extensively researched autonomic inhibition, but had little evident impact in this outside of Russian reflexology. The verbal-learning tradition spoke much of "inhibition" as a paraphrase for "negative transfer," but analyzed the phenomena so labeled in terms of associative competition (interference) and unlearning (cf. Underwood & Ekstrand, 1966) without appeal to inhibitory mechanisms as such. The skills-acquisition tradition had abundant need for inhibitional concepts to account for reminiscence, distribution-of-practice, and work-decrement phenomena (see McGeoch & Irion, 1952), but borrowed Hull's (1943, Ch. 16) postulated mechanisms of reactive inhibition (I_R) and conditioned inhibition ($_sI_R$) rather than exploiting its indigenous theory in this regard (see Irion, 1966, p. 19ff.). Ironically, Hull seems to have introduced these concepts mainly because he mistakenly (see Rozeboom, 1970, p. 116f.) thought them necessary to explain extinction, and failed to reconcile them with the rest of his system (see Gleitman, Nachmias, & Neisser, 1954). Even so, there is considerable evidence (see Boakes & Halliday, 1972; also Hearst, 1969; Jenkins, 1965; Kalish, 1969 p. 270ff.; Rescorla, 1969) that response inhibition is not merely a genuine phenomenon but abides by essentially the same conditioning principles that govern response activation. Moreover, while the nonPavlovian learning literature has restricted its view of the inhibitable to response processes, only the inertia of a dying S–R outlook blocks extension of inhibition theory to sensory suppressions as well. Consequently, just as expectancies provide a mechanism for selective sensory enhancement of input features, so may conditioned arousal of the inhibitory counterpart of a sensory process—a negative expectancy—be conjectured to suppress perceptual vividness of a received input feature (a mechanism for *inattention*) and perhaps also assist in perception of negative features, i.e., noticing respects in which the environment is lacking.*

H. Generalization and Discrimination

Learning theorists have never been able to decide exactly how to relate the concepts of "generalization" and "discrimination" (cf. Brown, 1965). Both terms have been variously applied to (a) the difference in strength with which, for o at t, two stimuli S_i and S_j respectively elicit a given process R, (b) the extent to which shifts in the R-evocativeness of S_i for o at t transfer to S_j, and (c) how distinct are o's central representations of S_i and S_j (see footnote, p. 227). On the whole, "generalization" has been most commonly understood as (b), while "discrimination" focuses upon (a) and (c), the last presumably determining o's capacity to discriminate in sense (a). Senses (a)–(c) are in decreasing order of empirical determinability; moreover, importantly unlike (c), (a) and (b) do not require that S_i and S_j be action units for o at t. Behavioral research on generalization and discrimination has expanded remarkably during the past two decades (cf. Gilbert & Sutherland, 1969; Kalish, 1969; Riley, 1968; Mostofsky, 1965; Terrace, 1966), with discrimination having received

* The relation between positive and negative expectancies envisioned here is analogous—and likely much more than just analogy—to the relation between positive and negative visual afterimages, and to the mutually cancellative "efference copy" and "reafference copy" of motor action (von Holst, 1954).

much the greater share of the action. No brief summary of this area's complexities can aspire to more than travesty, but its key concerns may be condensed as (1) the extent to which the sense-(b) generalization between two stimuli results from their sense-(c) discriminability or differential tuning of o's sensitivity to components of those stimuli, and (2) how far sense-(b) generalization of excitation and inhibition or some theory of feature selection can explain the development of discrimination in sense (a). Next to feature selection (see "Attention," below), most relevant of this for perception theory is the generalization/discriminability issue: Under what conditions if any do manifest changes in generalization between S_i and S_j for o reflect corresponding changes in the similarity between o's percepts of S_i and S_j, and by what mechanisms might these resemblance changes occur? Much data have accrued to show that discrimination training on two stimuli S_i and S_j (i.e., reinforcing a response to one while extinguishing it to the other) decreases generalization along multiple stimulus dimensions, most evidently those on which S_i and S_j differ but also to some extent ones on which they are alike* (e.g., Arnoult, 1957; Honig, 1969; Kalish, 1969, p. 222ff.; Thomas et al., 1970; Warren & McGonigle, 1969). Conversely, there is also some evidence that equivalence training on S_i and S_j (i.e, reinforcing both or extinguishing both to the same response) increases generalization at least between S_i and S_j themselves and perhaps between other stimuli as well (e.g., Honig, 1969). Behavior-theoretic interpretations of such learned generalization phenomena have taken two main forms, incremental (mediational) and decremental.† The former, a close kin of "sensory integration" theory (Section III, B, above), is the classic S–R approach: Under equivalence training, external stimuli S_i and S_j, with respective internal counterparts s_i and s_j, presumably become conditioned to a common response r_m whose sensory feedback s_m brings it about that the respective sensory consequences of S_i and S_j are no longer just s_i and s_j but the more similar $s_i + s_m$ and $s_j + s_m$ (Hull, 1939; Miller & Dollard, 1941, p. 74f.). Conversely, discrimination training supposedly attaches distinctively different mediation-response feedbacks s_m and s_n to S_i and S_j, respec-

---

* The concept of stimulus "dimension" has been treated confusingly in this literature through insufficient appreciation that entities located in a multidimensional space must logically have a position on *each* dimension of that space, not on just some of them, even if some values on those dimensions are anomolous. Thus when o is trained to discriminate a blank stimulus display from one containing a horizontal bar, it is misleading to say—as has become common—that the blank is not on the bar-tilt dimension at all; for *having no bar* is simply another alternative to features in the non-exhaustive set {*containing a bar tilted x degrees*}.

† Views of perceptual learning developed outside of behavior theory divide in this very same way (see Tighe & Tighe, 1966).

tively, thus revising the contrast of their sensory consequences from s_i versus s_j to $s_i + s_m$ versus $s_j + s_n$—an "acquired distinctiveness of cues" (Lawrence, 1949; Miller & Dollard, 1941, p. 73). However, despite the undeniable reality of incremental effects in, e.g., semantic generalization (cf. Feather, 1965) and verbal mediation (cf. Jenkins, 1963), it is doubtful that they suffice for learning of *sharp* discriminations and equivalences (cf. Estes, 1970, p. 171ff.; Rozeboom, 1970, p. 127ff.), or for the general steepening of generalization gradients by discrimination training (see especially Terrace, 1966, p. 307ff.). Some mechanism of the decremental sort seems also needed. In the latter, S_i and S_j are treated as complexes of features or elements, some but not all of which are common to both. Discrimination training on S_i versus S_j is then held to delete their shared elements from behavioral effectiveness (or equivalence training to delete their distinctive ones). How to achieve such differential cue neutralization, however, remains a theoretical puzzle; for, Hull's last-gasp proposals to this effect notwithstanding (Hull, 1952, p. 64ff.), orthodox $S–R$ principles cannot achieve it (Rozeboom, 1970, p. 127) unless the unwanted stimulus components can be suppressed by orienting behavior. From its earliest days, the mathematical models approach to learning has simply postulated, without attempting deeper explanation, that irrelevant stimulus elements become ineffectual (see Bush & Mosteller, 1951, and numerous later papers collected in Neimark & Estes, 1967), and esentially the same is true of more recent "attention" theories which presume reduced selection of irrelevant cues. It is, of course, only sound science to diagnose a system's functions before conjecturing mechanisms which account for them; but despite its good intentions, learning theory cannot yet authoritatively advise perception theorists how, beyond receptor orientations, organisms manage to enhance the distinctiveness of elementwise overlapping complex inputs. Even more profoundly lacking at present are nonincremental theories of how stimulus elements themselves become differentiated, i.e., how similarity induction between action units can be decreased.

I. Attention

Although problems of stimulus selection had been tugging at the sleeve of behavior theory ever since the continuity/discontinuity controversy of the 1930's (see Kimble, 1961, p. 128ff.; Riley, 1968, p. 118ff.), it took a convergence of American mathematical modeling and the British outlook on input processing (e.g., Broadbent, 1958) to coalesce assorted strands of conditioning research into what, during the mid-1960's, became an explosion of attention to attention. The evidence is now overwhelming that the degree to which a stimulus feature S_i sensorily present to o at t has the X-wise effect on o which, learning-theoretically, it ought to—i.e., the degree to which S_i has action-unit salience for o's value of X at t—is a local parameter whose empirical determinants, moreover, are to some small extent becoming identified (Egeth, 1967: Honig, 1969; Jenkins & Sainsbury, 1969; Kamin, 1969; Lovejoy, 1968; Mackintosh, 1965; Mostofsky, 1970; Sutherland & Mackintosh, 1971; Thomas, 1969, 1970; Trabasso & Bower, 1968; Wagner, 1969a, 1969b; Warren & McGonigle, 1969). Of especial importance for perception theory in this development are (a) its working of behavioral indicants of stimulus salience into a nonphenomenological data base for attention theory, and (b) its present emphasis upon stimulus selection by *dimensions* rather than by specific features. That is, the currently dominant conjecture is that when o is set at t to attend α and disregard β, α and β are *sets* of feature alternatives (e.g., *color* and *shape* rather than just *red* and *square*) such that o will be affected (unaffected) by whatever value of dimension α (β) holds for o's input at that time even if that value falls outside the region of o's past experience on that input dimension. If this thesis holds up even limitedly,* the concept of stimulus "dimension" will assume a psychonomic significance far weightier than its casual treatment to date now enables it to bear. Moreover, if stimulus selection really does turn out to parse pretty much by dimensions, it is surely not the case that all axes of the infinitely many different ways to dimensionalize stimulus space (e.g., height and width versus shape and size of stimulus objects) are equally available to o's attentive mechanisms at t. The really big perception-theoretic payoff of behavioral attention theory will come when the latter begins to account for which stimulus dimensions o *can* attend to at t.

J. Stimulus-Configurational Phenomena

In Section II, I claimed that the probability with which a stimulus complex T elicits response R in o at t must be a concatenative function of the R-tendency strengths individually evoked by those features of T which are action units for o at t. Logically necessary or not, this has in any event been a standing assumption of learning theorists. Consequently, some have found the fact that an organism can be trained to make the same response R to each of two stimulus features S_1 and S_2 when these are presented separately, yet to withhold R when S_1 and S_2 occur together, inexplicable unless the

---

* The feature-positive versus feature-negative data of Jenkins and Sainsbury (1969) make clear that the two values of a binary dimension (feature present versus feature absent) do not capture attention with equal strength.

sensory effects of concurrent input features are so modified by "afferent interaction" among them that if S_1 unaccompanied by S_2 is received as s_1, and S_2 alone as s_2, S_1 and S_2 together are received as $s_1' + s_2'$, where s_1' differs from s_1 and s_2' from s_2 (Hull, 1943, Ch. 13; Razran, 1965b). On the face of it, a principle of afferent interaction should have major perceptual implications; however, not only is the theory of this unworkable,* it has been motivated by the gratuitous presumption that logically complex environmental features cannot themselves be action units. Actually, it is not at all behavior-theoretically anomalous to suppose that o can learn to do R in response to complex features S_1-but-not-S_2 and S_2-but-not-S_1, to inhibit R in response to S_1-and-S_2 and neither-S_1-nor-S_2, and that simple features S_1 and S_2 meanwhile lose R-wise action-unit status for o through whatever mechanism attenuates the salience of irrelevant cues. That such complex stimulus "patterns" can function as cues in their own right has, in fact, become a recent mathematical modeling orthodoxy (e.g., Atkinson & Estes, 1963, p. 239ff; Estes & Hopkins, 1961).

More profound in its theoretical implications is the configural phenomenon of relational responding wherein, e.g., given a choice between stimulus object A and another object B to which A stands in relation ϕ (larger than, darker than, etc.), o's preference is strongly for A even though he has previously been reinforced for choosing B over another object C to which B is ϕ-related and has never previously encountered A (see, e.g., Hebert & Krantz, 1965; Reese, 1968). Despite the efforts of Spence, the main S–R spokesman on this point, to explain such "transpositional" phenomena as an artifact of approach and approach-inhibition tendencies generalized to new situations by similarity induction from nonrelational stimulus features of the training situation,† it is hard not to conclude that relational responding is generally real. That the class of perceivable stimulus features includes relations is not the deep issue here; most crucially at stake is some behavior-

---

* If this interaction principle were taken seriously, the enormous complexity of de facto stimulation totalities would result in no stimulus feature ever having the same sensory consequence on more than one occasion—whence the effects of past experience on present responding would have to derive from a principle of similarity induction sufficiently broad to undercut the sharp discriminability between s_1 and s_1' presumed by this hypothesis.

† For a comprehensive summary and discussion of this approach, see Reese (1968, p. 273ff.) Spence's model has to cook its generalization parameters just right if it is to obtain transposition, and cannot pretend to explain many forms of relational behavior (e.g., oddity selection and matching-to-sample); but a more penetrating criticism is that the model is not even logically coherent. The response supposedly being generalized is *approach,* but approach to what? (The only answer which even begins to make sense is "approach to the eliciting stimulus," but that works only if no more than one input feature can be evocatively effective at a time.)

theoretic recognition of perception's *propositional* composition (cf. O'Neil, 1958). When *o* chooses square *A* over square *B* by virtue of having learned to select the larger of two co-present squares, the stimulus complex which elicits this behavior is not just an unstructured aggregate of concurrent features, say *square-A + square-B + larger-than,* in which the relation is merely another isolated term. Rather, these features must occur in *o*'s input as parts of an integrated whole from which *o* can determine that *A,* not *B,* is the proper choice, i.e., a percept of *A's-being-a-larger-square-thàn-B* as distinct from *B's-being-a-larger-square-than-A.** Once one is attuned to appreciate it, the afferent importance of propositional structure (i.e., what distinguishes a grammatically well-formed sentence or sentential clause from a mere list of its constituent terms) is evident even in simultaneous discrimination between nonrelational features: If *o* learns at a T-maze choice point to pass through the gate marked with a circle and avoid the one with a triangle, his input must be something like *circle-on-left-gate, triangle-on-right-gate* rather than just *circle, triangle, left-gate, right-gate.*

In short, the responding of organisms to complex stimulus configurations makes clear that the set of action units received by *o* at *t* from his environment cannot adequately be described by a simple list of feature elements; at least some action units have a complex formal structure involving predication and probably other logical operations (e.g., negation) as well. Unfortunately, no mainstream approach to learning has yet evolved a theoretical framework within which the behavioral role of this structure can be expressed. Even so, recent efforts to interpret concept-attainment phenomena as a learning of "principles" or "rules" (e.g., Gagné, 1966; Hunt, 1962; cf. also Rozeboom, 1972b, p. 66f.) foreshadow the type of theory needed here.

K. Et Cetera

We may conclude by noting with even greater brevity than before a residuum of cryptoperceptual issues in learning theory. *Transfer of training* (cf. Ellis, 1965), which is the skills-acquisition and verbal-learning version of the concept of generalization, has an implicit concern for stimulus-selection principles through which different tasks are psychologically similar. The verbal-learning distinction between *nominal stimuli* and *functional stimuli* (cf. Underwood, 1963) emphasizes that the cues which actually

---

* See Rozeboom (1960, 1969). Alternatively, *o* might perceive, say, *A is a middle-sized square, B is a small square,* and from there infer *A is a larger square than B;* but either way, propositional structure plays an essential role in determining the input's consequences.

affect o at t are an o-determined selection from those to which o is exposed. Whatever else may be involved, the *intentional versus incidental learning* contrast (cf. McLaughlin, 1965) reflects an influence of cognitive set in human input processing. Finally, an exceptionally important notion which first appeared in surprisingly modern form at the very outset of skills-acquisition research (Bryan & Harter, 1899) and has figured in a variety of recent verbal-learning themes, notably *stimulus integration, response learning, meaningfulness and familiarity,* and *coding* (e.g., Goss, 1963; Mandler, 1954, 1967; Tulving & Madigan, 1970, p. 461ff; Underwood & Schulz, 1960), is that repeated activation of a complex sensory or sensorimotor process eventually gives it a *unitary* character which it initially lacks. This unitization is shown by various increased efficiencies in, e.g., reaction time and association formation, but perhaps most striking is the lessened demands of a unitized process on memory span and immediate recall (Melton, 1963; Miller, 1956). It does not seem inappropriate to think of complex but unitized processes as "concepts" in a sense envisioning an essential similarity between linguistic meaning units and comparable organizations wherein sensory or motor components dominate. Very likely, stimulus reception does not become full-blooded cognitive perception as we know it until rather high levels of afferent unitization are achieved. Were accounts of "sensory integration" (Section III B, above) to emphasize *integration,* rather than just the learned joint activation of sensory elements, and to seek insight into its still enigmatic psychonomic character, these might yet constitute the most satisfactory theory of perception now available.

References

Arnoult, M. D. Stimulus predifferentiation: Some generalizations and hypotheses. *Psychological Bulletin,* 1957, **54**, 339–350.

Atkinson, R. C. The observing response in discrimination learning. *Journal of Experimental Psychology,* 1961, **62**, 253–262.

Atkinson, R. C., & Estes, W. K. Stimulus sampling theory. In R. D. Luce, R. R. Bush, & E. Galanter, (Eds.), *Handbook of mathematical psychology.* Vol. II. New York: Wiley, 1963. Pp. 121–268.

Berlyne, D. E. Attention as a problem in behavior theory. In D. E. Mostofsky (Ed.), *Attention: Contemporary theory and analysis.* New York: Appleton, 1970. Pp. 25–49.

Bilodeau, E. A. (Ed.) *Principles of skill acquisition.* New York: Academic Press, 1969.

Boakes, R. A., & Halliday, M. S. (Eds.) *Inhibitional learning.* London: Academic Press, 1972.

Bolles, R. C. *Theory of motivation.* New York: Harper, 1967.

Boring, E. G. *Sensation and perception in the history of experimental psychology.* New York: Appleton, 1942.

Bourne, L. E. *Human conceptual behavior*. Rockleigh, New Jersey: Allyn & Bacon, 1966.

Brett, G. S. *Brett's history of psychology*. (Edited and abridged by R. S. Peters) Cambridge, Massachusetts: MIT Press, 1965.

Broadbent, D. E. *Perception and communication*. Oxford: Pergamon, 1958.

Brown, J. S. Generalization and discrimination. In D. I. Mostofsky (Ed.), *Stimulus generalization*. Stanford, California: Stanford Univ. Press, 1965. Pp. 7–23.

Bruner, J. S. On perceptual readiness. *Psychological Review*, 1957, **64**, 123–152.

Brunswik, E. The conceptual framework of psychology. In Neurath, O. (Ed.) International encyclopedia of unified science. Vol. 1, Part 2. Chicago, Illinois: Univ. of Chicago Press, 1952. Pp. 656–760.

Bryan, W. L. & Harter, N. Studies in the physiology and psychology of the telegraphic language. *Psychological Review*, 1897, **4**, 27–53.

Bryan, W. L., & Harter, N. Studies on the telegraphic language. The acquisition of a hierarchy of habits. *Psychological Review*, 1899, **6**, 345–375.

Buchner, D. N., & McGrath, J. J. *Vigilance: A symposium*. New York: McGraw-Hill, 1963.

Bush, R. R., & Mosteller, F. A model for simple generalization and discrimination. *Psychological Review*, 1951, **58**, 413–423.

Calkins, M. W. Association. *Psychological Review*, 1894, **1**, 476–483.

Davies, D. R., & Tune, G. S. *Human vigilance performance*. London: Staples Press, 1970.

Ebbinghaus, H. *Memory*. New York: Teachers College, Columbia University, 1913 (German original: 1885.)

Egeth, H. Selective attention. *Psychological Bulletin*, 1967, **67**, 41–56.

Ellis, H. *The transfer of learning*. New York: Macmillan, 1965.

Estes, W. K. *Learning theory and mental development*. New York: Academic Press, 1970.

Estes, W. K., & Hopkins, B. L. Acquisition and transfer in pattern-vs.-component discrimination learning. *Journal of Experimental Psychology*, 1961, **61**, 322–328.

Feather, B. W. Semantic generalization of classically conditioned responses: A review. *Psychological Bulletin*, 1965, **63**, 425–441.

Fitts, P. M. Perceptual-motor skill learning. In A. W. Melton (Ed.), *Categories of human learning*. New York: Academic Press, 1964. Pp. 244–285.

Gagné, R. M. *The learning of principles*. In H. G. Klausmeier & C. W. Harris (Eds.), *Analyses of concept learning*. New York: Academic Press, 1966 Pp. 81–95.

Gibson, J. J. *The perception of the visual world*. Boston, Massachusetts: Houghton, 1950.

Gilbert, R. M., & Sutherland, N. S. (Eds.) *Animal discrimination learning*. New York: Academic Press, 1969.

Gleitman, H., Nachmias, N., & Neisser, U. The S–R reinforcement theory of extinction. *Psychological Review*, 1954, **61**, 23–33.

Goss, A. E. Comments on Professor Noble's paper. In C. N. Cofer & B. S. Musgrave (Eds.), *Verbal behavior and learning: Problems and processes*. New York: McGraw-Hill, 1963. Pp. 119–155.

Guthrie, E. R. Association by contiguity. In S. Koch (Ed.), *Psychology: A study of a science*. Vol. 2. New York: McGraw-Hill, 1959. Pp. 158–195.

Hearst, E. Excitation, inhibition and discrimination learning. In N. J. Mackintosh & W. K. Honig (Eds.), *Fundamental issues in associative learning*. Halifax: Dalhousie Univ. Press, 1969. Pp. 1–41.

Hebert, J. A., & Krantz, D. L. Transposition: A reevaluation. *Psychological Bulletin,* 1965, **63,** 244–257.

Heidbreder, E. An experimental study of thinking. *Archives of Psychology, N.Y.,* 1924, **11,** No. 73. Pp. 1–175.

Heidbreder, E. The attainment of concepts. III. The process. *Journal of Psychology,* 1947, **24,** 93–118.

Hess, E. H. Ethology: An approach toward the complete analysis of behavior. In R. Brown, E. Galanter, E. H. Hess, & G. Mandler. *New directions in psychology.* Vol. I. New York: Holt, 1962. Pp. 159–266.

Hilgard, E. R. *Theories of learning.* (1st ed.) New York: Appleton-Century, 1948.

Hilgard, E. R., & Bower, G. H. *Theories of learning.* (3rd ed.) New York: Appleton, 1966.

Honig, W. K. Attentional factors governing the slope of the generalization gradient. In R. M. Gilbert & N. S. Sutherland (Eds.), *Animal discrimination learning.* New York: Academic Press, 1969. Pp. 35–62.

Hull, C. L. Quantitative aspects of the evolution of concepts. *Psychological Monographs,* 1920, **28**(1, Whole No. 123).

Hull, C. L. The problem of stimulus equivalence in behavior theory. *Psychological Review,* 1939, **46,** 9–30.

Hull, C. L. *Principles of behavior.* New York: Appleton, 1943.

Hull, C. L. *A behavior system.* New Haven, Connecticut: Yale Univ. Press, 1952.

Hunt, E. B. *Concept learning: An information processing problem.* New York: Wiley, 1962.

Irion, A. L. A brief history of research on the acquisition of skill. In E. A. Bilodeau, (Ed.), *Acquisition of skill.* New York: Academic Press, 1966. Pp. 1–46.

Jenkins, H. M. Generalization gradients and the concept of inhibition. In D. Mostofsky (Ed.), *Stimulus generalization.* Stanford, California: Stanford Univ. Press, 1965. Pp. 55–61.

Jenkins, H. M., & Sainsbury, R. S. The development of stimulus control through differential reinforcement. In N. J. Mackintosh & W. K. Honig (Eds.), *Fundamental issues in associative learning.* Halifax: Dalhousie Univ. Press, 1969. Pp. 123–161.

Jenkins, J. J. Mediated associations: Paradigms and situations. In C. N. Cofer & B. S. Musgrave. *Verbal behavior and learning: Problems and processes.* New York: McGraw-Hill, 1963. Pp. 210–245.

Jerison, H. J., & Pickett, R. M. Vigilance: A review and re-evaluation. *Human Factors,* 1963, **5,** 211–238.

John, E. R. *Mechanisms of memory.* New York: Academic Press, 1967.

Kalish, H. I. Stimulus generalization. In M. Marx (Ed.), *Learning: Processes.* New York: Macmillan, 1969. Pp. 207–297.

Kamin, L. J. Selective association and conditioning. In N. J. Mackintosh & W. K. Honig (Eds.), *Fundamental isues in associative learning.* Halifax: Dalhousie Univ. Press, 1969. Pp. 42–64.

Kendler, H. H. "What is learned?"—A theoretical blind alley. *Psychological Review,* 1952, **59,** 269–277.

Kimble, G. A. *Hilgard and Marquis' conditioning and learning.* New York: Appleton, 1961.

Koffka, K. *Principles of Gestalt psychology.* New York: Harcourt, 1935.

Köhler, W. *Gestalt psychology.* New York: Liveright, 1929.

Konorski, J. *Integrative activity of the brain.* Chicago, Illinois: Univ. of Chicago Press, 1967.

Lawrence, D. H. Acquired distinctiveness of cues. I. Transfer between discriminations on the basis of familiarity with the stimulus. *Journal of Experimental Psychology,* 1949, **39**, 770–784.

Lovejoy, E. *Attention in discrimination learning.* San Francisco, California: Holden-Day, 1968.

Lynn, R. *Attention, arousal and the orientation reaction.* Oxford: Pergamon, 1966.

MacCorquodale, K., & Meehl, P. E. Edward C. Tolman. In W. K. Estes, S. Koch, K. McCorquodale, P. E. Meehl, C. G. Mueller, Jr., W. W. Schoenfeld, & W. S. Verplanck, *Modern learning theory.* New York: Appleton, 1954. Pp.177–266.

McGeoch, J. A., & Irion, A. L. *The psychology of human learning.* New York: Longmans, Green, 1952.

Mackintosh, N. J. Selective attention in animal discrimination learning. *Psychological Bulletin,* 1965, **64**, 124–150.

Mackworth, J. F. Vigilance, arousal, and habituation. *Psychological Review,* 1968, **75**, 308–322.

McLaughlin, B. "Intentional" and "incidental" learning in human subjects: The role of instructions to learn and motivation. *Psychological Bulletin,* 1965, **63**, 359–376.

Maier, N. R. F., & Schneirla, T. C. *Principles of animal learning.* New York: McGraw-Hill, 1935.

Mandler, G. Response factors in human learning. *Psychological Review,* 1954, **61**, 235–244.

Mandler, G. Organization and memory. In K. W. Spence & J. T. Spence (Eds.), *The psychology of learning and motivation.* Vol. 1. New York: Academic Press, 1967. Pp. 328–372.

Melton, A. W. Implications of short-term memory for a general theory of memory. *Journal of Verbal Learning and Verbal Behavior,* 1963, **2**, 1–21.

Miller, G. The magical number seven, plus or minus two: Some limits on our capacity for processing information. *Psychological Review,* 1956, **63**, 81–97.

Miller, N. E. Liberalization of basic S–R concepts: Extensions to conflict, behavior, motivation, and social learning. In S. Koch (Ed.), *Psychology: A study of a science.* Vol. 2. New York: McGraw-Hill, 1959. Pp. 196–292.

Miller, N. E., & Dollard, J. C. *Social learning and imitation.* New Haven, Connecticut: Yale Univ. Press, 1941.

Morgan, C. L. *Introduction to comparative psychology.* London: Scott, 1894.

Mostofsky, D. I. (Ed.) *Stimulus generalization.* Stanford, California: Stanford Univ. Press, 1965.

Mostofsky, D. I. (Ed.) *Attention: Contemporary theory and analysis.* New York: Appleton, 1970.

Neimark, E. D., & Estes, W. K. (Eds.) *Stimulus sampling theory.* San Francisco, California: Holden-Day, 1967.

Norman, D. A. (Ed.) *Models of human memory.* New York: Academic Press, 1970.

O'Neil, W. M. Basic issues in perceptual theory. *Psychological Review,* 1958, **65**, 348–361.

Osgood, C. E. A behavioristic analysis of perception and language as cognitive phenomena. In J. S. Bruner, E. Brunswik, L. Festinger, F. Heider, K. F. Muenzinger, C. E. Osgood, & D. Rapaport. *Contemporary approaches to cognition.* Cambridge, Massachusetts: Harvard Univ. Press, 1957. Pp. 33–40.

Pavlov, I. P. *Conditioned reflexes.* London & New York Oxford Univ. Press, 1927.

Pavlov, I. P. *Lectures on conditioned reflexes.* New York: International Univ. Press, 1928.

Pikas, A. *Abstraction and concept formation.* Cambridge, Massachusetts: Harvard Univ. Press, 1966.

Pribram, K. H. *Language of the brain: Experimental paradoxes and principles in neuropsychology.* Englewood Cliffs, New Jersey: Prentice-Hall, 1971.

Ratner, S. C. Habituation: Research and theory. In J. H. Reynierse (Ed.), *Current issues in animal learning.* Lincoln, Nebraska: Univ. of Nebraska Press, 1970. Pp. 55–84.

Razran, G. The dominance-contiguity theory of the acquisition of classical conditioning. *Psychological Bulletin,* 1957, **54,** 1–46.

Razran, G. Russian physiologists' psychology and American experimental psychology: A historical and a systematic collation and a look into the future. *Psychological Bulletin,* 1965, **63,** 42–64. (a)

Razran, G. Empirical codifications and specific theoretical implications of compound-stimulus conditioning: Perception. In W. F. Prokasy (Ed.), *Classical conditioning: A symposium.* New York: Appleton, 1965. Pp. 226–248. (b)

Razran, G. *Mind in evolution.* Boston, Massachusetts: Houghton, 1971.

Reese, H. W. *The perception of stimulus relations.* New York: Academic Press, 1968.

Rescorla, R. A. Pavlovian conditioned inhibition. *Psychological Bulletin,* 1969, **72,** 77–94.

Riley, D. A. *Discrimination learning.* Rockleigh, New Jersey: Allyn & Bacon, 1968.

Rozeboom, W. W. "What is learned?"—An empirical enigma. *Psychological Review,* 1958, **65,** 22–33.

Rozeboom, W. W. Do stimuli elicit behavior?—A study in the logical foundations of behavioristics. *Philosophy of Science,* 1960, **27,** 159–170.

Rozeboom, W. W. The concept of "memory." *Psychological Record,* 1965, **15,** 329–368.

Rozeboom, W. W. Conditioned generalization, cognitive set, and the structure of human learning. *Journal of Verbal Learning and Verbal Behavior,* 1967, **6,** 491–500.

Rozeboom, W. W. Compositional structure in recall. *Journal of Verbal Learning and Verbal Behavior,* 1969, **8,** 622–632.

Rozeboom, W. W. The art of metascience. In J. R. Royce (Ed.), *Toward unification in psychology.* Toronto: Toronto Univ. Press, 1970. Pp. 54–163.

Rozeboom, W. W. Comments on Professor Hammond's paper. In J. R. Royce & W. W. Rozeboom (Eds.), *The psychology of knowing.* New York: Gordon & Breach, 1972. Pp. 321–327. (a)

Rozeboom, W. W. Problems in the psycho-philosophy of knowledge. In J. R. Royce & W. W. Rozeboom (Eds.), *The psychology of knowing.* New York: Gordon & Breach, 1972. Pp. 25–109. (b)

Sheffield, F. D. Theoretical considerations in the learning of complex sequential tasks from demonstration and practice. In A. A. Lumsdaine (Ed.), *Student response in programmed instruction.* Publ. No. 943. Washington, D. C.: Nat. Acad. Sci.—Nat. Res. Counc. 1961. Pp. 13–32.

Sherrington, C. *The integrative action of the nervous system.* New Haven, Connecticut: Yale Univ. Press, 1906.

Skinner, B. F. *The behavior of organisms: An experimental analysis.* New York: Appleton, 1938.

Skinner, B. F. *Science and human behavior.* New York: Macmillan, 1953.

Sokolov, E. N. *Perception and the conditioned reflex.* New York: Macmillan, 1963. (Russian original: 1958.)

Sutherland, N. S., & Mackintosh, N. J. *Mechanisms of animal discrimination learning.* New York: Academic Press, 1971.

Taylor, C. *The explanation of behavior.* London: Routledge & Kegan Paul, 1964.

Terrace, H. S. Stimulus control. In W. K. Honig (Ed.), *Operant behavior: Areas of research and application.* New York: Appleton, 1966. Pp. 271–344.

Thomas, D. R. The use of operant conditioning techniques to investigate perceptual processes in animals. In R. M. Gilbert & N. S. Sutherland (Eds.), *Animal discrimination learning.* New York: Academic Press, 1969. Pp. 1–33.

Thomas, D. R. Stimulus selection, attention, and related matters. In J. H. Reynierse, (Ed.), *Current issues in animal learning.* Lincoln, Nebraska: Univ. of Nebraska Press. 1970. Pp. 311–356.

Thomas, D. R., Freeman, F., Svinicki, J. G., Burr, D. E. S., & Lyons, J. Effects of extradimensional training on stimulus generalization. *Journal of Experimental Psychology, Monograph,* 1970, **83**, No. 1, Part 2.

Thompson, R. F., & Spencer, W. A. Habituation: A model phenomenon for the study of neuronal substrates of behavior. *Psychological Review,* 1966, **73**, 16–43.

Thorndike, E. L. Animal intelligence. An experimental study of the associative processes in animals. *Psychological Review Monograph Supplements,* 1898, **2** (**4**, whole No. 8).

Tighe, L. S., & Tighe, T. J. Discrimination learning: Two views in historical perspective. *Psychological Bulletin,* 1966, **66**, 353–370.

Tolman, E. C. *Purposive behavior in animals and men.* New York: Appleton, 1932.

Tolman, E. C. Principles of purposive behavior. In S. Koch (Ed.), *Psychology: A study of a science.* Vol. 2. New York: McGraw-Hill, 1959. Pp. 92–157.

Trabasso, T., & Bower, G. H. *Attention in learning.* New York: Wiley, 1968.

Tulving, E., & Donaldson, W. (Eds.) *Organization and memory.* New York: Academic Press, 1972.

Tulving, E., & Madigan, S. A. Memory and verbal learning. *Annual Review of Psychology,* 1970, **21**, 437–484.

Underwood, B. J. Stimulus selection in verbal learning. In C. N. Cofer & B. S. Musgrave (Eds.), *Verbal behavior and learning: Problems and processes.* New York: McGraw-Hill, 1963. Pp. 33–48.

Underwood, B. J., & Ekstrand, B. R. An analysis of some shortcomings in the interference theory of forgetting. *Psychological Review,* 1966, **73**, 540–549.

Underwood, B. J., & Schulz, R. W. *Meaningfulness and verbal learning.* Philadelphia, Pennsylvania: Lippincott, 1960.

von Holst, E. Relation between the central nervous system and the peripheral organs. *British Journal of Animal Behavior,* 1954, **2**, 89–94.

Voronin, L. G., Leontiev, A. N., Luria, A. R., Sokolov, E. N., & Vinogradova, O. S. *Orienting reflex and exploratory behavior.* Washington, D.C.: *Amer. Inst. Biol. Sci.* 1965. (Russian original; 1958.)

Vygotsky, L. S. *Thought and language.* Cambridge, Massachusetts: MIT Press, 1962. (Russian original: 1934.)

Wagner, A. R. Incidental stimuli and discrimination learning. In R. M. Gilbert & N. S. Sutherland (Eds.), *Animal discrimination learning.* New York: Academic Press, 1969. Pp. 83–111. (a)

Wagner, A. R. Stimulus validity and stimulus selection in associative learning. In N. J. Mackintosh & W. K. Honig (Eds.), *Fundamental issues in associative learning*. Halifax: Dalhousie Univ. Press, 1969. Pp. 90–122. (b)

Warren, J. M., & McGonigle, B. Attention theory and discrimination learning. In R. M. Gilbert & N. S. Sutherland (Eds.), *Animal discrimination learning*. New York: Academic Press, 1969. Pp. 113–136.

Watson, J. B. *Behavior: An introduction to comparative psychology*. New York: Holt, 1914.

Woodworth, R. S. *Experimental psychology*. (1st ed.) New York: Holt, 1938.

Wyckoff, L. B., Jr. The role of observing responses in discrimination learning. Part I. *Psychological Review*, 1952, **95**, 431–442.

Zeiler, H., & Wyckoff, L. B. Observing responses and discrimination learning. *Quarterly Journal of Experimental Psychology*, 1961, **13**, 129–140.

B. **Current Psychological Emphases**

Chapter 12

THE HISTORICAL AND PHILOSOPHICAL BACKGROUND OF COGNITIVE APPROACHES TO PSYCHOLOGY

W. J. DOWLING AND KELYN ROBERTS

"Cognitive psychology" is a fuzzy term, referring to many disparate and often conflicting approaches across the history of psychology. In spite of this fuzziness, there are certain trends and concerns which characterize this family of psychologies and which roughly distinguish them from the families called "behaviorist," "functionalist," etc. Cognitivists tend to be concerned with active, internal processes of the organism which organize ˉ experience and action. Cognitivists have tended to view the explanation of purposive action as a central concern and to emphasize the great variety of human behavior which suggests a highly creative organism. These active internal processes are generally regarded as a complex system of structures, applicable to a variety of processes such as perceiving, thinking, communicating, and acting. Many cognitivists also defend the legitimacy and value of labeling these inferred internal processes with such terms as "perception," "strategy," "belief." This raises problems of the status of phenomenologically based data—the status of conscious experience. This chapter is structured around the four characteristics of cognitive psychology: purposiveness, creativity, structure, and conscious experience. First, there is a brief review of the philosophical background from Descartes to the nineteenth century. Second, there are more detailed reviews of the history of cognition over the past 100 years grouped under the four topic headings.

For general historical perspective we have relied on Brett (1962), Boring (1950), Janet and Seoilles (1902), and Höffding (1900). The reader is referred to them for expansion on the more general points. We wish to caution the reader that this brief chapter is highly selective and falls far short of representing the complexity of the field. We have chosen to emphasize those aspects most pertinent to *Handbook of Perception* and to largely ignore some approaches to personality and clinical psychology which in a broader sense would be grouped under "cognitive" [see, e.g., Wann (1964) or Breger (1969)]. We also wish to direct the reader's attention to a burgeoning literature which goes well beyond the confines of this essay. In addition to Neisser's (1967) *Cognitive Psychology* and a new journal of that name, there are recent books by Reitman (1965), Gibson (1969), Paivio (1971), Chomsky (1972), Lindsay and Norman (1972), and earlier papers by Boring (1953), Bruner (1957), Campbell (1959), and Hebb (1960) which exemplify some of the modern conceptions of the traditional cognitive issues.

I. HISTORY OF PHILOSOPHICAL THEORIES

Contemporary cognitive theorizing begins in the seventeenth century with Descartes (1596–1650). Descartes proposed that man's nature was inherently dualistic with a mechanistic body and a creative and rational mind. In addition, he posited certain innate ideas such as the self and God. Knowledge of one's own mind was through direct experience.

Descartes' mechanism was extended to the mind by Locke (1632–1704). Locke viewed all knowledge as derived from experience and tried to eliminate the concept of innate ideas. Experience was shaped by reason but occasionally through mere contiguity irrational connections were formed in the mind. For Locke, too, knowledge of the mind was immediately given. Complex ideas, though not connected directly with experience, were constructed out of the experiential simple ideas.

Hume (1711–1776) argued that reason was subservient to the "passions," including emotion and interest in the basis of all experience (Kemp Smith, 1941). Hume thus arrived independently at the same kind of reaction against the hyperrationality of Cartesianism that Spinoza (1632–1677) had earlier formulated. But for Hume as well as the Cartesians, the mind was directly accessible to one's own conscious experience.

Both the rationalist Cartesians and the British empiricists exhibit a definite trend toward mechanistic explanations of mental phenomena. Both camps relied on direct phenomenological experience as data. Descartes,

Locke, and Hume all believed in the purposive character of reason and thinking. They differed in what they held as the sources of knowledge, its units and the types of relations that govern its organization.

Kant (1724–1804) attempted a synthesis between what he took to be Hume's skepticism and the Cartesian emphasis on disembodied reason. The result was a closely interacting system integrating experience and reason. Kant claimed that neither could exist without the other—what we know through introspection is an amalgam of the two. Kant specified the content of the mind but remained doubtful about the possibility of its objective study through science. It was in this Kantian philosophical atmosphere that Fechner (1801–1887) instituted his famous program of psychophysics, opening the way for experimental psychology. Among other things, Fechner was establishing the possibility of the mathematicized science of psychology that Kant had denied.

II. PURPOSIVENESS

The purposive, the ends-directed, the seemingly teleological aspect of behavior has been repeatedly emphasized by cognitive psychologists. Wundt was concerned with what he viewed as "mental" causative factors such a volitions and intentions (Mischel, 1970), and one could argue that it was the purposive character of these causative factors which led to distinguish so rigidly between the mental and physical types of causation. The behaviorist program swept away concern with the mental, including the purposive. However, a concern with the purposive was kept alive in European psychology by Külpe and the Würzburgers who emphasized the role of *aufgabe* as the "conscious task or purpose that precedes a course" (Boring, 1950), and by McDougall (1919) with his "conation." And in the face of the traditional American-pragmatist concern with values the strict denial of purpose could not last.

It remained for behaviorists with a cognitive orientation such as Tolman (1932) to attempt to reinstate the purposive in American psychology. Tolman wanted to accomplish this without an appeal to the conscious-experience aspect of the purposive. His program was to show the necessity of "mental" hypothetical constructs to an adequate explanation of behavior—"cognitive maps," "vicarious trial and error," "hypotheses." This necessity is succinctly captured in Campbell's (1969) observation that "when stimulus is defined as single-receptor activation, and response as muscle contraction, almost no stimulus–response consistencies are in fact found, particularly for higher animals." Cognitivists generally view Tolman's "purposive behaviorism" as a salutary influence in the experimental psychology of the 1930's, but sometimes wonder about the logic of labeling purely behavioral referents with terms having primarily conscious-experience connotations (Breger, in Breger, 1969).

The gestalt psychologists of the 1930's and 1940's also emphasized purposiveness and ends-directedness. Köhler (1938) argues from the pervasiveness of "requiredness" in conscious experience to a milder dualism than Wundt's. And the gestalt social psychologists emphasized the role of motivational "interest" in the cognitive realm (Heider, 1958) and what Asch (1952) calls the "isomorphism of experience and action."

Cognitive behaviorism and gestalt psychology coalesced with the influence of Freud in the development of Bruner's (1957) concern with the observer's determination of his own perceptual experience. Bruner saw the observer's motivational interests, purposes, and expectations as important determiners of perception, and stimulated considerable research on these particular problems.

One remaining trend important to the reinstatement of purposiveness has been the development of designs for computer analogs of complex ends-directed action. Tolman's (1951) schematic sowbug, and Ashby's (1952) homeostat prefigure Newell, Simon, and Shaw's (1958) problem-solving programs. One of the long-term trends leading to contemporary cognitive psychology has been a concern with the development of adequate mechanistic models of teleological processes in the mind. Work on computer-oriented models of perception and thinking (reviewed by Reitman, 1965) approaches this goal more closely than ever before.

III. CREATIVITY

Another facet of the active person is his creativity. For the cognitivist there does not appear to be a simple correlation between external events and actions. Instead there seems to be some mechanism or function of choice that guides and directs behavior. This mechanism can be most clearly demonstrated in linguistic cognitive structures which seem to remain relatively constant throughout the life of the person. Theories of these functions vary, but typically involve some notion of a constructive or generative rule system, combined with some meaning or deep-structure system relatively independent of the environment. This problem has appeared in many forms. As seen above, Descartes phrased the problem in terms of other minds. Language is the principal source of evidence that others are not mere machines. For the British associationists and Kant the problem becomes one of the construction of general ideas to match experience. For Wundt, creative synthesis was necessary for an experience to be formed. For Chomsky (1957, 1965, 1972) creativity is necessary to account for the richness and diversity of natural language.

Wundt regarded apperception as the fundamental act of will. Apperception had an active and a passive form coresponding to the two forms of creative activity: impulse and choice. All psychic activity involved a "creative synthesis" resulting in qualitatively new entities and not merely a summation of prior states as in physical causation (Brett, 1962).

Although Gestalt psychology was a reaction against Wundtian elementism, the Wundtian emphasis on creativity in perception was retained in the new approach. Not only is the person's own experience created psychologically but meaning and value were part of that experience, part of the emergent wholes which make up our cognitive structures. Some of these assumptions about creativity and meaning were echoed by Bartlett (1932) for whom both the situation and the ongoing psychological schema determine the emergent meaning. This approach to meaning and perception has been extended and formalized in analysis-by-synthesis models and tentative interpretation systems such as Winograd's (1972).

Chomsky (1965, 1972) and his adherents (McNeill, 1970) develop the argument for creative activity along two lines. One is that language is rule-governed and involves indefinitely many utterances; the rule system is open-ended. In order to generate and understand utterances one applies the rules in a creative, generative fashion. Second, given the enormous variability of speech data the child hears, and its disorganized presentation in the child's environment, Chomsky doubts that the child could induce an appropriate adult rule structure. Rather, the child must select among alternative innate hypotheses. It is important to realize that the two issues raised here of creativity in language use and innateness of linguistic structure may well be answered independently of each other.

IV. STRUCTURE

Insofar as the nineteenth century left psychology with conceptions of mental structure, those conceptions tended to be weak or vague. James (1890) relied almost entirely on a simple structure of associations. And even though he at times emphasized the structural complexity of wholes (for example in his point that a sentence is more than just a loose collection of words), James provided no explicit indication of what those complex structures might be. Wundt, though Blumenthal (1970) makes a good case for his interest in structural models, failed to go very far beyond simple associationism. The principal sources of structural thinking in contemporary cognition are the Gestaltists, Piaget, Chomsky, and information-processing oriented psychologists.

The Gestalt reaction to Wundt's particular kind of structuralism turned his problem upside down. For Wundt the primary sensory data were elementary color patches and the like, and the concepts of structure were invoked to explain how meaningful percepts were constructed out of them. The Gestaltists denied the primacy of the sensory elements. They asserted that the primary data of perception involved whole objects. The observer could not help committing the Wundtian "stimulus error" (Boring, 1950) by incorporating interest and meaning in his object percepts. The problem of structure thus became phrased as the problem of explaining what sorts of *physical* configurations would be perceived as whole objects or figures—"*Gestalten.*" Hence the structural principles of figural organization: similarity, contiguity and common fate.

The foregoing shows clearly the contrast between Wundt's dualism and that of the Gestaltists. Wundt made his main distinction between directly known sensations and the inferred world of object-percepts and their objects. The Gestaltists distinguished between more or less directly known object-percepts and inferred physical objects. The "more or less" occurs because what is directly known is supposed to be a brain state. Error with respect to physical objects may occur when brain states are systematically deviant, as in optical illusions (Köhler, 1938). These dualisms and a third alternative, neutral monism, are discussed below in the section on conscious experience. (Neutral monism denies the direct knowledge of anything except the conscious contents of the fleeting moment.)

Gestalt social psychology, especially that of Lewin and Heider, developed influential structural models. Lewin's (1936) life-space was a dynamic structure aimed at explaining experience and action or purposive behavior. As Campbell (1963) has shown, Lewin's phenomenological model had a great affinity to Hull's (1952) behavioristic system. The differences in emphasis are found in Lewin's here-and-now dynamism and in his incorporation of conscious experience.

Heider's (1958) models of both social interaction and cognitive consistency have had a seminal influence on both social psychology and cognitive psychology. The cognitive consistency model in particular has spawned a large amount of theory and research relevant to the study of cognition (Abelson *et al.,* 1968).

Piaget's work in outlining the developmental sequence of cognitive structures has been very influential. First, his work has stimulated much further work in the numerous content areas he has investigated, and second, his approach, method, and theory, have been emulated in other areas such as the development of syntax (Brown, 1965). However, it seems to us that his definition of "structure" (Flavell, 1971; Piaget, 1970) was unnecessarily restrictive. The defining properties of structures are "totality," "transformations," and "self-regulation." Piaget defined a "structure as a system of transformations that has laws proper to the system as a totality (in contrast to properties specific to the system's elements)" and whose operation does not go beyond the system's boundaries. The requirement that the laws of the structure should be independent of the relational properties of the elements seems arbitrary. Lewin's and Heider's models, for example, were constructed to put most of the burden of operation of the model on the properties of elements and to keep the overall rule system to a minimum, such as simply positing a "force field" in which the elements interact. This seems to us a purely semantic dispute. On the other hand, the lack of interaction between different cognitive structures would appear to be severely limiting for a complete theory of cognition.

This trend toward thorough structuralism can be seen in modern linguistics and psycholinguistics. Chomsky's (1957) structural linguistic model for syntax has had a profound impact on cognitive psychology as recent psycholinguistic reviews have shown (Miller & McNeill, 1969; McNeill, 1970).

Though modern behaviorism acknowledged the need for a structure of experience with concepts such as cognitive maps (Tolman, 1951) and habit-family hierarchies (Hull, 1952), the structural organization was assumed to be dependent on occurrences in the real world rather than on internal organizing principles. Cognitive theorists emphasized the flexible, self-organized characteristics of the organism and the great detail in which the cognitive information was cross-classified. In this regard the information-processing metaphor held theoretical promise, with the empirical evidence for limited processing capacity demanding an active recoding of information in order to bypass the seemingly narrow input and output channels. The concepts of addressable information and organized programs stored in the same memory constituted a natural metaphor of organized information and organized processes to utilize that information. Current theoretical structures range from dictionaries to hierarchical organizations to complex net organizations of both data and program (Norman, 1970; Winograd, 1972). Perhaps most importantly for the cognitive psychologist, a self-recursive program containing a hierarchy of subroutines along with organized data structures is a mechanistic account of the mind which is purposive and creative (Minsky, 1968).

V. CONSCIOUS EXPERIENCE

The status of conscious experience in psychology is bound up with a cluster of closely related problems. The most concrete of these problems is whether phenomenological reports are admissible as data. Somewhat less concrete is the question of the admissibility of terms referring to conscious experience and the mind into psychological theory. Most abstract of all are questions of the relationships between the mental and the physical. In the history of modern psychology these questions have tended to be settled with only partial independence of one another. The past century has seen a swing from strict Cartesian mind-body dualism to a behaviorist material monism. This has been followed by attempts to recapture the mental for psychology via less extreme dualisms (Köhler, 1938) or neutral monisms (Boring, 1953; Hebb, 1960).

Like Descartes, Wundt (1907) distinguished rigidly between the directness of observation of "inner" mental events and the indirection by which "outer" physical events are known. Wundt expanded this distinction between inner and outer into a whole philosophy of science in which psychology, having privileged access to the immediately known inner world, was given priority over physics which had to be satisfied with an outer world known only through a tenuous chain of inference. The privileged position of knowledge of the inner self in Wundt's epistemology led directly to his reliance on self-observation or introspection as the chief method of the science of psychology.

The American pragmatists, from the beginning intimately involved with the development of experimental psychology, had begun as early as the 1860's to chip away at the underpinnings of Wundt's position. In his 1869 essay "Questions Concerning Certain Faculties Claimed for Man," Peirce (1931–1958) denied the availability of immediate, infallible knowledge of either the outer or the inner worlds. Peirce concludes: "There is no reason for supposing a power of introspection; and, consequently, the only way of investigating a psychological question is by inference from external facts." By this Peirce meant not to deny the possibility of psychology as a science of the mind, but only its supposed privileged access to indubitable data. This position of Peirce had progressively more and more influence on the thinking of James. Traces of it can be found in the *Principles of Psychology* (James, 1890, especially Ch. 10), but it is not until the paper "Does Consciousness Exist?" that James (1904) gave the new approach to epistemology and psychological method full expression. Peirce and James both rejected the notion of directly accessible sensations, while still holding to the importance of mental experience as proper subject matter for psychology. This was an important step in the direction of a cognitive behaviorism (as Hebb, 1960, points out) since if consciousness is merely inferred in the observer himself, one's access to others' conscious experience is for scientific purposes just as direct as access to one's own conscious experience. This position of Peirce and James gained wider and wider currency under the label of neutral monism, so much so that Russell (1928) was able to say that "in the English-speaking world, the greatest influence in the overthrow of German idealism was William James."

The psychology of internal cognitive processes inferred from both conscious experience and behavior, typified by Boring's (1963) papers of the 1930's disappeared from the mainstream of American psychology during the 1920's and 1930's while two extreme positions on either side took its place. The dominant influence in the 1920's was that of radical behaviorism (Watson, 1924), a materialistic monism which denied the necessity for including mental terms in psychological theory. The rise of behaviorism can be seen as a reaction to the extreme idealism of Wundt's approach. Peirce (1931–1958), James (1904) and Russell (1921) started the rejection of Wundtian introspectionism by questioning the directness of conscious experience. The behaviorists carried this trend to the opposite extreme by denying the relevance of conscious experience entirely. A third stream of reaction to Wundt was the Gestalt movement. As noted above the Gestaltists developed a dualism between the mental and the physical. Cognitive psychology has tended toward neutral monism (Hebb, 1960) or a "cognitive behaviorism" involving an attack on the mind via converging operations (Garner, Hake, & Eriksen, 1956). However, Gestalt psychology helped maintain the balance necessary to the development of cognitive psychology during the 1930's by keeping alive a concern for internal cognitive processes and the contribution of the organism to his own experience.

A most profound influence on cognitive theory since the 1950's has come from the idea of the electronic computer as a model of mental processes. This influence has served to dispose of some of the problems of mind-body interaction which concerned psychologists of the 1890's. For example, Wundt and his contemporaries believed that the principle of conservation of energy required a strict mind-body parallelism (Boring, 1950). However, in an age when control systems operating on small amounts of energy determine the pattern of operation of huge machines have become extremely common, Wundt's reliance on physical laws of conservation appear based on a false analogy. (Low energy control of high energy systems were operative in nineteenth century factories, but the principles of such control don't seem to have sunk in at that time.) A second way in which the computer analogy has freed thinking about mind-body relations is in switching the concern from considerations about energy to considerations about flow of information. Phrased in information-processing terms, many of the old mind-brain puzzles go away. For example, while it is difficult to imagine what it would mean for a brain or computer to carry on some purely "mental" activity such as "seeing" a picture, it is easy to conceive of brain, or computer, or mind carrying out the processing of visual information and producing an appropriate response. The reasons cognitive theorists offer for using mental terms is their value as a shorthand and a heuristic. Sperry (1965) argues, as did James (1890), that the term "mind" is needed because the phemomena under discussion are too complex to be phrased meaningfully in non-mental terms.

VI. EPILOGUE

The history and philosophy of cognitive psychology is crucial to understanding the particular directions and energies psychology has possessed as a discipline and as a science. We have tried to set forth some of the important issues as we see them and, hopefully, as they have been seen by others. We would argue that much of the energy and effort within any science depends on the relation of the scientist to the domain of study. If nothing else, we seem closely connected to the study of the human mind. That this study is difficult and misleading is a truism. Certain men and theories have gripped us more than others; we can see the influence of older theories, of other ideas. There are many possibilities and ideas left to be explored that do offer understanding into how man is an active organism, setting his own path and understanding himself. There is much to be explored.

References

Abelson, R. P., Aronson, E., McGuire, W. J., Newcomb, T. M., Rosenberg, M. J., & Tannenbaum, P. H. (Eds.) *Theories of cognitive consistency: A sourcebook.* Chicago, Illinois: Rand McNally, 1968.
Asch, S. E. *Social psychology.* Englewood Cliffs, New Jersey: Prentice-Hall, 1952.
Ashby, W. R. *Design for a brain.* New York: Wiley, 1952.
Bartlett, F. *Remembering.* London & New York: Cambridge Univ. Press, 1932.
Blumenthal, A. L. *Language and psychology.* New York: Wiley, 1970.
Boring, E. G. *A history of experimental psychology.* (2nd ed.) New York: Appleton, 1950.
Boring, E. G. A history of introspection. *Psychological Bulletin,* 1953, **50,** 169–189.
Boring, E. G. In R. I. Watson & D. T. Campbell (Eds.), *History, psychology, & science: Selected papers.* New York: Wiley, 1963. Pp. 253–318.
Breger, L. (Ed.) *Clinical-cognitive psychology.* Englewood Cliffs, New Jersey: Prentice-Hall, 1969.

Brett, G. S. In R. S. Peters (Ed.), *History of psychology.* Cambridge, Massachusetts: MIT Press, 1962.

Brown, R. *Social psychology.* Glencoe, Illinois: Free Press, 1965.

Bruner, J. S. On going beyond the information given. In *Contemporary approaches to cognition.* Cambridge, Massachusetts: Harvard Univ. Press, 1957. Pp. 41–69.

Campbell, D. T. Methodological suggestions from a comparative psychology of knowledge processes. *Inquiry,* 1959, **2,** 152–182.

Campbell, D. T. Social attitudes and other acquired behavioral dispositions. In S. Koch (Ed.), *Psychology: A study of a science.* Vol. 6. New York: McGraw-Hill, 1963. Pp. 94–172.

Campbell, D. T. A phenomenology of the other one: Corrigible, hypothetical, and critical. In T. Mischel (Ed.), *Human action: Conceptual and empirical issues.* New York: Academic Press, 1969. Pp. 41–69.

Chomsky, N. *Syntactic structures.* The Hague: Mouton, 1957.

Chomsky, N. *Aspects of a theory of syntax.* Cambridge, Massachusetts: MIT Press, 1965.

Chomsky, N. *Language and mind.* New York: Harcourt, 1972.

Flavell, J. S. Stage-related properties of cognitive development. *Cognitive Psychology,* 1971, **2,** 421–450.

Garner, W. R., Hake, H. W., & Eriksen, C. W. Operationism and the concept of perception. *Psychological Review,* 1956, **63,** 149–159.

Gibson, E. J. *Principles of perceptual learning and development.* New York: Appleton, 1969.

Hebb, D. O. The American revolution. *American Psychologist,* 1960, **15,** 735–745.

Heider, F. *The psychology of interpersonal relations.* New York: Wiley, 1958.

Höffding, H. *A history of modern philosophy.* (Transl. by B. E. Meyer) New York, Macmillan, 1900.

Hull, C. L. *A behavior system.* New Haven, Connecticut: Yale Univ. Press, 1952.

James, W. *Principles of psychology.* New York: Holt, 1890.

James, W. Does "consciousness" exist? *Journal of Philosophy, Psychology and Scientific Methods,* 1904, **1**(18).

Janet, P., & Seoilles, G. *A history of the problems of philosophy.* Vol. 1. New York: Macmillan, 1902.

Kemp Smith, N. *The philosophy of David Hume.* London & New York: Cambridge Univ. Press, 1941.

Köhler, W. *The place of value in the world of facts.* New York: Liveright, 1938.

Lewin, K. *Principles of topological psychology.* New York: McGraw-Hill, 1936.

Lindsay, P. H., & Norman, D. A. *Human information processing.* New York: Academic Press, 1972.

McDougall, W. *Introduction to social psychology.* London: Methuen, 1919.

McNeill, D. The development of language. In P. A. Mussen (Ed.), *Carmichael's manual of child psychology.* New York: Wiley, 1970. Pp. 1061–1162.

Miller, G. A., & McNeill, D. Psycholinguistics. In G. Lindsey & E. Aronson (Eds.), *Handbook of social psychology.* Vol. 3. Reading, Massachusetts: Addison-Wesley, 1969. Pp. 666–794.

Minsky, M. *Semantic information processing.* Cambridge, Massachusetts: MIT Press, 1968.

Mischel, T. Wundt and the conceptual foundations of psychology. *Philosophy and Phenomenological Research,* 1970, **31,** 1–26.

Neisser, U. *Cognitive psychology.* New York: Appleton, 1967.

Newell, A., Simon, H. A., & Shaw, J. C. Elements of a theory of human problem solving. *Psychological Review,* 1958, **65,** 151–166.

Norman, D. A. (Ed.) *Models of human memory.* New York: Academic Press, 1970.

Paivio, A. *Imagery and verbal processes.* New York: Holt, 1971.

Peirce, C. S. *Collected papers.* C. Hartshorne & P. Weiss (Eds.), Vols. 1–6; A. W. Burks (Ed.), Vols. 7–8. Cambridge, Massachusetts: Harvard Univ. Press, 1931–1958.

Piaget, J. *Structuralism.* (Transl. by C. Maschler) New York: Harper, 1970.

Reitman, W. R. *Cognition and thought.* New York: Wiley, 1965.

Russell, B. *The analysis of mind.* London: Allen & Unwin, 1921.

Russell, B. *Sceptical essays.* London: Allen & Unwin, 1928.

Sperry, R. W. Mind, brain and humanist values. In J. R. Platt (Ed.), *New views on the nature of man.* Chicago, Illinois: Univ. of Chicago Press, 1965. Pp. 71–92.

Tolman, E. C. *Purposive behavior in animals and men.* New York: Appleton, 1932.

Tolman, E. C. *Behavior and psychological man.* Berkeley: Univ. of California Press, 1951.

Wann, T. W. *Behaviorism and phenomenology.* Chicago, Illinois: Univ. of Chicago Press, 1964.

Watson, J. B. *Behaviorism.* New York: Norton, 1924.

Winograd, T. Understanding natural language. *Cognitve Psychology,* 1972, **3**(3).

Wundt, W. *Outlines of psychology.* (Transl. by C. H. Judd) New York: G. E. Stee-hert & Co., 1907.

Chapter 13

CHOOSING A PARADIGM FOR PERCEPTION

RICHARD L. GREGORY

I. INTRODUCTION

The strange fact that we can perceive external objects raises questions which are related to central issues in the philosophy of science. By comparing strategies by which sensory data are used for cognition with the use of data in science, we may find that the explicit methods of science can illuminate the processes of perception. A basic mystery is how sensory patterns give rise to perceptions far richer (and yet generally appropriate) than available sensory data. If we regarded perceptions as internal patterns, formally equivalent to the monitored shapes of perceived objects and no more, then this essential problem would not arise. Perceptions then would be like pictures, much as in a camera, related by geometrical transforms to profiles and surface texture of objects available to the senses. This is very much the view of perception taken by the Gestalt school, especially by Köhler (1920), who supposed that there are physical brain traces, related isomorphically to the shapes of perceived external objects. Circular objects were supposed to give circular traces, square objects square-shaped traces, and so on. This supposed direct correspondence of external characteristics with scaled down but essentially similar brain states, is to say that we have diminished replicas of reality in our heads. It is to say that for every house we see there is, while seeing it, a tiny toy house formed of electrical potentials in the brain. However, the retinal image (and here we may consider viewing with a single eye) will be flat but the brain model is supposed to be three-dimensional; so already the perception is going beyond the given data, by some process already starting to look mysterious. When we consider seeing a house with a green roof, are we to suppose that the corresponding part of the brain turns green? This is not considered by Köhler, or other what might be called "toys in the brain" theorists. But, if they considered the point, they would have to say either that the brain does turn green (against which we have very strong evidence) or that although *shapes* are represented by corresponding identical shapes, other characteristics of objects—color, temperature, hardness, taste, sound, and so on—are not represented in this "toy" way; but by some kind of code. But if color and hardness are represented not directly by the brain changing in hardness and color, but by a code—so that the physical brain states are very different from what they represent—then why should we suppose object shapes to be represented by brain shapes? Here we see a simple argument, challenging a way of thinking about perception. The ridiculousness of the green brain consequence of extended isomorphism jolts belief in the Gestalt concept of perception, perhaps more so than by experiments alone, for they would have to be interpreted with presuppositions.

If descriptive passages (in written or printed language) rather than drawings or photographs had been taken as essentially similar to perception, then the history of perceptual theories would surely have been very different. If it had always been clear that descriptions given by a language, having symbols quite unlike the things described, can serve for many purposes better than pictures then a quite different concept would have been available for considering perception.

This situation is familiar throughout science. A few observations, or a simple argument, may quite change prevailing opinion, perhaps to give significance to much that was obscure. It seems that science is highly dependent on certain general concepts for making sense of observations; even the most general concepts, or ways of thinking, can be challenged and are sometimes overthrown by what are then seen as crucial facts, or arguments of special significance. This approach to the philosophy of science has been most ably and cogently thought out and presented by Thomas S. Kuhn, in his book, *The Structure of Scientific Revolutions* (1962) (revised edition, 1970, from which quotations will be drawn). Kuhn calls the most general and basic (often implicitly held) concepts in science "paradigms." Examples are natural selection and relativity. They dominate generations of scientists, and may be essentially questioned by only a few scientists: the majority design their experiments, make their predictions and teach according to the prevailing paradigm. The question here is: Do we have an accepted paradigm for perception? It's lack, according to Kuhn would prevent perception being a "normal science." Lack of a paradigm would prevent experiments or theories having the power they have in the normal sciences which are dominated by a paradigm—which may however turn out to be inadequate and would perhaps be overthrown by a scientific revolution. Paradigms relate facts, select facts, and make us see facts in a certain light. According to Kuhn they have fashions, and they may turn out to be clearly inappropriate. So they are not to be identified with "truth," in any absolute sense.

Paradigms serve not only to relate facts: they can make facts and questions respectable. They can affect profoundly the structure of science as a social activity, and the reputations and professional standing of scientists. Nearly all scientists work within a paradigm and spend their lives filling in its structure. A very few break through to basic new ways of thinking, perhaps to initiate a "scientific revolution." Although discoveries are often difficult to date and discoverers are difficult to name, Kuhn sees revolutions as at least sometimes initiated by individuals, now celebrated in the history of science: men such as Newton, Lavoisier, and Einstein. A new discovery or a new technique can, he suggests, also produce a change of paradigm; thus (p. 7), "the scientist's world is qualitatively transformed as well as quantitatively enriched by fundamental novelties of either fact or theory." These remarks apply to "normal" science. Is the study of perception a "normal science"? We do not seem to have generally accepted ways of relating or selecting data or theoretical positions held much more cogently than as "schools" of thought concerning the nature of perception. As a result, there are few standards of what is "good science" in perception, or indeed in psychology generally. One might even argue that the case, in Kuhn's terms, is worse than this, for philosophies of perception are clustered around not only talented men (and this might be defended) but around particular experimental techniques—almost as though techniques are accepted as lode stones, each leading to some unique truth. Does this happen in sciences other than those surrounding and forming psychology? If so, they should worry too! What we lack, I submit, is a paradigm broad enough to allow communication between people concerned with understanding the phenomena and underlying processes of perception. This lack may be due in part to perceptual research being undertaken under the auspices of many kinds of scientific establishment. We find neurophysiologists, biochemists, opticians, ophthalmologists, experimental psychologists, and computer programmers all concerned with pattern recognition and scene analysis. It is interesting that all these—and of course artists—have techniques and special knowledge capable of increasing our understanding of perception. But evidently perception is not a normal science in

Kuhn's sense. We should consider how to select or devise an adequate paradigm.

We should not expect Kuhn to be able to tell us how to find a paradigm, but he does make useful comments (p. 156):

> When a new candidate for a new paradigm is first proposed, it has seldom solved more than a few of the problems that confront it, and most of these solutions are still far from perfect. Until Kepler, the Copernican theory scarcely improved upon the predictions of planetary position made by Ptolemy. . . . Ordinarily it is only much later, after the new paradigm has been developed, accepted, and exploited that apparently decisive arguments—the Foucault pendulum to demonstrate the rotation of the earth or the Fizeau experiment to show that light moves faster in air than in water—are developed. Producing them is part of normal science, and their role is not in paradigm debate but in post revolutionary texts.

In short, we must not expect everything to drop into place or every problem to disappear.

As a further hazard, it is possible for an inappropriate paradigm to suggest an important observation or inspire an effective invention. Kuhn gives an example both instructive and amusing from the history of electrical science: the invention of the Leyden jar of about 1740. At that time, the principal paradigm for electrical phenomena was that electricity is some kind of a fluid. What better then to collect electrical fluid in, than a glass jar? They tried glass jars and they worked—for quite the wrong reasons! Such a success could presumably perpetuate a failing, or select a nonsense paradigm.

Some aspects of perception are mentioned explicitly by Kuhn. He considers ambiguous figures (such as Necker cubes and Jastrow's duck–rabbit figures (Figs. 1 and 2) as related to changes of paradigm. Thus (p. 111):

> . . . during revolutions scientists see new and different things when looking with familiar instruments in places they have looked before. It is rather as if the professional community had been transported to a different planet where familiar objects are seen in a different light. . . . It is as elementary prototypes

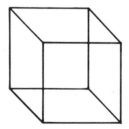

Fig. 1. The orientation-ambiguous Necker cube.

FIG. 2.   An object-ambiguous figure—Jastrow's duck-rabbit.

for these transformations of the scientist's world that the familiar demonstrations of a switch of visual gestalt prove so suggestive. What were ducks . . . before the revolution are rabbits afterwards.

Kuhn points out that in science changes of "view," unlike perception, are generally irreversible. He cites the Stratton (1897) reversing goggles experiments, to illustrate how changed data can be rearranged to fit an existing paradigm (Kuhn, 1970, p. 112) and also discusses the Bruner and Postman (1949) study on perception of incongruity using playing cards with suits having red and black switched, so that clubs and spades are red, diamonds and hearts black. Some of the subjects in this experiment suffered not merely confusion but acute distress. Thus, for one subject: "I can't make the suit out, whatever it is. It didn't look like a card that time. I don't know what color it is now or whether it's a spade or a heart. I'm not even sure now what a spade looks like. My God!" Scientists, as Kuhn points out, occasionally behave like this.

Perceptual demonstrations and experiments in perceptual psychology make Kuhn (p. 113): "suspect that something like a paradigm is prerequisite to perception itself." How similar are spontaneous changes in perception (as in the duck–rabbit figure) and changes of scientific paradigm? Kuhn discusses this (p. 114 et seq.) in these terms:

> The subject of a gestalt demonstration knows that his perception has shifted because he can make it shift back and forth repeatedly while he holds the book or piece of paper in his hands . . . unless there were an external standard with respect to which a switch of vision could be demonstrated, no conclusion about alternative perceptual observations could be drawn. . . . With scientific observation, however, the situation is exactly reversed. The scientist can have no recourse above or beyond what he sees with his eyes and his instruments. If there were some higher authority by recourse to which his vision might be shown to have shifted, then that authority would itself become the source of his data, and the behaviour of his vision would become a source of problems.

These problems are, of course, the problems of perception.

II. THE SELECTION OF PARADIGMS BY DATA

Kuhn has much to say about the *invention* of new paradigms, but less about how the best of existing paradigms may be *selected*. Clearly shopping around existing paradigms and selecting the best is very different from inventing a new one: it should be easier, and the decision might be based explicitly on available empirical data. To invent and accept for consideration a new paradigm, Kuhn points out, involves to a high degree "subjective" and "aesthetic" considerations, because its structure and its implications have not yet been worked out. To judge between existing rival candidates is a matter of selecting, rather than inventing.

Paradigms select facts. How can we select a paradigm? We shall try, by challenging candidates with facts. We shall put up for consideration six paradigm candidates (which will be described briefly) and each will be challenged in turn with ten questions. We shall set up a kind of examination game. Paradigm candidates may receive or lose credits for their answers (or ability to provide a basis for what seems a possible answer) to a series of questions. The questions are somewhat arbitrarily chosen, the candidates will not be fully described, and the scoring will be idiosyncratic. So this will be just like any other examination: the kind of test we have to pass to be allowed to answer and ask questions to become professors!

III. PERCEPTUAL FACTS TO CHALLENGE PARADIGM CANDIDATES

FACT 1. That Perceptions of Objects Go Beyond Available Sensory Inputs (or Data)

Behavior can be appropriate though it goes beyond available sensory data in virtually any typical situation, for example, sitting down in a chair, or taking a spoonful of food. The point is this: retinal images cannot directly monitor the strength of the chair, or the palatability of the food. But the behavior is appropriate to the chair's strength or the food's quality though these, being nonoptical, cannot be directly monitored by eyes.

Q. 1. How does indirectly relevant sensory data mediate appropriate behavior?

FACT 2. That Appropriate Behavior Can Continue through Gaps in Sensory Inputs

Consider a laboratory eye–hand tracking experiment, in which the hand moves a joystick to keep a marker on a moving target, displayed on an oscilloscope screen. If the target is removed, from time to time (by Z-modulation), no significant errors may occur, provided the target's course is familiar. To take everyday examples of the same point: we do not have to watch the ground continuously, or steps of a staircase, when we walk. There are visual data gaps with every blink, and every shift from fixation of the eyes from ground or stairs, but behavior continues to be appropriate and uninterrupted through data gaps.

Q. 2. How is skilled behavior maintained during temporary absence of sensory input?

FACT 3. That in Skills There May Be No Delay between Sensory Input and Output Behavior

Consider again an eye–hand tracking experiment. For a familiar track (such as a sine wave, or a more complicated repeating course) there is, on average, *no* delay between the target the subject is following and the marker spot he is controlling. Errors may be equally distributed ahead and behind the target. On the other hand, if the target moves in a novel way, then there will in general be a time lag between target and marker: there will be a delay of about 0.5 seconds before the error is corrected. But we know that there is an irreducible physiological lag between "stimulus" and "response": so there is a problem about skills.

Q. 3. How can skilled behavior have zero average delay between sensory input and behavior output?

FACT 4. The Probable Objects Are Perceptually Favored over Improbable Objects

Consider the hollow mold of a face (Fig. 3). Although in fact hollow, it appears as a normal face—with the nose sticking out instead of in as it actually is in the mold face—in spite of normal lighting, texture, and even some stereopsis from the two eyes. A photograph of a hollow face always looks like a normal face, and a mold seen directly looks like a face until viewed very close, with both eyes, when it suddenly does look hollow. We may assume that the hollow face looks like a normal face because hollow faces are extremely unusual, and so have a low probability.

Q. 4. Why are improbable objects more difficult to see than probable objects, of similar form?

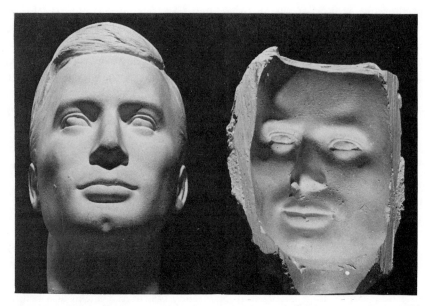

Fig. 3. Hollow mold of a face (in spite of normal lighting, texture, etc., this appears as a face though, in fact, it is hollow. Evidently the prior probability determines the perception.)

FACT 5. That Intense Pattern Stimulation of the Retina May Produce Corresponding Aftereffects (Afterimages), Added To Any Immediately Subsequent Perceptions

Afterimages occur essentially as a function of stimulus intensities, spatial and temporal distributions, and colors. They are not evoked only by special forms or patterns: in other words, *any* form or pattern can produce an afterimage, and transfer to any other pattern or to no pattern.

Q. 5. Why can any pattern produce an afterimage, precisely related to the given pattern?

FACT 6. That Spatial Distortions Occur with Some Figures

It is a fact that many simple line figures appear distorted. Perceptual distortions may be measured by setting an adjustable line to the same apparent length as a line in the illusions figure appearing shrunk or expanded. The perceptual distortions are in this sense "objective." It is known (from observation of illusion figures in stabilized retinal images) that these distortions occur undiminished in the absence of effective eye movements, so we know that their origin is not to be attributed to errors of fixation. We also know that they are not retinal in origin, for they occur undiminished when the figures are divided up between the eyes and observed by binocular fusion. We therefore know that their origin is in the brain. There are several extant theories attempting to explain these distortions, and the theories cross possible paradigms. It is this that makes the study of illusions particularly interesting.

Q. 6. Why are distortions observed in many figures?

FACT 7. That Spontaneous Changes of Perception (Perceptual Ambiguity) Occur with Unchanged Sensory Input, with Many Figures and Objects

Best known of these effects are (a) figure–ground reversals, such as those demonstrated by Rubin (Fig. 4); (b) changes in orientation, such as the Necker cube (Fig. 1); (c) changes from one apparent object to another, such as Jastrow's duck–rabbit figure (Fig. 2).

We know that all these continue to occur (though with lower frequency) with stabilized retinal images—so eye movements are not necessary, though changes of fixation can initiate such perceptual changes. We know that for these and many other ambiguous figures, there is only a small number of alternative perceptions (in the Necker cube, two, or possibly three if the figure is seen as flat; in the duck–rabbit, two; for the figure–ground, two).

FIG. 4. Figure-ground ambiguity—a Rubin figure.

We know that some three-dimensional objects will change perceptually. Wire cubes are an example. [There are accompanying shape changes with such object reversals (Gregory, 1970).]

Q. 7. How can some line figures and some three-dimensional objects change perceptually, with no change of sensory input?

FACT 8. That There Can Be Impossible (Paradoxical) Perceptions

Several simple line figures, such as the Penrose triangle (Fig. 5) or the three prongs (Fig. 6) appear as impossible objects. We know that paradoxical perceptions can be given also by three-dimensional objects, viewed from critical position (Figs. 7a and b).

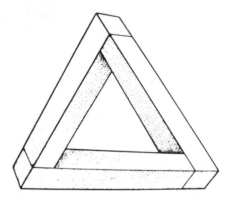

Fig. 5. A paradoxical figure, devised by L. S. and R. Penrose.

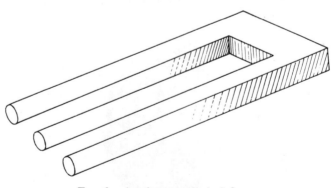

Fig. 6. Another paradoxical figure.

Fig. 7. a. A photograph of an actual object which—from a critical viewing position—appears paradoxical. b. The same object viewed from a "noncritical" position. It is no longer paradoxical and its true three-dimensional form is seen.

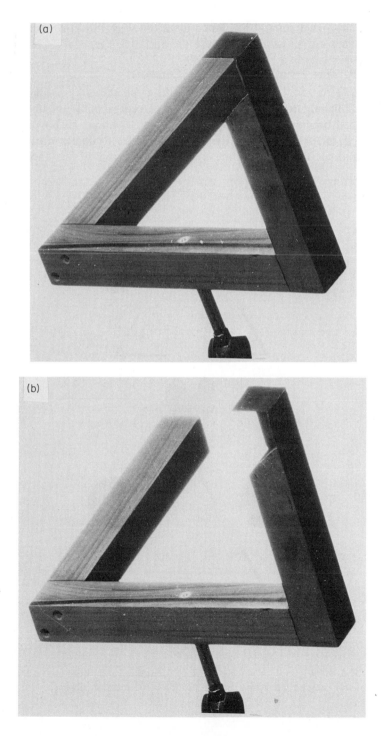

Q. 8.   How can we see logically impossible objects?

FACT 9. That There Can Be Illusory Contours

Certain line figures can produce marked perceptual contours, and regions of modified brightness (enhanced, or reduced, by about 10%) over large areas and far removed from physical contours (examples are given in Figs. 8 and 9). These illusory areas seem to lie in front of the "incomplete" figures.

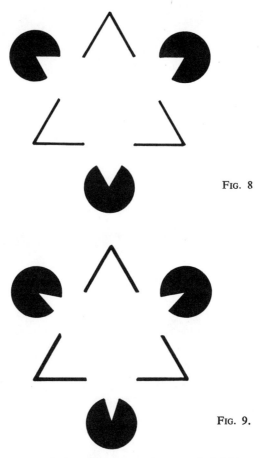

Fig. 8

Fig. 9.

FIGS. 8 & 9. Figures producing illusory contours and brightness differences (these effects may be due to perceptual postulates of masking objects).

Q. 9. How can contours and large regions of enhanced, or reduced, brightness be created by simple line figures?

FACT 10. That Visual Distortions Can Occur Across Illusory Contours

Some, and perhaps all, of the classical distortion illusions can occur without physical contours, across illusory contours. This is a new finding (Gregory, 1972) but is readily checked by the reader (see Figs. 10 and 11).

Q. 10. How can visual distortions be generated across illusory contours?

IV. SUMMARY OF THE QUESTIONS (For Reference)

We have now selected ten challenge questions derived from brief discussions of what seem to be some basic issues. The questions concern phenomena which are in most instances well known and in all instances can be readily checked. However, there is nothing "absolute" about the choice of questions. It may be felt that they "unfairly" challenge some candidates, while ignoring the weak spots of others: but the reader is free to play the candidate baiting game with his questions.

To follow the discussion from here, it will be necessary to refer to the ten challenge questions. We shall now summarize them for easy reference.

Q. 1. How does sensory input give appropriate behavior, when the input is not directly relevant to the object situation (e.g., how do we see a table as hard?)?

Q. 2. How is skilled behavior maintained through (temporary) absence of sensory input?

Q. 3. How can skilled behavior have *zero* average delay though there is physiological delay between input and output, due to neural conduction times?

Q. 4. Why are highly improbable objects more difficult to see (or recognize) than probable objects of similar form (e.g., a hollow mold face appearing as a normal face)?

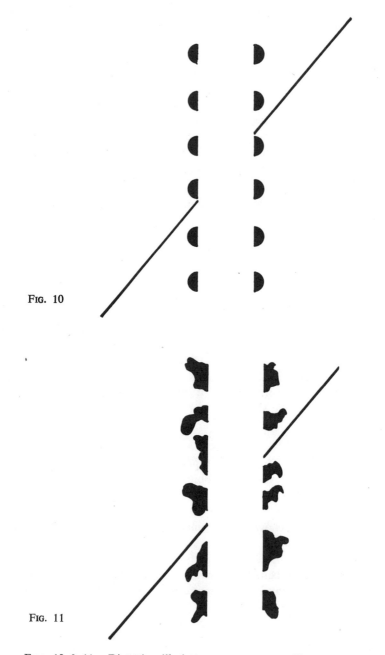

FIG. 10

FIG. 11

FIGS. 10 & 11.   Distortion illusions can occur across illusory contours or regions of enhanced or diminished brightness.

Q. 5. Why do afterimages exactly correspond to the stimulus pattern?

Q. 6. Why are measurable distortions observed in many situations (such as the classical visual distortion illusion figures)?

Q. 7. Why do some line figures and some three-dimensional objects spontaneously change perceptually with no change of sensory input? (E.g. the Necker cube, the duck–rabbit, and skeletal wire shapes such as cubes)?

Q. 8. How can perceptions be of (logically) impossible objects [e.g., the Penrose impossible triangle figure, the three prongs figure; the three-dimensional object (Figs. 7a and b) which though it is an object appears impossible when viewed from a critical position]?

Q. 9. Why are illusory contours and areas of changed brightness created in some simple line figures (Figs. 8 and 9)?

Q. 10. Why do distortions, equivalent to classical visual illusion distortions, occur across illusory contours (Figs. 10 and 11)?

V. THE PARADIGM CANDIDATES CHALLENGED BY QUESTIONS

Since this cannot be much more than a play-exercise at candidate baiting, we should not expect to see all suggested candidates here; and they mutate, from time to time, to produce many varieties and sports. We shall put up six candidates, all having adherents and being at least historically significant. It will be necessary at this stage to summarize briefly our candidates. If the summaries are cartoons, I hope they will catch something of the essential likeness of their subjects.

CANDIDATE A: Reflexes and Tropisms

Primitive organisms are generally held to respond to light, very much as they are supposed to respond to chemical gradients. They are supposed to respond "automatically" to selected physical features of their environment which are *monitored* by specific sense endings. Most monitored characteristics are of immediate importance for survival (temperature, humidity, toxicity, etc.). Some may be associated with other characteristics which are important. For example, darkness may be associated with shelter, so that although bright light itself may not be harmful, or dim light beneficial, the safe situation may be fairly reliably indicated by light intensity. A physical monotonic gradient leading to safety (or food or whatever) has predictive use, if monitored and accepted for "tropistic" behavior, even if what is monitored is not directly useful, as food or shelter or any other need.

Which of our ten questions would tend to preclude this as a candidate paradigm for human perception, especially of vision? Here are some possible answers. (In each case, the answers: *A. 1, A. 2,* etc. refer to the corresponding challenge question: *Q. 1, Q. 2,* etc.)

A. 1. By monitored characteristics (which, although they themselves are unimportant) are highly correlated with characteristics which are important for the behavior. For these tropisms to be useful there must be physical monotonic functions to "goals"—so this is limited to fortunate situations.

A. 2. Behavior should cease when input stimuli cease (apart from inertia) or it should become random.

A. 3. Not possible if output is controlled directly by input and there is physiological delay between input and output.

A. 4. Neural systems (or sense endings) must be "tuned" to accept only what are generally reliable inputs. If the "tuning" were not sharp enough to reject features correlated with other situations then the wrong object will be "recognized," and the behavior will generally be inappropriate.

A. 5. Because the receptor system (or associated "upstream" systems) suffer selective sensitivity changes, which will modify later stimulus patterns as transmitted neurally.

A. 6. Neural mechanisms mediating tropism might become adapted, or unbalanced, in many ways. In some stimulus situations there may be other stimuli, not rejected producing errors.

A. 7. Might alternative reflexes or tropisms be selected by a stimulus?

A. 8. No meaningful answer seems possible here.

A. 9. No meaningful answer seems possible here.

A. 10. No meaningful answer seems possible here.

CANDIDATE B: Gestalten, and Isomorphic Brain Fields

This candidate (cf. Köhler, 1920) postulated physiological processes to explain perceptual phenomena, such as preference for "closed" objects and tendency to closure. The essential notion is that external shapes are represented by corresponding shaped brain traces (circles by circles, ellipses by ellipses, and presumably houses by "toy" brain-trace houses). The emphasis is very much on visual (and sometimes musical) form, other characteristics being virtually ignored. Direct evidence for the postulated physiological states was seldom claimed. We have given some comments on this at the beginning of this paper.

A. 1. No answer, except (as for Candidate A above) when available sensory input happens to be highly and appropriately correlated with important non-sensed features.

A. 2. Behavior should cease or become, in general, inappropriate when sensory input ceases. (Inertial continuation will soon generate errors.)

A. 3. There must be physiological delay for modification of the supposed isomorphic brain traces. Zero delay between input and output is essentially impossible.

A. 4. No clear answer, unless there are supposed to be physiological restraints to the forms isomorphic brain traces can adopt, and that these are related to the probabilities of objects. [This is very much what Hebb says in relation to his phase sequences (Candidate C) but these he supposes are representing inductive generalizations, and so should be related to probabilities of objects. The brain traces in the Gestalt paradigm candidate are however not supposed to be much affected by experience. They are supposed to be subject to physical stability principles—tending to adopt minimal energy configurations (such as circles), shapes of "good figure" and "closure"—but according to *their* physical characteristics, not the characteristics, or probable characteristics, of external objects.]

A. 5. Intense stimulation would be supposed to affect the physiological system representing shapes; the effects to be transferred in time to later perceptions, while the physiological effect lasts.

A. 6. Distortions are attributed to a supposed tendency of generally isomorphic brain traces to adopt forms of minimal potential energy, e.g., ellipses tending to circles.

A. 7. Are the brain traces supposed to be metastable according to their physical properties? (This would not explain why shapes such as ducks and rabbits are stable.)

A. 8. No sensible answer.

A. 9. That certain shapes (e.g., patterns of dots) set up an isomorphic trace which fills gaps (as is supposed to occur in phi-movement).

A. 10. That the figures give sufficient features to select traces, which are distorted according to their tendencies to minimal energy configuration, and that these fill in gaps which distort other features of the figures as they would be distorted if the figures were complete(?).

CANDIDATE C: Phase Sequences

"Phase sequences" and "assemblies of phase sequences" (Hebb, 1949) are postulated physiological embodiments of what F. C. Bartlett (1930) called "schema." They are supposed to be developed by experience and to represent neurally the progress and results of inductive generalizations based on instances associated with success or failures. This idea may be traced back to William James (*Principles of Psychology,* 1890), for James also postulated physiological processes to explain perceptual phenomena. The candidate differs from the Gestalt candidate by basing the phase sequences almost entirely on experience and by denying (cf. Hebb, 1949, p. 51 et seq.) that brain fields are isomorphically related to external shapes (so this is not a "toys in the brain" notion).

A. 1. By inductively derived relations from past associations.

A. 2. By the phase sequence continuing. It might have predictive power, providing the present situation turns out to be essentially similar to situations represented by instances from the past. (There would be very limited ability to deal with new situations unless phase sequences have elaborate logical structures, but this is not envisaged.)

A. 3. There might be zero delay if the phase sequences control behavior, provided they are predictive.

A. 4. Improbable objects would not have developed phase sequences and so might not—or could not—be seen.

A. 5. Changes of sensitivity (e.g., on the retina) transfer to other situations.

A. 6. No particular answer; but this candidate could accept several kinds of explanation without special difficulty.

A. 7. Alternative phase sequences selected by the current sensory data

(?). The fact that perceptions change *spontaneously* with ambiguous figures and objects might be described in terms of satiation of the physiological trace systems (cf. Pritchard, Heron, & Hebb, 1960).

A. 8. Aspects, or parts, of different phase sequences combined; to produce, for these figures, some kind of neural incompatibility or conflict (?).

A. 9. Sufficient sensory input to select a phase sequence, normally representing an object (?).

A. 10. The selected and completing phase sequence providing "internal" contours or features to produce the usual distortions as though there were external contours (?).

CANDIDATE D: Pick-Up of Information from the External Ambient Array

This candidate is what we may call a "passive" account of perception. Perceptions are not supposed to be in any sense "created" by the brain, but are rather supposed to be selections of reality, or of the "external (optical) ambient array." Thus, a perception is for this candidate part of the world itself. Retinal images and brain processes are left out of this account; at times denied. In philosophical terms, this would be an embodiment of what many philosophers (rather rudely) call "naive realism." It is propounded by J. J. Gibson (1950, 1966) and E. J. Gibson (1969).

A. 1. Selected optical features are supposed to carry their own information, for example, texture gradients to give distance and form directly, without inference. Information is supposed to be in the world itself (not from brain-stored probabilities, derived by inductive generalizations, as an "active" candidate might say). It is not clear how *nonoptical* properties are supposed to be given directly from the visual "ambient array." This is a serious problem, as behavior is essentially appropriate to nonoptical object properties, such as hardness. They are supposed to be discovered from active exploration of objects; but it does not seem clear how they are then given as part of the "ambient array."

A. 2. This should not happen for this candidate, for if perceptions are selections of the "external ambient array," when this is unavailable perception and controlled behavior should cease. But behavior can continue uninterrupted through data gaps, in familiar situations.

A. 3. This would be expected if selected reality is itself perception. But zero delay would be impossible if the "ambient array" is selected by the senses—which have physiological delay. It is not clear whether information processing (taking time) is accepted or denied by this candidate. (I shall assume it is wrongly denied and mark down correspondingly.)

A. 4. No ready answer is given, when there had been sufficient perceptual learning for relevant information from the external array to be selected. Consider the case of the hollow face. When lighting is normal (the source above the hollow face, and so on) then the texture gradients will be typical. But if texture gradients, etc., *determine* depth, why should it appear like a normal face, with the nose sticking out, when in fact it is hollow and the nose sticks in?

A. 5. As propounded, the retinal image is unimportant (or even sometimes regarded as nonexistent). Perception is not considered in terms of the retinal image as an interface between the neural system and the world, and so it is not clear how afterimages could occur.

A. 6. This candidate tends to deny that illusions or such phenomena occur. Perceptions should not be distorted, if they are "passive" selections of what is outside, for surely it is not the *world* which is distorted.

A. 7. Perceptual ambiguities, also, are not considered seriously. But the world itself cannot be ambiguous; so at least these perceptions cannot be samples of the world. (Ambiguities such as Necker cube reversals appear to counter this candidate at a basic logical level, and no answer is provided.)

A. 8. The world cannot be logically impossible but some perceptions are "of" logically impossible objects (e.g., Figs. 5–7b), so at least these perceptions cannot be samples of the object world. (So perceptual paradox also counters this candidate at a logical level.)

A. 9. Contours, or other perceptual phenomena, should not be created if perceptions are selections of reality.

A. 10. There should be neither created contours, distortions, or any other phenomena of perception. If perceptions are merely selections of the physical world, there could be no phenomena except those of physics.

CANDIDATE E: Perceptions as Hypotheses

This candidate's history goes back at least to von Helmholtz (see 1963) (Hermann L. F. von Helmholtz, 1821–1894) and especially to his concept of "unconscious inference," and perceptions as "unconscious conclusions." Von Helmholtz believed that purely physiological concepts are inadequate, that psychological concepts are needed, and that these should be closely related to epistemology. Like Kuhn, writing later, he did not regard these "unconscious inferences" as just like other thinking. For example, take this passage from *Perceptions in General*:

> because they are not free acts of conscious thought, these unconscious conclusions from analogy are irresistible, and the effect of them cannot be overcome by a better understanding of the real relations. It may be ever so clear how we get an idea of a luminous phenomenon in the field of vision when pressure is exerted on the eye; and yet we cannot get rid of the conviction that this appearance of light is actually there at the given place in the visual field. . . . It is the same way in the case of all the images that we see in optical instruments.

Von Helmholtz argues that strong associations between retinal optical patterns and other object-characteristics are built up by association through individual experience, to give perceptions of objects as inductively based inferences, of the form:

> This retinal shape has (nearly) always occurred when there is an external table.
> This retinal shape is present.
> Therefore there is (probably) an external table.

Helmholtz points out that sensations are selected according to whether they are likely to be relevant for recognizing objects. He has the following passage in italics: *"We are not in the habit of observing our sensations accurately, except as they are useful in enabling us to recognise external objects. On the contrary, we are wont to disregard all those parts of the sensations that are of no importance so far as external objects are concerned."* He goes on to point out that special talent is needed to observe for the first time (discover, indeed) entoptic phenomena—though the stimuli are present from time to time in all normal retinas. The outstanding discoverer of object-irrelevant, but perceptually highly interesting entoptic phenomena, was the nineteenth century physiologist J. E. Purkinje, whose observations can be repeated by anyone, though they were perhaps never before seen by any human being. Again, here we have pre-echos of the selective power of "paradigms", this time in perception itself. As for science, we seem to see the power of assumptions about the world on how we see it.

There are hints—looking back they may appear strong hints—of a development of the notion of perception as inference in K. J. W. Craik's book, *The Nature of Explanation* (1943). Craik stresses the importance of thinking about brain function in terms of symbolic activity, carried out by its physiological processes. Craik's central notion is that the brain *models* aspects of reality. There are also remarkably "modern" comments on language; as in the following passages: (TNE p. 81 et seq):

> . . . language has a more important function than such mere description. It must evolve rules of implication governing the use of words, in such a way that a line of thought can run parallel to, and predict, causally determined events in the external world. The ability of a particular 'line of thought' to do this is the test of its correctness as an explanation: if it is successful, it 'works'—it 'covers' the facts. Some may object that this reduces thought to a mere 'copy' of reality and that we ought not to want such an internal 'copy'; are not electrons, causally interacting, good enough? Why do we want our minds to play the same sort of game, with laws of implication instead of causal laws to determine the next step? The answer, I think, is first, that only this internal model of reality—this working model—enables us to predict events which have not yet occurred in the physical world, a process which saves time, expense, and even life.

Craik's term 'models' hardly conveys the importance to perception, on this view, of (unconscious) inference. It might be best, here, to describe perceptions as hypotheses: hypotheses based on sensory data. [The notion that perceptions are logically equivalent to hypotheses in science has been argued by the present writer (Gregory, 1970): so it may come as no great surprise if this paradigm candidate ends up in a strong position.]

A. 1.   The perceptual hypotheses allow inferences from present data to non-sensed object characteristics, e.g., a brown mottled image to wood hard, strong, easily scratched.

A. 2.   Perceptual hypotheses (as do hypotheses in science) could have the power to predict future events. If behavior is controlled not by current sensory input but by hypotheses, built from elements of the past, and selected by current data, then provided the hypothesis is appropriate, behavior can continue through data gaps and remain appropriate.

A. 3.   Once an adequate hypothesis is selected, it may give zero delay performance by predicting the immediate future. There will, however, be a time lag selecting each hypothesis, and it will fail to predict correctly in exceptional conditions—to generate what may be systematic errors or illusions.

A. 4.   We should expect on general grounds that hypotheses of high prior probability will be selected by less evidence than will hypotheses of low prior probability, if any reasonably efficient

Bayesian selection procedure is adopted. (Note that this is not a physiological but a logical explanation. This is not a physiological but a strategy explanation of the "hollow face effect," where what is seen is probable from past data, but incorrect for the present object.)

A. 5. Intense stimulation may selectively affect retinal (or more central) local sensitivities: these local changes in sensitivity will affect transmission of succeeding images.

A. 6. Distortions may occur because stored object hypotheses could not have scale parameters included (except very roughly) because objects (such as tables and houses) may have *any* size or be at *any* distance over a wide range. Size and distance must therefore be given by current sensory data, since these parameters cannot be part of stored hypotheses, for most normal objects. Available scaling information is essentially ambiguous (e.g., perspective shrinking, and convergence of parallel lines), and so assumptions are necessary to interpret it, to use it for scale setting. If these assumptions are misplaced (e.g., accepting converging lines presented on the plane of a picture, or an illusion figure, as generated at the retina by changing distance, then corresponding errors of scale must occur (Gregory, 1958). (They would occur quite apart from the physiology involved, generated by a misplaced strategy which might be mediated by brain cells, transistors, or elastic bands.)

A. 7. Each alternative perception is regarded as an hypothesis. The Necker cube (or the duck–rabbit figure) have features which select not one, but two or more reasonably likely hypotheses, which are entertained in turn (perhaps for testing) and which *are* the perceptions.

A. 8. Hypotheses, or descriptions, can be logically impossible. Paradoxes may be generated by following false assumptions, which turn out incompatible. (It is very difficult to see what, other than descriptions or hypotheses, can be paradoxical.)

A. 9. In these figures, we may suppose the gaps to be due probably to an object in front of a figure and hiding parts of it. If the evidence for such a masking object were sufficient, then an hypothesis of such a masking object might be created (Harris and Gregory, 1973).

A. 10. If the classical distortions are due to mis-set size scaling (due to inappropriately applied assumptions, normally required for giving three-dimensional hypotheses from two-dimensional images) then the same might apply to hypotheses which are not in fact related closely to external objects.

CANDIDATE F: Feature Analysers, and "Grandmother Cells," Representing Objects

We return to an essentially physiological candidate, of great prestige at the present time, following the discovery of D. Hubel and T. N. Wiesel (1962) that certain shapes (orientation of lines, movement and so on) produce activity (firing) of certain cells in the striate cortex. Should we think of the feature detectors as signalling or as "describing" objects? A problem arises when we think of perception as more than response to simple patterns: how, for example, is the letter "A" represented? We can imagine each of the three lines stimulating orientation selective cells, the firing of these cells representing the three lines. But how are they put together to form the perception of the letter "A"? If the cells signaling these orientations provide evidence for the hypothesis letter "A," then we have paradigm D, above, with more knowledge of how hypotheses are mediated. If, on the other hand, we maintain a purely physiological paradigm, then the concept becomes one of supposing that there are cells sensitive to complex shapes and finally complete objects—"grandmother cells" as the joke goes. On the perceptual hypothesis alternative, there should not be a close relation between the physiological activity (at the striate area) and specific perceptual phenomena. There are implications here as to how recorded physiological activity should be interpreted in terms of perceptual phenomena on these alternative paradigm candidates.

It seems that an essential issue is: "How far do perceptions go beyond available sensory data?" Like most of the other candidates, this essentially physiological candidate has no power to bridge data gaps.

A. 1.   There would have to be established correlations from previous experience, related to current sensory features represented neurally in this way. (But this takes us back to candidate D.)

A. 2.   Appropriate output should cease with interruption to input, if the output is directly controlled by the input.

A. 3.   Zero delay seems impossible, because the output is dependent upon the input, and there is irreducible physiological delay between input and output.

A. 4.   There may be more fully developed analyzers for familiar objects.

Unfamiliar objects may have no analysers (no "grandmother cells") and so fail to be recognized.

A. 5. Changes of sensitivity will transfer to other situations.

A. 6. Cellular interactions, such as lateral inhibition might produce shifts of signaled contours in the presence of neighboring contours (cf. Blakemore, 1970).

A. 7. Not clear why there should be these particular ambiguities and stabilities but neural systems having meta stable states; analogous to computer "flip flop" circuits have been proposed (Attneave, 1972) but why should physiological stable states correspond (especially to biologically unimportant and unfamiliar) objects?

A. 8. Not clear how paradoxical perceptions could occur. (Why should logically conflicting analyzers be selected by features of these figures? Could there be logically impossible "grandmothers"?)

A. 9. Activation of line detector or other feature-sensitive cells, especially in the striate cortex, by features which are present in the figure. Activated cells normally representing *complete* lines may be activated though there are gaps in these lines. (There are however serious objections to explaining these filled-in, illusory contours as due to striate feature detector activity, cf. Gregory, 1972.)

A. 10. Once the feature detector cells are firing as though the features are complete, distortions might be generated by lateral inhibition or other interactive cellular effects as for the usual "complete" figures. But the figures do not seem to have "trigger features" suitable for activating these line feature detectors.

VI. THE CANDIDATES' SCORES

To continue the scoring game, we may construct a table (Table I) relating the six candidates' answers (or lack of answers) to the ten questions, each question being marked out of a maximum of five points. It seems clear that some of the answers are very much better, and much more plausible, than others.

Our marking for brevity's sake will not be justified in detail. The reader may well mark differently. He might discover from this why he differs, and what would be *his* chosen Paradigm. Will we ever reach even temporary agreement?

TABLE I

PARADIGM CANDIDATES

Questions	A	B	C	D	E	F	
Q. 1	1	1	4	1	4	1	12
Q. 2	0	1	4	0	4	0	9
Q. 3	0	0	4	0	4	0	8
Q. 4	2	1	4	2	5	4	18
Q. 5	5	5	5	0	5	5	25
Q. 6	3	1	1	0	5	4	14
Q. 7	3	1	4	0	5	3	16
Q. 8	0	0	3	0	5	0	8
Q. 9	0	1	3	0	4	2	10
Q. 10	0	1	3	0	4	2	10
	14	12	35	3	45	21	130 / 130

VII. CONCLUSIONS

Given these challenge questions, and the paradigm candidates outlined here, candidate "E", *Perceptions as hypotheses, based on stored and sensed data,* wins the contest. The only near runner-up is candidate "C", *The phase sequence theory,* of D. O. Hebb. These two candidates have much in common. The main difference is that "E" is phrased in terms of supposed "software" logical processes, without specific reference to underlying neural processes carrying out hypothesis building and selecting, while candidate "C" postulates specific neural processes (phase sequences) as the basis of perception. Why should postulated physiology reduce the score (as it seems to) for candidate "E"? And is it this *particular* postulated physiology, or is *any* postulated physiology, a handicap rather than a merit? These are questions at the edge of our paradigm-thinking. We do want, ultimately, to tie up physiology with cognitive processes (and here "E" and "C" agree) but there is a danger in setting up supposed physiological restraints (using concepts such as neural adaptation or changes of synaptic resistance) as bricks for a cognitive paradigm. More specifically, it might be better to think of inductive generalizations as the basis of much learning rather than say physiological reflexes. Here J. S. Mill has the essential formulation rather than Pavlov. Just how the nervous system represents the logic is a secondary—though certainly important—question: *What* is performed must first be understood. This situation is not new in the history of other sciences, including physiology. It was essential to see the heart as a pump—to see its function, and to relate hearts to other kinds of pumps— to begin to understand it and pose appropriate experimental questions.

Similarly for the lens of the eye, it is optical not physiological concepts which are necessary in the first instance, and they must not be forgotten. There are in all these cases physiological restraints (such as limited optical accommodation to distance and to the heart's capacity as a pump) but we can make out a strong case for not selecting or basing paradigms on restraints of this kind. Considering the eye as an optical system: the paradigm comes from general considerations of image formation. The physiological restraints must be considered in terms of this very general paradigm.

The vital question is: "How are restraints set up to be appropriate for carrying out operations needed for current situations, or problems?" Hebb's answer is that paths of conductivity, giving more or less spontaneous activity, are developed from past situations and are set going as "phase sequences" for later similar situations. This might be regarded as a suggested physiological embodiment of Bartlett's "Schema," with the added richness of Hebb's insights, and the sense of safety and progress that reference to possible physiological bases or mechanisms often rightly engenders. If such rather simple physiological modifications, activities, and restraints appeared adequate we should endorse Hebb's suggestion and his candidate would emerge as the all out winner. But since he wrote, it is clear partly from developments (and paradoxically especially from lack of developments) in artificial intelligence that the schema notion, and so its supposed physiological basis, is far too inflexible and crude to serve for perception. At the present time we simply do not know in detail what operations the physiology has to carry out. Our situation here may be compared with what we need to know to understand or describe even a simple calculating machine. There are circuits (or mechanisms) which perform operations within appropriate restraints, so that suitable operations are performed for the problem in hand. Each state of the machine can be described in terms of electronics or mechanics; but to understand that it is multiplying, or extracting roots or whatever, we must know what these operations are in terms of mathematics, logic, or other strategy procedures. There may be many kinds of circuits or mechanisms for carrying out necessary operations, and for many purposes it is irrelevant what they are, until the machine produces errors or is overloaded in some way. Exciting as it is, Hebb's Phase Sequence Candidate is too like the electronic engineer describing what the machine may be doing, before he knows the logical or strategy operations it is carrying out by means of its supposed or known circuits. This candidate is too exciting. It suggests answers before we have formulated appropriate questions. The "perceptual hypothesis" notion seems to raise the kinds of questions requiring answers before we can understand the significance of the underlying physiology.

Limitations of research techniques can limit and bias how we think. To overcome this, so far as possible, we should surely select paradigms on the *most general possible considerations.* The "facts" and "questions" used here were chosen to be general, in this sense, so that we might see the wood without falling over the trees. The "perceptions as hypotheses" notion just won over the "perceptions as physiological phase sequences" notion, because it is not clear that such physiological characteristics and restraints are essentially relevant to how the brain carries out cognitive functions.

The Gestalt isomorphic brain traces were in this sense a similar notion but more dangerous, for we should not expect logic procedure appropriate to many situations to be carried out by following simple restraints (such as minimal energy configurations) which will in general be arbitrary with respect to the logic of the problems to be solved. We cannot, then, include physiology into our cognitive paradigm before we have established which physiological characteristics are performing the necessary operations for deriving perceptions from data. Although the "hypothesis" notion does not begin to answer physiological questions, it does not preclude physiological data or concepts. It should in time allow us to understand the physiology of perception functionally. Without recognizing the logical functions carried out by physiological processes—understanding, in our sense, is impossible. To understand we need concepts based not so much on contingent properties of nervous systems as on considerations sufficiently general for nervous systems to appear as special cases. We now see the lens of the eye as a special case of an image-forming system. Hopefully, in the future, we shall come to see brains as special cases of cognitive systems. When this day arrives we shall have found an adequate paradigm of perception.

References

Attneave, F. Multistability in perception, *Scientific American,* 1971, **225**, 6, 62–71.

Bartlett, F. C. *Remembering.* London & New York: Cambridge Univ. Press, 1930.

Blakemore, C., Carpenter, R. H. S., & Georgeson, M. A. Lateral inhibition between orientation detectors in the human visual system. *Nature* (London), 1970, **228**, 37–39.

Bruner, J. S., & Postman, L. On the perception of incongruity: A paradigm. *Journal of Personality,* 1949, **18**, 206–223.

Craik, K. J. W. *The nature of explanation.* London & New York: Cambridge Univ. Press, 1943.

Gibson, E. J. *Principles of perceptual learning and development.* New York: Appleton, 1969.

Gibson, J. J. *The perception of the visual world.* London: Allen & Unwin, 1950.

Gibson, J. J. *The senses considered as perceptual systems.* Boston, Massachusetts: Houghton, 1966.

Gregory, R. L. Eye movements and the stability of the visual world. *Nature* (London), 1958, **182**, 1214–1216.

Gregory, R. L. *The intelligent eye*. London: Weidenfeld, 1970.

Gregory, R. L. Cognitive contours. *Nature (London)*, 1972, **238**, 51–52.

Harris, J. P., & Gregory, R. L. Fusion and rivalry of illusory contours. *Perception*, 1973, **2**, 235–247.

Hebb, D. O. *The organisation of behaviour*. New York: Wiley, 1949.

Hubel, D., & Wiesel, T. N. Receptive fields, binocular interaction and functional architecture in the cat's visual cortex, *Journal of Physiology (London)*, 1962, **160**, 106.

James, W. *Principles of psychology*. New York: Holt, 1890.

Köhler, W. Physical Gestalten. In W. H. Ellis (Ed.), *Source book of Gestalt psychology*. London: 1938. (Originally published: 1920.)

Kuhn, T. S. *The structure of scientific revolutions*. Chicago, Illinois: Univ. of Chicago Press, 1962.

Kuhn, T. S. *The structure of scientific revolutions*. (rev. ed.) Chicago, Illinois: Univ. of Chicago Press, 1970.

Pritchard, R. M., Heron, W., & Hebb, D. O. Visual perception approached by the method of stabilised images. *Canadian Journal of Psychology*, 1960, **14**, 67.

Stratton, G. M. Some preliminary experiments on vision. *Psychological Review*, 1896, **3**, 611.

Stratton, G. M. Vision without inversion of the retinal image. *Psychological Review*, 1897, **4**, 341.

von Helmholtz, H. In J.P.C.S. Southall (Ed.), *Handbook of physiological optics*. New York: Dover, 1963. (Originally published: 1867.)

Chapter 14

THE VISUAL SYSTEM: ENVIRONMENTAL INFORMATION

R. M. BOYNTON

I. INTRODUCTION

"Ecological optics" is the name given by James J. Gibson to characterize a new branch of optical science which, for the study of vision, he believes to be more useful than the existing branches of physical, geometric, and physiological optics. He appears to take inspiration from a fellow maverick, the Italian physicist Vasco Ronchi. To quote from Gibson (1966, p. 222),

> Ronchi (1957) has argued eloquently that optics cannot be defined merely as the science of light, its origin, propagation, and detection by instruments; it must have some ultimate reference to an eye. Optics is the science of *vision*, not of *light*. Otherwise, [Ronchi] asserts, there are contradictions at the very heart of the discipline. But Ronchi, a physicist, assumes that an eye transmits nervous impulses that are "turned over to a mind which studies their characteristics and compares them with the mass of information in its files. . . ."

Gibson continues,

This is precisely what I, a psychologist, do not assume. Instead of making the nervous system carry the whole burden of explaining perception, I wish to assign part of this burden to light itself. Ecological optics is my way of doing so. This concerns light that is relevant to an eye, leaving aside radiation that is *irrelevant*. But I do not assume that light is *dependent* on an eye, as Ronchi seems to do.

This quotation is from Chap. 10 of Gibson's book, *The Senses Considered as Perceptual Systems* (1966). (The present chapter borrows its title from Chap. 10 of that book.) Among the characteristics shared by the books of Gibson and Ronchi is their polemical nature. Ronchi lists, and has published separately (1958) 20 "embarrassing questions" to which traditional optics cannot, in his view, provide satisfactory answers; because of this, he tends to denounce the whole subject of optics as conventionally treated. Gibson, in his turn, adds at the conclusion of his Chap. 10 three "supplementary notes," one each for students of optics, visual sensation, and philosophy, which make fascinating reading. The first begins: "Anyone who has studied modern optics as this mixed body of knowledge exists today will be puzzled, and perhaps offended, by what is here called ecological optics." To this writer, it is not so important whether one is puzzled or offended by Gibson. The important question is whether visual science will best be advanced by descriptions couched in his new form of "optics," which has few moorings to the established branches of the subject. Believing that the contrary is the case, I have taken it as my main task to recast Gibson's Chap. 10 in terms of the accepted branches of optics, hopefully doing so in a straightforward and relatively nonpolemical fashion.

Ecological optics can be considered as an attempt to extend a visually relevant optical analysis to include events outside the eye. It is not true that, with the discovery of an image on the retina of the eye, the contributions of optics to the science of vision will be exhausted when the details of our knowledge about this imaging process are filled in. Von Helmholtz was the monumental contributor to this effort to treat the eye as an optical system, yet his three-volume *Physiological Optics* (1924) deals with much more than eyeball optics. There are many good reasons, which I have discussed elsewhere (Boynton, 1967), why it is best not to restrict "physiological optics" to the optics of the eye.

II. HISTORICAL NOTES

An early attempt at ecological optics was made by that most influential physiologist of all time, Galen of Pergamon (129–201 A.D.) who was a strong proponent of the "emanation theory" of vision. Taking a lead from

Plato, Galen proclaimed that rays from the pupil of the eye were discharged in the direction of perceived objects.* In the presence of light, these rays were said to interact somehow with the perceived object, to be then returned to the lens of the eye. Meanwhile, a visual spirit, originating in the brain, was said to flow into the lens where it interacted with the returning rays. Vision was assumed to occur when the visual spirit, thus charged with a message from the object, was flushed back to the brain through a supposedly hollow optic nerve.

A record of some of the Greek accomplishments (and mistaken notions) was preserved through the middle centuries in the Arab culture, where some efforts at natural philosophy continued. Outstanding among such Arab philosophers was Ibn-al-Haitham, also known as Alhazen (965–1039 A.D.). He rejected the emanation theory, and apparently was the first to become convinced that some kind of optical image was formed in the eye. This conviction probably arose because of his knowledge of the pinhole camera, which he may actually have discovered. This simplest of optical devices (known today to almost everyone as the proper one to use when observing solar eclipses) is of fundamental importance to an understanding of this chapter.

If a very small hole is punched into the side of a box (see Fig. 1a) a small amount of light will be allowed to enter the dark enclosure within. Provided that some sort of screen is placed inside, an image† of external objects can be captured at any distance from the pinhole: the closer the screen to the hole, the brighter and smaller the image will be. Much important information about the external world is obviously represented in such an image, despite various limitations (it is two-dimensional, dim, and not particularly sharp). By viewing such an image, one can perceive identifiable objects, located in proper geometric relation to other objects and their surrounds.

In Alhazen's time, there was no evidence to support the view that a pinhole camera had anything in common with the eye. It was known that light entered the eye through the pupil, but the pupil of the eye is much too large to act as a pinhole [see Fig. 1(b)]. Indeed, if one enlarges the opening of the pinhole to the size of the eye's pupil, the image within the camera would be almost totally degraded.‡ Because dissection was prohibited by the

* Most of the material in this section is taken from Polyak (1957).

† The term "image," as used here, implies a distribution of light emerging from a surface which, when viewed, produces a visual sensation more or less resembling that which would be elicited instead by exposing the eye to the distribution of light emitted or reflected from tangible objects.

‡ This will be true unless the image were moved to such a long distance from the pinhole that the larger aperture would, effectively, again become a pinhole. An

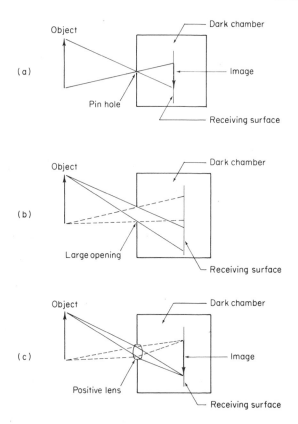

Fig. 1. (a) Pinhole camera. The only light from the ends of the object which can gain admittance to the dark chamber is that which is directed toward the pinhole. Consequently there is a constrained beam of light within the dark chamber, moving in the directions shown. A receiving surface placed anywhere within the chamber will register a dim and moderately sharp image of the object. (b) If the pinhole is enlarged to the size shown, light from the head and tail of the arrow-object (and from other points along it as well) will be diverging as it enters the dark chamber. The tip of the object will be poorly imaged as a large circle of light upon the receiving screen; other points along the object will register likewise, thus producing a grossly overlapping string of circles and a very badly blurred image. (c) If the large hole in the chamber is filled with a positive lens, the diverging light can be focused as shown upon a receiving surface, and a bright, sharp image may be achieved. For a given distance of the object from the lens, this image will be in good focus only at a particular distance of the receiving surface from the lens.

---

enormous camera would be required for this, and the resulting image would again be very dim, just as for the image formed by a true pinhole at a shorter distance. Needless to say, no such enormous distances are found within the eye, whose diameter is about 1 inch.

Arab religion, Alhazen and others of his day had to lean heavily upon Greek anatomy and belief, much of which (like the idea of a hollow optic nerve) was faulty. Thus there could have been little more than a suspicion on Alhazen's part that an image might exist somewhere within the eye. After the teachings of Galen, Alhazen believed that it was located in the lens.

During the Italian renaissance, the great scientist-painter Leonardo da Vinci (1452–1519) gave thought to these problems. He too was aware of the pinhole camera; aided by its use, he became a leader in the development of perspective drawing which had been completely unknown, for example, to the Greeks. He also became convinced that there was some kind of an image in the eye, and he attempted to sketch how the image-forming rays might behave. But nothing whatever was yet known about the laws of light refraction, and for all his genius and effort, Leonardo was not destined to discover these laws. In his attempts, he was seriously hampered by a curious but not unusual preoccupation: he thought that the image in the eye had to be right-side up.

Johannes Kepler (1570–1630) was a seventeenth century astronomer who, believing in the heliocentric theory of Copernicus, tested it by building telescopes with which to make stellar observations. In so doing, he developed new concepts in optics, and he appears to be the first person to have understood correctly how positive lenses actually work [including their role, illustrated in Fig. 1(c), in permitting the enlargement of the pinhole of a camera]. Proceeding from his understanding of these relations, Kepler reasoned that the lens of the human eye was required to form an image within, and therefore he was able to conclude that the image could not be formed within the lens itself. The vitreous humor, which fills the space between lens and retina, did not seem to be a likely candidate either, so he inferred that the receptive layer for vision was at the back of the eye. However, Kepler was curiously mistaken concerning a basic optical fact: he did not believe that significant refraction took place at the cornea of the eye. Had he known that it does, he might well have helped to perpetuate the myth of an image in the lens. In any event, he was correct in believing in a retinal image characterized as small in size, upside down, and systematically related to points in space.

In 1595, an Italian named Aranzi actually had cut a hole in the back of an animal eye, and by placing a translucent screen there, directly observed the image that Kepler was later to imagine. There is no evidence that Kepler knew of Aranzi's discovery, which had created remarkably little attention. In Germany, following Kepler's theoretical work, Scheiner successfully repeated Aranzi's experiment, the importance of which was then immediately recognized. Probably for this reason, Scheiner's name is usually associated with this demonstration.

The discovery of the retinal image was of monumental importance for the proper understanding of vision, since it immediately became clear that emanations from the eye were not needed in order to see, and that the image on the retina contained the essential geometric information required for spatial vision.

III. THE EYE AS A CAMERA

A popular lay view today, which probably began with Kepler and was later reinforced by advances in photographic science, is that the "eye works just like a camera."

The eye most emphatically does *not* work just like a camera, and the differences are worth discussing.* The eye is a living organ, while the camera is not. In a camera, light passes through the image-forming optics of high refractive index, and then back again into air before striking the film plane. In the eye, high-index media are encountered as light enters the eye at the outer surface of the cornea, but the light never again returns to air. The control of pupil size begins with the action of light upon the identical photoreceptors that initiate the act of vision, while the camera's photoelectric analog, when there is one, is located so that the light falling upon the photocell is *not* affected by the size of the opening in the iris diaphragm. The lens surfaces in most cameras are sections of spheres, to which an optical analysis developed for spherical components can properly be applied. There is no spherical surface anywhere in the eye. The camera lens is homogeneous in its refractive index (or at most contains a few such distinct elements, each of which has this property). The lens of the eye is layered like an onion, with the refractive index of each layer differing slightly from the next. Cameras have shutters and utilize discrete exposures, either singly or in succession. The pupil of the eye is continuously open. Cameras must be aimed by someone; the eye is part of a grand scheme which does its own aiming. Images produced by photographic cameras must first be processed and then viewed or otherwise analyzed; the image produced upon the retina is never again restored to optical form, and the mechanisms responsible for its processing are perhaps a billionfold more complex than those used in photography. This list could be expanded,

---

* The term "camera" literally implies only a darkened enclosure and not necessarily all the peripheral equipment that is associated with a photographic camera. The analogy between the eye and a photographic camera is discussed here.

but the point should by now be clear enough. Despite these important differences, the idea of the retinal image, "just like a camera," was an important insight. But preoccupation with the retinal image as a starting point for the analysis of vision has led to a limited view of the subject, one that has been vigorously challenged in the writings of James J. Gibson.

In 1959, writing in the first volume of Koch's *Psychology, a Study of a Science,* Gibson put forward the beautiful idea (p. 466) of a "flowing sea of energy . . . in which the organism is immersed. . . ." Somewhat later, in his book *The Senses Considered as Perceptual Systems* (1966), he introduced his concepts of ecological optics by saying (p. 12) that "Terrestrial airspaces are . . . filled with light; they contain a flux of interlocking reflected rays in all directions at all points. This dense reverberating network of rays is an important but neglected fact of optics, to which we will refer in elaborating what may be called *ecological* optics."

In Gibson's book, then, the earlier concept of a "sea of energy" has been replaced by a "dense interlocking network of rays." Unfortunately, the ray as used by Gibson is nearly as obscure a concept as the ray proposed by Galen. In using the ray conceptualization, contact with physical reality is lost, and what is left is purely geometric in nature.* Rays are considered, for example, to come from the edges of objects. However, no special properties are actually possessed by the edges of objects which enable them, in preference to homogeneous surfaces, to spray rays into the environment. In much of what follows, an attempt will be made to put the "sea of energy" back into the system.

Because of the eye–camera analogy, the subject of vision has too often been treated as if there were but one object in the visual world. In introductory psychology books, this object is sometimes a tree; opticists prefer arrows like those of Fig. 1. One or the other of these is viewed by an observer whose eye, for unexplained reasons, always remains stationary with respect to this single, clear, and presumably luminous stimulus. It is worth noting, as Gibson does, that the real world is much more complicated than this. Sources of light radiate energy that is reflected in very complicated ways from environmental surfaces: only some tiny percentage of the available light will enter the eye of an observer who is located somewhere in this environment. Being free to move within his environment, an observer samples different portions of the sea of radiant energy within which he is immersed. At the region in space where an eye happens to be located at a particular moment, light energy is moving in many directions. The problem that the visual apparatus faces is one of extracting meaningful

---

* This is true also for geometrical optics, an established branch of optical science (see Section IV of this chapter).

information from this complex distribution of light, which Gibson calls the "optic array."

IV. THE RELATION OF GEOMETRICAL OPTICS TO ECOLOGICAL OPTICS

Geometrical optics is a discipline concerned with methods whereby it is possible to predict, at least approximately, the location of images formed by optical systems. Instead of dealing with light as waves or photons (physical optics), the ray concept is utilized. The path of a ray corresponds, roughly, with the flight path of a photon: because this path is linear within a homogeneous medium, and changes predictably with a sudden change of medium, straight lines may be drawn to represent such paths, and very powerful techniques for doing this have been worked out which are based upon some very simple laws.

A ray may be drawn in any arbitrary direction from any point in object space. When a ray in air enters a different medium, for example the glass of a lens, it is refracted (bent) at the initial interface, and is refracted again as it comes out the other side. A well-designed lens focuses the rays on the image side, as shown in Fig. 1(c), but actually there is always a complex, three-dimensional collage of more-or-less intersecting rays. (A cross section taken through these produces a "spot diagram," whose compactness can provide a basis for assessing the quality of the image of a point source.)

There are two important respects in which the methods of geometrical optics, and the ray concept upon which these are based, deviate from the realities of physical optics. (1) The quality of the image is always worse in fact than the calculations of geometrical optics predict. As an important example of this, the quality of the image of a fine black line produced by an optical system like the eye should, according to geometrical optics, produce an image having 100% contrast, no matter what the width of the line. In fact, contrast will approach zero as the width of the line approaches zero (see Fig. 2). (2) Geometrical optics has nothing whatever to say about the *intensity* of the light. The density of rays might seem to bear some relation to this, but does not, because the optical designer is free to trace the paths of as few or as many rays as he wishes. Moreover, there is nothing about a particular ray to denote the density of photon traffic along its path. This could be as many as 10 million per microsecond or as few as 1 per hour: geometrical optics predicts the same image. But the performance of real optical systems, including those which have the eye as the final com-

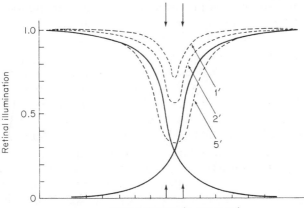

FIG. 2. Retinal illuminance produced by completely black lines of the widths indicated, seen against a bright background (dotted curves). The curve for a 2-min line has been derived by adding the distributions of the two edges shown by the solid lines. The other dotted curves were similarly constructed by moving the edge gradients closer together or farther apart than the distance shown. Edge gradients are from Westheimer and Campbell (1962).

ponent, is critically dependent upon intensity. Thus an important variable is left out.

V. CONTOUR

Very little seems to have been written about geometrical optics as the subject relates to the imaging of complex scenes, although the camera lenses that are designed with the help of the principles of geometrical optics are most often used for such purposes. What is it that we are in fact interested in imaging? The answer, Gibson (1966) stresses, is *contour*.

From the standpoint of photometry, contour concerns abrupt changes in luminance as one scans across the physical scene. As I look out the window of my study I see a dark tree; its left edge is outlined clearly against the bright snow in the background. I am confident that any other normally sighted person, assuming the same vantage point, would see this contour in the same location. This prediction could be more objectively specified and tested with the aid of a surveyor's transit, and it is virtually certain that two operators of this essentially visual instrument would give almost the same readings.

Suppose that we replace the optical system of the transit with an electronic telephotometer with a very small acceptance angle, and also replace the eye with a photocell. As the instrument is swung around until it just points toward the edge of the tree, the output delivered by the photocell abruptly decreases. For a purely geometric specification, then, we would expect the same result whether human vision were employed to specify the contour or, alternatively, the photometer-photocell device were used. Although the specification may in principle be made in purely physical terms, it is difficult, tedious, and (for some purposes) not particularly informative to do so. In this limited sense we may wish to accept Gibson's viewpoint, which considers contours, faces, facets, and textures in the real world which are defined and specified only by visual observation.

But for the purpose of trying to understand how an eye, located somewhere in the environment, is actually able to extract the useful information that is optically located there, a purely geometric specification is a poor point at which to begin such an analysis, because such a specification of the stimulus clearly implies that a visual observation *already has been made*; thus one is caught up in a tautology which can explain nothing. Gibson neatly sidesteps this problem (he thinks) by proclaiming that the optic array, at the point where the eye or other detector is located, already contains the information necessary for vision. This is why, for him, there is no need to be particularly concerned about the mechanisms in whatever pickup device that is used to analyze the array; one needs to know only about the array itself. Although Gibson has quite a bit to say about eyes in the early chapters of his book, he makes the following statement in his "Supplementary Note for Students of Visual Sensation" at the end of Chap. 10:

> The reader who knows the facts of visual psychophysiology and psychophysics may wonder why no reference has been made to them in this chapter. Nothing has been said about the measuring of light intensity in patches by methods of photometry, or about the sensation of brightness that theoretically ought to correspond to the luminance of each patch in the optic array, or about the nature of this correspondence. The reason is that these elegant quantitative studies become irrelevant to perception, if the assumptions made in this chapter are correct. . . .

We may doubt that a blind man would be much impressed by the viewpoint just stated. He would probably want to know, if the detection of the optic array is so trivial and uninteresting a problem, why no one has been able to build for him a device that will do this with anything like the fidelity of real vision.

VI. USEFUL PROPERTIES OF LIGHT

Light is a form of energy admirably suited to provide detailed spatial information. There are several reasons for this. First, in air, most light travels in reasonably straight lines. Not all of it does, and that which is scattered or refracted is critically important for vision, both outside as well as within the eye. In a homogeneous medium, image-forming rays travel in straight lines, and thus it is possible to learn something about the location of a source of light, provided only that a means exists to determine the direction of travel of the light originating from that source: the light must, of course, have come from somewhere along the line of travel. With two such sightings, the location of the source could be pinpointed by triangulation (a common procedure in navigation), but the eye does not do this.

A second useful property of light is the very high velocity at which it travels. Over terrestrial distances, this has the advantage, not shared by our other distance senses, of permitting essentially instantaneous contact with distant sources.

A third useful property of light is the manner in which it interacts with surfaces. Probably the most important correlate of the perception of a surface is its diffuse reflectance—the amount of light which is reflected back over a wide range of angles, relative to what is incident at a particular angle. A diffusely reflecting surface reflects light in a manner that is largely independent of the location of the source that illuminates it, making relatively easy the identification of that light as "belonging" to a surface, rather than to the source.

The concept of light as flying photons seems best for purposes of understanding vision, although physicists tell us that photons do not have a precise location in space at a given time. But for visual purposes it is convenient and not overly misleading to think of them as tiny, speeding bullets, so small that they can be packed into very small spaces without interacting (for example, there is negligible interaction between the concentrated beams emerging from two slide projectors crossing at right angles). Once created, a photon moves eternally in a straight line unless interacting with matter; if this happens, the light either will be absorbed and the photon will "die" (usually being converted into heat) or it will be reflected or refracted at one angle or another. (Other possibilities exist, but are of secondary importance for visual perception.)

VII. THE DENSE NETWORK OF RAYS

The poorly lit and sparsely furnished room of Fig. 3 was invented by Gibson to introduce and illustrate his concepts of ecological optics. We borrow it here to illustrate the present version of the subject.

The single lamp suspended from the ceiling emits photons in a variety of directions. A real light bulb, like the one depicted, must have a finite surface area from which such photons are emitted. For convenience, we will

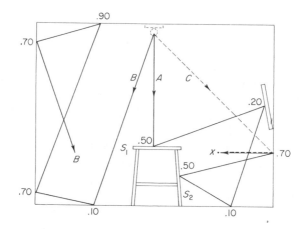

FIG. 3. A tiny sample of the paths that might be taken by photons emitted from a light source in the ceiling of a room. The numbers shown are the assumed diffuse spectral reflectances of various surfaces in the rooms, used for purposes of calculation (see Table I).

pretend instead that the lamp is a "point source" and imagine that all of the emitted light emerges from a common point at the center of the bulb. When the lamp is heated to incandescence, photons are generated. For any single photon it is impossible to predict the direction of its movement, but statements can be made concerning the *probability* that a photon will be emitted in a particular direction. The higher this probability, the higher is the intensity of the source in that direction.

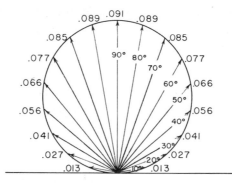

FIG. 4. A perfectly diffuse surface with a reflectance of 1.0 reflects light in the manner shown in this diagram. Each vector has a length which is proportional to the probability that a quantum incident at point *p* will be reflected in the direction shown, ±5°. The probabilities given at the arrow tips sum to 1.0. Reflectance at angles less than 5°, which is very small, is ignored in these calculations.

Consider a photon emitted in direction A, heading toward the top of the stool. As already noted, the path traced out by the movement of this particle is the physical manifestation of a "ray." For simplicity, assume that the top of the stool (and all other surfaces in the room) has the special property of being 'perfectly diffuse." (This concept is described and explained in Fig. 4). The *reflectance R* of a perfectly diffuse surface specifies the fraction of incident light that will be reflected in one direction or another. The top of the stool has a reflectance of 0.50, which means that half the incident photons are absorbed, while the other half are reflected (which is the same as saying that, for any given photon, the probability of reflection is 0.5). The probability that a single photon, starting in the direction A, will later travel in direction X as a result of the particular series of reflections shown, can be calculated by application of the following formula:

$$p = p_{r1}p_{\theta 1} \cdot p_{r2}p_{\theta 2} \ldots p_{rn}p_{\theta n}$$

where p_{rn} is the probability that a photon incident upon surface n will be reflected in some direction θ_n, and $p_{\theta n}$ is the probability that a photon, (if reflected) will be contained within an angle $\theta \pm 5°$. The result of these calculations is shown in Table I. There is about one chance in a billion that this particular series of events will occur.

Another photon reaching point X, traveling in the direction shown, could arrive there by an entirely different route. The dotted lines in the diagram provide an example of a much shorter route (C). No detector, whether an eye or otherwise, would be able to discriminate, at the final common path, which of these two routes had been traversed. It is necessary to imagine a few million ray paths like the ones shown (path B provides one more example) to begin to develop some notion of what Gibson has in mind when he refers to a "dense network of rays." It would be hopeless to attempt a full diagram of this network, since the entire room would soon be blackened with rays.

TABLE I   Calculation of Photon Path Probabilities

Surface	Probability of reflection	Angle θ	Percent of reflected light within $\theta \pm 5°$	Cumulative probability
Top of stool	0.50	20°	0.027	0.0135
Picture (right)	0.20	30°	0.041	0.00011
Floor	0.10	30°	0.041	0.000,000,46
Side of Stool	0.50	80°	0.089	0.000,000,020
Wall	0.70	70°	0.085	0.000,000,001,2

A major consequence of this dense network is that, for each point in the room, there will be rays incident there from every point of every surface (except for the obstruction of rays caused by the interposition of a completely absorbing object). This fact makes it possible for an eye, as it moves within the room, to pick up information about surfaces from almost any point within it. Such a point, when arbitrarily chosen for optical analysis, is called a "station point" by Gibson.

VIII. THE STATIONARY CONVERGENCE POINT

In a homogeneous medium, the light emitted from a point always diverges. Therefore, the entire dense network of rays which blackens our conceptual space consists of overlapping sets of diverging rays, each set being associated with some particular point of emission. Nevertheless, Gibson wrote, in his 1959 chapter in Koch's Volume 1 (p. 472) that "there in a whole array of focusable light converging to *any* given location in the open air. This may be termed the optical aray, one sector of which is picked up by an eye. . . ." This statement is, physically and optically, *unconditionally wrong. Focusable* light *never* converges, but always diverges; it is the job of an optical system, for example a lens, to produce the convergence that causes the focus. The erroneous concept is retained unaltered in Gibson's book, where we find an observer (see Fig. 5) placed in the same room illustrated here in Fig. 3. Rays from the edges of objects are shown

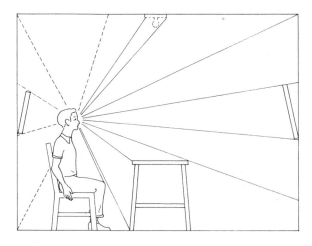

FIG. 5. The effective array at a stationary convergence point according to Gibson (1966).

converging toward the eye; Gibson's figure caption explains that "The solid lines represent the sample of the total optic array that is admitted to a human eye in a given posture. The dashed lines (which are intercepted by the head and body of the observer) represent the remainder of the array, which is available for stimulation but not effective at this moment."

Since this is wrong, is it just nonsense that Gibson proposes? Fortunately, no, but a type of additional analysis, not offered by Gibson, must now be entered into in order to make sense of it.

IX. A MAGIC CUBE

Let us demarcate, for purpose of analysis, a cubic foot of space within a room, perhaps a three-dimensional version of the one sketched in Fig. 6. Consider the cube to be located in mid-air, remote from the source of light or any of the surfaces or objects in the room. Within this cubic foot of space, there will exist a dense and complex distribution of paths of moving photons, a sample of the dense network of rays just discussed. Three such rays are illustrated in Fig. 6. Here the rays have been shown as they exist outside and inside the cube, all passing through the internal point x. The total number of rays that could be drawn through x is indefinite. Similar arrays of arrows should also be imagined as passing through all possible points within the cube, and many more arrows than the number shown should be imagined as passing through each point.

Think now about what would happen if a head were positioned so that one of its eyes were entirely located within this cubic foot of space. One consequence would be that no rays could pass through the space from behind the head, so that the distribution of light in the cube would be altered thereby. Otherwise, the incoming distribution of rays (the "optic array," in

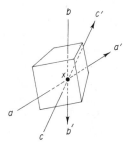

FIG. 6. A "magic cube." The reader is asked to imagine that photons exist only within the cube, along the three paths shown by the dotted lines.

Gibson's terminology) would be unaltered. This provides the correct notion that the optical basis for vision is totally contained within the optic array in the *region* where the eye is located.

Think now about something much more difficult to imagine, something physically impossible, yet instructive to consider: suppose that, by some magic, all incident photons outside the cube now cease to exist, but that somehow their distribution within the cube is the same as it would have been otherwise. For example, imagine that photons that ordinarily would come in along the path c–c' (Fig. 6) are now, instead, suddenly generated at the interface where that ray strikes the cube. Having instantaneously assumed the speed of light, these photons now exist only while passing through the cube (including point x) until they reach the interface on the opposite side–a flight path that would require about a tenth of a nsecond. Here they suddenly disappear again. In other words, no incident energy exists outside the cube, but the radiant energy within the cube is nevertheless assumed to be distributed exactly as before, when there was a real light source in a real room with real objects and therefore a full distribution of light within.

What would happen if the eye were located, as before, within such a cube, assuming again that the flow of photons within it were the same as that occurring in an actual, lighted room, except that photons exist only within the cube? The inescapable answer is that the observer would see the same room, containing the same objects, as he would see if the photons existed also outside the cube. There would be no basis for him to know that photons now exist only within the cube; thus he would perceive the consequences of this photon flow as a truly three-dimensional, full-color "reproduction." Indeed, he could even swing his head around within the cube and thus perceive "objects" that had formerly been "obscured" by the back of his head.

Modern holographic techniques produce a pale version of this sort of thing, where three-dimensional objects are seen where none physically exist. Seeing objects in a mirror is actually a better example of the phenomenon: if a tube is held before the eye and objects are viewed by reflection in a mirror, there is no basis for knowing that the objects do not actually exist at the point in space where they seem to be.* The main point should by now be clear: if the distribution of light that would have been produced by the reflected light from real objects could somehow be reproduced without the objects actually being there, the visual end result would be the same. This *Gedanken* experiment emphasizes that we are not

---

* It is easy to take the commonplace for granted. Seeing objects in a mirror is probably the most compelling "optical illusion" of them all.

in visual contact with objects, or edges, facets, faces, or textures. We are in contact only with photons.

X. POINT SOURCES AND POINT SINKS

The intensity of a point source is a measure proportional to the numbers of photons that are moving, per unit solid angle, in a particular direction with respect to the source. A convenient way to represent the intensity of a source is by a series of vectors drawn from a point: the angle of the vector indicates the direction in which intensity is to be specified, whereas the length of the vector specifies the intensity at that angle (see Fig. 4). The full intensity distribution from a point source could be represented by a three-dimensional solid, inside of which the reference point would be located. Imagine, for example, an oddly shaped lump of clear plastic, and visualize within it some arbitrary point which can be taken to represent the location of the point source. Vectors drawn from the point to the surface of the plastic could then represent the intensity of the source in various directions. Because three-dimensional representation is difficult, intensity diagrams of this sort are usually represented as two-dimensional plane sections through the internal point. The intersection of one of these planes with the surface of the plastic would then specify the location of arrowheads of the vectors of intensity, each drawn from the common internal point.

The point source, used in this way, has some of the same conceptual properties and physical limitations as does the stationary convergence point of Gibson, since real sources also have a finite volume and no source of zero volume could emit any light.

It is possible to consider the stationary convergence point in the same way that point sources have been treated, excepting that the direction of the vectors is reversed. Since we have chosen to deal with the distribution of light which is converging toward a point, we may again describe this in terms of a three-dimensional solid. Each point on the surface is located at a distance from the internal stationary convergence point which represents the intensity (photons per unit solid angle) incident toward the internal point; the location of a point on the surface of the object relative to the internal point defines a vector drawn from the surface point to the internal point. Thus the geometry of the situation is exactly the same as for the measurement of the intensity of light from a point source, excepting that the direction of the light is reversed; thus it seems reasonable to refer to this new measurement as *negative intensity,* implying (falsely) that all of the incident light dies at the point, which then becomes a *point sink.*

In principle, all of the richness of achromatic detail inherent in the visual

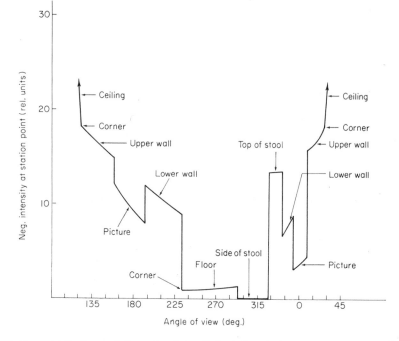

FIG. 7. Distributions of "negative intensity" at the stationary convergence point where the eye is located in Fig. 5. Zero degrees is taken as directly ahead of the eye (to the right in Fig. 5) and other angles are specified according to the usual geometric convention (270° is straight down, 180° is behind the head, and 90° would be straight up). Negative intensities associated with light reflecting from the ceiling, which would be very high compared to those calculated, are not shown. In making these calculations, the reflectances of the various surfaces are as given in Table I; the "picture" hanging on the left-hand wall is assumed to have a reflectance of 0.5. The stool is assumed to be solid. All surfaces are assumed to be perfectly diffuse, and only that light which has been once reflected is used in making the calculations.

environment could be specified by such a set of vectors defining the negative intensity distribution around a point sink.

In Fig. 7, this has been attempted for Gibson's room, and the result is represented in Cartesian coordinates. This representation assumes that the illuminance can be calculated anywhere in the room by application of the inverse-square law:

$$E = I/d^2$$

where I is the intensity of the source in a given direction and d is the distance from the source to the surface. Secondary reflections from other surfaces, of the sort described earlier, have been disregarded, as well as tertiary and still higher-order reflections.

The purpose of this exercise is to breathe some physical life into the geometric concepts introduced by Gibson. In referring to Fig. 5 Gibson states:

> It should be especially noted that the lines in this diagram have a different character from those in previous diagrams, corresponding as they do to the edges and corners of surfaces facing in different directions. They are no longer beams of light shrunken to lines; they are the boundaries between pencils of rays. They are no longer the paths of photons; they are relations. Hence they no longer represent energy but information. . . . A relation, I think, cannot be said to carry energy. A boundary, margin, border, contour, or transition is nevertheless justly considered as a stimulus for an eye, or more exactly, stimulus *information* for an eye, and this is the central problem of [ecological optics].

The point of view being taken here is very different. My emphasis is upon the undeniable fact that the eye is not actually in contact with Gibson's boundaries, margins, borders, contours, etc., but only with photons that enter the eye as a result of reflection from surfaces. With this in mind, the boundaries of which Gibson writes are properly conceived as being associated with rapid rates of change in the negative intensity diagram just introduced.

XI. THE PICKUP DEVICE

In order to respond to such rapid rates of change, there must be a detector which can differentially respond according to the angle of incidence of the incoming quanta. To understand the evolution of vision requires knowing how biological devices have developed which are capable of extracting intelligence from the optic potential, the "sea" of radiant energy. Many problems of visual perception are also concerned with trying to understand how such adaptively useful information can be got from this complex array of flying photons. This, it seems to me, is a proper starting point for the analysis of vision. I agree with Gibson that the retinal image, often so considered, is not.

How might one choose to build a device to tell us what we need to know about this light distribution? One possible solution would utilize a tiny bit of stuff that not only absorbs light, but which also can keep account of (1) the quantity of light absorbed, e.g., number of photons, (2) the energy distribution of this absorption (the basis for color), and (3) the direction from which each absorbed photon came. It turns out that no such a device has evolved. The reason for this is essentially connected with the fact that the energy of a photon is terribly small. In order to have good vision when an absorption takes place, it is nevertheless necessary to have some kind of a signal generated which, although too small to lead by itself to a visual sensation, can combine with a very few other such signals—perhaps a half-dozen at the absolute threshold.

The visual photopigments which do this absorbing are basically the same in all living creatures so far studied. They contain stored energy which is released when a photon is absorbed. But all evidence strongly indicates that the signal that is produced by this energy release simply indicates that the absorption has occurred, and nothing more. The signal does not tell what the energy of the absorbed photon was, or from what direction it came. Such a response is called a *univariant* response, and it just seems to be the nature of things that this is what the visual system utilizes.

Faced with this limitation, how could we build a pickup device to provide evidence about direction? One way would be to take a convex surface and stud it with directional light pipes. Visualize an array of blackened soda straws sticking out of a sphere. We could then place photopigment at the base of each pipe and, if we had some way to record which pigment did the absorbing, we would have a way of knowing something about the direction from which the absorbed photon came. In this case, information about direction would be converted into a spatial code, so that the direction of light incidence would be signaled by which of an array of spots of photopigments were activated. (Clearly there would be a need for some sort of neural network inside the sphere in order to interpret all this.) What has just been described is, in fact, much like the compound eye of the housefly and also that sacred crab of the visual physiologist, *Limulus polyphemus*.

This of course has turned out not to be the optimal solution. We humans see better than the crab does, and our eyes work differently. Our eyes share with the crab's the fact that information about direction is converted into a spatial code, but it is done differently. Assuming a fixed position of the eye and, for the moment, a pinhole pupil located at a station point, the negative intensity distribution at that point reveals itself as a positive illuminance distribution on the retina.

A device that can analyze the distribution of negative intensity at a stationary convergence point is the pinhole camera, already discussed. If the light actually died at the station point, the pinhole camera would record nothing. But it does not die: photons cross at the pinhole so that the distribution of positive intensities inside the camera corresponds spatially and quantitatively to the distribution of negative intensities outside. From all of the rays in the dense network, the pinhole camera samples only that subset which converges at the pinhole. Thus, despite the fact that all light in the network diverges from the various points that either radiate or reflect it, there is an array of (nonfocusable) light converging to any given location in open air: Gibson's trick is to ignore all light except that which happens to pass through this point.

But we have seen that a pinhole pupil would produce an eye that would see very poorly. Something must be done to enlarge the entrance port without destroying the retinal image, and we find that the human eye does this in the same basic manner as do all optical systems which focus light to produce images, just as Kepler first demonstrated.

Each luminous point in space irradiates photons in many directions, some in the direction of our eye. For the stationary eye with a fixed but finite pupil, there is from each point in space a cone of light, made up of photons traveling in similar, but significantly different directions. Each of these rays must have the same meaning if we are correctly to infer its origin. The job of the optical system of the eye is somehow to map this diverging light back as nearly as possible into a point. This is done by the optical system of the eye; each point on the retina receives a converging bundle of rays. The absorption of light by molecules of photopigment located there encodes the fact that the source of the light was located somewhere along a particular line in space, this line having a particular direction with respect to the eye. The accommodative mechanism of the eye allows this point to be sharply imaged for sources located along this line at a variety of possible distances from the eye.

It is thus not sufficient to consider only the network of rays converging at a station point, since the entrance port of the eye with its finite pupil is not located at a point but occupies an area. A pickup device that can deal only with the optic array at a point must be severely limited in its performance.

The nodal point, in optics, describes where a pinhole would have to be located, in air, to form the same geometric image as that actually produced by the optical system. In the eye, this is located just behind the lens of the eye. This is a very useful conception for calculating visual angles and for approximating the location of retinal images as these relate to the external patterns of light. But there is in fact no such point or pinhole, nor is there air in the eye, so that photons do not actually cross at the nodal point of the eye, not even a subset of them.

XII. SUMMARY

It should be mentioned that the analysis given in this chapter deliberately avoids any consideration of many complex aspects of the visual environment that are important for perception. Color vision is possible because of the varying energies of photons entering the eye; these in turn are related to the selective reflectances, with wavelength, of the surfaces from which photons reflect. Perfectly diffuse surfaces do not exist in nature, although there are some which come very close to it. Most surfaces exhibit specular (mirror-like) and diffuse reflectance at the same time, giving us evidence of their smoothness and probable feel. Specular reflectance provides information about the color of the source of illumination of the objects, an important cue for color constancy. The imperfect optical system of the eye means that a negative intensity distribution like that of Fig. 7, when translated into a positive light distribution on the retina, will be less sharp (for example, the infinitely steep gradients of Fig. 7 will have a finite slope).

In summary, the following points are stressed. Gibson is correct when he says that visual information is potentially contained in the optic array at a stationary convergence point. But it is not possible to build an optical device, including an eye, which is located at a point, or whose entrance port is punctate, if the device is to have decent sensitivity and resolving power. The point is nevertheless a useful analytic concept, and can be treated as a point sink, around which the distribution of "negative intensity" describes the salient features of the visual environment. Positive-power optics, which focus light, can be used (and have evolved in the eye) to allow large entrance ports. The distribution of light at the station point is not focusable, as Gibson maintains, since focusable light is confined to that which *diverges* from each of the elements from which it radiates, and therefore necessarily occupies a finite area. Although there is a sense in which it seems correct to assert that all information about the visual environment is contained at a station point in the optic array that is found there, this differs little from the ray tracing exercise of the geometrical opticist who uses the nodal point concept to predict the approximate location of an image. Neither geometrical nor ecological optics is in the least useful for deciding how to build a device capable of picking up the information. Rays are not real, while photons are; the characteristics of salient contours in the outside world should be defined in terms of distributions of negative intensity at the station point, and not tautologically in terms of rays arbitrarily drawn from elements of the environment that have already been deemed, through the use of vision, to be visually significant.

References

Boynton, R. M. Progress in physiological optics. *Applied Optics,* 1967, **6,** 1283–1293.
Gibson, J. J. Perception as a function of stimulation. In S. Koch (Ed.), *Psychology, a study of a science.* Vol. 1. *Sensory, perceptual, and physiological formulations.* New York: McGraw-Hill, 1959. Pp. 456–501.

Gibson, J. J. *The senses considered as perceptual systems.* Boston, Massachusetts: Houghton, 1966.

Polyak, S. L. *The vertebrate visual system.* Chicago, Illinois: Univ. of Chicago Press, 1957.

Ronchi, V. *Optics: The science of vision* (Transl. by E. Rosen) New York: New York Univ. Press, 1957.

Ronchi, V. Twenty embarrassing questions. (Transl. by E. Rosen) *Atti della Fondazione Georgio Ronchie Contributi dell' Istituto Nazionate di Ottica,* 1958, **13,** 3–20.

von Helmholtz, H. In J. P. C. Southhall (Ed.), *Treatise on physiological optics.* Vols. I, II, and III. New York: Dover, 1924. (Originally published 1909.)

Westheimer, G., & Campbell, F. W. Light distribution in the image formed by the living human eye. *Journal of The Optical Society of America,* 1962, **52,** 1040–1045.

Chapter 15

A NOTE ON ECOLOGICAL OPTICS

JAMES J. GIBSON

The foregoing chapter on ecological optics, by R. M. Boynton, is both a description and a critique of what I believe to be an emerging discipline. The critique is welcome, but the description is so incomplete that I take this opportunity to say so, even at the risk of sounding ungracious.

A chapter on the subject could have been written by me, and the reader may wonder why I did not grasp the opportunity. The reason is that ecological optics cannot be treated in one chapter. It claims to be more than a special branch of optical science; it is more radical and more far-reaching than that. It is the basis for a new theory of vision and is itself based on a new conception of the environment to be perceived. It implies a new answer to the old question of how knowledge is possible. I have doubts that "visual science will be advanced" by it—more likely visual science will be upset although, of course, an upset is sometimes an advance. For these reasons, ecological optics needs to be treated in the context of a whole book on visual perception, and such a book is forthcoming.

I argue that the established branches of optics are appropriate for the study of visual sensations but not for the study of visual perception. I maintain that visual perception is not based on having sensations but on attention to the information in light. The essence of ecological optics is the demonstration that there *is* information in ambient light. The common assumption of physical, geometric, and physiological optics, however, is that there is *no* information in light, that is, no information about the ordinary things from which the light is reflected. A good deal of hedging goes on in perceptual theory today in the attempt to avoid facing this issue, but I am convinced that it is unavoidable. And this is the reason why ecological optics is theoretically crucial. The kind of optics one accepts determines one's theory of perception.

Students of traditional optics, like students of sensory physiology, tend to be impatient with what they consider philosophical issues. They like to believe that science progresses by the accumulation of facts, not by polemics. Yet when Boynton asserts (pp. 300–301) that "we are not in visual contact with objects, or edges, facets, faces, or textures. We are in contact only with photons," this assertion is loaded with epistemology. It is a strictly philosophical conclusion. I disagree with it. There is a misunderstanding of the metaphor of "visual contact," one that goes back to Johannes Müller, and it is one that I discussed repeatedly in *The Senses Considered as Perceptual Systems* (Gibson, 1966). It leads to the doctrine that all we can ever *see* (or at least all we can ever see *directly*) is *light*.

The heart of ecological optics is the concept of the ambient optic array at a point of observation. The ambient *array* is to be distinguished from the ambient *light*. The former constitutes stimulus information; the latter constitutes stimulus energy. Boynton thoroughly approves of the concept of ambient light energy coming to a point (I call it a "Boynton point") but he is doubtful of the concept of a purely relational array or structure. He catches me up for having once defined it in terms of rays, and he is quite right to do so. The formula of a "dense intersecting network of rays" was a mistake; all I meant to imply by it was that the steady state of illumination in a living-space is *projective*. I now define an ambient optic array as a nested set of adjacent *solid angles,* not *rays,* each solid angle corresponding to one of the large faces or small facets of the environment. The solid angles are separated by contours or contrasts. These contours I take to be mathematically definite, and to be independent of an observer. So defined, the array as such is invariant from noon to sunset.

In this theory contours or contrasts are optical facts, and are more important for useful vision than intensities. It becomes reasonable to assume that some mechanism of the visual system registers contours directly, without first having to register the different intensities in the form of brightness sensations on either side of each contour and only thus to detect the differences. This is what I meant by suggesting that visual sensations were irrelevant for visual perception; I meant sensations, not sensitivity. Boynton, like most of us until recently, identifies the problem of information pickup with that of having sensations, but this is a confusion. The mechanism of information pickup entails sensitivity but is not one of getting and then interpreting the so-called data of sense.

Boynton says that, for me, "there is no need to be particularly concerned about the mechanisms in whatever pickup device is used to analyze the array; one needs to know only about the array itself." But of course I *do* need to be concerned with the mechanisms of information pickup; the difference between us is that I am led to postulate a device that samples the structure of the ambient array whereas he is led to postulate a device that operates on a set of neural signals from the retinal mosaic.

We are both suspicious of the eye–camera analogy, although I go further than he does in rejecting the usefulness of the concept of the retinal image. He still believes that "the discovery of the retinal image was of monumental importance for the proper understanding of vision" (p. 290). I maintain that it was only important for the understanding of *vertebrate* vision, the kind of vision based on the chambered eye, and that the optic array is more important for vision in general, which can be based on either the chambered eye or the compound eye. In short I maintain that the chambered eye with an image-forming lens is only one way of sampling the information in ambient light; the eye consisting of tubes each pointing in a different direction achieves the same end without a focusing lens and with no focused image. The seeing of the environment does not, then, depend on the formation of an image. This conclusion has quite radical implications for perception. I am not quite sure whether Boynton accepts it or not.

In this connection he again points out my error in 1959 of conceiving an ambient array as a dense set of rays. I did say that the array consisted of "focusable light," thinking only of the eye with a lens and forgetting that "focusable light never converges but always diverges; it is the job of a lens to produce the convergence that causes the focus" (p. 298) Boynton is right. Rays radiate. What converges are visual solid angles. But he is not right, I think, in saying that the error is carried over into my 1966 book.

Incidentally, I now call the apex of all the visual angles in an array a *point of observation,* not a *station point.* The reason is that a point of observation is almost never stationary, and the structure of an optic array is almost never frozen but changing. The station point of a picture projected on a transparent plane, in perspective geometry, is not to be confused with the point of observation for an ambient array, in ecological optics. The two are not so similar as I once thought. The "laws of perspective" are not the same as the invariants in an optic array.

Boynton has become convinced that ambient light as well as radiant light should be accorded some treatment in optics. He proposes that intensity vectors toward a point (a *point sink*) should be recognized as well as intensity vectors from a point (a *point source*). How is this conception of ambient *light,* drawn from physical optics, related to my conception of an ambient *array,* drawn from a new sort of abstract geometrical optics? This is an important question. I want to say that the former is stimulus energy while the latter is stimulus information. But he does not agree, and wishes to "breathe some physical life into the geometric concepts" that I have introduced. The reader is invited to reconcile these different formulas, if he can.

The purpose of ecological optics is not to explain the visibility of stars, or lighthouses, or spectral colors. It is not to improve the design of optical instruments or the prescribing of spectacles. It is not concerned with dazzle, or afterimages. Its purpose is to explain how animals see their environment, chiefly illuminated surfaces, and this explanation has been sadly neglected. Ecological optics is less concerned with seeing light than with the seeing of things by *means* of light. Consequently, I believe that it can *bracket* the disciplines of radiometry, photometry, and psychophysics and base itself on the *invariant* properties of an optic array. These geometric concepts may well prove to be more lifelike than the physics of photons.

The invariants in a changing optic array over time permit the student of vision to investigate problems that otherwise he could not touch. Traditional optics, physical, geometric, and physiological, simply cannot handle the fact that we live in a cluttered environment of opaque surfaces and hence that some things are hidden at some points of observation. But ecological optics invites the study of occluding edges, angular and curved, and the changing occlusion that results from a moving point of observation. Any surface is revealed by an appropriate movement, both the back side of an object and the background of it. Disocclusion at one edge is usually accompanied by occlusion at another. The optical transitions that specify the changing occlusion have been worked out (Gibson, Kaplan, Reynolds, & Wheeler, 1969). The perception is of *one surface behind another*. The observer does not see a patchwork with depth added; he does not see space; he does not see a figure on a ground. He perceives an occluded surface without having any sensations to correspond with that surface. Presumably the perception is based on an invariant over time.

A frozen optic array therefore is never in one-to-one projective correspondence with the cluttered environment that we actually perceive. Still less is a retinal image or a picture of some selected sector of the cluttered environment. What we see is not a projection, an image, or a picture, but a layout of surfaces. And the information for perceiving this layout is got by noticing what is invariant under changes of the array produced by the exploratory movements of the observer himself.

References

Gibson, J. J. *The senses considered as perceptual systems.* Boston, Massachusetts: Houghton, 1966.

Gibson, J. J., Kaplan, G. A., Reynolds, H. N., & Wheeler, K. The change from visible to invisible: A study of optical transitions. *Perception and Psychophysics,* **5**, 113–116.

Chapter 16

INFORMATION PROCESSING

RALPH NORMAN HABER

If it is possible to be in the midst of a revolution of which most of the protagonists are unaware, then the information processing approach to the study of perception is such a revolution. It has caused a fundamental change in the way research is done and in the way ideas are formulated. But these changes have been relatively unheralded, and with only a few important exceptions, they have been unnoticed as individual contributions. In total, however, the impact has been immense and as far reaching as any other single set of changes in perception in the past century. It is still very much with us, and the final outcome is not yet clear, although most of us in the middle of it see it as incredibly fruitful and with long-lasting implications for both the theory and the data of perception. Needless to say, this reviewer of the current scene is particularly convinced.

Having sounded such a call to arms, it should be easy to describe the revolution. Some of the players will emerge over the next few pages. But the action is more difficult to specify, until a context or perspective is developed. For the moment, it should be sufficient to say that an information processing approach places heavy stress on processing as an active, multistage activity, and uses a very flexible concept of information as that which is being processed.

I. ORIGINS OF INFORMATION PROCESSING APPROACHES

Processing models in psychology are not new. Freud's psychoanalytic theory of motivation and personality is explicitly a processing model. What is processed for him is energy which undergoes numerous investments, cathexes, and shifts as a function of development and experience. This concept of energy processing holds a central place in Freud's theories, even though he had to redefine energy in a way somewhat differently from the typical connotations used by psychologists or neurologists of his day. We shall note a similar change in the concept of information in information processing theories.

There have been processing theories in perception as well. The microgenetic analysis stressed by Werner and his colleagues at Clark is a prime example (see Flavell & Draguns, 1957, for a general review). Werner argues that perception should be characterized as a temporal growth process—a growth in clarity. The time scale is microgenetic, extending over a few hundred milliseconds after the onset of stimulation. Werner stresses the growth of contours and offers his research on metacontrast (especially 1935) as evidence that if a new contour is introduced adjacent to one which is not yet fully developed, the latter's growth is disturbed and perception is attenuated. Kaswan and Young (1963) use this approach to study the growth of contours quantitatively. They show that very fine detail specified by contours does not appear "at once," but rather the subject requires time in order to make fine acuity judgments.

Microgenetic theory, either in its original form given by Werner or as expressed by subsequent research, has not suggested any operations to distinguish the characteristics of this slow growth, especially in ways that might differentiate it as continuous or as going through discrete stages. Whether this has been a determinant of the relatively small impact that the microgenetic approach has had on perceptual theory and research is not clear to me, but this lack of specification has clearly limited the usefulness of this otherwise important contribution.

Thus, neither Freud nor Werner is a father of information processing. In fact, the paternity cannot be traced to psychologists at all. Rather, I see three clear antecedents, ones that have affected nearly all of psychology, but whose impact on perception has been felt simultaneously. These are the communication theory of Shannon and Wiener, the definition of information as a metric for communication, and the arrival of digital computers as a computational and analogic device. All three can be dated to the time of the second World War, and attracted psychological attention immediately after the war. Needless to say, these three are themselves closely related to each other.

The communication theory of Shannon and Wiener, stemming from work at the Massachusetts Institute of Technology and at Bell Telephone Laboratories, reached general publication in 1949. It was developed to apply to telephone switchboard systems, although its general application has been far greater. Of relevance to this discussion, they provided a model of communication in terms of channels over which messages are transmitted. Their goal was to describe such a system with statistical concepts of complete generality, that is, independent of the specific types of channels, the types of senders and receivers, and most critically, the nature or the content of the information flowing through the channels. The importance to perceptual theorizing of this model is the ease with which it could be applied to human perceptual systems, which are viewed as communication channels (see Fig. 1). Statistical procedures were available to define various characteristics of transmission of signals in noise, of the information content of the messages themselves, and of capacity of the channels. All of these could be defined independently of which system and what kind of signals are being communicated.

The second antecedent stems from the same sources and creators, but deserves mention in its own right. Shannon specified information content that was independent of the physical units of the stimulus and of the response. This was in terms of uncertainty reduction, or a change in the number of alternative possibilities the events being communicated could represent. Since these could be specified in theory for any particular type of communication, this concept of information provided a metric that was not dependent upon the events themselves. Hence, the information in a word, or in Morse code, or in speech heard in noise, or categorical judgments, or in a picture pattern, all could be defined by uncertainty: How much do we have to learn about the event in question to distinguish it from all possible events that could have been involved in the communication?

This is not the place to review the impact of this definition on perception on the rest of psychology (see Courtis & Green, 1963, and Garner, 1962, for two such reviews). For perceptual research it provided a critical ingredient—a means to compare across different stimuli in different experimental settings to arrive at a more general statement about perceptual processes. As I will note in a later section, few of those who use informa-

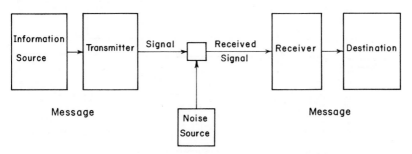

FIG. 1.   A general form of a communication channel described by Shannon.

tion processing concepts today still use the Shannon and Wiener information definition. But the impetus to information processing approaches would not have been nearly as strong had it not been for this initial antecedent.

The third antecedent was the explosive growth in the use of digital computers which began shortly after World War II. It was not the use per se, but the awareness by psychologists of the existence and capabilities of computers. We began to speculate on similarities of computer operations and human behavior, and even to simulate such tasks as perceptual learning, recognition, problem-solving, thinking, and gaming. We took over both the terminology of computer function—channels, gating, serial and parallel, memory, storage buffers, and the like (see Fig. 2)—and began to build our own theories of perception around similar concepts. The construction of a program became a perceptual theory—complete with flow chart, subroutines, processors, buffers, memory, comparators, decision matrices, receiver operating characteristics, and so forth.

Each of these antecedents appeared in full bloom within a few years after the end of World War II and were well known to all workers in perception by the early 1950's. Almost immediately several important developments of research and theorizing were published that today can almost be put in the category of antecedents. I will single out only a few of these, admitting that I am slighting some important and influential work.

Clearly, the most important of these has been the Signal Detection Theory, begun by Tanner and Swets in 1954, stemming from work at MIT

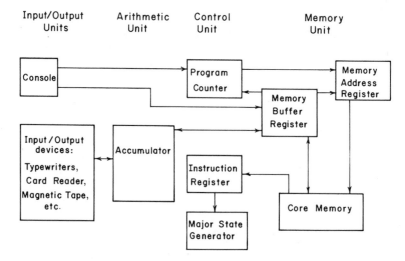

FIG. 2. A typical architecture of a digital computer.

on statistical communication theory and related decision theory. Its impact has led to major reinterpretations of even the centuries-old concept of sensory thresholds. The critical principle is that the subject's response, whether in a psychophysical experiment or to any stimulation in a natural environment, represents a decision or an evaluation of sensory evidence that he has observed against a criterion or whether that observation could have arisen from noise alone or from a signal imbedded in noise. Thus, this theory forces a recognition that every observation task facing a perceiver requires him to differentiate target signals, defined by the task, from irrelevant signals and from noise inherent in every communication channel.

A second development has stemmed from the seminal paper by Stroud (1956) on the quantization of time in the visual system—his perceptual moment hypothesis. Stroud argues that the visual system—probably more peripherally than the cortex—integrates stimulation over time, based on a time gating pulse of perhaps 100 milliseconds in frequency. All events occurring with a temporal frequency in excess of this are grouped into the same time unit or moment, and are therefore temporally indistinguishable. Within the moment, energy is integrated over time. Without the need for further assumptions, he provides explanations for critical duration in temporal integration, for Bloch's law, for flicker fusion, for perceptual simultaneity, and a number of other important temporal phenomena in vision and visual perception. Stroud's hypothesis has by no means met with universal favor, either theoretically or in terms in empirical verification or consistency. On the other hand, it has been remarkably influential on work concerning temporal information processing in vision.

A third development arose in England, and while it has been exported to some extent, its major impact is still communicated by Englishmen, initially Cherry (1953), and especially Broadbent (1958, 1971). They began with the experiments on dichotic listening, in which each ear receives a different message and the subject is asked to attend selectively to one message, or to a particular characteristic of a message which may appear in either ear. Many variations of this type of task have been used. These are reviewed by Broadbent (1971) and Moray (1970). The importance of the work has stemmed from the ease with which it has led both to general models of information processing and to predictions about the specific components of selective perception. Broadbent can, in a number of senses, be considered the contemporary father of information processing, especially with his 1958 book.

The fourth development, also in 1958, did for vision what Broadbent's book did for audition: it elaborated a model and a powerful set of operations for the study of visual information processing. Sperling's dissertation (published in 1960) reintroduced, after nearly a century, the poststimulus sampling procedures as a means to analyze the course of information as it is initially represented and held in the first of several memory systems. Sperling, along with Broadbent, provided clear evidence for a rapid decay buffer storage as an early stage of processing (see below). Sperling's work also provided a means of assessing the stages at which information recoding and losses occur. This became more explicit in his 1963 experiments. The basic form of the model he proposed in that paper (see Fig. 3) is still contained in virtually every other model subsequently published.

Another development has stemmed from another book and paper. Miller's book in 1951 on language and especially his review article in 1956 have served to change the course of much of perceptual and judgmental research. In the latter, he both shows the value of a definition of information free of the context of the stimulus content, and also recognizes its limitations. His distinction between bits of information—precisely defined in terms of uncertainty reduction—and chunks of information less elegantly defined in terms of the stimulus or response units being employed in the particular experiments—paved the way for much of the information processing developments to come. His book in 1960 (Miller, Galanter, & Pribram) has also come to serve as a similar landmark.

The sixth development from the early antecedents was Attneave's work (1954) on the application of information theory to psychology, especially to problems on perception. He explored a vast range of applications and the kind of explanatory and predictive power that can be drawn from the information theory analyses. His major contributions (see especially his 1959 book), stem from attempts to define patterns and forms in terms of their information content as uncertainty reduction and then to examine how

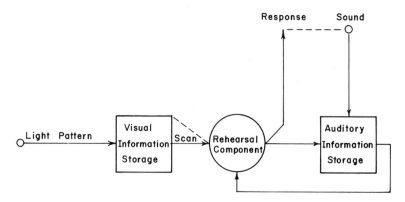

Fig. 3. An information processing model for visual memory tasks proposed by Sperling in 1963.

such measures relate to psychophysical investigation of form perception. I will have more to say on this later.

Finally, this list could not be complete without mention of the incredibly influential book by Hebb in 1949. This work has had impact on nearly every other development in information processing, even though Hebb would not have described himself as an information processing modeler. He was unusual, though, because of his interest in determining how central representations of visual stimulation are established, microgenetically and onto-genetically. Rather than drawing computer-program-like flow charts, however, he examined in terms of neural networks how the nervous system might create the representations. Although specific details of his ideas have undergone a number of modifications, the general principles underlying his analyses have not been improved upon or even significantly altered.

Hebb undertook his work in part to provide a neurophysiological means to understand how perception develops and functions. Parallel to his work although substantially independent from it, were equally important contributions on the neurophysiological components of perception. The lateral inhibitory system research of Hartline and Ratliff is now central to many aspects of information processing interpretations of visual phenomena. Equally critical is the work on the receptive field organization of the visual system brought to such prominence by Hubel and Wiesel. While there were some earlier publication on receptive fields, the vast majority of this research post-dates 1960. Perhaps its greatest importance for information processing analyses lies in the promise it offers to explain how distinctive visual features are extracted from pattern stimulation and transmitted to the cortex as relatively simple coded representations of characteristics of the stimulus.

This list is by no means exhaustive, and it is highly selective. I want to try to show both the range of the early work and the rapidity with which information processing approaches spread. The history, of course, is still in progress. The next decade may find as dramatic a shift and as rapid a development as the last two decades, as difficult as this is to imagine.

A number of assumptions or principles are characteristic of information processing theorizing and research. The next few sections describe the most salient of these.

II. THE UNITY OF SENSATION, PERCEPTION, MEMORY, RETRIEVAL, COGNITION, AND KNOWLEDGE

Although distinctions among these "typical" areas of experimental psychology have been diminishing in recent years of their own accord, information processing theories insist that they must all be treated within a single system of theory and research. Separation can only be made on the basis of expediency, or to delimit the range of discourse within the single article or line of research. This unity stems from a new awareness of the extensive flow of information, and the feedback and feedforward processes across these areas. Thus, we cannot understand how memory is organized without knowing how the information to be remembered was perceived and initially categorized. Conversely, the strategies used for perception depend in part on what fate the information will undergo in memory, and so forth. Obviously, to a researcher concentrating at one end of this continuum, the events and processes near the other end exert relatively little impact. Thus, students of long-term memory are usually not very concerned with the initial perception of the stimulus items, if only because they guarantee an adequate input by using long viewing times and relatively slow rates of presentation.

This continuity has become more obvious theoretically when the computer antecedents of information processing are recognized. Although we place arbitrary division between computer processes (referring to the memory as distinct from the accumulator, for example), the operations of a computer must be all considered together when analyzing either its functions or the way a particular program is handled.

The explicit recognition of this continuity has highlighted a number of very critical theoretical and methodological problems. The important breakthrough for this began for perception with a paper of Garner, Hake, and Eriksen (1956) who focus on the difficulties of distinguishing between perception and memory in word recognition research. They apply the concept of converging operations to perception, a point of view also stressed about the same time by Broadbent (1958). They argue persuasively that for each proposed mechanism, stage, process, or model that might be offered to explain or interpret a particular empirical result, the experimenter or theoretician must provide some experimental operation in the experiment that will differentiate that mechanism, stage, process, or model from all other possible ones. I have illustrated this recently in the following way:

> A processing approach such as the one being proposed here requires very careful attention to converging operations. Most specifically, whenever it is proposed that a process occurs between time t_0 and t_1 (or locus L_0 and L_1), it is required not only that a measure of the information content be made at both t_0 and t_1, but also that some additional manipulation or measure be taken "to converge" on the changes observed between t_0 and t_1. For example, finding an information loss between t_0 and t_1 is open to many interpretations, such as interference, fading trace, selective encoding, and probably others.

However, a poststimulus sampling cue introduced at various intervals of time between t_0 and t_1 could provide information about the time course of the loss of content. Hence, poststimulus sampling is one converging operation. Manipulating the stimulus content could provide another converging operation. For example, if two sets of stimuli were used, one composed of items known to be prone to interference and another known to be resistant to interference, and no differential loss between the two sets of stimuli occurred between time t_0 and t_1, then this converging operation would suggest that interference was probably not involved in the process accounting for the loss. Without these two converging operations, and probably several others as well, merely reporting the loss from t_0 to t_1 indicates relatively little about the underlying process. It is for this reason that information-processing analyses cannot usually be applied to old data. If the converging operations were not included at the time, it is usually impossible to differentiate possible interpretations or processes. Nor are such analyses often applicable to data collected for other reasons or within the context of other points of view (Haber, 1969b, p. 3).

A great impetus of the information processing approach has been its success in specifying converging operations. Needless to say, not all experiments converge on a single explanation, but this has been as much a function of the growing complexity and sophistication of the explanations as of any paucity of convergence of operations and design. I will return to the problems arising from the complexity of conceptualization after I have commented about the heart of the information processing revolution—the staging of processes.

III. SPECIFICATION OF STAGES

An information processing approach assumes that if the appropriate operations could be devised, it should be possible to sample and examine the contents of stimulation at every point in time, and at every level in the nervous system. Comparing those samples over time and location with the original stimulus and with the perceiver's responses (be they description of his perceptual experience, or his detection, recognition, reaction time, identification, or other discrete responses) would indicate the nature of the processing of that stimulus into perceptual experience and responses. This is analogous to what a verbal learning theorist does when he analyzes the changes in the contents of memory over time since initial memorization (e.g., Waugh & Norman, 1965). In doing this he attempts to make statements about the reorganization of memorial processes as a result of time, limited capacity of retention, interference, and other competing demands upon cognitive activity.

Information processing analyses assume that the total time from stimulus onset to the occurrence of a perceptual response can be divided into intervals, each characterized by a different operation. Using this assumption, we can create a block design of these intervals, labeling each block according to its operation, connecting the blocks to suggest the order that the operations are performed, and paralleling the blocks to suggest operations that are simultaneously performed. Then we can begin a careful program of experimentation derived from aspects of this design: have the intervals been divided up correctly, are the order of operations correct, is the overall organization of the processing of information correct, and so forth. These types of questions and the experiments derived from them represent the crux of information-processing analyses (Haber, 1969b, pp. 2, 3).

This approach makes explicit that perception, as an experience or awareness by the perceiver of having been stimulated, cannot be immediate. Rather, it is an end product of a number of separable operations, stages, or processes, each of which occur in sequence (or parallel sequences), and take time to complete. Immediacy of perception as a temporal assumption is perhaps a straw man or a dead horse by now, although it has had an illustrious history in theories of perception. Certainly, introspective analysis rarely permits one to observe any stages or separate processes—perceptual experience certainly seems immediate. Gestalt psychology did much to advance this view, and Gibson (for example, 1959, 1966) has fueled the assumption in his strong rejection of any memorial components in perception. However, being unaware of stages or the lapse of time does not disprove information processing concepts, but it has taken rather elaborate experiments to demonstrate these stages.

A second implication of the information processing approach is a recognition of how processing is limited by the channels through which information flows. This, of course, comes as no surprise. We have had concepts of limitation—span of perception, forgetting, selective attention—for a century. Channel capacity is also a central concept in the information theory model. Now we have a better procedure to look for the stages at which the recoding of information takes place and to examine the determinants of loss or change in content. The points in time where recoding takes place are central ones in information processing theories and analyses, and interest is centered on such points almost exclusively.

It is with the specification of stages or separable processes that most of the excitement and controversy has arisen, and most of the power of converging operations has been displayed. In editing the collection of papers on Information Processing Approaches to Visual Perception in 1969, I noted several different operations in use to converge on staging (Haber, 1969b).

One of these is a presentation of visual noise display following the stimulus as a way to precisely control the amount of time the perceiver has to extract information from the initial central representation of the display. This procedure was initiated by Sperling (1963). With its use it is possible

Time ——————➤

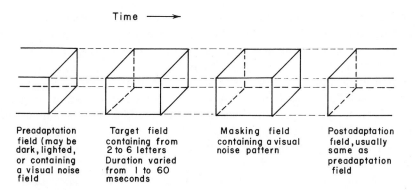

| Preadaptation field (may be dark, lighted, or containing a visual noise field | Target field containing from 2 to 6 letters Duration varied from 1 to 60 mseconds | Masking field containing a visual noise pattern | Postadaptation field, usually same as preadaptation field |

FIG. 4. The sequence of stimulus events used by Sperling (1963) in his experiment on information extraction.

to distinguish the content of an initial visual information storage or iconic storage from that which is further processed into a short-term memory storage. Figure 4 shows a design as originally used by Sperling (1963) and employed by many others since. Sperling's assumption was that the onset of the visual noise mask served to disrupt, terminate, or otherwise interfere with the extraction of information contained in the representation of the first flash. His results, shown in Fig. 5, were not only consistent with this

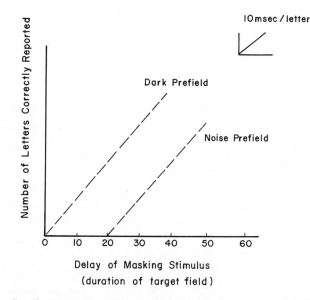

FIG. 5. Sperling's (1963) results showing the number of letters correctly reported as a function of the delay of the visual noise mask for arrays of two through six letters, respectively.

assumption, but further provided evidence which he interpreted as a serial readout of letters from a visual information storage at a rate of one letter per 10 milliseconds of processing time. Subsequent work (especially 1967) led him to modify this interpretation because he noticed that the serial position data were not consistent with a serial processing model. See Figure 6 for his revised model. A detailed debate has been in progress ever since on the factors that determine this readout, with a number of critical variables being added to the list. The issues are far from settled, but the power of the operation has permitted the debate to be very fruitful as well as exciting.

As an aside, a parallel debate has been concerned with the original assumption underlying the operation itself. Does visual noise as a second visual presentation serve to interrupt the processing of information contained in the first presentation, or does it degrade the contrast of the first through a temporal integration with it? Eriksen (especially 1966) suggested that the visual noise did not actually interrupt processing, but merely degraded the clarity of the representation. The balance of present evidence, at least as I see it in 1973, is that both integration and interruption effects occur, at least over the first 50–75 mseconds after the offset of the presentation.

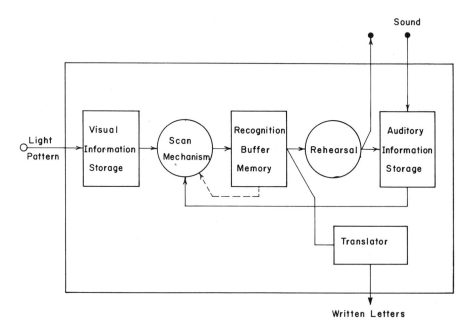

FIG. 6. The 1967 revision of Sperling's (1963) model, now showing a parallel extraction of information from the visual information storage buffer.

Therefore, it behooves experimenters to take both of these into account, even though the visual noise procedure may have been intended only to produce interruption.

A second powerful operation, also introduced by Sperling (1960), is contained in a poststimulus sampling design. Since the output from short-term memory of information from brief visual presentations of unrelated items rarely exceeds five items, Sperling sought a means of avoiding this limitation. He did this by signaling the perceiver to report only part of the presentation. Figure 7 sketches the procedure in which the perceiver is shown twelve letters in three rows of four letters each. The indicator in this experiment was a low, middle, or high pitched tone signaling the perceiver to report one of the three rows, respectively, thereby providing the post-stimulus cue.

Figure 8 shows the typical pattern of results in which the number of letters available (12 times the number reported from the indicated row divided by four) drops as the indicator is delayed. This procedure circum-vents the limitation on reports (since the perceiver never has to report more than four letters) while still permitting a precise sampling of information extraction. It is from this type of evidence that Sperling concluded that the initial representation of brief visual stimulation is a rapidly decaying visual storage. The poststimulus sampling design, as initiated by Sperling, has found widespread use as a means of tapping the amount of information available at a given point in the information processing network, while at the same time avoiding any limitation due to subsequent processing or channel or memory capacity problems.

A third operation has come from the revival of Donder's subtractive

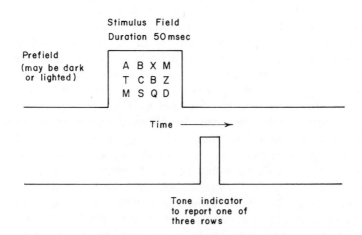

FIG. 7. A sequence of stimulus events used by Sperling (1960).

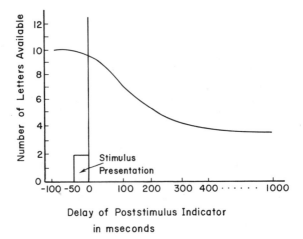

FIG. 8. Sperling's (1960) results showing the number of letters available as a function of the delay of the indicator.

procedures in reaction time research (see Sanders, 1967, for a symposium covering the range of research using this procedure). It is impossible to overestimate the importance of this procedure, for it permits precise estimates of the time that a brief internal process takes without having to measure the process directly. The two most influential applications of reaction time procedures can serve as brief examples. The first is Sternberg (see 1969, for a review). The general paradigm is to present a target character to the perceiver and then to flash an array of items which may or may not contain the target. The perceiver must make a choice reaction response as rapidly as possible. Reaction time typically increases as the number of targets in the display increases, with a steeper slope for those arrays which do not contain an instance of the target. This effect is interpreted as a sequential scanning of the items in the array which terminates as soon as the target is found. The rate of scanning is between 30–50 milliseconds, depending upon practice. A second procedure, developed by Posner (see Posner & Mitchell, 1967) is used to assess processing in a visual classification task. Perceivers are shown a pair of letters to which they must respond "same" or "different" as rapidly as possible. When the classification is to be made in terms of the names of the letters (for example, both AA and Aa would be called same), perceivers are substantially faster on physical matches (AA) than on name matches (Aa). In this way, Posner is able to distinguish matching on the basis of visual features from matching of names. Both of these approaches have generated prolific literatures and have made major contributions to information processing analyses.

Finally, there are a class of operations concerned with the vast variety of stimulus magnitude and similarity manipulations. These include varying the number of items in a display and examining what happens to reaction time or recognition. Another is to vary the stimulus items within a single display in terms of their visual similarity or similarity or some other relevant dimension such as acoustic confusibility, where acoustic representations are under investigation.

This list is greatly abbreviated and fails to illustrate the complexity and creativity of the research in information processing, but I hope that it does at least begin to indicate that range.

IV. DEFINITION OF INFORMATION

The information processing revolution began with a new definition of information, one which reflected the amount of uncertainty reduction being communicated, quite independent of the particular content of the uncertainty being reduced, the stimuli, the responses, or even the communication channels being employed. Initially heralded as a major breakthrough, the promise of this definition has not been fulfilled, and it plays a relatively small role in information processing research now, or in any research in perception at all. In retrospect, it was not this aspect of the information processing revolution that endured, even though at the beginning it looked like the most important.

Its failure has been in large part empirical rather than theoretical. It just did not work. Since it turned out to be relatively easy to calculate the amount of information contained in a stimulus or in a response, widespread use was made of this metric. But when it was correlated with reasonable dependent variables, the relationships were by and large negligible. Thus, the amount of information in a pattern does not correlate with ratings of complexity, simplicity, or similarity to other patterns, nor does it predict recognition, recall, speed of perception, threshold, or any number of other measures. There are a few exceptions to this generalization in the literature, some of the most interesting of which are summarized and discussed in Berlyne's new book (1972), but in substance the metric failed to provide a useful description of form. The success with judgmental tasks has been much better (for example, Garner, 1962) for which information is computed over the number of different stimuli to be judged, or the number of possible attributes each may possess. This task is probably closer to the original Shannon and Wiener situation than most others that psychology presents.

The failure has been dramatic when the meaningfulness of the material becomes a relevant variable. This led Miller (1956) to reject the information definition and substitute a much more pragmatic one—one which he named chunks of information, to replace the concept of bits. Miller reviewed an impressive amount of literature which tended to point to a limit of immediate short-term memory of about seven items of information, plus or minus two, that is, between two and three bits. A similar limit is found for unidimensional absolute judgment tasks and for a variety of others as well. But as soon as a perceiver recognizes that the items might be related to each other, as when letters spell words, then this limit blows up. To illustrate with only a slight exaggeration, the limit of perceptual short-term memory should be seven unrelated line segments, or seven unrelated letters if the seven line segments can be organized into letters, or seven unrelated words if the letters spell words, or seven unrelated simple sentences if the words are organized semantically or syntactically, or seven ideas, or seven cosmic thoughts, and so forth. While it may be possible in theory to carry out an uncertainty reduction and analysis on each of these levels, it seems quite unlikely that they would be equivalent and it has not proved very amenable to do so in practice.

Rather, Miller suggests that the unit of information ought to be the subjective units being employed by the subject in the particular task. Thus, if letters are presented which spell words, then the response units are words. The experimenter needs converging operations to determine whether the perceiver is processing units made up of line segments, letters, or the entire word.

Thus, the refinement in definition offered by uncertainty reduction has had to be replaced by sophistication in experimental design and converging operations. Few researchers seem to want to retain the more refined definition, although there is still an occasional attempt to use it. Information theory measures seem unlikely to be revived, because the assumptions underlying these calculations cannot be met for the processing of meaningful material, in which the rules governing the recombinations of units do not simply follow the principles of uncertainty reduction. In any event, the judgment of history seems to portend this, at least empirically. The principles are just not used.

V. TYPES OF INFORMATION PROCESSING MODELS

Because the model of a digital computer has been one of the strong antecedents of the information processing revolution, it is not surprising that most theories generated by believers read like computer programs, at least through the level of a flow chart. Although each theorist has some unique properties to his model, only several basic styles have appeared, depending upon which part of the information processing continuum draws the greatest attention. I do not intend to reconstruct or even review these models in any detail, since they are changing too rapidly under the influx of perhaps 50 to 100 relevant publications per month in the research literature. I would like to distinguish three general classes, however, and suggest a few salient features of each class. Classes can be differentiated simply by which aspect of an information processing continuum the model selects to attend to.

At the input end, where the interest is greatest in what was traditionally called perception, Sperling (beginning with 1963, see Figs. 3 and 6) has proposed a model of how visual stimulation reaching the retina is transformed and held in a brief buffer (visual information storage in his notation, but more generally called iconic memory, following Neisser's 1967 systematization) and then recoded into an acoustic representation and held and rehearsed in short-term memory. Broadbent provided a parallel model which stressed acoustic inputs, but otherwise specified very similar stages in processing, although he placed greater emphasis on a filter process to select among incoming channels of stimulation. Neither Broadbent nor Sperling, nor their followers or detractors have paid much attention to the very early stages of processing. They leave out the problems of how receptor stimulation expressed as a spatial-temporal pattern on the retina is encoded into some organized neural pattern of activity which presumably forms the content of the first central or iconic buffer storage.

The second class of models has been constructed by theorists interested in memory more than in perception. Melton (1963) probably had first crack at this type, although Norman (1970) and Atkinson and Shiffrin (1968) provided the greatest range of detail. If anything, the research literature is expanding even faster for the memory-related information processing models and their empirical consequences. These models pay little attention to input variables, recognizing only that stimulation precedes storage. Such models usually denote some form of iconic stage, but generally begin to differentiate the processing after information reaches succeeding stages. Substantial focus is placed on rehearsal, recognition, acoustic representation for linguistic material, the processes which underly forgetting or memory loss, and retrieval and responding as distinct from storage. While Sperling's 1967 model (Fig. 6) was designed to account initially for perceptual variables, he does include processes more akin to traditional memory variables, so he bridges the gap.

The third type of model focuses on problem-solving behavior and on verbal associative learning, and does not pay much attention to perceptual or memorial processes as such. The beginnings of this date to Newell, Shaw, and Simon's work on problem solving (1963). These are reviewed in some detail by Reitman (1965), who himself has been a substantial contributor to this field. These models are often only remotely related to the preceding two types in that they make little reference to empirical verification of the stages. Their major concern is whether a computer program can be written and operated on a computer that will take a problem or a list of items to be associated and produce a solution or mimic the nature of the learning curves normally found. Whether or not the steps or the processes used are the same or similar to those used by human beings solving or learning the same problem is not answered by these models. I consider this a drawback of some seriousness, since as such, the models do not tell us much as they could about information processing by humans. On the other hand, they still have the potential to do this.

There have also been some computer models of perceptual processes as distinct from problem-solving ones. The most notable one is by Rosenblatt (1958), brought up to date by Minsky and Papert (1969). This type of model is concerned primarily with the organization of the neural network necessary for perceptual discrimination between stimulus patterns. It is a powerful model in theory, but as yet, it suffers from the same drawbacks as the problem-solving and thinking computer simulations mentioned above. We still have to wait and see.

One or two other remarks are necessary about models. Every one of the models has been constructed to account for the processing of linguistic or other symbolic stimuli, principally natural language. While no doubt exists about the importance of such processing and the prominent role reading and linguistically-bound thought plays in the lives of most human beings, it is by no means the only information processing that occurs. Specifically, these models say nothing and probably can say little about the processing of pictorial stimuli, nor in general about how we come to have knowledge about the spatial arrangement about the objects around us. It is to be hoped that information processers become more interested in such problems. Hochberg (e.g., 1970) has probably worried more within the context of such models about both of these omissions. But much more is needed than what can be done by one man, no matter how creative and energetic he is.

A second comment has been raised by a number of workers, most recently by Broadbent (1971). He notes that psychological theories, models, and hypotheses often are so complex that they far outstrip the abilities of reasonable experiments to test between alternative versions. Complex theories cannot be verified by simple experiments no matter how loud we shout or proclaim it. Only with converging operations can we distinguish explicitly between predictions from one model and formulations from alternative ones. An experiment should be designed to eliminate as many alternative explanations of an effect as possible. Simple experiments based upon overblown theories cannot hope to do this.

While Broadbent's argument could and should be applied to many areas of psychology, the information processing models often represent natural targets. He argues that we should formulate our theories to a degree of complexity with the bounds that our experiments can handle—to distinguish between alternative explanations. While I agree in principle with this point, I feel that in practice the information processing modelers have been among the most sophisticated of psychological researchers. While our models are complex and multistaged—including Broadbent's own work—most research, and Broadbent is here most prominent, is replete with means of converging between different explanations, processes, or sequences. But it is better to be forewarned of the pitfalls set for the unwary when we construct global theories, or depend upon the operations of the computer program to tell us all the answers./

Figure 9 is perhaps the most realistic model in terms of the complexity of the phenomena being studied by information processing approaches. But is there any hope that our experiments will bring it under control?

VI. CONCLUSION

I have tried in this brief chapter to communicate a sense of the information processing approach to the study of perception. I have stressed its

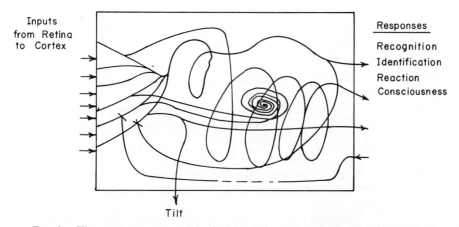

Fig. 9. The most current model of visual information processing showing both serial and parallel processes indicating all of the feedback and feedforward loops.

historical antecedents and early developments without becoming embroiled in the headlines of current controversies and excitements. That history is not very old, and nearly all of the earliest workers are still major contributors today. It will be interesting to see what a similar account written 10 years hence will look like, and which developments of today will continue to hold their promise. I cannot wait to see it!

References

Atkinson, R. C., & Shiffrin, R. M. Human memory: A proposed system and its control processes. In K. W. Spence & J. T. Spence (Eds.), *The psychology of learning and motivation*. Vol. 2. New York: Academic Press, 1968.

Attneave, F. Some informational aspects of visual perception. *Psychological Review*, 1954, **61**, 183–193.

Attneave, F. *Applications of information theory to psychology*. New York: Holt, 1959.

Berlyne, D. E. *Aesthetics and psychobiology*. New York: Appleton, 1972.

Broadbent, D. E. *Perception and communication*. Oxford: Pergamon, 1958.

Broadbent, D. E. *Decision and stress*. New York: Academic Press, 1971.

Cherry, C. Some experiments on the reception of speech with one and with two ears. *Journal of the Acoustical Society of America*, 1953, **25**, 975–979.

Courtis, M., & Green, R. T. Information theory and figure perception. *Bulletin of the British Psychological Society*, 1963, **16**, 4.

Eriksen, C. W. Temporal luminance summation effects in backward and forward masking. *Perception and Psychophysics*, 1966, **1**, 87–92.

Flavell, J. A., & Draguns, J. A. A microgenetic approach to perception and thought. *Psychological Bulletin*, 1957, **54**, 197–217.

Garner, W. R. *Uncertainty and structure as psychological concepts*. New York: Wiley, 1962.

Garner, W. R., Hake, H. W., & Eriksen, C. W. Operationism and the concept of perception. *Psychological Review*, 1956, **63**, 317–329.

Gibson, J. J. Perception as a function of stimulation. In S. Koch (Ed.), *Psychology: A study of a science*. Vol. 1. New York: McGraw-Hill, 1959. Pp. 456–501.

Gibson, J. J. *The senses considered as perceptual systems*. Boston, Massachusetts: Houghton, 1966.

Haber, R. N. (Ed.) *Information processing approaches to visual perception*. New York: Holt, 1969. (a)

Haber, R. N. Introduction. In R. N. Haber (Ed.) *Information processing approaches to visual perception*. New York: Holt, 1969. Pp. 1–15. (b)

Hebb, D. O. *The organization of behavior*. New York: Wiley, 1949.

Hochberg, J. E. Attention, organization, and consciousness. In D. Mostofsky (Ed.), *Attention*. New York: Appleton, 1970. Pp. 99–124.

Kaswan, J., & Young, S. Stimulus exposure time, brightness, and spatial factors as determinants of visual perception. *Journal of Experimental Psychology*, 1963, **65**, 113–123.

Melton, A. W. Implications of short-term memory for general theory of memory. *Journal of Verbal Learning and Verbal Behavior*, 1963, **2**, 1–21.

Miller, G. A. *Language and communication*. New York: Appleton, 1951.

Miller, G. A. The magic number seven, plus or minus two. *Psychological Review,* 1956, **63**, 81–97.

Miller, G. A., Galanter, E., & Pribram, K. *Plans and the structure of behavior.* New York: Holt, 1960.

Minsky, M., & Papert, S. *Perceptrons.* Cambridge, Massachusetts: MIT Press, 1969.

Moray, N. *Attention: Selective processes in vision and hearing.* New York: Academic Press, 1970.

Neisser, U. *Cognitive psychology.* New York: Appleton, 1967.

Newell, A., Shaw, J. C., & Simon, H. A. Empirical exploration with the logic theory machine. In E. A. Feigenabum & J. Feldman (Eds.), *Computers and thought.* New York: McGraw-Hill, 1963. Pp. 109–133.

Norman, D. A. (Ed.) *Models of human memory.* New York: Academic Press, 1970.

Posner, M. I., & Mitchell, R. F. Chronometric analysis of classification. *Psychological Review,* 1967, **74**, 392–409.

Reitman, W. R. *Cognition and thought: An information processing analysis.* New York: Wiley, 1965.

Rosenblatt, F. The perceptron. A probabilistic model for information storage in the brain. *Psychological Review,* 1958, **65**, 286–418.

Sanders, A. (Ed.) *Attention and performance.* Amsterdam: North-Holland Publ., 1967.

Shannon, C. E., & Wiener, W. *The mathematical theory of communication.* Urbana: Univ. of Illinois Press, 1949.

Sperling, G. The information available in brief visual presentations. *Psychological Monographs,* 1960, **74** (11, Whole No. 498).

Sperling, G. A model for visual memory tasks. *Human Factors,* 1963, **5**, 19–31.

Sperling, G. Successive approximations to a model for short-term memory. *Acta Psychologica,* 1967, **27**, 285–292.

Sternberg, S. Memory scanning: Mental processes revealed by reaction time experiments. *American Scientist,* 1969, **57**, 421–457.

Stroud, J. M. The fine structure of psychological time. In H. Quastler (Ed.), *Information theory in psychology.* Glencoe, Illinois: Free Press, 1956. Pp. 174–207.

Tanner, W. P., & Swets, J. A decision-making theory of visual detection. *Psychological Review,* 1954, **61**, 401–409.

Waugh, N. C., & Norman, D. A. Primary memory. *Psychological Review,* 1965, **72**, 89–104.

Werner, H. Studies in contour. I. Quantitative analyses. *American Journal of Psychology,* 1935, **47**, 40–64.

Chapter 17

AUTOMATA

PATRICK SUPPES AND WILLIAM ROTTMAYER *

I. INTRODUCTION

The subject of this chapter is still in an embryonic stage and consequently the survey we present does not have a finished character. From many directions there is great current interest in the relation between perception and the theory of automata, because, increasingly, emphasis is on understanding how processing of energy as it impinges on the peripheral nervous system in the form of sensations is performed by the organism. From another standpoint, there is great interest in computer science in understanding how machines can be taught to perceive and to learn perceptual concepts.

The problem of providing a proper survey of the work in computer science relevant to the general theme of perception and automata is far from simple. It would be inappropriate in this handbook to give a detailed account of the work in computer science. On the other hand, a good part of the work we describe has originated in the context of computer efforts at pattern recognition or perception. Because the bibliography of this effort is now in itself substantial, we cannot hope to give the reader a really adequate account of what has been done.

To illustrate methods of approach we have given an undue emphasis to our own work, an emphasis not commensurate with its importance. We have used it in several places as an example to give the reader a sense of methods. We have also tried in the bibliography to give a number of leads

* Research connected with this article was partially supported by National Science Foundation Grant NSFGJ-443X.

into the literature, and we urge the reader to follow them up in order to get a detailed sense of the approaches that currently seem promising.

Since the bulk of the theoretical work on perception (including our own) has been on vision, we confine ourselves almost exclusively to remarks in this area. We begin by offering an abstract characterization of the perceptual process, which may be used to describe all of these approaches. Each approach is obtained by placing different restrictions on the abstract characterization, which allows one to pinpoint the essential features of each approach succinctly and to compare and contrast the differences between them.

We think of a perceptual device as being capable of telling whether what it perceives (a scene) has a certain property. Thus there are only two possible outputs: 1 (corresponding to a yes answer) and 0 (corresponding to a no answer). A device that can do this must be rather complex. Seven different features must be specified in order to define such a device mathematically:

1. $\mathcal{D}$, the form of the original perceptual data, e.g., the state of the retina; mathematically, $\mathcal{D}$ is a family of structures (sets together with relations on the set) rather than simple sets.

2. Φ, the preprocesser, which looks at elements of $\mathcal{D}$ and outputs (coded) information about them; Φ is fixed (no learning), and hopefully fairly simple.

3. C, the set of possible outputs of Φ; alternatively, the possible inputs to Ω; coded information about elements of $\mathcal{D}$.

4. $\mathcal{R}$, the feedback (reinforcement); it may be a function of the answer.

5. Λ, the learning component, whose input is $\mathcal{R}$ and output is $\mathcal{P}$.

6. $\mathcal{P}$, the set of possible particular programs Ω can use to compute its answer; $\mathcal{P}$ is the output of Λ.

7. Ω, the processer, whose inputs are elements of C and $\mathcal{D}$, and which outputs the final answer; a general type of computing device that must be programmed to be able to handle any particular problem.

Schematically,*

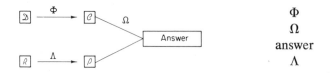

$$\Phi$$
$$\Omega$$
$$\text{answer}$$
$$\Lambda$$

Thus, Φ, Λ, and Ω are components of the computing devices, while $\mathcal{D}$ and $\mathcal{R}$ define the perceptual situation (environment). The question is al-

---

* Formally, Φ, Λ, and Ω are functions: $\Phi: \mathcal{D} \to C$, $\Lambda: \mathcal{R} \to \mathcal{P}$ and $\Omega: C \times \mathcal{P} \to \{0,1\}$ (1 is true or yes, 0 is false or no).

ways what particular devices can do in given situations. Thus the objects of study in the abstract are structures $\langle \mathcal{D}, \mathcal{R}, \mathcal{C}, \mathcal{P}, \Phi, \Lambda, \Omega \rangle$. In general, $\mathcal{C}$ and $\mathcal{P}$ are determined by the choices of the other five elements and are not of independent interest.

Let us agree that the ultimate goal is to define $\mathcal{D}, \mathcal{R}, \Phi, \Lambda$, and Ω, so that the resulting overall system has roughly the same perceptual abilities as a human being. (For specific purposes, one might want to improve on human performances, e.g., make the receptors more sensitive or eliminate lapses of attention.) This goal is unlikely to be achieved immediately. Thus it seems wise to try to reach it by a series of steps, starting with systems that are extremely limited by human standards and trying to improve them. It is not a telling criticism of a particular system that it cannot match human performance, because every system proposed so far is deficient in some respect. Because this is a new area, it is natural to try to apply knowledge gained from other areas. Indeed, one way to distinguish different approaches is to specify what already known body of knowledge the approach is based on.

A satisfactory overall system would be able to do two things: (a) perform in a manner roughly equivalent to humans, and (b) learn in the way that humans do. Neither of these capabilities is presently simultaneously realizable. There are thus two approaches, each of which emphasizes one aspect and neglects the other. An artificial-intelligence approach emphasizes (a) and neglects (b), while a learning approach emphasizes (b) and neglects (a). Thus artificial-intelligence devices can perform tasks more complicated than learning devices, but learning devices are more adaptable and need less specific programming.

It is natural to ask questions that do not depend on the learning process about any approach. Suppose one has placed restrictions on Φ and Ω. What sorts of things can the resulting device do (given an appropriate element of $\mathcal{P}$) and what can it not do (given any element of $\mathcal{P}$)? The former question is about the *power* of the device, the latter about its *limitations*. These questions depend solely on $\mathcal{P}$, the whole range of possible programs for Ω. How particular elements of $\mathcal{P}$ are obtained, which is the whole of the learning question, is irrelevant. To put the matter a little differently, asymptotic learning studies (those that ignore practical questions like length of time and amount of memory) deal with whether Λ will eventually find a correct element of $\mathcal{P}$. They usually read "If there is at least one correct element in $\mathcal{P}$, then procedure Λ will eventually find a correct one." In order to apply such a theorem to a particular case, one needs to know that the antecedent clause is true. Conversely, if it is known that the antecedent clause is false then Λ cannot be successful, and wasted effort may be avoided. Questions about the truth or falsity of the antecedent clause are questions about the power and limitations of the device. These are the questions of interest. The main part of this chapter summarizes three approaches to the problem, keeping these considerations in mind.

The perceptron approach discussed in Section II is a learning approach. It originated from considering how the brain might be organized to solve perceptual problems. Our work, discussed in Section III, is also a learning approach. It is based on stimulus-response learning theory, rather than models of the brain, however. A connection can be made (Suppes, 1969) between stimulus-response theory and automata, and we try to exploit this connection. The work in Section IV on picture-parsing illustrates an artificial intelligence rather than learning approach. In Sections II–IV we neglect learning and concentrate on questions of the power and limitations of the different approaches. Remember, however, that the choices of Φ and Ω made in Sections II and III were made to facilitate learning. Learning is discussed in Section V. We note that this characterization of the problem is based on the work of Minsky and Papert (1969) and Block's remarks on their work (Block, 1970), as well as on our own thinking.

In addition to the historical importance attached to visual perception, there are other reasons for concentrating on it in the present chapter. Perhaps the best is that our understanding of the geometry of visual perception is very much better than the geometry of any of the other senses. With the single exception of the auditory processing of language, almost all the applications of automata to perception have been restricted to visual perception. It is perhaps worth pointing out the theory we develop in Section III can be applied almost without change to tactile perception. We take the notions of straight line and intersection as primitive. Consequently, given a drawing with raised lines, for example, a Braille drawing, a person can gather the information necessary for perception by tactile methods. The fact that this would require moving the fingers and hence would take time is not essential, since what is required is that the device at some time have all the information at its disposal, not that it be gathered all at once. Of course, hypotheses about motion are always an important part of visual perception as well. We shall not pursue this tactile theory, but it will be obvious to the reader that the technical developments in Section III apply without serious change to such tactile perceptions.

The remainder of this section is devoted to some general remarks about automata. The first automata of which we have precise details and of which we have any serious historical information appeared in the second or third century B.C. in Alexandria. Perhaps the most striking example is the mobile theatre of Hero of Alexandria, which had a large number of moving parts, including wine flowing from the statue of Bacchus and the sounds of drums and cymbals. The ancient literature also gives a fairly detailed description of how the mobile theatre was built and of its mechanical principles of construction. The more practical applications were to hydraulic clocks or other forms of water clocks. Needham (1965) has also emphasized the independent development of mechanical toys, clocks, and other devices in China.

From the fifteenth century on there are numerous examples of mechanical automata doing a surprisingly wide variety of things, ranging from clocks to toys and mechanical conjurers. Many subtle functions are performed by these mechanical automata and from a surprisingly early date. What is missing by and large, however, is any sort of development bearing on the central concern here, that of perception. In the few cases where a mechanical automaton depended upon some kind of input, the input was too simple to treat it as a case of perception. To take a modern instance, an elevator that keeps its door open as long as a light beam is interrupted more often than every 10 or 15 seconds is an example of a very simple automaton depending upon an extremely simple visual input, but we would not want to treat it as a case of perception. It is not our point here to draw a sharp distinction. We do want to emphasize that in the long history of mechanical automata, including even efforts at talking automata in the eighteenth century, problems of perception scarcely entered. For example, in 1779, the Imperial Academy of Science of St. Petersburg set as the subject for its annual prize investigation into the nature of sounds, in particular of the vowels, and the building of a device capable of reproducing them. The prize was won by Kratzenstein, who used a bellows that forced air into tubes of different shapes. Methods of this kind were extended to some words and phrases, but no conceptually interesting results were obtained. Even in the twentieth-century development of mechanical robots prior to the introduction of computers in the late 1940's, little attention was paid to perception. The theoretical ideas developed in this chapter and the literature referred to make clear why this was the case. The subject is difficult, and progress is even now relatively slow.

Although, as indicated, most of the current conceptual work that is specifically oriented toward perception is concerned with visual perception, the work on generative grammars in the late 1950's by Chomsky and others provides one close link between automata and perception, in this case the perception of spoken speech. Much of the formal work has not been concerned with the details of phoneme perception or with the more elementary distinctive features of phonemes, but it has been implicitly assumed that the distinctive features of the "meaningful" elements, for example phonemes, of spoken speech are finite in number, and a theory of language built up from a finite vocabulary has been extensively developed. A good introduction to these matters is to be found in Chomsky and Miller (1963).

Assuming without detailed justification that speech can be broken down into a sequence of discrete elements made up from a finite set of such elements, we can then ask what kinds of abstract machines are required to process speech of different levels of complexity. Put in this abstract way the problem may be seen as far removed from perception, but as we shall see in several different contexts in this chapter, once the restriction to a finite set of basic elements is made, a good many subtle distinctions can be introduced and certain theoretically interesting questions can be answered.

We turn now to a brief sketch of the general theory of automata and the languages a given class of automata can recognize or accept. We begin with the definition of a finite automaton which is close to the definition originally given by Rabin and Scott (1959).

DEFINITION 1. *A structure* $\mathfrak{A} = \langle A, V, M, s_0, F \rangle$ *is a finite (deterministic) automaton iff**
  (i) *A is a finite, nonempty set (the set of states of $\mathfrak{A}$),*
  (ii) *V is a finite, nonempty set (the alphabet or vocabulary),*
  (iii) *M is a function from the Cartesian product $A \times V$ to A (M defines the transition table of $\mathfrak{A}$),*
  (iv) *s_0 is in A (s_0 is the initial state of $\mathfrak{A}$),*
  (v) *F is a subset of A (F is the set of final states of $\mathfrak{A}$).*

The generality of this definition is apparent. It is also indicative of the weakness in a certain sense of the general notion of a finite automaton. About the only restrictions are that the sets A and V be finite. On the other hand, these finite restrictions are critical.

It is evident that we can have some extremely trivial models of Definition 1. Here is the simplest: $A = \{s_0\}$, $V = \{0\}$, $M(s_0,0) = s_0$, $F = \phi$, where ϕ is the empty set (also later the empty sequence).

Perhaps the simplest nontrivial example of a finite automaton is the following. We have a two-letter alphabet consisting of the symbols "0" and "1," and two internal states, s_0 and s_1. The transition function of the automaton is defined by the following tabulation:

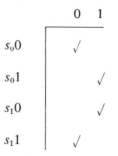

	0	1
$s_0 0$	✓	
$s_0 1$		✓
$s_1 0$		✓
$s_1 1$	✓	

---

* Throughout, "iff" is used as an abbreviation for "if and only if."

Finally, we select the internal state s_1 as the only member of the set F of final states. In saying that this is the simplest nontrivial automaton, we mean that the transition table depends both on the internal state and the input letter. From a more general conceptual standpoint, it is clear that the device is itself pretty trivial.

We next describe the language that a given finite automaton can accept or recognize. First, V^* is the set of all finite sequences of elements of V, including the empty sequence ϕ. The elements of V^* are called *sentences, strings,* or *tapes.* If $\sigma_1, \ldots, \sigma_n$ are in V, then the sequence $\sigma_1\sigma_2 \ldots \sigma_n$ is in V^*; in other words, we shall usually show elements of V^* by juxtaposing names of elements of V.

Second, the function M can be extended to a function from $A \times V^*$ to A by the following recursive definition for s in A, x in V^* and σ in V

$$M(s,\phi) = s$$
$$M(s,x\sigma) = M(M(s,x),\sigma).$$

Thus, for the two-state, two-letter-alphabet automaton introduced above, we may compute M for the string $x = 101$ by using this recursive definition.

$$
\begin{aligned}
M(s_0,101) &= M(M(s_0,10),1) \\
&= M(M(M(s_0,1),0),1) \\
&= M(M(s_1,0),1) \\
&= M(s_1,1) \\
&= s_0,
\end{aligned}
$$

and so the string 101 is not accepted, because the final state is s_0, not s_1, the only member of F. More formally, we have

DEFINITION 2. *A string x of V^* is accepted by $\mathfrak{A}$ iff $M(s_0,x)$ is in F.*
It is also customary to call strings that are accepted by $\mathfrak{A}$, *sentences* of $\mathfrak{A}$.

DEFINITION 3. *The language accepted by $\mathfrak{A}$ is the set of all sentences of $\mathfrak{A}$.*
In the literature, the language accepted by $\mathfrak{A}$, which we shall denote $L(\mathfrak{A})$, is often called the *set of tapes accepted by $\mathfrak{A}$.*
There is a natural notion of equivalence for automata which is weaker than the natural isomorphism of states and transitions for given inputs.

DEFINITION 4. *Two automata are (weakly) equivalent iff they accept the same language.*
In order to talk about the languages accepted by automata as defined independent of any machine concepts, we must introduce the general concept of a *grammar.*
Let V be a finite, nonempty set. Then V^* is the set of all finite sequences

of elements of V. Let ϕ be the empty sequence. Then $V^+ = V^* - \{\phi\}$. V is the *vocabulary*. V^* is the set of *strings* or *tapes*.

DEFINITION 5. *A structure $G = (V,N,P,S)$ is a phrase-structure grammar iff*

    (i) *V, N, and P are nonempty finite sets,*
    (ii) *$N \subseteq V$,*
    (iii) *$P \subseteq V^+ \times V^*$,*
    (iv) *$S \in N$.*

The standard terminology is this. The set N is the set of *nonterminal* symbols, or variables. $V_T = V - N$ is the set of *terminal* symbols. The set P is the set of *productions*. If $\langle \alpha, \beta \rangle \in P$ we ordinarily write: $\alpha \to \beta$. Finally, S is the *start* symbol.

DEFINITION 6. *If γ and δ are in V^* then $\gamma\alpha\delta \Rightarrow {}^G\gamma\beta\delta$ iff $\alpha \to \beta$ is a production, i.e., $\langle \alpha, \beta \rangle \in P$.*

DEFINITION 7. *Derivation of γ_m from γ_1, with $\gamma_1, \gamma_m \in V^*$. $\gamma^1 \underset{G}{\Rightarrow} {}^*\gamma_m$ iff $\exists\, \gamma_2, \ldots, \gamma_{m-1} \in V^*$ such that*

$$\gamma_1 \underset{G}{\Rightarrow} \gamma_2, \ldots, \gamma_{m-1} \underset{G}{\Rightarrow} \gamma_m.$$

DEFINITION 8. *The language generated by a grammar G, denoted $L(G)$, is:*

$$L(G) = \{w|w \in V_T^* \,\&\, S \underset{G}{\Rightarrow} {}^*w\}.$$

DEFINITION 9. *Two grammars G_1 and G_2 are (weakly) equivalent iff $L(G_1) = L(G_2)$.*

Example 1

As an example, here is a tiny subfragment of English, for which we make no claims of empirical correctness.*

$$N = \{S, NP, VP, PN, Adj\,P, Adj, N, Art, V_1, V_2\}$$
$V_T =$ a small set of English words
$P =$ the set of following production rules

1. $S \to NP + VP$	5. $Adj\,P \to Adj$
2. $NP \to PN$	6. $Adj\,P \to Art$
3. $NP \to Adj\,P + N$	7. $VP \to V_1$
4. $Adj\,P \to Adj\,P + Adj$	8. $VP \to V_2 + NP$

---

* The nonterminal symbols have an intuitive meaning taken over from classical grammars: S for sentence, NP for noun phrase, VP for verb phrase, PN for proper noun, AdjP for adjective phrase, Adj for adjective, N for noun, Art for article, V_1 for intransitive verb, and V_2 for transitive verb.

Here is a sample derivation:

1.	S	Axiom
2.	NP + VP	By Rule 1
3.	Adj P + N + VP	By Rule 3
4.	Adj P + Adj + N + VP	By Rule 4
5.	Art + Adj + N + VP	By Rule 6
6.	Art + Adj + N + V_2 + NP	By Rule 8
7.	Art + Adj + N + V_2 + PN	By Rule 2
8.	The large ball hit John	By Lexical Rules

We turn now to types of grammar. *Type* 0 *Grammars* are characterized by Definition 5. To obtain a *Type* 1 or *Context-Sensitive Grammar*, we add the restriction that for every production $\alpha \to \beta$, $|\alpha| \le |\beta|$, where $|\alpha|$ is the length of α, or the number of symbols in α. This restriction can be shown equivalent to

$$\alpha_1 A \alpha_2 \to \alpha_1 \beta \alpha_2$$

with $\beta \neq \phi$ and $A \in N$.

To obtain *Type* 2 or *Context-Free Grammars,* we add the stronger restriction: if $\alpha \to \beta \in P$ then

(i) α is a variable, i.e., $\alpha \in N$,

(ii) $\beta \neq \phi$.

To obtain *Type* 3 or *Regular Grammars,* we add the still stronger restriction: any production must be of the form

(i) $A \to aB$

or, (ii) $A \to a$,

with $A, B \in N$, $a \in V_T$. (We can have instead of (i), $A \to Ba$.)

For an example of a regular grammar, we may slightly change our previous example.

Example 2

$$N = \{S,NP,VP,Adj\ P\}$$
$$V_T = \{PN,N,Adj,Art,V_1,V_2\}.$$

If we drop Rule 8 and rewrite Rule 1 as 1′, $S \to NP + V_1$, we can immediately check that the grammar is regular. To rewrite Rule 8 is more troublesome and requires more variables, i.e., elements of N. We leave the details to the reader. In general, it is not easy to see if a *language* has a grammar of a given type.

We turn now to relations between languages and automata.

There are four basic theorems about the types of automata that can recognize or process the four types of languages, Types 0–3. It is too far from our main concern to give a detailed treatment of these matters, but we will use them later in discussing picture-parsing grammars and in remarks on coding for automata. Consequently we review the classical results briefly. The reader is referred to Chomsky and Miller (1963) and Chomsky (1963), or to the excellent recent textbook Hopcroft and Ullman (1969).

The first basic theorem is that a language is recognized by a finite automaton if and only if it has a regular grammar. Intuitively this means that the structure of the language is simple. A critical property for example is the absence of imbeddings.

The next basic theorem for context-free languages requires the notion of a pushdown automaton, and we describe the character of such automata in an informal way. The new idea introduced is that in addition to having a finite number of control states, as in the case of the finite automaton, the pushdown automaton has a pushdown store, which is a restricted form of memory. The automaton can put structural information in the store, but it can make state transitions only in terms of the top symbol on the store—the store operates like a stack of cafeteria trays on the principle of "first in and last out." In addition, a special store-vocabulary is provided the machine and the transition function depends not just on the input symbol and the current state as in the case of the finite automaton, but also on the top symbol of the store. The basic theorem is that a language can be recognized or processed by a pushdown automaton if and only if it has a context-free grammar.

For the consideration of context-sensitive and Type 0 languages we need to introduce the concept of a Turing machine. A Turing machine has a single read-write head. Given an internal state and the scan of an input letter, the Turing machine executes a move by changing its internal state, printing a nonblank symbol on the cell scanned (thereby replacing the symbol scanned), and moving its head left or right one cell. As in the case of a finite automaton the set of internal states is finite as is the input alphabet. A language is of Type 0, that is, has a Type 0 grammar, if and only if it is accepted by some Turing machine. The general class of Type 0 languages is so large that they are themselves of little interest. For example, there are Type 0 languages that are recursively enumerable but not recursive. This means that there is no mechanical decision procedure for deciding whether or not a string made up of the terminal vocabulary is or is not a sentence of the language. It is generally felt that languages are always recursive and consequently Type 0 languages form too large a class. We emphasize that problems of vagueness and unclarity about the grammar of a language are quite separate from the question of whether or not it is recursive.

A linear bounded automaton is a Turing machine that stays within the squares of the tape on which the input is placed. The basic theorem for context-sensitive languages is that a language is context-sensitive if and only if it is accepted by some linear bounded automaton. With reference to the remark just made about recursion, it should also be noted that any context-sensitive language, that is, any language that has a context-sensitive grammar, is recursive.

II. PERCEPTRONS

In this section we summarize the work of Minsky and Papert (1969), but also use the review of their work in Block (1970). Earlier relevant work is summarized in Rosenblatt (1959, 1962). The power and limitations of perceptrons are presented, with the discussion of learning being postponed until Section V. We begin with some brief historical remarks, then define perceptrons and the perceptual situation dealt with by Minsky and Papert, give their main results, and conclude with comments on the significance of their results.

The perceptron, as a relatively simple linear device, has had some surprising successes, notably Samuel's checker player (Samuel, 1959, 1967). These successes, plus the perceptron's appealing similarity to known physiological structures, led to the widespread belief that it was a satisfactory model for the perceptual process. Although no concrete model that has abilities even remotely resembling human capabilities has ever been produced, this belief has persisted. Minsky and Papert felt that the perceptron was not an adequate model of the perceptual process, and that its successes were limited to applications where a linear weighing of evidence was appropriate. Further, they felt that even in these cases the evidence to be weighed had to be judiciously chosen to make a correct overall solution feasible. Since many of their colleagues were unconvinced, they set out to prove their conjecture. It is these results that we summarize, and we begin with the definition of a perceptron.

The perceptron approach can be defined generally (without confining it to a particular context) by placing the appropriate restrictions on the preprocessor Φ and the processor Ω. The basic idea is that Φ computes the answers to many simple questions, and Ω combines these answers linearly to answer a more complex question. There are two big attractions (besides its similarity to physiological structures) to this approach: Ω is simple (so learning can be studied easily) and Φ operates in parallel (computing many things at once). The preprocessor Φ answers a question by stating whether a statement, $P(X)$, is true of X. Formally, P can be represented as a function from all the possible values of X into $\{0,1\}$ with 0 corresponding to P being false, and 1 to P being true. Since Φ operates in parallel, it can compute more than one predicate P at a time. Hence, the predicates must be calculable independently. This means that Φ must consist of a set of predicates, rather than one predicate. Let φ's henceforth represent typical elements of Φ. This definition of Φ determines the nature of the output of Φ, which must consist of n-tuples of 0's and 1's. The processor Ω takes as its inputs the n-tuples of 0's and 1's ($\langle X_1, X_2, \ldots, X_n \rangle$) and $(n+1)$-tuples of real numbers ($\langle \alpha_1, \alpha_2, \ldots, \alpha_n, \theta \rangle$, where the α_i's are coefficients and θ is the threshold) and is defined by

$$\Omega(\langle X_1, X_2, \ldots, X_n \rangle, \langle \alpha_1, \alpha_2, \ldots, \alpha_n, \theta \rangle) = \begin{cases} 1 & \text{if } \sum_{i=1}^{n} \alpha_i X_i > \theta, \\ 0 & \text{otherwise.} \end{cases}$$

A predicate ψ is said to be a *linear threshold function* with respect to Φ if there are coefficients α_i and a threshold θ such that $\Omega = 1$ if ψ is true, and $\Omega = 0$ if ψ is false. The set of all linear threshold functions with respect to Φ is denoted by $L(\Phi)$. The coefficients and threshold come from the set $\mathcal{P}$ of "programs"; hence, $\mathcal{P}$ is the set of all $(n+1)$-tuples of real numbers. How particular elements of $\mathcal{P}$ are selected to make a specific calculation is a learning question and is discussed in Section V.

The general definition of perceptrons, as stated formally, is uninteresting. Because there are no restrictions on the predicates in Φ, it is possible to choose a complex partial predicate that "does all the work" and, hence, trivializes Ω. (For any ψ, simply make ψ an element of Φ, and Ω the identity function.) What is needed to capture the intuition behind perceptrons is to restrict the partial predicates to being "simple" functions. This cannot be done with complete generality since there is no general theory for the simplicity of functions. However, in particular contexts it is possible to give satisfactory ad hoc definitions of simplicity. Technically speaking, the data $\mathcal{D}$ must be specified before a precise notion of simplicity can be given.

Minsky and Papert use two different definitions of $\mathcal{D}$, which gives rise to two different theories: an algebraic theory and a geometric one. Although the results of the geometric theory are of primary interest to us, we mention certain general concepts that are best defined in terms of the algebraic theory.

Let $\mathcal{D}$ be the class of all finite sets. (Minsky and Papert take $\mathcal{D}$ to be the class of all sets, but their main results are proved for families of finite sets.)

An arbitrary element of $\mathcal{D}$ is denoted by R and is called a retina. Thus R denotes an arbitrary finite set with no structure. The domains of the φ's, the predicates in Φ, are subsets of R. Since the domains are not in general all of R, the φ's are called *partial predicates*. The complex predicate, ψ, computed by Ω, has as domain all of R. To specify ψ, it is necessary to specify R. Normally, we are not interested in predicates tied to a certain R, but rather in predicate schemes defined for a family $\mathcal{D}$ of R's, and we shall let ψ also represent a predicate scheme. Formally, ψ is a function from $\mathcal{D}$ into the set of predicates defined on elements of $\mathcal{D}$, such that $\psi(R)$ is some predicate defined on R.

We are now in a position to define an appropriate definition of simplicity for predicate schemes, but this requires two preliminary definitions.

DEFINITION 10. *For any element φ of Φ, $S(\varphi)$, called the support of φ, is the smallest subset S of R such that for every subset X of R, $\varphi(X) = \varphi(X \cap S)$.*

Intuitively, the support of φ is the subset of R on which φ "really depends." As examples let $\psi(X)$ hold iff X is not empty. Then the support of ψ is the whole retina R. In contrast, if $\psi(X)$ holds iff $\{p_1,p_2\}$ is in X, then $\{p_1,p_2\}$ is the support of ψ.

DEFINITION 11. *The order of a predicate ψ is the smallest number k, for which there is a set of predicates Φ such that $|S(\varphi)| \leq k$ for all φ in Φ and $\psi \in L(\Phi)$.*

Using the first of the examples of support, where R is the support of ψ, the order of ψ in contrast is 1, because we take as Φ the set of completely local predicates φ_p: $\varphi_p(X)$ holds iff p is in X. Then the support of any φ_p is just $\{p\}$ and $|S(\varphi)| = 1$, and $\Psi(X) = \Sigma\varphi_p(X) > 0$.

DEFINITION 12. *A predicate scheme ψ is of finite order, in fact of order $\leq k$, on a family of sets $\mathcal{D}$ if for every element R of D, $\psi(R)$ has order $\leq k$.*

Henceforth, we are no longer interested in predicates (only predicate schemes), so we follow Minsky and Papert and call predicate schemes predicates. All the results mentioned below about predicates are really about predicate schemes. The last definition, then, is the operative one. The smaller k is, the simpler the predicate (scheme). This is the intuitive idea. The important use of the definition is to rule out predicates *not* of finite order as being calculable by a perceptron. This would follow if there were some limit on the supports of the elements of Φ, a restriction which seems reasonable and gives the theorems more than just technical interest.

In the geometric theory an element R of $\mathcal{D}$ is obtained by dividing a rectangular region of the Euclidean plane into equal squares. The set of squares is R, and the set of all such R's is $\mathcal{D}$. For a subset Y of a rectangular region, a corresponding subset in an appropriate R is given by x is in X if at least one point of Y lies in the square x. For example, X is a circle if it can be obtained from a real circle Y by this rule. However, apparent errors may occur near the "limits of resolution" because of this; e.g., small circles will not look very round, and serious problems may result when dealing with real figures. Minsky and Papert avoid these problems by starting with figures defined on R and then deal only with translations which are a multiple of the length of the sides of a square and 90 degree rotations.

Two squares in R are *adjacent* if they have a common edge. A subset X of R is *connected* if for every two squares in X there is a path of adjacent squares connecting them.

THEOREM 1. *The predicate* $\psi(X)$ *iff* X *is connected is not of finite order. In fact, it is of order* $\geqq C|R|^{\frac{1}{2}}$.

This is one of the most significant theorems in the book of Minsky and Papert. The algebraic theory was developed as a tool for proving it. Minsky and Papert felt that the partial predicates must be in some sense "local," and that it would prove impossible to compute "global" functions on the basis of these "local" ones. Their paradigm of a global feature was "connectedness." Recognition of connectedness by a different device is discussed in Section III.

A *component* of a figure is the set of all squares connected to a given square. A *hole* of a figure is a component of the complement (where squares touching only at a corner are considered to be adjacent). Every figure is assumed to be surrounded by an outside that does not count as a hole. A predicate is *topologically invariant* if it remains unchanged whenever the figure is distorted without changing connectedness or inside-outside relations of its parts.

THEOREM 2. *Let the Euler number* $E(X) = |$ *components*$(X)| -$ *holes* $|X|$. *Then the only topologically invariant predicates of finite order are functions of the Euler number.*

The above results are negative. The following results are positive.

We first mention some familiar geometrical properties that have low finite order.

THEOREM 3. *The following predicates are of order* 3: *convexity, solid rectangles, and hollow rectangles.*

THEOREM 4. *Except for resolution problems, the predicate that* X *is the perimeter of a complete circle is of order* 4.

The following results depend on "stratification," a technique which simulates serial computation in the parallel framework. Stratification requires such large coefficients that it is not achievable in a practical way, but it is of theoretical interest.

THEOREM 5. *Let* R *consist of a line of squares, infinite in both directions. Then the predicate that X has a symmetry under reflection is of order* ≤ 4 *for all finite X.*

THEOREM 6. *Let* R *consist of two infinite lines of squares A and B. Then the predicate that the (finite) figure in A is a translate of the figure in B is of order* ≤ 5.

That context can be crucial is illustrated by the following pair of theorems.

THEOREM 7. *The predicates that X is a solid square and X is a hollow square are of order* ≤ 3.

THEOREM 8. *The predicate that X is a hollow square in context is not of finite order.*

In general, it seems that most of the predicates "in context" are not of finite order, although this is proved only for a few predicates. Insofar as this is the case, it is a serious limitation on perceptrons.

Without casting doubt on the ingenuity and importance of Minsky's and Papert's work, for our purposes the significant issue is the continuing potentiality of the perceptron approach to perception. As Block (1970) points out, Minsky and Papert have defined perceptrons in such a way that only the simplest type of perceptron may be called a perceptron. These simple perceptrons have received a great deal of attention, but they were accorded this interest only because they were seen as the simplest type in a series of progressively more complicated models. It seemed wise to study the simplest case thoroughly before proceeding to the more complicated models, which are the objects of real interest. Minsky and Papert probably do not do justice to the view that the simple perceptron is only of temporary interest.

In addition, their geometric results are tied to their definition of $\mathfrak{D}$, i.e., the type of retinas they deal with. It seems plausible that all their results (with minor modifications) would hold if one divided the plane into, e.g., hexagons, rather than squares. However, there are other choices for $\mathfrak{D}$, e.g., line drawings, for which it is not so obvious that the same results would hold.

In conclusion, it seems that Minsky and Papert have not established that the perceptron approach should be abandoned in trying to model the perceptual process. They have shown that there are good reasons for following other approaches. We turn to some relatively simple alternatives in the next two sections.

III. AUTOMATA AND LINE DRAWINGS

The intuitive idea behind the approach discussed in this section is to keep the preprocessor Φ simple and to have the processor Ω act like an automaton (not necessarily a finite one). An automaton acts "serially" rather than in "parallel" and, hence, differs considerably from the perceptrons of the previous section.

An automaton takes as its input a string of symbols that has on the surface no natural geometric properties. In order to do geometry with an automaton, it is necessary to code a figure with geometric properties so that it is an appropriate input for an automaton. There is no straightforward way to code all the usual geometric properties into a string of symbols. The solution to this problem is to choose some natural coding and then to investigate which geometric properties can and which cannot be recognized.

The above considerations suggest the following choices. Let $\mathcal{D}$ consist of only straight-line drawings, which are henceforth called *figures*. For each figure in $\mathcal{D}$, label the vertices with capital roman letters, followed when necessary by primes. Each line in the figure is represented by an *n*-tuple of labels. A tape for the figure can then be obtained by listing the *n*-tuples, in any order, and separating them with a comma. As an example, take Fig. 1. Label the vertices, using any order. Thus, a tape for the figure is ABCDE, AG,BF,GCH,HD.

Any permutation of the labels or rearrangement of the order in which the lines are listed will also yield a tape for the figure. This method of coding figures requires a minor change in the way elements of the vocabulary V are written. We now use a comma, a prime symbol and the capital roman letters, e.g., A, B, . . . , A', B', . . . are labels. We list conditions that elements of V^*, the set of finite sequences of elements of the

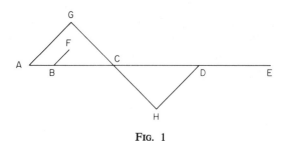

Fig. 1

vocabulary V, must satisfy to be codings of figures, with the least interesting first (and we omit obvious conditions on the labels themselves as letters followed by a possibly empty sequence of primes).

1. Commas must not appear at the beginning or end of the tape, nor may two commas follow each other.

2. Every sequence of labels coding a line segment of a figure must contain at least two distinct labels, but no label may occur twice.

3. There must be no "geometric" impossibilities. There is no complete characterization of these impossibilities, but they seem to be obtainable from a real drawing by deleting one vertex, e.g., ABC,ADE,BE,DC which is a coding for Fig. 2 with the vertex F omitted.

Intuitively, we have a straightforward method for coding figures as input tapes for automata, including Turing machines. Whatever sort of computing device is used, it will be limited by the limitations of its input.

The results fall into two categories: negative (what geometric information cannot be retrieved from a coding) and positive (what can be retrieved). The positive results are listed first, without proof, since the proofs are complex. The negative results are susceptible to shorter proofs, so we either give or indicate the main ideas in these proofs.

A coding is *connected* if there is a sequence $\langle b_0, b_1, \ldots, b_n \rangle$ for every pair of lines c, d such that $b_0 = c$, $b_n = d$ and for all i, $1 < i < n$, b_i has a vertex in common with b_{i-1} and b_{i+1}. A *component* of a coding is a maximal connected subset of the coding.

Note that a coding is connected if a figure for which it is the coding is connected.

THEOREM 9. *There is an effective procedure (thus a Turing machine) for listing the components of a coding and, hence, for recognizing connectedness.*

We say that AB is a *segment* in a coding if there is a line $b = qArBt$ in the coding, where q, r, and t may be either empty or nonempty. An n-tuple

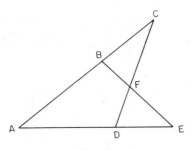

FIG. 2

$V_1V_2 \cdots V_n$ of the vertices which occur in a coding is a *polygon* if $V_1V_2, V_2V_3, \ldots, V_{n-1}V_n, V_nV_1$ are segments in the coding.

Note that if an *n*-tuple is a polygon in a coding, then the elements of the *n*-tuple list, in order, the vertices of a polygon in any figure which the coding is a coding of.

THEOREM 10. *There is an effective procedure (thus a Turing machine) for listing all the polygons in a coding.*

The procedures mentioned above are "reasonable," i.e., they do not require simply running through all possibilities. However, they require the capabilities of a Turing machine, rather than that of a finite automaton. The ability to look over the same *n*-tuple more than once becomes necessary, because no particular order has been specified for the elements on the tape. With suitable arrangement of lines, a pushdown automaton, for example, can recognize whether a given *n*-tuple of vertices is a polygon. How far this reduction of computing capabilites can be carried without requiring a particular arrangement of the elements on the tape is a topic for further investigation.

We now turn to some negative results.

THEOREM 11. *It is not always possible to tell whether a polygon in a figure is concave or convex given only a coding for the figure.*

Proof

Figures 3A and B have the same, or equivalent, codings.

THEOREM 12. *It is not always possible to tell what line segments are inside (outside) of a closed figure (which must be a polygon) given only a coding for the figure.*

Proof

Figures 4A and B have the same coding.

THEOREM 13. *It is not always possible to recognize the simple regions in a figure [areas enclosed by a polygon but not crossed by any (broken) line], given only a coding for the figure.*

and

FIGS. 3A and B

FIGS. 4A and B

Proof

Figures 5A and B, each of which contains two hexagons and a quadrilateral, have the same coding.
In the first, the two hexagons are the simple regions, in the second the quadrilateral and a hexagon.

The above results are the rule, not the exception. Indeed, they hold for almost all relatively complex figures. Combined, the three results indicate that most topological properties are lost by this method of coding.

Additions can be made to the coding to alleviate some of the above difficulties and, hence, make the resulting tapes more closely resemble ordinary geometry. These possibilities shall not be discussed here.

IV. PICTURE-PARSING GRAMMARS

In the preceding two sections we have been concerned with automata or automatonlike devices that begin by observing local properties of a figure and build up, either from parallel or serial processing, the computations for a complex predicate. Another important approach that has developed in the past decade is to look at the more global characteristics of figures to see whether a grammar can be written for figures that is similar to the kind of grammars that have been written for languages. The connection with automata is then made directly by the theorems relating grammars and automata as outlined in the introductory section.

Because of the extensive interest in automatic pattern recognition by computers, the literature on picture-parsing grammars, or grammatical description of pictures, is now enormous, and it is not possible to review even the most important articles that have been published. Most of the

FIGS. 5A and B

published work has appeared since 1960. The early work of Eden (1961, 1962) and Narasimhan (1962, 1964, 1966) has been influential in subsequent developments. An important step in making the connection with grammars completely explicit and formal was taken by Shaw (1969), and we shall mainly use some of his examples to illustrate the theory.

How a picture language is intended to work can be illustrated by considering a simple grammar for generating those letters of the alphabet that are made up only of line segments. We shall follow with slight modifications an example used by Shaw (1969). The terminal vocabulary, V_T, consists of h, v, l, r, four operation symbols $+, -, \times$, and $*$, and parentheses. The meaning of $h, v, l,$ and r is that they are segments of given length, with h being horizontal; v, vertical; l, a left diagonal; and r, a right diagonal. To interpret the operation symbols a direction is also given each segment, so that we can refer to the head and tail of each of the four primitive elements as shown in Fig. 6. The meaning of the operation symbols is reflected in

FIG. 6. Primitive elements.

just the four possible concatenations of heads and tails. For example, letting $\frown$ stand for the operation of concatenation,

$$r + l = \text{head } (r) \frown \text{tail } (l) \qquad \wedge$$
$$l + r = \text{head } (l) \frown \text{tail } (r) \qquad \vee$$
$$h - v = \text{head } (h) \frown \text{head } (v) \qquad \urcorner$$
$$h \times v = \text{tail } (h) \frown \text{tail } (v) \qquad \llcorner$$
$$r * l = \text{tail } (r) \frown \text{tail } (l) \ \& \ \text{head } (r) \frown \text{head } (l).*$$

Also, the head and tail of $S_1 O S_2$ for any of the four operations 0 is the head of S_2 and the tail of S_1.

The picture grammar is simply stated in terms of these operations, requiring in this version only the single nonterminal symbol S. There are eight rules of production

$$S \rightarrow (S + S)$$
$$S \rightarrow (S - S)$$
$$S \rightarrow (S \times S)$$
$$S \rightarrow (S * S)$$
$$S \rightarrow \text{atom, where } r, l, h \text{ and } v \text{ are atoms.}$$

---

* The operations are not always well defined for all primitive elements. Here $r * l$ is not defined, but $r * r = r$, for example, and another example is given in text.

The capital letter A has the following derivation, which of course is not unique:

S
(S + S)
(r + S)
(r + (S + S))
(r + (S + l))
(r + ((S * S) + l))
(r + ((S * h) + l))
(r + (((S + S) * h) + l))
(r + (((r + 1) * h) + l)).

The terminal expression for the letter F is $(v + (h \times (v + h)))$, and for the letter L is $(h \times v)$; other examples are easily constructed.

The selection of primitive elements for such picture grammars could be guided by knowledge of the special types of receptor cells in the retina or other sensory organs, but this direction has not been pursued very far as yet. The main thrust, as indicated, has been toward pattern recognition and related problems in "perceptual" uses of computers. The theoretical and technical developments are now substantial, and it will be surprising if some of the methods and results do not prove highly useful in the study of perception by living organisms. Some steps in this direction are outlined in Barlow, Narasimhan, and Rosenfeld (1972).

The kind of grammar just exhibited has a number of defects when applied to pictures.

1. A good case can be made for parallel processing rather than sequential processing as required by a pushdown automaton for a context-free grammar. In a parallel grammar every instance of the left member is replaced by the right member of the production rule. The power of such grammars is essentially the same as that of the phrase-structure grammars defined in Section I; this is proved in Rosenfeld (1971). Use of such parallel grammars could lead to perceptually more appropriate picture grammars.

2. The grammar given above is context-free, but there is a variety of evidence that context-sensitive rather than context-free grammars are more useful for analysis of pictures. For example, using h and v as given above we can generate the set of all squares with horizontal base and n units per side, but even the simple language for this set is context-sensitive. The tendency in linguistics, on the other hand, is to restrict the base grammar to being context-free and then to apply transformations to this base. Increasing divergence between grammars for pictures and grammars for linguistic utterances seems likely in the future.

3. Most of the picture grammars as yet developed apply to line drawings and seldom if ever to pictures with continuous gradients of shading and color over the entire surface. How well the present framework can be successfully modified to analyze such "richer" scenes is not yet clear.

V. LEARNING

This section is divided into three parts. The first gives an abstract characterization of a learning situation, the second deals with perceptron learning, and the third with automaton learning.

In the general situation, learning takes place in a series of trials. Each trial is defined by (a) the state of conditioning at the beginning of the trial, (b) the presented object (stimulus), (c) the sampled stimuli, (d) the response given, (e) the reinforcement received, and (f) the new state of conditioning at the beginning of the new trial. Item (f) actually belongs to the next trial, and often the first five elements will not all be distinct. For example, sometimes no distinction may be drawn between the presented and sampled stimuli. A learning procedure is specified by saying how the state of conditioning changes from one trial to the next, and this depends on the reinforcement schedule used, to which we now turn.

The types of reinforcement for learning perceptual patterns mainly fall under one paradigm. There is a set $\mathcal{D}$ of perceptual displays and a subset G of $\mathcal{D}$ that we want the device to learn to select. On each trial, the device responds *yes* to the presented display d if it classifies d as a member of G, otherwise it responds *no*. If the answer is correct, it receives positive reinforcement (e_1), and if the answer is incorrect, it receives negative reinforcement (e_2). This type of reinforcement we call *standard reinforcement*.

The first goal is to find learning procedures that, given standard reinforcement, will eventually learn always to respond correctly. Second, one wants the learning procedure to be "reasonable." Although no precise definitions of "reasonable" are available, it is an important consideration, and we comment on some of the issues involved.

For perceptrons, the state of conditioning is the set of coefficients that is being used. It is convenient mathematically to order the coefficients by ordering the k partial predicates in Φ. One can then think of the coefficients and the values of the partial predicates as k-dimensional vectors. Let us choose the most general model and let the coefficients be real numbers. The states of conditioning are then vectors in the k-dimensional vector space over the real numbers, and the values of the φ's are elements of the k-dimensional vector space over $\{0,1\}$.

We let $A = \langle \alpha_1, \alpha_2, \ldots, \alpha_k \rangle$ and $\Phi(d) = \langle \varphi_1(d), \varphi_2(d), \ldots, \varphi_k(d) \rangle$ where $d \in \mathcal{D}$ and $\mathcal{D}$ is the domain of the φ's. This allows us to write $\Sigma_i \alpha_i \varphi_i(d)$ as $A \cdot \Phi(d)$. The response is *yes* if $A \cdot \Phi(d) > 0$ and *no* otherwise. The set of reinforcements E is $\{e_1, e_2\}$. The sample space X consists of all possible experiments; each experiment is a sequence of trials. In the present situation a trial is simply a triple $(A, d, e,)$, where A is a state of conditioning, d an object in $\mathcal{D}$ and e a reinforcement.

A particular event is a subclass of the sample space, e.g., the event of the first reinforcement being e_2 is the set of all experiments in which e_2 occurred on the first trial. For convenience, let A_n be the state of conditioning at the beginning of trial n and d_n be the object on trial n. The dimension of the two necessary vector spaces is defined by k.

DEFINITION 13. *A structure* $\Lambda = (\mathcal{D}, \Phi, E, X)$ *is a* perceptron learning model *if and only if the following axioms are satisfied:*

(i) *If e_1 occurs on trial n, then $A_{n+1} = A_n$.*

(ii) *If e_2 occurs on trial n and $A_n \cdot \Phi(d_n) < 0$, then $A_{n+1} = A_n +$* $\Phi(d_n)$.

(iii) *If e_2 occurs on trial n and $A_n \cdot \Phi(d_n) > 0$, then $A_{n+1} = A_n -$* $\Phi(d_n)$.

We are now in a position to state the well-known learning theorem for perceptrons. (For the history of this theorem, see Minsky & Papert, 1969.)

THEOREM 14. (*Perceptron Convergence Theorem*). *For any set $\mathcal{D}$ and any subset G of $\mathcal{D}$, if there is a vector A such that $A \cdot \Phi(d) > 0$ iff $d \in G$, then in any perceptron learning model given standard reinforcement there will only be a finite number of trials on which the conditioning vector changes.*

The force of "any perceptron learning model" is that the choice of A_1 does not affect the result. Also, instead of saying trials on which "the conditioning vector changes" one could say equivalently "e_2 occurs" or "Ω responds incorrectly." If there are only a finite number of changes, then Ω will eventually make no mistakes. This is equivalent to saying that Ω can distinguish the elements of G *from those of* $\mathcal{D} - G$, *provided that* every type of element in both G and $- G$ occurs infinitely often in an experiment.

The conditions of the theorem require a vector A such that $A \cdot \Phi(d) > 0$ *iff $d \in G$*. This condition can be stated in other terms by saying that G and $\mathcal{D} - G$ are linearly separable. If the two sets are not linearly separable, the theorem simply does not apply. The vector that the procedure eventually finds will not necessarily be the vector A.

The simplicity of this learning procedure is appealing. The perceptron learns only on trials where it responds incorrectly, which is plausible. Also, it approaches the final answer step by step, with each change bringing it closer to the final answer. Contrast this with the procedure used by a similar device, the homeostat. The homeostat uses only integer coefficients (which do not decrease its power). It learns by having an enumeration of all k-tuples of integers available, and every time it makes a mistake it goes to the next k-tuple. Sooner or later it finds one that works. It does seem implausible to have an enumeration of all k-tuples available, but this could be solved by setting up some random guessing procedure. Often, the real objection to the homeostat is that it seems to learn primarily from a "lucky guess." On the other hand, "real" learning requires a gradual acquisition of an ability. Although this intuition is widespread, it should not be accepted uncritically. The same intuition favored linear conditioning models over all-or-none conditioning models, and yet the latter have proved to fit the data of many concept-formation or concept-identification experiments better (Suppes & Ginsberg, 1963).

In any discussion of reasonableness, the question of time (measured in number of trials) is bound to arise. If a learning procedure requires an inordinately large number of trials to the last expected error, we regard it as unreasonable or impractical. Note that the perceptron convergence theorem says nothing about rate of learning. What counts as "unreasonable" is difficult to formulate precisely; it is also difficult mathematically to estimate the rate. Minor modifications (which do not affect the convergence theorem) in the choice of the starting vector or the learning procedure (e.g., add $2\Phi(d)$ rather than $\Phi(d)$) can greatly affect the learning rate. That the homeostat probably takes longer than the perceptron to learn is a definite disadvantage. We emphasize, though, that this problem is entirely different from the preceding one of "gradualness" versus "lucky guess."

We turn now to automaton learning. As mentioned in the introduction, stimulus-response learning theory is the basis of the automaton approach. After formulating an appropriate general stimulus-response model with the appropriate restrictions, the asymptotic convergence theorem is stated. However, to avoid a large number of technical details, we formulate the concepts and axioms of the theory informally. A mathematically explicit development is to be found in Suppes (1969) and Rottmayer (1970).

The following characterization of an all-or-none conditioning model is standard, except that the notion of a subtrial is introduced. A subtrial corresponds to what is usually called a trial, but no reinforcement or conditioning takes place. Conditioning occurs only after a series of subtrials, now called a trial. A subtrial corresponds to an automaton making one transition, a trial to processing a whole tape. The definition requires seven primitive concepts. There is the set S of stimuli and the set R of responses. The set E of reinforcements contains only two elements, e_1 and e_2; e_1 is the positive reinforcer, e_2 the negative one. The fifth primitive concept is a measure μ of saliency on the set of stimuli. The concept of subtrial requires the introduction of $\mathcal{M}$ which is a sequence of positive integers m_n. Each m_n indicates the number of subtrials on trial n. This notion is necessary in defining the next primitive concept, that of the sample space X. Each element of X represents a possible experiment, i.e., an infinite sequence of trials, where each trial n has m_n subtrials. Each trial is an (m_n+2)-tuple consisting of three things: (a) the conditioning function at the beginning of the trial which is a partial function from S into R, where $C(\sigma) = r$ means σ is conditioned to r and $C(\sigma)$ undefined means σ is unconditioned; (b) m_n triples of the form (T,s,r) where T is the set of presented stimuli, s is the set of sampled stimuli and r is the response on a subtrial; and (c) the reinforcement which occurred. The final concept is the probability measure P on the appropriate algebra of events (subsets) of X. All probabilities must be defined in terms of P.

In the following axioms of the theory it is assumed that all events on which probabilities are conditioned have positive probability. There are three kinds of axioms: sampling axioms, conditioning axioms, and response axioms.

Sampling Axioms

S1. *On every subtrial a set of stimuli of positive measure is sampled with probability 1.*

S2. *If the same presentation set occurs on two different subtrials, then the probability of a given sample is independent of the subtrial number.*

S3. *Samples of equal measure that are subsets of the presentation set have an equal probability of being sampled on a given subtrial.*

S4. *The probability of a particular sample on trial n, subtrial m, given the presentation set of stimuli, is independent of any preceding subsequence of events.*

Conditioning Axioms

C1. *On every trial with probability 1 each stimulus element is conditioned to at most one response.*

C2. *If e_1 occurs on trial n, the probability is c that any previously unconditioned stimulus sampled on a subtrial will become conditioned to the response given on that subtrial, and this probability is independent of the particular subtrial and any preceding subsequence of events.*

C3. *If e_1 occurs on trial n, the probability is 0 that any previously unconditioned stimulus sampled on a subtrial will become conditioned to a response different from the one given on that subtrial, and this probability is independent of the particular subtrial and any preceding subsequence of events.*

C4. *If e_1 occurs on trial n, the conditioning of previously conditioned sampled states remains unchanged.*

C5. *If e_2 occurs on trial n, the probability is 0 that a previously unconditioned stimulus sampled on a subtrial will become conditioned.*

C6. *If e_2 occurs on trial n, the probability is d that any previously conditioned stimulus sampled on a subtrial will become unconditioned, and this probability is independent of the particular subtrial and any preceding subsequence of events.*

C7. *With probability 1, the conditioning of unsampled stimuli does not change.*

Response Axioms

R1. *If at least one sampled stimulus is conditioned to some response, then the probability of any response is the ratio of the measure of sampled stimuli conditioned to this response to the measure of all the sampled conditioned stimuli, and this probability is independent of any preceding subsequence of events.*

R2. *If no sampled stimulus is conditioned to any response, then the probability of any response r is a constant guessing probability p_r that is independent of n and any preceding subsequence of events.*

The conditioning method used in the theory just stated is simple. Conditioning occurs on trials where there is a correct response, and deconditioning occurs on trials where there is an incorrect response. Thus learning occurs on all trials, not only on incorrect trials as in the perceptron model. The method of learning actually resembles a homeostat more than a perceptron as far as "gradualness" is concerned.

We can prove the following theorem about stimulus-response theory as formulated above.

THEOREM 15. *If $\mathcal{D}$ is any set of perceptual displays and G is a subset of $\mathcal{D}$ that can be recognized by a finite automaton, then there is a stimulus-response model that can also learn to recognize G, with performance at asymptote matching that of the automaton. (We can regard the codings of the figures in G as being a language, so that in terms of Definition 4 the* theorem says the stimulus-response model will at asymptote be weakly equivalent to any finite automaton that can recognize the figures in G.)

As far as time is concerned, the theorem is actually proved by placing a lower bound on the rate of learning. This lower bound is unreasonable, but the actual rate will be much faster. Still, the learning would probably be classified as slow, and perhaps as unreasonably slow. Minor modifications may increase the rate of learning, just as many variations are available for perceptrons.

In closing, we note that both learning procedures assumed an arbitrary starting point and simple *yes/no* reinforcement. This is the most difficult learning situation, and a slow rate of learning can probably be expected. This difficult situation is the correct one for proving asymptotic or convergence theorems. It is probably not the correct situation for the detailed study of perceptual learning. The ordinary learner does not have an arbitrary starting point, and in most situations he is given more information about what to do than simply being told *yes* or *no* after each response. Development of more complex and more realistic learning models is beyond the scope of this chapter.

References

Barlow, H. B., Narasimhan, R., & Rosenfeld, A. Visual pattern analysis in machines and animals. *Science,* 1972, **177**, 567–575.

Block, H. D. A review of "Perceptrons: An introduction to computational geometry." *Information and Control,* 1970, **17**, 501–522.

Chomsky, N. Formal properties of grammars. In R. D. Luce, R. R. Bush, & E. Galanter (Eds.), *Handbook of mathematical psychology.* Vol. 2. New York: Wiley, 1963. Pp. 125–155.

Chomsky, N., & Miller, G. A. Introduction to the formal analysis of natural languages. In R. D. Luce, R. R. Bush, & E. Galanter (Eds.), *Handbook of mathematical psychology.* Vol. 2. New York: Wiley, 1963. Pp. 269–321.

Eden, M. On the formalization of handwriting. *American Mathematical Society of Applied Mathematics Symposium,* 1961, **12**, 83–88.

Eden, M. Handwriting and pattern recognition. *IRE Transactions on Information Theory,* 1962, **IT-8**, 160–166.

Hopcroft, J. E., & Ullman, J. D. *Formal languages and their relation to automata.* Reading, Massachusetts: Addison-Wesley, 1969.

Minsky, M., & Papert, S. *Perceptrons.* Cambridge, Massachusetts: MIT Press, 1969.

Narasimhan, R. A linguistic approach to pattern recognition. Report No. 121, 1962, University of Illinois, Digital Computer Laboratory.

Narasimhan, R. Labeling schemata and syntactic description of pictures. *Information Control,* 1964, **7**, 151–179.

Narasimhan, R. Syntax-directed interpretation of classes of pictures. *Communications of the Association for Computing Machinery,* 1966, **9**, 166–173.

Needham, J. *Science and civilization in China.* Vol. IV; 2. London and New York: Cambridge Univ. Press, 1965.

Rabin, M. O., & Scott, D. Finite automata and their decision problems. *IBM Journal of Research and Development,* 1959, **3**, 114–125.

Rosenblatt, F. Two theorems of statistical separability in the perceptron. *Proceedings of a symposium on the mechanization of thought processes.* London: HM Stationery Office, 1959.

Rosenblatt, F. *Principles of neurodynamics.* New York: Spartan Books, 1962.

Rosenfeld, A. Isotonic grammars, parallel grammars and picture grammars. In B. Meltzer & D. Michie (Eds.), *Machine intelligence 6.* New York: American Elsevier, 1971. Pp. 281–294.

Rottmayer, W. A. A formal theory of perception. Technical Report No. 161, 1970, Stanford University, Institute for Mathematical Studies in the Social Sciences.

Samuel, A. L. Some studies in machine learning using the game of checkers. *IBM Journal of Research and Development,* 1959, **3**, 210–229.

Samuel, A. L. Some studies in machine learning using the game of checkers. Part II. *IBM Journal of Research and Development,* 1967, **11**, 601–618.

Shaw, A. C. A formal picture description scheme as a basis for picture processing systems. *Information and Control,* 1969, **14**, 9–52.

Suppes, P. Stimulus-response theory of finite automata. *Journal of Mathematical Psychology,* 1969, **6**, 327–355.

Suppes, P., & Ginsberg, R. A fundamental property of all-or-none models, binomial distribution of responses prior to conditioning, with application to concept formation in children. *Psychological Review,* 1963, **70**, 139–161.

Chapter 18

THE DEVELOPMENTAL EMPHASIS

ELIANE VURPILLOT*

Over the last few decades, the developmental aspects of the various psychological processes have occupied an increasingly important place in research. This is the result of a combination of factors as different as the development of the experimental method, the discovery of measuring techniques suited to the human infants, and the dissemination of Piaget's theory.

Ten years ago, in a remarkable book on nativism and empiricism in perception, Hochberg observed that there was little more to say about the problem originally posed by empiricists, i.e., "Whether we can have any idea of space at all which is not learned through experience. . ." (Hochberg, 1962, p. 326). However, after 300 years of controversy about nurture versus nature, there is still an interest in finding out how much perception owes to the individual's contact with his environment and how much of it is determined by the anatomic and functional characteristics of his central nervous system. Such an interest has inevitably led to the systematic study of the development of perception in the child.

---

* Translated by Peter Graham.

I. ASSOCIATIONISM, OR THE GESTALT THEORY

The increase in research into the perception of the child began to take place at the turn of the century, with the controversy between associationists and Gestaltists over the innate or acquired nature of perceptual organization. The associationists' model made a distinction between perceptions and sensations, and supposed that a baby at birth only had a set of multiple and independent sensations; these sensations were thought to organize themselves gradually according to the laws of association and constitute perceptual structures whose form was determined by the nature of the baby's contacts with the environment and whose strength was a function of the frequency of occurrence of these contacts. In the associationist view, all perception is acquired. The Gestaltist model, on the other hand, sees all perception as a field effect, which appears as soon as sensory stimulations are received.

The organization of any field (whether it be physical, cerebral, or perceptive) taken in its broadest sense, in structured units of various kinds, obeys a certain number of laws, known as laws of organization. When the physical properties and the spatial or other relationships that exist between the elements of a given field are known, it is possible to forecast how this field is going to organize itself, what units will be formed, and the degree of relative strength of each of them.

The laws that determine how the forces within a field operate are always the same whether it is a physical field, a cerebral field, or a perceptual field. It is the *isomorphism* between the three spheres, and particularly that existing between the cerebral field and the perceptual field, which produces the adequacy and structural harmony between the perceived world and the physical world.

In the physical world, the interplay of forces is determined by objective relationships of size, orientation, and position between the various elements. The form taken by a perception is therefore chiefly determined by the physical characteristics of the object. On the level of the cerebral field, however, the activity of the neurons can change with their degree of maturation. Modern Gestaltists, therefore, suppose that perceptual processes such as figural aftereffects (Köhler & Wallach, 1944) or optico-geometric illusions (Köhler & Fishback, 1950), are liable to a certain degree of evolution with age, through the rate of permanent satiation of the brain tissue.

In order to substantiate their theory, the Gestaltists and their pupils attempted to prove the universality and the precocity of the laws of organization of forms by demonstrating, for instance, the existence of optico-geometric illusions in animals of widely differing species, such as the pigeon (Warden & Baar, 1929), the minnow (Herter, 1930), and the chicken (Winslow, 1933), as well as in very young children.

It should be remembered that the earliest genetic studies used verbal instructions and did not generally involve children under 4; the number of contacts that a 4-year-old child has already had with its environment is such that its performances do not enable one or other of the two schools to be vindicated.

During the first quarter of this century, another controversy arose between the champions of classical associationism and the believers in syncretism (Renan, 1890) or globalism. The former held that as the perception of elements always precedes the perception of a whole, the child ought to be able to perceive details more easily than the whole and display a good differentiation (Cramaussel, 1924, 1927). In the opinion of the latter, on the other hand, the young child has an overall and chaotic vision of objects and is more able to distinguish a whole than its parts, producing as a result poor performances in differentiation tasks (Claparède, 1909, 1925; Decroly, 1929; Luquet, 1913, 1927; Segers, 1926). Later the notion of syncretism evolved somewhat: research showed that, in fact, the child had a better perception of either a whole or its details depending on the physical characteristics of the stimulus and that the child's handicap resided in its inability to take in simultaneously several levels of perceptual organization of a single object (Dworetzki, 1939; Elkind, Koegler, & Go, 1964; Meili, 1931; Vurpillot, 1972).

The essential fact to be remembered is that the controversies between associationists and Gestaltists, and between associationists and the champions of syncretism gave a vital impetus to modern genetic study of perception.

Research over the last 30 years has differed from previous research in that as a whole it has been both methodologically and statistically more sophisticated, and better adapted to collecting information rather than verifying predictions that are based on a given theory. Three main trends have emerged from this research. They can best be defined in the form of the following questions: (1) Can one speak of perception as soon as the child is born? (2) What interaction is there between maturation and exercise? (3) What role does the subject's action play in its perception?

II. DOES THE BABY PERCEIVE AS SOON AS IT IS BORN?

Of all the research devoted to perception in the child over the last 15 years, the most considerable and the most original in its technique as well as in its contribution has been focused on the infant during its first year. At the present time there exists an impressive body of data that shows that as soon as it is born the human infant has a differentiated behavior in response to the different values of certain stimuli. It is therefore quite certain that its sensory receptors are much more sensitive than was thought for a long time. What is less certain is whether the responses obtained are mechanical, so to speak, and totally determined by the properties of the stimulus, or whether, between the arrival of neural excitation in the primary projection areas of the cortex and the command of the motor response, any psychological processes of organization, differentiation, or identification take place. In short, at what point in the life of an infant is it possible to start talking about perceptual structures?

Some of the most eminent people in this field incline toward the hypothesis of a primitive lack of organization. Spitz (1965) considers the newborn infant to be a psychologically undifferentiated organism devoid of consciousness or perception. It is possible to point to a relationship between variations in the stimuli and differences in the reactions; but, he goes on, if something does in fact occur between stimulus and response, it is not a psychological process. Any excitement of the peripheral sensory receptors is transmitted to the autonomic nervous system and triggers off emotional manifestations. And so up until the age of 2 months, at least, the environment constitutes for infants no more than a source of disturbance. When the stimuli are sufficiently strong, they bring a visceral sensitivity into action and trigger off observable responses; but the relationship between stimulus and response is lacking in meaning; and according to Spitz without meaning or consciousness there can be no perception.

Various functions and structures gradually emerge from the initial state of indifferentiation under the influence of two distinct processes: maturation, defined by the blooming of innate forms, functions and organs, and development, defined by appearance of forms, functions and behaviors resulting from exchanges with the environment. The mother or her substitute is closely bound up with the infant's whole emotional experience, and is an indispensable intermediary between it and its environment. The good relationship between mother and child is the basis of all communication between the latter and its environment, whether perception, the construction of forms, permanent and invariant objects, or cognitive and mnemonic structures are involved.

In books devoted to the infant which he wrote a relatively long time ago (Piaget, 1936, 1937), but which have not been contradicted by any of his recent writing, Piaget postulated that "at birth, no impression of space is given except for the perception of light and the accommodation that goes with this perception (the pupillary reflex to the degree of illumination and the palpebral reflex to dazzle). Everything else, i.e., the perception of forms, sizes, distances, positions, etc., is gradually formulated at the same time as the objects themselves" (Piaget, 1950, p. 87). At the beginning, the object is indistinguishable from the sensory impressions that accompany the action and only exists as an extension of this action. During the first months, action alone gives constant qualities to the object; the sensorimotor schema serves as a link with "sensory pictures" (proximal stimuli), gives them a meaning, and enables them to be recognized and differentiated. Owing to a progressive coordination of several sensorimotor schemas, the sensory pictures gradually dissociate themselves from the action and constitute permanent and invariant objects.

In contrast with these two positions, which can both be said to fall into the category of structured theories of development, there exists a vast body of data collected by young-child psychologists which has resulted in other conclusions. Two names are particularly important: Fantz, who has had a decisive influence on the development of research into infants' perception, and Bower, whose originality resides in the fact that he has tackled such crucial problems as the validity of the laws of perceptual organization in the infant (Bower, 1965), the permanence of the object (Bower, 1967, 1971), and the relationship between touch and vision (Bower, Broughton, & Moore, 1970). Without putting forward any theory of development, these authors attempt to show, by adducing a good deal of precise data, that infants' perception displays a certain degree of organization from birth.

Bower demonstrates that long before it is able to relate the information it obtains through various sensory channels or the variations in stimuli and its own action, the infant reacts in a way that is adapted to certain modifications in its environment. Thus, in one of Bower's experiments (Bower et al., 1970), 6-day-old infants already seem able to perceive visually the solid nature of an object. But Bower, who is much less assertive than many of his colleagues and extremely ingenious in his conceptions of experimental situations, by no means concludes that the infant's perception displays the same degree of organization as that of an adult. He even goes so far as to attribute an acquired nature to certain laws of organization, such as proximity for instance, which is something he has in common with a functionalist such as Brunswik (Brunswik & Kamiya, 1953).

III. INTERACTION BETWEEN MATURATION AND EXERCISE

It is extremely difficult to study the respective roles of maturation and exercise in the evolution of human behavior, although certain electrophysiological information is available (electroencephalograms, electroretinograms) concerning the activity of sensory receptors and the cerebral cortex, as well as the modification of some of their parameters with age. The comparison of such information with the anatomic characteristics of neurons as revealed in autopsy does not tell us all that much about the role of maturation in development. And so animals are generally used for this kind of research: sensory deprivations are inflicted on them at variously early stages and for variously long periods, and the behavioral, physiological, and anatomic modifications resulting from them are studied. The first researches point to the irreversibility of the catastrophic consequences of sensory deprivation at a very early stage, whereas adult animals seem little affected by equally long deprivation, which led to the conclusion that the lack of exercise of one function such as vision prevents the nervous maturation of the visual system from occurring normally.

The development of the technique of planting microelectrodes in the neurons of cats and monkeys at various points of their visual system and the study of their receptive fields (Hubel & Wiesel, 1959, etc.) enabled very precise information to be gained concerning neuronic activity. We now know that each visual neuron is specialized and responds electively to luminous stimuli which fall on one particular zone of the retina and which have well-defined characteristics as far as their form and orientation is concerned. The study of neuronic activity in the cells of the visual system in cats, subjected at a very early stage to various kinds of visual deprivations, resulted in a rapid degradation of the functioning of these neurons, particularly from the point of view of their sensitivity to the formal properties of the stimuli. Moreover, research into the behavior of baby monkeys (Fantz, 1965) has shown that just like human newborn babies they were able to respond differentially, from birth, to patterned and to plain cards, but that this ability to differentiate disappeared when these animals were brought up in darkness or in diffused light. It would seem, therefore, that the deprivation of varied visual stimuli results in the loss of an innate ability. In that case, the perceptual deficiency of animals brought up in darkness must be due not to an interruption of nervous maturation, nor to an anatomic degeneration of the cells, but to their functional degradation.

IV. THE ROLE OF ACTION IN PERCEPTUAL DEVELOPMENT

A great many writers on the subject point to the observer's activity in perceptual mechanisms, but the way in which this activity influences perception is viewed in widely differing ways depending on the theoretical context that is chosen.

A. J. J. Gibson's Approach

The movement of sensory receptors in response to a stimulus constitutes an activity of a sensorimotor type whose most obvious role is to gather rich and diversified information. Several writers consider this function of exploratory activity to be one of the fundamental factors of the organization and evolution of perceptions.

J. J. Gibson (1950, 1966) considers optical texture, defined by the distribution of areas of varied intensity at the level of the proximal stimulus, and its transformations during the movements of an individual, or of the objects he is looking at, to be the foundation of the visual perception of the physical world. Each point of fixation has a corresponding proximal stimulus and a certain distribution of luminous intensities which reach the retinal receptors. When an immobile observer moves his gaze over his environment, the localization of the point of fixation changes and with it the content of the proximal stimulus. When the observer himself moves, whether or not his point of fixation changes at the same time, the content of the proximal stimulus changes, and it changes also when it is not the observer but a part of the environment that moves. When one remembers that in any case an individual does not fixate the same point for more than a fraction of a second, except in exceptional or artificial cases, it becomes clear that his visual perception of the environment is based on a succession of changing proximal stimuli. But the transformation that links the proximal stimuli together has certain characteristics which differ depending on whether this transformation originates from a movement of physical objects, a movement of the observer, or simply a movement of his visual receptors. More particularly, it occurs that during these transformations certain relationships remain unchanged within the distribution of intensities, invariances that are proper to each type of modification on the level of the physical world. The observer thus has at his disposal a sufficiently rich and differentiated amount of information to obtain a satisfactory perceptual knowledge of his environment.

Although the observer records in the succession of proximal stimuli all that he needs in order to become aware of the physical world, it does not follow that he is immediately capable of using it in its entirety. He has to learn to analyze the content of the proximal stimuli in order to discover what J. J. Gibson calls variables of a higher order, such as the spatial order or the temporal evolution of the stimuli, and to link them with perceptions of surfaces, of objects, and of movement.

The proximal stimulus contains all the possible information, and it is in an already organized form. The sole perceptual progress resides in an increasingly subtle differentiation of an increasing number of variables

(Gibson & Gibson, 1955). This differentiation consists of a perceptual learning process in which the simple repetition of stimuli plays a leading role. The perception of a stimulus is above all determined by the individual's sensory equipment, which itself depends on the nature of his nervous system and on his degree of maturation, and secondly by the ability he has acquired, thanks to his contacts with his environment, to isolate the variables of a higher order (E. J. Gibson, 1969). Gibson expects perceptions to become more subtle with age, but sees this evolution as the result of a perceptual learning process similar to the one which can be observed in an adult during a new task. Gibson therefore feels that the observer's action comes into play in an almost mechanical way, as a source of transformation with the proximal stimuli. It matters little whether the movement of the observer is active or passive, or whether consequences of his action are favorable to him or not.

B. Piaget's Approach

From 1942 to 1961, Piaget and his collaborators published an important corpus of research on the development of perception; its results were synthesized by Piaget in *The Mechanism of Perception* (1961). Piaget's views on perception display two distinct, though not independent, characteristics. First, Piaget presents a probabilistic model which is intended to explain the effects of primary field effects, and secondly he is at pains to demonstrate that primary perceptual structures of a quasimechanical origin are gradually complemented by other perceptual structures which he terms secondary and which are due "to constructions and reconstructions of perceptual activity" (Piaget & Stettler von Albertini, 1954). The term field effect, which is borrowed from the Gestaltists, does not refer to a field of forces but to a field of centration defined by the "immediate interactions that occur between simultaneously perceived elements during a single fixation of the gaze" (Piaget, 1967, p. 4). In other words, a field effect is relative to the content of a single proximal stimulus; as soon as there is any movement of the gaze and perception takes in several proximal stimuli at once, perceptual activity comes into action, taking us out of the sphere of pure field effects.

1. THE THEORY OF RELATIVE CENTRATIONS

The theory of relative centrations is aimed at explaining primary field effects through different probabilities of encounters between the subject's receptor elements and the stimulations issued from the physical elements of the stimulus.* It is postulated that (1) the perceived size of a part of a drawing—segment, angle, or interval—is directly proportional to the density of encounters carried out on this element; and (2) all other things being equal the density of encounters will tend to be stronger on the longer of the two lines (or segments, intervals, angles, etc.). The relative physical sizes of the lines of a drawing and their situation in relation to the point of fixation determine the probable density of encounters between the subject's receptor elements and each particular element of the drawing, and, as a result, the relative perceived size of the various parts of this drawing as well as its form, since Piaget defines it by relationships between sizes.

2. The Influence of Perceptual Activities

Perception resulting from a single field of centration (or proximal stimulus) is therefore deforming by nature. An exact correspondence between perceived stimulus and physical stimulus can only result from a compensation between deformations and therefore from the relating of elements perceived in different fields of centration. Perceptual activities are above all sensorimotor, and are observable in the form of movements of the sensory receptors. But these movements can be complemented or replaced by non-observable intellectual activities relating various stimulations recorded at various times. Piaget then talks of spatiotemporal transports, anticipations, schematization, and putting into reference. What these activities have in common is that they establish relationships between elements which did not possess any because they were too far apart in space or time to belong to a single field of centration. In doing so, they modify the relative densities of encounters over the elements involved and, consequently, their perceived size. Their coming into action can then result either in an improvement of perception, insofar as the perceived sizes will be closer to the physical sizes, or on the contrary in a deterioration.

When the proportions of the elements of a drawing are such that the probable densities of encounters are very different over these, any perceptual activity that tends to equalize these densities, by the multiplication of the points of fixation for example, is bound to cause a compensation of the deformations. This is the case, for instance, of field effects known as primary opticogeometric illusions, whose intensity is diminished by perceptual activity.

---

* Where geometric drawings are involved, the elements of the stimulus can be likened to small fractions of lines, fractions whose angular size could, for instance, be determined by the separating power of the eye. As for the subject's elements, it would seem preferable to consider them to be abstract units without attempting to give them an anatomic or physiological support whose localization at the present time involves insoluble problems.

In another connection, a perceptual activity that causes either a localized increase in encounters by an unequal distribution of ocular fixations, or a relating of distant elements of different sizes, introduces a heterogeneity in the densities of encounters that the structure of the drawing did not render predictable and gives rise to fresh deformations. In either case, the process is the same: a homogenization of the densities of encounters over all the elements favours an accurate perception, whereas a heterogeneity in the densities of encounters results in deformations. In this way, the unity of the mechanisms of perception is established.

In young children, exploration activities are neither exhaustive nor systematic (Vurpillot, 1968; Zaporozhets & Zinchenko, 1966), and the cases of relating, which are few, generally take place between close elements (Piaget & Stettler von Albertini, 1954; Piaget & Vinh-Bang, 1961). Perceptual activities develop with age, side by side with the child's intellectual development and influence perception in two ways, by changing primary perceptual structures or field effects, and by enabling the construction of secondary perceptual structures in the form of perceptual schemas arising from the relating and integration into a single form of elements previously perceived as isolated units.

C. Russian Psychologists and the Theory of the Image

The Russian perception psychologists (Ananiev, Wekker, Lomov & Yarmolenko, 1959; Leontyev & Gippenreiter, 1966; Zaporozhets, 1965; Zaporozhets & Zinchenko, 1966; Zinchenko & Ruzskaya, 1960) also see the action of the child as playing a fundamental role in the development of perceptions, but their theoretical framework differs from that of Piaget. Taking Sechenov and Pavlov as their reference, they see a reflex origin in mental processes and consider that perception contains both motor components and sensory components. They see the adaptation of a human being to his environment as a corresponding of two sets, that of the states of the stimulus and that of the states of the observer, in such a way that the actions of the latter conform with the properties of the former.

The transition of the states of the stimulus to the states of the subject takes place according to a code that retains the spatiotemporal distribution of the characteristics of the object that originates stimulation; this code is called "image" (Wekker, 1966). Images have an origin in which the individual's activities, particularly that of exploration, are preponderant. It is the scanning of the object by the sensory receptors that organizes the image's spatial structure, since it enables a temporal series of distinct and separate states to be transformed into a unitary, organized, and complete spatial structure. Insufficient scanning results in the formation of an incomplete and distorted image and consequently a partially adapted response.

D. Held and the Distinction Between Active and Passive Movements

Any living being, brought up in normal conditions, possesses a range of sensorimotor coordinations that enables him to move in a way that is adapted to his environment. In some species, for instance the chicken and the frog, these coordinations are present from birth and have no flexibility (Hess, 1956; Sperry, 1951). It is reasonable then to suppose that they are inscribed in the nervous system of these animals. In other species, such as man and monkey, these coordinations emerge at a given age, towards the fourth month in the human infant, and are flexible, as was shown by research into adjustment to the wearing of prismatic spectacles. Held and his collaborators (Hein, Held, & Gower, 1970; Held, 1965; Held & Bauer, 1967; Held & Hein, 1963) have put forward the hypothesis that the acquisition or modification of visually controlled behaviors can only take place if the subject is able to establish a causal relationship between a transformation of sensory stimuli and a self-produced movement. The movements of a human being are only involved in the origin of the perception of the environment if they result from an active movement; passive movements, for Held, have no influence. He differs here with Gibson.

V. CONCLUSION

Research into the development of perceptions is on the increase, and goes a long way toward explaining the upsurge of genetic psychology. What is to be deplored, however, is the general lack of interrelation between data and theory. We have theories about the development of perceptions which are convincing because of their internal logic, but whose every prediction is only half-heartedly verified experimentally by their authors. Moreover, there is an increasing amount of extremely well-executed research that lacks theoretical perspective. This has become so true that because it is not planned with this in mind research does not supply the sort of data that enables the predictions of the various theoretical models to be contrasted and compared.

References

Ananiev, B. G., Wekker, L. M., Lomov, B. F., & Yarmolenko, A. V. *Osyazanie v protsessakn poznaniya i truda.* (Touch in the processes of cognition and work) Moscow: Publ. House Acad. Pedagogical Sci. RSFSR, 1959.

Bower, T. G. R. The determinants of perceptual unity in infancy. *Psychonomic Science*, 1965, **3**, 323–324.

Bower, T. G. R. The development of object-permanence: Some studies of existence constancy. *Perception and Psychophysics*, 1967, **2**, 411–418.

Bower, T. G. R. The object in the world of the infant. *Scientific American*, 1971, **225**, 30–38.

Bower, T. G. R., Broughton, J. M., & Moore, M. K. The coordination of visual and tactual input in infants. *Perception and Psychophysics*, 1970, **8**, 51–53.

Brunswik, E., & Kamiya, J. Ecological cue-validity of "proximity" and of other Gestalt factors. *American Journal of Psychology*, 1953, **66**, 20–32.

Claparède, E. *Psychologie de l'enfant et pédagogie expérimentale.* Geneva: Kundig, 1909.

Claparède, E. *Sur la perception syncrétique. L' Educateur*, 1925, **3**, 42–43.

Cramaussel, E. Ce que voient des yeux d'enfant. *Journal de Psychologie Normale et Pathologique*, 1924, **21**, 161–169.

Cramaussel, E. Expériences au jardin d'enfants. *Journal de Psychologie Normale et Pathologique*, 1927, **24**, 701–718.

Decroly, O. *La fonction de globalisation et l'enseignement.* Bruxelles: Lamertin, 1929.

Dworetzki, G. Le test de Rorschach et l'évolution de la perception. Etude expérimentale. *Archives de Psychologie (Geneve)*, 1939, **27**, 233–396.

Elkind, D., Koegler, R. R., & Go, E. Studies in perceptual development. II. Part-whole perception. *Child Development*, 1964, **35**, 81–90.

Fantz, R. L. Ontogeny of perception. In A. M. Schrier, H. F. Harlow, & F. Stollnitz (Eds.), *Behavior of nonhuman primates.* Vol. 2. New York: Academic Press, 1965. Pp. 365–403.

Gibson, E. J. *Principles of perceptual learning and development.* New York: Appleton, 1969.

Gibson, J. J. *The perception of the visual world.* Boston, Massachusetts: Houghton, 1950.

Gibson, J. J. *The senses considered as perceptual systems.* Boston, Massachusetts: Houghton, 1966.

Gibson, J. J., & Gibson, E. J. Perceptual learning: Differentiation or enrichment? *Psychological Review*, 1955, **62**, 32–41.

Hein, A., Held, R., & Gower, E. C. Development and segmentation of visually controlled movement by selective exposure during rearing. *Journal of Comparative and Physiological Psychology*, 1970, **73**, 181–187.

Held, R. Plasticity in sensory-motor systems. *Scientific American*, 1965, **213**, 84–94.

Held, R., & Bauer, J. A. Visually guided reaching in infant monkeys after restricted rearing. *Science*, 1967, **155**, 718–720.

Held, R., & Hein, A. Movement-produced stimulation in the development of visually guided behavior. *Journal of Comparative and Physiological Psychology*, 1963, **56**, 872–876.

Herter, K. Weitere Dressversuche an Fischen. *Zeitschrift fuer Vergleichende Physiologie*, 1930, **11**, 730–748.

Hess, E. H. Space perception in the chick. *Scientific American*, 1956, **195**, 71–80.

Hochberg, J. E. Nativism and empiricism in perception. In L. Postman (Ed.), *Psychology in the making.* New-York: Knopf, 1962. Pp. 255–330.

Hubel, D. H., & Wiesel, T. N. Receptive fields of single neurones in the cat's striate cortex. *Journal of Physiology (London)*, 1959, **148**, 574–591.

Köhler, W., & Fishback, J. The destruction of the Müller-Lyer illusion in repeated trials. II. Satiation patterns and memory traces. *Journal of Experimental Psychology,* 1950, **40,** 398–410.

Köhler, W., & Wallach, H. Figural after-effects. An investigation of visual processes. *Proceedings of the American Philosophical Society,* 1944, **88,** 269–357.

Leontyev, A. N., & Gippenreiter, Y. B. Concerning the activity of man's visual system. In *Psychological research in the U.S.S.R.* Moscow: Progress Publishers, 1966. Pp. 361–392.

Luquet, G. H. *Les dessins d'un enfant.* Paris: Felix Alcan, 1913.

Luquet, G. H. *Les dessin enfantin.* Neuchatel & Paris: Delachaux et Niestlé, 1927. (2nd ed., 1967)

Meili, R. Les perceptions des enfants et la psychologie de la Gestalt. *Archives de Psychologie (Geneve),* 1931, **23,** 25–44.

Piaget, J. *La construction du réel chez l'enfant.* Neuchatel & Paris: Delachaux et Niestlé, 1937 (2nd ed. 1950).

Piaget, J. *La naissance de l'intelligence chez l'enfant.* Neuchatel & Paris: Delachaux et Niestlé, 1936.

Piaget, J. *The origins of intelligence in children.* (Transl. by M. Cook) New York: International Universities Press, 1952.

Piaget, J. *The construction of reality in the child.* (Transl. by M. Cook) New York: Basic Books, 1954.

Piaget, J. *Les mécanismes perceptifs.* Paris: Presses Universitaires de France, 1961.

Piaget, J. Le développement des perceptions en fonction de l'âge. In P. Fraisse & J. Piaget (Eds.), *Traité de psychologie expérimentale.* (2nd ed.) Vol. VI. *La perception.* Paris: Presses Universitaires de France. 1967. Pp. 1–62.

Piaget, J., & Stettler von Albertini, B. Observations sur la perception des bonnes formes chez l'enfant par actualisation des lignes virtuelles. *Archives de Psychologie (Geneve),* 1954, **34,** 203–242.

Piaget, J., & Vinh-Bang. Comparaison des mouvements oculaires et des centrations du regard chez l'enfant et chez l'adulte. *Archives de Psychologie (Geneve),* 1961, **38,** 167–200.

Renan, E. *L'avenir de la science.* Paris: Calmann Levy, 1890.

Segers, J. E. Recherches sur la perception visuelle chez des enfants âgés de 3 à 12 ans et leur application à l'éducation. *Journal de Psychologie Normale et Pathologique,* 1926, **23,** 723–753.

Sperry, R. W. Mechanisms of neural maturation. In S. S. Stevens (Ed.), *Handbook of experimental psychology.* New York: Wiley, 1951. Pp. 236–280.

Spitz, R. A. *The first year of life. A psychoanalytical study of normal and deviant development of object relations.* New York: International Universities Press, 1965.

Vurpillot, E. The devlopment of scanning strategies and their relation to visual differentiation. *Journal of Experimental Child Psychology,* 1968, **6,** 632–650.

Vurpillot, E. *Le monde visuel du jeune enfant.* Paris: Presses Universitaires de France, 1972.

Warden, C. J., & Baar, J. The Müller Lyer illusion in the ring dove Tintor Risorius. *Journal of Comparative Psychology,* 1929, **9,** 275–292.

Wekker, L. M. On the basic properties of the mental image and a general approach to their analogue simulation. In *Psychological research in the U.S.S.R.* Moscow: Progress Publishers, 1966. Pp. 310–333.

Winslow, C. N. Visual illusion in the chick. *Archives of Psychology, N.Y.,* 1933, **23,** 1–83.

Zaporozhets, A. V. The development of perception in the preschool child. *Monographs of the Society for Research in Child Development*, 1965, **30** (Monog. 100), 82–101.

Zaporozhets, A. V., & Zinchenko, V. P. Development of perceptual activity and formation of a sensory image in the child. In *Psychological research in the U.S.S.R.* Moscow: Progress Publishers, 1966. Pp. 393–421.

Zinchenko, V. P., & Ruzskaya, A. G. Sravnitel'ngi analiz osyazaniya i zreniya. Soobschenyi VII. Nalychnge uroveni vospriyatiya formy u detei doshkolnogo vozrasta. (Comparative analysis of touch and vision: Communication VII. The observable level of perception of form in children of preschool age) *Doklady Akademia Pedogogicheskikh Nauk. RSFSR*, 1960, **4**, 85–88.

Chapter 19

PHENOMENOLOGY

DAGFINN FØLLESDAL

Since the middle of the eighteenth century, the term phenomenology has been used in philosophy for a variety of theories of *phenomena,* "that which appears," "that which is given" (Lambert, Kant, Sir William Hamilton, Eduard von Hartmann, C. S. Peirce, Stumpf). Hegel used the term for his theory of the stages of development of the spirit (phenomenology of the spirit).

In our time, "phenomenology" is primarily used for the philosophy of the Czecho-German philosopher Edmund Husserl (1859–1938). Husserl's phenomenology has developed into one of the major trends in contemporary philosophy and has also been a main influence on Heidegger and Sartre's existentialisms.

I. A GENERAL SURVEY OF PHENOMENOLOGY

A. Intentionality

The general theme of Husserl's phenomenology is intentionality, the peculiarity of consciousness to be directed, to be as if it is consciousness *of* something. Husserl's concern with intentionality was inspired by his teacher, Franz Brentano (1838–1917), who in turn acknowledged indebtedness to the scholastics, particularly Thomas Aquinas. According to Brentano:

> Every mental phenomenon is characterized by what the scholastics in the Middle Ages called the intentional (and also mental) inexistence of an object, and what we could call, although in not entirely unambiguous terms, the reference to a content, a direction upon an object. (Brentano, 1874, p. 85; 1924 and 1955, p. 124; Chisholm, 1960, p. 50)

This may sound commonplace, but it leads to difficulties, for example, when we try to apply the principle to a person who has hallucinations or to a person who thinks of a centaur. Brentano held that even in these cases our mental activity, our thinking, or our sensing is directed toward some object. The directedness has nothing to do with the object's being real, Brentano held: The object is itself contained in our mental activity, "intentionally" contained in it.

However, even though the view that the objects of acts are real leads to difficulties in the case of centaurs and hallucinations, the view that the objects are unreal, whatever that may mean, also leads to difficulties in the case of many other acts, for example, acts of normal perception. It seems that, on that view, what we see when we see a tree is not the real tree in front of us, but something else, which we would also have seen if we were hallucinating. So, the view that every act is directed toward an object leads to a dilemma.

Husserl resolved this dilemma by proposing an analysis of consciousness where it is not crucial that there be an object toward which the act is directed, but where attention is focused on what the directedness consists in, what features of consciousness it is that make consciousness always be as if it is consciousness *of* something. Thus, in the case of perception, Husserl is interested in those features of consciousness that make an act of perception be as if it is of an object of such-and-such a kind, located in such-and-such a manner with respect to other objects and with respect to the perceiver. Husserl is also interested in those features of the act that make it an act of perceiving and not, for example, one of remembering or imagining.

B. The Noema

All these features of the act, both those that determine its object, if it has any, and those that determine its kind, Husserl calls the *noema* of the act, from Greek νόημα, that which is thought, that which is grasped.

Husserl conceives of the noema as an intensional entity, a "generalization of the notion of meaning to the realm of all acts" (1952, p. 89, 1.2–4). Just as the meaning of a linguistic expression determines which object the expression refers to, so the noema determines what the object of an act is—if the act has an object; some acts have a noema for which there is no corresponding object.

The object of the act is a function of the noema, that is, given the noema, the object, if any, is uniquely determined. The converse, however, does not hold, to one and the same object there may correspond several different noemata, depending upon the various ways in which the object can be experienced, whether it be perceived, imagined, remembered, etc., and depending upon its orientation, our point of view, etc.

To take an example from perception, let us consider the act of seeing a tree. When we see a tree we do not see a collection of colored spots, for example brown and green distributed in a certain way; we see a tree, a material object with back, sides, and so forth. Part of it, for example the back, we cannot presently see, but we see a thing which has a back. That seeing is intentional, object-directed, means that the near side of the thing we have in front of us is regarded only as a side of a thing, and that the thing we are seeing has other sides and features which are co-intended to the extent that the full thing is regarded as something more than the one side. The noema is the complex system of determination which unifies this multitude of features into aspects of one object.

C. Constitution

The object is hence intended as having a great number of properties, normally, as in the case of all material objects, many more than can ever be exhausted by our experience of it. Objects are *constituted* through our acts, Husserl said. This does not mean that they are caused by our acts or brought about by our acts, but just that in the act the various components of consciousness are interconnected in such a way that we have an experience as of one full-fledged object. All there is to the existence of an object hence corresponds to components in the act. In the case of physical objects, the inexhaustible character of what is experienced is a characteristic feature of the act and of what it is to be a physical object. However, in the extended sense of the term "constitution," Husserl says, an object—whether it is physical or not—" 'constitutes' itself within certain connections of consciousness which bear in themselves a transparent unity so far as they carry with them essentially the consciousness of an identical X" (Husserl, 1913, §135).

Incidentally, Husserl's use, here and many other places, of the reflexive form "an object constitutes itself" is an indication that he did not regard the object as being brought about by the act. Husserl considered phenomenology as the first strictly scientific version of transcendental idealism, but he also held that phenomenology transcended the traditional idealism-realism distinction, and in 1934 he wrote in a letter to Abbé Baudin: "No ordinary 'realist' has ever been as realistic and as concrete as I, the phenomenological 'idealist' (a word which by the way I no longer use)". (Letter quoted in Kern, 1964, p. 276n.) Husserl did not try to "reduce" reality to consciousness. According to Husserl, there is a certain givenness in our experience of the world, an ego-foreign element enters, the hyle, to which we will come in Section II,A. For more on Husserl's concept of constitution, see Sokolowski (1970).

D. Transcendence

Objects which in principle can never be exhausted by our experience, like material objects, are called *transcendent* by Husserl; thus the tree in our example is a transcendent object. Regardless of how long we go on experiencing it, walking around it to see it from other points of view and using other of our senses, there remains more to be known about the tree, and the possibility always remains that we will discover that we have been wrong and will come to reconstitute the object, that is come to have a noema which is so different from the earlier noemata as to be incompatible with them and hence be a noema of a different object.

E. The Noesis

The noema is an abstract entity; Husserl conceived of it very much like a Platonic idea. It is, hence, not a component of the act which has the noema, this act being a temporal event. Corresponding to the noema, the meaning given in the act, there are, however, meaning-given elements in the act, certain experiences which Husserl calls noeses, from Greek νόησις, the activity of the reason. An act is a collection of such noeses, that together give the act the noema it has. Sometimes, as in the case of perception, a second kind of experiences, the so-called hyle are found as components of acts. However, this will be discussed in Section II,A.

Husserl says that the noesis provides the multiplicity, the noema the unity in our acts. He also says, however, that there is a close parallelism between noema and noesis, and it seems that the differences there are are mainly due to the noema being abstract and timeless, the noesis concrete and temporal, much like a type and a token.

F. Phenomenological Reduction; Phenomenological Analysis

Husserl holds that noemata are known through a special kind of reflection, in which the noema of one act is made the object of another act. This second, reflective act has of course, like all acts, its noema which is a noema *of* the noema of the first act, that is it is a noema with the noema of the first act as its object. The noema of the reflective act is hence different from the original noema, since if it were the same, it would have had the same object as the original noema. Similarly we can also reflect on the noesis or hyle of acts. This special kind of reflection on noemata, noeses, and hyle Husserl calls *the phenomenological reduction,* and the analysis that is carried out in such reflection is what Husserl calls *phenomenological analysis.* The phenomena to be studied in phenomenological analysis are hence noemata and noeses and to a lesser extent the hyle. Phenomenology is basically such a reflective study of these three basic factors in intentionality or constitution. Phenomenology is thus for Husserl fundamentally different from psychology, which Husserl regards as a natural science. In psychology one observes acts, etc., in the natural, object-directed attitude and studies their regularities, causal connections, etc.

G. Intension

The basic notions of phenomenology, the notion of noema and correspondingly that of noesis, are so-called *intensional* notions (cf. Section I,B). Such notions normally have to be appealed to in any analysis of intentionality (with *t*) and acts, but they are notoriously obscure and have resisted centuries of efforts at clarification. There arise both the question of what such intensional objects are and how one gets to know anything about them. We have briefly seen how Husserl sought to answer these two questions. Instead of pressing these questions further, let us go on to consider his theory of perception.

II. THE PHENOMENOLOGICAL THEORY OF PERCEPTION

A. Hyle

What has been said so far concerning acts and their directedness, holds for all acts, including acts of perception. What is specific about acts of perception is that in them our senses play a role, in providing certain boundary conditions which the noema has to fit. These boundary conditions are found in all acts of perception, and also in some other acts in which our senses play a role, for example, acts of remembering brought about by sensory impressions. According to Husserl, whenever our senses are stimulated, we have certain experiences called hyle or hyletic data, from the Greek word for matter (ὕλη). These experiences are not by themselves experiences of an object, but they normally occur as components of more comprehensive experiences, acts, which in addition to the hyle contain experiences of an intentional kind, the noeses. The noesis "informs" the hyle, so that this multitude of visual, tactile and other data is unified into a set of appearances of one object.

Although Husserl sometimes calls the hyletic data sense data (*Empfind-ungsdaten*), they are very different from what other philosophers have called sense data. Hyletic data are not what we perceive in our acts, like the noeses they are experiences that contribute to determining what we perceive. Husserl criticizes Brentano for confusing hyletic data and the qualities of the objects that we experience, calling both sorts of entities "physical phenomena."

The color, shape, and various other features of an object are objects of our acts, and are experienced in the way we experience physical objects. They are objective entities, experiencable by various subjects from various perspectives. The round shape of a tabletop, for example, may be experienced as round, elliptic, etc., depending on our point of view. Likewise, its color will appear differently depending on light conditions, whether we wear colored glasses, etc., and a tone will sound differently depending on the acoustics of the room and our location in it, etc. Shapes, colors, sounds, etc., are *perspected variables,* Husserl says, as opposed to the *perspective variations* through which we are aware of them. These perspective variations are examples of what Husserl calls hyletic data. The perspected variable and the perspective variations are interdependent, linked through the complex system of determinations which we have called the noema. Part of what the phenomenology of perception sets out to do, is to explore these basic principles of perception according to which the perspective variations are linked up together, so as to be perspectives of one perspected variable.

It is, however, only within the context of the full act, with its noetic components, that the hyle can be identified with perspective variations. To quote Husserl: "The pure perceptual data . . . are not themselves perspectives, but they become perspectives through that which we also call apprehension (Auffassung), just that which gives them the subjective function of being appearances of the objective" (1962, p. 163, 1.14–17).

In a full act, all the noetic and hyletic components together make it an act with some particular object. Within the act there are certain subunits, certain noeses informing certain hyle into a perspective of the act's object. It is these various perspectives that Husserl somewhat misleadingly calls sense data.

In one of the best books on the subject, Aron Gurwitsch (1966) criticizes Husserl for holding that hyletic data "remain really unchanged with regard to the different noeses operating upon them." Gurwitsch argues that "data devoid of all articulation, hyletic data in the strict sense, do not exist at all. What is given depends on the structural connections within which it appears." (Gurwitsch, 1966, p. 256.)

However, Husserl was well aware of this difficulty. In Husserl (1913, § 85), he characterizes the hyle-noesis schema as provisional, and in a manuscript dating from between 1918 and 1921 he writes:

> We can not place side by side two components in intuition, sense and filling. We can only obtain the difference by contrasting the empty and the filled sense, that is, through a synthesis of intuition and empty consciousness. Perhaps could we say: the abstract identical, that we call sense with regard to different acts of consciousness, is an essence (sense-essence), which particularizes in a special mode, and in two basic modes: in the mode of intuition [*Anschaulichkeit*] (and within the realm of perception in the mode of primordial intuition [*originäre Anschaulichkeit*]) and in the mode of non-intuition, the empty mode. (1966, p. 363, 1.18–27)

There are hence no noeses-independent hyletic data that can be reidentified from one act to another. The hyle can perhaps only be characterized as something ego-foreign that enters into our acts and limits us in what we can experience, that is, limits the stock of noemata that are possible in a given situation. The assortment is never narrowed down to just one, it is fundamental to the phenomenological view on perception that the material factors never uniquely determine the noema of an act nor even its object.

B. Example

By way of illustration of the preceding, let us turn to the tree example again. We noted how, when we see a tree we see something with a number of sides and aspects that we do not presently see. The noema of our act has a number of components that are not filled by hyle. By moving around and using our senses more and more of these components can be filled. While we do this, some of the components that are presently filled will no longer remain filled, but they still remain determined, due to our memory of past filling. During this process, the noema is continuously being replaced by a series of more and more rich and refined noemata of the object, and as long as our further experience remains harmonious, we come to have an ever better confirmed belief in there being a tree in front of us and its having

the properties we attribute to it. However, if a conflict comes up in this
process, if we come to have hyle that are incompatible with our noema, an
"explosion" of the noema takes place, and the noema is replaced by a
noema of a different object. Thus, if we go around the tree and find no
backside, we no longer say that we see a tree, but perhaps that we see a
stage prop or have an hallucination.

C. Hallucinations

When one hallucinates, one has hyle that fits in with some components of
a noema of some ordinary physical object, but other hyle are missing, corresponding, for example, to other senses. For an hallucination there is no
object, we only have some hyle and a noema and noesis as if there were
some object there.

Hallucinations are different from misperceptions in that in the case of
the hallucination there is no noema of any object that can replace the
original noema and fit harmoniously in with all our further use of our
senses. In the case of hallucination, the hyle one has cannot be regarded as
brought about by some causal chain in which the object of the act plays a
part, there being no object of the act. Instead, the hyle are regarded as due
to the influence of illness, drugs, etc., on the organism. Studies concerning
the causal origin of the hyle are of course not part of phenomenology, but
of psychology. That is, they take place in the natural attitude, not in the
reflective phenomenological attitude.

D. Illusions

Illusions are, together with hallucinations, a source of some of the major
philosophical problems of perception and at the same time a touchstone
for the adequacy of any theory of perception. Particularly theories like
Husserl's, according to which we are perceiving physical objects and their
properties and not sense data, often turn out to be inadequate to handle
illusions.

According to Husserl, illusions are transcendent objects (1913, § 42);
like material objects in general they can be observed by different observers,
and noemata of illusions contain determinations of the various hyle we will
have when we move around, put a measuring rod along the object, etc.
Illusions differ from ordinary physical objects in the pattern of determinations in the noema being different from what it normally is.

Thus, for example, consider the well-known illusions where two equal
lines appear to be of unequal length. Looking at the two lines, I may be

aware that I am having an illusion and expect that the two lines will come out the same length when measured by a measuring rod. In this case I am, at least so far, correctly perceiving an object. Or, being unfamiliar with this illusion, I may expect the readings of the measuring rod to be different, in which case there is no object corresponding to my noema. I am misperceiving, due to my being confronted with an object so unlike anything I have experienced so far.

E. Later Developments

Among the very many philosophers who have been influenced by Husserl, Maurice Merleau-Ponty (1908–1961) has made the most notable contributions to a phenomenological theory of perception. Merleau-Ponty rejects certain of Husserl's views, including his "idealism" which we discussed in Section I, C. Instead, Merleau-Ponty emphasizes and develops further ideas from Husserl's latest years. In particular, Merleau-Ponty focuses on the role that the human body plays in perception (Merleau-Ponty, 1945).

Another main contributor to a phenomenological theory of perception is Aron Gurwitsch (1901–1973), who in Gurwitsch (1966), and other works discusses Husserl's theory of perception and develops it further. Gurwitsch deviates from Husserl on certain points, taking into account the findings and notions of Gestalt psychology, which both historically and systematically is closely related to phenomenology.

References

Brentano, F. *Psychologie vom empirischen Standpunkt.* Leipzig: Duncker & Humblot, 1874. (Reprinted in Philosophische Bibliothek. Hamburg: Felix Meiner, 1924, 1955.) (English transl. by D. B. Terrell of Vol. I, Book 2, Ch. I, in Chisholm, 1960.)

Chisholm, R. *Realism and the background of phenomenology.* Glencoe, Illinois: Free Press, 1960.

Gurwitsch, A. *Studies in phenomenology and psychology.* Evanston, Illinois: Northwestern Univ. Press, 1966.

Husserl, E. *Ideen zu einer reinen Phänomenologie und phänomenologischen Philosophie. Erstes Buch: Allgemeine Einführung in die reine Phänomenologie. (Jahrbuch für Philosophie und phänomenologische Forschung.* Vol. I.) Halle a.d.S: Niemeyer, 1913. [New, expanded ed. by W. Biemel (*Huuserliana* III). The Hague: Nijhoff, 1950.] [English transl. by W. R. Boyce Gibson, London: Allen & Unwin, 1931; New York: Collier Books (Paperback), 1962.]

Husserl, E. *Ideen zu einer reinen Phänomenologie und phänomenologischen Philosophie. Drittes Buch: Die Phänomenologie und die Fundamente der Wissenschaften.* Ed. by M. Biemel (*Husserliana* V) The Hague: Nijhoff: 1952.

Husserl, E. *Phänomenologische Psychologie, Vorlesungen Sommersemester 1925.* Ed. by W. Biemel (*Husserliana* IX) The Hague: Nijhoff, 1962.

Husserl, E. *Analysen zur passiven Synthesis. Aus Vorlesungs- und Forschungsmanuskripten, 1918–1926.* Ed. by M. Fleischer (*Husserliana* XI) The Hague: Nijhoff, 1966.

Kern, I. *Husserl und Kant. Eine Untersuchung über Husserls Verhältnis zu Kant und zum Neukantianismus* (*Phenomenologica* 16). The Hague: Nijhoff, 1964.

Merleau-Ponty, M. *Phénoménologie de la perception.* Paris: Gallimard, 1945. (English transl. by C. Smith. New York: Humanities Press, 1962.)

Sokolowski, R. *The formation of Husserl's concept of constitution* (*Phenomenologica* 18). The Hague: Nijhoff, 1970.

Supplementary Reading

Husserl, E. *Logische Untersuchungen.* 2 vols. Halle a.d.S.: Max Niemeyer, 1900–1901. 2nd rev. ed. with the 2nd vol. in two parts, 1913–1921. (English transl. by J. N. Findlay. New York: Humanities Press, 1970.)

Husserl, E. *Vorlesungen zur Phänomenologie des inneren Zeitbewusstseins.* Ed. by Martin Heidegger. (*Jahrbuch für Philosophie und phänomenologische Forschung.* Vol. IX). Halle a.d.S.: Niemeyer, 1928. [Edited by R. Boehm (*Husserliana X*). The Hague: Nijhoff, 1966.] (English transl. by J. C. Churchill. Bloomington: Indiana Univ. Press, 1964.)

Husserl, E. *Formale und transzendentale Logik. Versuch einer Kritik der logischen Vernunft.* (*Jahrbuch für Philosophie und phänomenologische Forschung.* Vol. X). Halle a.d.S.: Niemeyer, 1929. (English transl. by D. Cairns. The Hague: Nijhoff, 1969.)

Husserl, E. *Méditations cartésiennes. Introduction à la phénoménologie.* [Transl. from German by G. Peiffer & E. Levinas (Bibliothèque de la Société française de Philosophie). Paris: Colin, 1931; Paris: J. Vrin, 1947.] The original German text was first published in *Cartesianische Meditationen und Pariser Vorträge* Ed. by S. Strasser (*Husserliana* I). The Hague: Nijhoff, 1950. (English transl. by D. Cairns. The Hague: Nijhoff, 1960.)

Husserl, E. *Erfahrung und Urteil. Untersuchungen zur Genealogie der Logik.* Ed. by L. Landgrebe. Prague: Academia Verlagsbuchhandlung, 1939; Hamburg: Claassen & Gowerts, 1948; Hamburg: Claassen, 1954.

Chapter 20

TRANSACTIONAL AND
PROBABILISTIC FUNCTIONALISM

KENT DALLET

Perceptual theory begins in the world as we know it and attempts to explain how we come to know it. Part of the answer seems to be that we cannot find out about the world if we know nothing to begin with. Only by preliminary knowledge or assumption can we interpret sensory information to determine what we are confronting. The necessity of knowledge for the obtaining of knowledge is part of "intentionality" in the tradition of Brentano and Husserl, and it is central to both of the approaches to perception to be discussed in this chapter. Despite several resemblances in their views of reality, subjectivity, and the process of knowing, the two positions developed independently, from somewhat different philosophic antecedents. While Egon Brunswik's probabilistic functionalism was undoubtedly influenced by European phenomenology, his major philosophic allegiance was to the Vienna positivists, and most of his energies went toward establishing the necessity for an ecologically sampled probabilistic approach to perception. The perceptual transactionalists (Adelbert Ames, Hadley Cantril, William H. Ittelson, Franklin P. Kilpatrick, and others) took their name and their philosophy from John Dewey and Arthur F. Bentley.

Brunswik and the transactionalists begin with the same fact: that the pattern of excitation in sense organs is not an unequivocal sign of events in the world, but is ambiguously related to several possible external configurations of events. Brunswik speaks of the pattern of physiological excitation as the peripheral stimulus, while its labeled physical counterpart (light, sound, etc.) is the proximal stimulus, and the event to be discerned from these signs is the distal stimulus. Reference is also made to a region designated "central" for the purpose of referring to the knowledge or activity of a perceiver which allows him to predict a distal stimulus on the basis of its proximal or peripheral representatives. Whereas many early studies of sensory functioning dealt only with the relation between proximal and peripheral events, these functionalist traditions are mainly concerned with the relation between central and distal events. Both stress the availability of several sources of information for use in the inference of distal events, and both speak of the process as inferential, emphasizing the similarities between visual space perception with its constancies, and our general knowledge of reality. While both concentrated heavily on the spatial constancies, there was also an emphasis on person perception in the work of Brunswik and the transactionalists—perhaps because person perception is obviously inferential and knowledge-like, less dominated by the physiology of the senses. Both stress that perception has evolved to be a preparatory and on-going part of action in the world, serving to guide the perceiver with respect to distal events. It is this emphasis above all others which justified the title "functional" in the tradition of American "adaptive" psychology. Finally, both have stressed the conceptual problems involved in the terms "stimulus" and "response" so beloved of those who drew their inspiration from British empiricism. The stimulus is not the antecedent of perception, but an achievement of the perceiver which perceptual theory must struggle to account for.

I. TRANSACTION

The term was developed by Dewey and Bentley through many years of correspondence (Ratner *et al.*, 1964) which eventuated in *Knowing and the Known* (Dewey & Bentley, 1949). Dewey saw the Ames demonstrations in 1946 and corresponded with Ames (Ames, 1960). The beginnings of transactionalism can be traced to Dewey's classic paper on the reflex arc which appeared in the 1896 *Psychological Review* and has been reprinted several times (most conveniently in Dewey's *Philosophy and Civilization,* 1931). In that paper, Dewey pointed out that what is to be a stimulus for an organism depends on his prior and ongoing responses, in a circular process. Later, commenting on Bergson, Dewey stated "As soon as an integral and clear-cut object stands out, then the response is decided, and the only intelligent way of choosing the response is by forming its stimulus"

(Dewey, 1931, p. 221). Brunswik also pointed out (1956, p. 5) that an organism's stimuli are determined with reference to his behavior. The objects he deals with are things that are sit-on-able, pick-up-able, edible, and so on. The environment is the achievement of a perceiver, and the scientist's environment of facts and variables is no exception.

From Brunswik's writings one generally gets the impression that he assumes an external reality subject to different segmentation and packaging according to our purposes. However, the transactionalists (e.g., Ittelson, 1960) suggested that instead of starting with an external reality which influences the perceiver, we might turn the process around to examine how the perceiver creates, achieves, projects (Ittelson: "externalizes") a world to which the qualities of reality are attributed. Of course, to argue the priority of chickens and eggs is pointless, and indeed, the term "transaction" is intended to emphasize that perceiver and world are part of a single process. One does not influence or cause changes in the other, but instead the two exist in an interdependence too intimate to allow us to say that they are separate entities which "interact." Instead they are parts or aspects of one transaction. Dewey and Bentley devoted a good deal of effort to finding *le mot juste*. The term "field" was rejected because of the connotations it carried, presumably from Lewin's use of it (Ratner *et al.*, 1964, p. 167).

While it is hard to express the transactional view briefly, these aspects are worth noting in Dewey and Bentley. Perceiving and knowing have duration, they are processes. Perceiving is a form of action, it is a laying-hold-of, and the restriction of perceiving to sense perception is an unfortunate development (Ratner *et al.*, 1964, p. 222). Sense data are the result of a transaction, they are part of man-knowing-world. "Fact" is cosmos noted by a speck of cosmos (Dewey & Bentley, 1949, p. 74). "Since man as an organism has evolved among other organisms in an evolution called 'natural,' we are willing under hypothesis to treat all of his behavings, including his most advanced knowings, as activities not of himself alone, nor even as primarily his, but as processes of the full situation of organism-environment. . ." (Dewey & Bentley, 1949, p. 104). Transaction is "unfractured observation." A transaction can be viewed from one perspective or another so that each individual in it has his own view of the transaction, but one must struggle to avoid separating subject and object, self and not-self. William James said that "self" is a location marker, in which case everything becomes object or everything becomes subject, and we are face-to-face with Existence, *Dasein*, or whatever one wishes to call it. The dilemma of subject and object arises when we give special value to those aspects of our transactions which seem to transcend our own point of view, and assume that the intersubjective is somehow more "real" (Ittelson, 1960, p. 12ff.).

Of course, we do consider chickens and eggs apart from the rest of the universe, we continue to speak of interacting entities, and every transaction must be viewed in the context of the greater transaction Existence. So "transaction" is a way of looking at things in context. It is not the "true unit" of behavior.

Dewey and Bentley made passing reference to both Brunswik and Ames. Like Brunswik, they appreciated the concept of ecology as one which reduced the split between organism and environment by its emphasis on the ways in which organism and environment evolve together. In a footnote to *Knowing and the Known* (Dewey & Bentley, p. 142) they stated that "the recent work of Egon Brunswik goes as far, perhaps, on the transactional line as any," and in his *Conceptual Framework of Psychology* (1952, pp. 93–94) Brunswik returned the compliment. While Dewey had a high opinion of Ames, it was as "a doer rather than a literary man or a professor; it's the demonstrations that count; and they *prove* perception is transactional. . ." (Ratner *et al.*, 1964, p. 612). Dewey complained of Ames' shortcomings as a philosopher, shortcomings which Dewey felt tended to undo what had been accomplished by the demonstrations (Ratner *et al.*, 1964, p. 619). He maintained that Ames tended to overintellectualize the perceptual "assumption" (Ratner *et al.*, 1964, p. 611) and complained (p. 626) that Ames talked "99% biologically and 1% transactionally."

II. THE AMES DEMONSTRATIONS

Ames' work took its start from his observations with aniseikonic lenses (reprinted in Kilpatrick, 1961a). Some objects were distorted by the lenses as he would expect them to be distorted from his knowledge of physiological optics, while some objects did not show the expected distortion. Certain distortions were not apparent right away, but developed gradually with continued observation. For Ames, this indicated that the perceiver was not a passive participant, and the demonstrations were all designed to make the role of the perceiver more prominent (Ames, 1955). Each demonstration presents a pattern of stimulation to the retina which appears to have been created by one external configuration, but which is actually the result of another unusual distal configuration. Thus, a trapezoidal pattern such as might result from a rectangular window tilted away from us, is actually produced by a trapezoidal "window" at right angles to the visual axis. Since the position and shape of the window are deceptive, rotation of the window creates illusory patterns of motion. In another demonstration, what appears to be a normal-sized playing card at a certain distance, is actually a card half normal size and only half as far away. Since any retinal projection is basically two-dimensional, each peripheral stimulus can result from an infinite set of distal configurations. Binocular illusions are also possible, and in actuality binocular cues are not enough to negate many monocular illusions. The trapezoidal window is quite effective binocularly. Full plans and descriptions of the demonstrations are available in Ittelson (1952).

From the demonstrations we can conclude that space perception is based upon the use of several cues in a framework of assumptions and cue weightings contributed by the perceiver. The contents of sensory input are not self-explanatory and do not inform themselves. In addition to dramatizing this fact, the demonstrations make it possible to assess, in a preliminary fashion, exactly how various assumptions and cues are weighted relative to one another. And finally, the demonstrations create a situation in which it is possible to determine how the perceiver reacts and adapts when his assumptions are invalidated.

Perceptual assumptions commonly involve making certain features of a situation invariant at the expense of other features. This is sometimes referred to as a perceptual constancy, but the term constancy tells only half the story because as one aspect remains constant another is seen as variable. Apparent whiteness remains constant but illumination is seen to change. Shape remains constant (inappropriately rectangular in the case of the trapezoidal window) but apparent angle of regard changes. When two spots of light differing in intensity are presented side by side in one of Ames' demonstrations, the observer sees lights of equal intensity at differing distances. Adding a third light of intermediate intensity, the apparent variation in distance becomes more pronounced. Perceptually, a schema of equal intensities takes precedence over the schema of a graded series, perhaps because graded series are rare in nature. Linear perspective and "texture gradients" are instances of the equality-schema. The common tendency for distance to be affected when variations are introduced in shape, size, or intensity, would appear to have potential survival value in a world of movable objects which grow very slowly in comparison to the rate at which perception and motion commonly take place.

Assumptions and cue weightings—as Brunswik suggested—have a certain amount of situational specificity. While varying the size of a projected image makes it seem to approach or recede, the effect works better for a playing card than for an oak leaf, and better for an oak leaf than for a white rectangle. For Brunswik, the likelihood of situational specificity was one reason for advocating representative sampling of stimulus objects and observational settings.

III. BRUNSWIK'S "LENS MODEL" OF PERCEPTION

There are usually several ambiguous cues mediating any perceptual achievement (multiple mediation), and these cues can be used in various combinations to predict a distal event (vicarious functioning). Brunswik's main objection to the Ames demonstrations was that they restricted multiple mediation and vicarious functioning by providing an unrepresentative situation which failed to reproduce or violently misrepresented the cue-event relationships available in everyday perception. He did not seem to recognize the value of artificial situations for revealing assumptions and cue weightings engendered by ecological realities and not by the limited experiences available to the subject in the laboratory. Brunswik's preference was first to determine the degree of objective validity of various relations between distal and proximal events by representatively sampling the natural environment, and then to study how efficiently the observer made use of the available mediating relationships.

The lens model depicts the general situation outlined above. The distal event and its central counterpart in perception are linked by many parallel paths which represent individual cues and the processes by which these cues allow the perceiver to relate an inner process to a distal event. But whereas the distal event and the perceptual end-product are represented as unitary, the intervening "rays" are divergent in such a way that the distal object is fragmented and "disappears in the stimulus layer" of this process, just as the image of physical optics cannot be visualized everywhere along a bundle of rays passing through a lens. Since percept and object are coherent, while the mediating cues are probabilistic, fragmentary, and ambiguous, it can be said that organisms "produce between layers of reality correlations that leap across the intermediary layers" (Brunswik, in Hammond, 1966, pp. 522–523). In this way the world is extended far beyond receptor surfaces. Like perception, thought and even emotion can be viewed as an intentional attainment of distant objects, and may be more or less successful as the situation allows.

IV. PERCEPTUAL LEARNING AND DEVELOPMENT

The perceiver's rules for participating are presumed to result from past interactions with the environment. Ames considered past experience "more truly the cause of the visual impression" than the object, which serves as catalyst (Dewey suggested "occasion") for the percept (Ames, 1960, p. 3). While the tendency of the 1940's was to consider almost everything the result of personal experience, Ames (1960, p. 16) speaks of "past experience, personal and inherited," and I have already cited Dewey and Bentley's assertion that observer and environment evolved together, an evolution which can be taken in both personal and species context. Hence, the issue of nativism versus individual learning was not really joined.

Brunswik did learning experiments to show that observers could learn to be influenced by correlated cues (e.g., in the size-weight illusion), and he helped originate experimental work on probability-learning in order to show that rats and humans could respond appropriately to imperfect environmental contingencies. The transactionalists reported a number of observations on adaptation to the Ames demonstrations. For example, Kilpatrick (1961a, Chap. 9) considered the adaptations which take place when an individual discovers, by reaching for things with a stick, that the Ames distorted room is not as "normal" as it appears. One process is a reweighting of cues without changing any assumptions about how cues and distal realities are related. This might mean looking for certain "giveaway" cues, such as the moment when the trapezoidal window is seen edgewise, or textural details of construction in the distorted room. Such reweighting might take place suddenly, as in seeing a hidden figure. If this is not sufficient (and in the Ames demonstrations it usually is not, doing little more than strengthening our intellectual conviction that the situation is illusory), then a process of "formative" learning might begin, in which our perceptual assumptions are gradually changed.

Brunswik also proposed a developmental hypothesis to account for several sets of data indicating that perceptual constancy increases up to a certain age and then decreases slightly. He proposed that by adopting different attitudes, one could focus on the distal event or on the proximal cues. He supposed that young children were apt to focus on proximal cues, and learned gradually to "think" or "perceive" in terms of their distal correlates. In the process, the child's ability to maintain distal focus increases, and is reflected in higher scores on most measures of "constancy"—while his unmeasured ability to focus on proximal cues might become worse. Eventually some improvement in proximal cue estimation takes place—as when a child learns perspective drawing. By late adolescence, either distal or proximal focus can be achieved by adopting different attitudes, and there is a net decrease in mean constancy resulting from the experimenter's tendency to average results obtained under different attitudes. Peak constancy in averaged data represents a stage at which flexibility of attitudes has not been attained.

V. PERCEPTION AND OTHER KNOWLEDGE

Both schools of thought emphasized the continuity between perceptual and other knowledge. Brunswik called perception "ratiomorphic" (having the form of thinking), and suggested that whereas perception aims at an approximate knowledge which is never far wrong, thinking aims at greater precision, and might produce results either more accurate than perception, or else more inaccurate. His example was the estimation of size by perception, as opposed to its calculation in thought. Estimated size is roughly accurate, whereas computed size can be exactly right or radically wrong. Both Brunswik and the transactionalists acknowledged the similarity of their views to those of Helmholtz but indicated important differences, primarily arising from the fact that the newer "unconscious inference" is an hypothetical process and not a residue of conscious analytic thought.

Of special interest is Ames' concept of "ultrastimulus perception" (Ames, 1953, reprinted in Kilpatrick, 1961a). We believe we are uniformly aware of the visual field despite the fact that there is a blind spot, and despite the fact that acuity deteriorates markedly away from the fovea. Moreover, our awareness of our surroundings extends to objects beside and behind us, to surrounding rooms and corridors, streets and paths, virtually to the ends of the known universe. I am aware of offices down the hall, not as I have seen them through doorways, but as though I were looking directly through the walls. Perceptual knowledge is combined into a continually changing world, presumably as a convenience, because knowledge is more efficiently packaged this way. Ames admitted that despite his intellectual conviction that objects are part of a transaction involving himself, he continued to believe in an unchanging space-world existing in its own right. (It is interesting that Brunswik [1956, p. 39] also admitted that despite his belief that perception should be approached multivariately and probabilistically, he tended to think of experiments in the usual single-variable deterministic style.) Ways of looking are habits of thought and vice versa.

We externalize not only our conclusions about the "thatness" and "thereness" of perceptual objects, but also such attributes as value, beauty, causation, and solidity. Ames (1955, 1960) discusses perception as an apprehension of significances. Some significances are properties of objects, some are expectations (prehensions) of sequential events. Ames tried to reveal such prehensions by, for example, a demonstration in which one sees a steel ball fall and bounce, followed by the dead landing of a similar-appearing ball of putty. This produces the reaction of surprise which typically accompanies the unmasking of a perceptual illusion.

VI. PROBABILISM AND REPRESENTATIVE DESIGN

One of the marks of perception, as opposed to conjecture, is that the information dealt with is taken to be certain, and is used with confidence. When we are fooled by one of the Ames demonstrations, there is an emotional reaction of surprise, laughter, and unease. But if our perceptual inferences are probabilistic and fallible, why should we be confident? If perception is, as William James proposed, of probable objects, why does it not seem this way? Functionalism seems to have diverged from phenomenology.

Does the organism intend probabilistically and fully attain its intention, or does it intend with certainty and fall short in attainment? The criterion of certainty is probably appropriateness, and not accuracy. We underestimate the size and distance of the moon with full knowledge that it is much larger and farther away than we "see it" to be. An airplane in the sky certainly appears to move slowly despite contrary knowledge. "Certainty," it appears, is a part of a process which theory teaches us to call probabilistic. And our feelings of confidence are not usually inappropriate; the allowable margins of error for distant objects are enormous in those everyday situations to which perception is geared. Hence the gap between our feeling of certainty and the conclusion that perception is probabilistic, is not paradoxical.

It is neither pessimism nor a theoretical whim which makes perception itself and the generalizations of perceptual theory probabilistic. Neighboring variables interact, and are not always "the same"; the attitude of the observer is a little different each time; proximal cues are linked to distal events in differing ways or sometimes not at all; cues are used in place of one another and in different combinations. Although conventional univariate experiments seem to yield clear-cut results, Brunswik pointed out that such results are of "unscrutinized ecological generalizability," citing as an example the fact that the well-known vertical–horizontal illusion did not seem to be borne out in his data on everyday size estimation (Brunswik, 1956, p. 53).

VII. PERSONS AS STIMULUS OBJECTS

Brunswik's interest in person perception arose from the fact that it involved the inference of a "remote" attribute such as intelligence or likeability from a set of surface cues, none of which were especially good predictors of the trait in question. Heider (1958) developed this line of thinking to encompass motivational states and other underlying characteristics of persons, and it is worth noting here that Heider, in earlier papers (collected in Heider, 1959) helped to develop the ideas summed up in Brunswik's "lens model." Heider's papers are quite helpful in understanding Brunswik.

Among the transactionalists, persons were first used as value-laden stimuli viewed under conditions of perceptual conflict; in the distorted room, under biretinal rivalry, or at ambiguous distances. The experimental work is summarized by Ittelson and Slack (1958). However, Cantril, Kilpatrick, and others (Kilpatrick, 1961b) also expressed a position similar to Heider's, discussing traits of personality as examples of constancy similar to the traditional perceptual constancies. Not only do we conceive of others' variable behavior in terms of a relatively constant set of traits, but we also achieve conceptual constancy in predicting our own behavioral characteristics. Since self and other are part of the same transaction (despite our tendency to separate them, and despite our tendency to make the visual more "real" than the visceral), our experience with the one influences our experiences with the other. Deviant individuals, Kilpatrick suggests, might upset the self-constancy of all those who participate in the same social situation with them. To treat disturbed self-constancy, constancy of response from others is suggested. Ittelson (1960) also suggests that conventional psychotherapy helps modify our assignment of experiences as "internal" and "external." Both of these suggestions relate self-constancy to the classic idea of "projection."

VIII. CURRENT STATUS

It is my impression that many of the ideas which Brunswik and the transactionalists urged upon us have been incorporated into current thinking about perception without retaining a doctrinal label. Gibson's views (Chap. 15, this volume) seem to me to include a restatement of many of these ideas, as does Teuber's chapter in the *Handbook of Neurophysiology*. Much of the experimental work on perception with prisms, pseudophones, and the like, lends itself easily to discussion in terms of probabilistic and transactional functionalism. What have not been incorporated are the philosophical implications which do not have immediate consequences for research, although the recent upsurge of phenomenology (Chap. 19, this volume) might lead to a revival of interest in these aspects as well. While very few people today need to call themselves "transactionalists" or "Brunswikians," a great many will find that they have been thinking along similar lines, so that the ideas expressed in this chapter cannot seem as unusual as they might have seemed when they first appeared in the 1940's.

References*

Ames, A., Jr. Reconsideration of the origin and nature of perception. In S. Ratner (Ed.), *Vision and action.* New Brunswick, New Jersey: Rutgers Univ. Press, 1953. (Reprinted in Kilpatrick, 1961a.)

* Further references will be found in Kilpatrick (1961a) for the transactionalists,

Ames, A., Jr. *An interpretive manual. The nature of our perceptions, prehensions, and behavior.* Princeton, New Jersey: Princeton Univ. Press, 1955. (Reprinted in Ittelson, 1968.)

Ames, A., Jr. *The morning notes of Adelbert Ames, Jr.* (posthumously edited by H. Cantril) New Brunswick, New Jersey: Rutgers Univ. Press, 1960.

Brunswik, E. The conceptual framework of psychology. In O. Neurath *et al.* (Eds.), *International encyclopedia of unified science.* Vol. 1, No. 10. Chicago, Illinois: Univ. of Chicago Press, 1952.

Brunswik, E. *Perception and the representative design of psychological experiments.* Berkely: Univ. of California Press, 1956.

Dewey, J. *Philosophy and civilization.* New York: Minton, Balch & Co., 1931.

Dewey, J., & Bentley, A. F. *Knowing and the known.* Boston, Massachusetts: Beacon Press, 1949.

Hammond, K. R. (Ed.) *The psychology of Egon Brunswik.* New York: Holt, 1966.

Heider, F. *The psychology of interpersonal relations.* New York: Wiley, 1958.

Heider, F. On perception, event structure, and psychological environment: Selected papers. *Psychological Issues,* 1959, **1**, Part 3.

Ittelson, W. H. *Visual space perception.* Berlin & New York: Springer-Verlag, 1960.

Ittelson, W. H. Perception and transactional psychology. In S. Koch (Ed.), *Psychology: A study of a science.* Vol. 4 New York: McGraw-Hill, 1962.

Ittelson, W. H. *The Ames demonstrations in perception.* Princeton, New Jersey: Princeton Univ. Press, 1952. (Reprinted: New York; Hafner, 1968, together with Ames' *An interpretive manual.*)

Ittelson, W. H., & Slack, C. W. The perception of persons as visual objects. In R. Tagiuri & L. Petrullo (Eds.), *Person perception and interpersonal behavior.* Stanford, California; Stanford Univ. Press, 1958.

Kilpatrick, F. P. (Ed.) *Human behavior from the transactional point of view.* Hanover, New Hampshire: Trustees of the Institute for Associated Research, 1952. (Mostly reprinted, with some revision, in Kilpatrick, 1961a.)

Kilpatrick, F. P. (Ed.) *Explorations in transactional psychology.* New York: NY Univ. Press, 1961. (a)

Kilpatrick, F. P. Personality in transactional psychology. *Journal of Individual Psychology,* 1961, **17**, 12–19. (b)

Kilpatrick, F. P. Hadley Cantril (1906–1969): The transactional point of view. *Journal of Individual Psychology,* 1969, **25**, 219–225.

Postman, L., & Tolman, E. C. Brunswik's probabilistic functionalism. In S. Koch (Ed.), *Psychology; a study of science.* Vol. 1. New York: McGraw-Hill, 1959.

Ratner, S. *et al.* (Eds.) *John Dewey and Arthur F. Bentley. A philosophical correspondence, 1932–1951.* New Brunswick, New Jersey; Rutgers Univ. Press, 1964.

and in Hammond (1966) for Brunswik's probabilistic functionalism. Ittelson (1960) provides a well-integrated account of transactionalism and its implications.

AUTHOR INDEX

Numbers in italics refer to the pages on which the complete references are listed.

SUBJECT INDEX

A

Act
  as collection of noeses, 380
  noema of, 378–379
  of perception, 381–384
  phenomenologists view of, 378–383
  reflective, 381
  role of senses in, 381–384
Action units, 218, 223, 226
  complex structure of, 235
Activity, self-produced, 373
Activity of subject, 119–120, *see also*
    Act psychology; Bodily activity;
    Mental activity; related topics
  contributing to perception, 119–120
  exposing receptors to stimulation by
    objects, 119
  fixation reaction, 119
  role in information processing, 110
  optimizing state of receptors, 120
  function of receptors, 120
Act–object analysis, 7
Act psychology (Brentano), 113–114
  acts as mental activity, 114
  physical vs. perceptive worlds, 114
Adaptation, local, 117, 120
Afterimage
  as belief, 10
  correspondence to stimulus pattern,
    262–269
  persistence, 194
Ambient array, 273–274, 291–292, 294,
    298–299, 300, 305, 309–312, *see
    also* Ecological optics; Light; Optics
  defined, 310
  vs. internal organizational process,
    195
  distinct from ambient light, 310–311
Ambiguous figures, 186, 258–259, 263–
    264, 273, 274, 277, *see also* Figure–
    ground phenomena; Illusions
  figure–ground reversal, 263, 264, 269
  Jastrow's duck–rabbit, 258–259, 263,
    264

Necker cube, 258, 263, 264
  three-dimensional objects (wire cubes),
    264, 269
American pragmatism, 251
Ames demonstrations, 83–84, 390–391
  adaptation to, 393
  distorted room, 83–84, 393, 396
  role of the perceiver in, 390
  trapezoidal window, 195, 390, 393
Analogy, inference from, *see* Inference
    from analogy
Analycity as answer to skepticism, 48–
    50
Analysis-by-synthesis model, 141, 199,
    247
Analytic inspection of sensory fields, *see*
    Sensory fields; analytic inspection
    of
Aniseikonic lenses, 390
Appearing
  Theory of, 29–33
  two senses of, 29
Apperception
  active and passive forms of, 247
  attention required for (Leibnitz),
    126–127
  as focusing of attention, 128
Apprehension
  haptic, of specific form, 117
  of nonphysical surrogate, 63
  in phenomenological theory, 382
  of significances, 394
  span of, 129
Approach response, 234
Arousal pattern of electrocortical acti-
    vity, 134
Artificial intelligence revealing inflexi-
    bility of schema theory, 281
Assimilation-accommodation as orga-
    nizing principle for cognitive struc-
    ture, 162
Association, sensory-sensory, 224
Associationism, 79–80, 93–99, 247–248,
    see also Learning
  conflict with nativism, 99–105

5
B 6
C 7
D 8
E 9
F 0
G 1
H 2
I 3
J 4